Financial Inclusion for Inclusive Growth

About the Editor

Rajmani Singha M.Com. (Gold Medalist) and Ph.D. from Manipur University is currently working as Associate Professor of Finance and Accounting in the Department of Commerce, Manipur University. Before joining to the present position he has worked three years in Sherubtse College in Royal Government of Bhutan (which was affiliated to University of Delhi) as Lecturer. He has published two books and 42 research papers in national and international repute in his credit. In the last one and half decade, he has been attending and participating 40 national and 10 international seminar and conferences as paper presenter and also actively participating as discussant and rapporteur. His area of interest is Finance (Microfinance, Financial Management and Security Analysis and Portfolio Management), Accounting, Management and Marketing. He was the founder President of the Association of Commerce Alumni (ACA) Department of Commerce, Manipur University and also the founder President of Manipur University Alumni Association (MUAA). He has been consultant to several Microfinance Institutions and Non-Governmental Organizations of the State in particular and region in general. At present he is coordinating NSS Units working in different colleges under Manipur University as Programme Coordinator, NSS Cell. He has organized several programmes related to NSS like National Integration Camp, Training of Trainers on Life Skills Education, Capacity Building on Employability, Financial Management and Accounting practices for Micro and Small enterprises, etc.

Financial Inclusion for Inclusive Growth

Edited by

DR. A. RAJMANI SINGHA
Associate Professor of Finance
Department of Commerce,
Manipur University, Canchipur,
Imphal-3

CONCEPT PUBLISHING COMPANY PVT. LTD.
New Delhi - 110059

ISBN-13: 978-81-8069-968-9

First Published 2013

Published and Printed by

Concept
Since 1974

Concept Publishing Company Pvt. Ltd.
A/15-16, Commercial Block, Mohan Garden
New Delhi-110059 (India)
T: 25351460, 25351794, *F*: 091-11-25357109
E: publishing@conceptpub.com, W: www.conceptpub.com
Editorial Office: H-13, Bali Nagar, New Delhi-110 015, India.

Cataloging in Publication Data--Courtesy: D.K. Agencies (P) Ltd. <docinfo@dkagencies.com>

Financial inclusion for inclusive growth / edited by A. Rajmani Singha.
p. cm.
Contributed articles.
Includes bibliographical references and index.
ISBN 9788180699689

1. Financial services industry—India. 2. Rural poor—Government policy—India 3. Microfinance—India. I. Singha, A. Rajmani.

DDC 332.10954 23

Dedicated to

My Dear Father

Late Aheibam Kunjababu Singha

Preface

Inclusive Growth, one of the strategy of economic development implemented in the recent past has received renewed attention of the government for bringing overall development of the country. Growth is inclusive when there is an equality of economic opportunities made available to each and every stratum of people. Financial inclusion makes growth broad based and sustainable by progressively encompassing the financially excluded population. Thus, financial inclusion is no longer a policy choice but a policy compulsion. On the other hand, providing financial services to the poor has now become a matter of concern for almost all the developing countries of the world.

Financial inclusion is delivery of banking services at an affordable cost to the vast sections of underprivileged and low income groups. By financial inclusion we mean the provision of affordable financial services, viz., access to payments and remittance facilities, savings, loans and insurance services by the formal financial system to those who tend to be excluded. It is important to recognize that in the policy framework for development of the formal financial system in India, the need for financial inclusion and covering more and more of the excluded population by the formal financial system has always been consciously emphasized.

The essence of financial inclusion is in trying to ensure that a range of appropriate financial services is available to every individual and enabling them to understand and access those services. Apart from the regular form of financial intermediation, it may include a basic to frill banking account for making and receiving payments, a savings product suited to the pattern of cash flows of a poor household, money transfer facilities, small loans and overdrafts for productive, personal and other purposes, insurance of both life and non life, etc., while financial inclusion in the narrow sense, may be achieved to some extent by offering any one of these services, the objectives of "Comprehensive Financial Inclusion" would be to provide a holistic set of services encompassing all of the above. (NABARD, August 2008).

However, the success of the financial inclusion depends on the interest of the government and not on any policies. For example documentation that are required for opening a bank account is least in developed countries, what required is just the ID, but in developing nations lots of legal formalities are to be first completed. Therefore, simplification of the norms can give positive results for more inclusion of people within the ambit of finance and inclusive growth.

The present book is an attempt at providing a comprehensive and value oriented strategies for financial inclusion for inclusive growth of the country. The different sub-topics and topics in the form of ideas, thought, essay and case studies contributed by the scholars would certainly make an eye opener and use this volume a reference book on the desk top of academicians, research scholars and students of Commerce, Management and Economics who are interested to know more on finance in general and financial inclusion in particular.

The present volume is the outcome of the contribution made by the renowned scholars who are in the field within and outside the country. I would like to extent my profound gratitude and thanks to all of them especially to **Prof. Sujit Sikidar (Guwahati), Prof. Prahllad Debnath (Tripura), Prof. Kristiano Raccanello (Mexico), Dr. Felix, M.J. (Thailand), Dr. Clifford G. Machogu (Kenya), Dr. Jairus B. Amayi (Tanzania), Dr. Rudra P. Pradhan (IIT Kharagpur), Dr. Rohit Garg (HIM, Haryana), Dr. Kompalli Sasi Kumar (SSIM, Secunderabad), Dr. Ratan Borman (Assam), Dr. S.S. Mahapatra, (Sikkim), Dr. Gautam Patikar (Nagaland), Dr. L.S. Sharma (Mizoram)** and all paper contributors for their continued support, encouragement, inspiration to complete this task. Without their help it will be difficult task for me to complete this volume.

It is my pleasure to record the profound gratitude and thanks to **Prof. V.P. Giri (Mumbai), Prof. Apurba Nanda Mazumdar (Silchar), Prof. V.S. Pai (KIAMS, Karnataka), Prof. K. Birendra Singh (Manipur), Prof. B.B. Pradhan (Orissa), Prof. B. Ramesh (Goa),**

Prof. P. Kallu Rao (Mumbai), Prof. S.K. Sharma (Haryana), and Dr. Amritpal Singh (Guwahati) for their constant support, guidance and direction in making the present volume.

I would also like to express my sincere thanks to all my colleagues, students and non-teaching staff of the Department of Commerce Manipur University for their moral and physical support in the process of editing this volume within a short period of time.

My research students especially **Th. Surjit Meitei, Ksh. Ranjan Singh, O. Deepak Kumar Singh and K. Suraj Sharma (NYC)** have also made me indebted to them by their constant support and help as and when I asked for.

I am thankful to **Mr. A.K. Mittal, Nitin Mittal** and other members of Concept Publishing Company, Pvt. Ltd. Mohan Garden, New Delhi for taking pain in conversion of manuscripts to the present volume of the book in short period of time.

Last but not the least, my special thanks goes to my wife, **Sulochana Ahanthem**, my sons **Suraj, Lanchenba**, my mother, uncles and brothers for their constant support and encouragement and also for bearing with me as I was continuously involved with editing of this volume.

Finally, the Almighty God, whose benevolence and blessings shower to complete this effort within the stipulated time.

A. Rajmani Singha
Imphal

Contents

Section-II
Financial Inclusion and Microfinance

Section-III
Financial Inclusion and Commercial Banks

Section-IV
Financial Inclusion and ICT

Section-V
Financial Inclusion and Micro Insurance

Section-VI
Financial Inclusion and Rural Development

Section-VII
Financial Inclusion and Entrepreneurship Development

List of Contributors

1. A. Rajmani Singha (Dr), Associate Professor, Department of Commerce, Manipur University; *Email:rajaheibam2@gmail.com*
2. Ayekpam Ibemcha Chanu (Dr.) Assistant Professor, Department of Commerce, Assam University, Diphu Campus, Diphu, Karbi Anglong, Assam; *Email:chanu. ibemcha@rediffmail.com*
3. Chanambam Nalini Devi (Dr.) Assistant Professor, Pachhunnga University College, Aizawl, Mizoram; *Email: nalinidevi72@gmail.com*
4. Clifford G. Machogu (Dr.) Senior Lecturer, Kabianga University College, Kericho- Kenya; *Email:cgm4@rediffmail.com*
5. C. Vanlalkulhpuia Research Scholar, Department of Management, Mizoram University, Aizawl; *Email: puia virgo@rediffmail.com*
6. Elangbam Nixon Singh (Dr.) Associate Professor, Department of Management, Mizoram University, Aizawl; *Email: singhnixon@yahoo.co.in*
7. Felix. M.J. (Dr.) Assistant Professor, SDA College, Bangkok, Thailand; *Email: marthonohjessan@mail.coj*
8. Gautam Patikar (Dr.) Assistant Professor, Department of Commerce, Nagaland University; *Email: gautam_patikar@yahoo.com*
9. H. Ramananda Singh (Dr.) Associate Professor, Department of Business Administration, Assam University, Silchar, Assam; *Email: hao_rama@rediffmail.com*
10. Jairus B. Amayi (Dr.) Lecturer, Accounting and Finance, Faculty of Business Administration, St. Augustine University of Tanzania, P.O. BOX 6369, Mwanza Tanzania; *Email:drjbamayi@yahoo.com*
11. K. Aparna (Dr.) Assistant Professor, Department of Business Management, Telangana University, Andhra Pradesh; *Email:aparnaruthwik@gmail.com*

12. K. Gyanendra Singh (Dr.) Assistant Professor, Department of Social Science, National Institute of Technology, Mizoram; *Email: gyanendra_eco@yahoo.com*
13. Kompalli Sasi Kumar (Dr.) Associate Professor—Finance, Siva Sivani Institute of Management, NH-7, Kompally, Secunderabad-14; *Email: kompalli99@ rediffmail. com / sasikumarkompalli@gmail.com.*
14. Kristiano Raccanello (Dr.) Associate Professor and Researcher, Fundación Universidad de las Américas Puebla (Mexico), Department of Economics; *Email: kristiano.raccanello@udlap.mx.*
15. Ksh. Ranjan Singh, Research Scholar, Department of Commerce, Manipur University; *Email:kshetrirs@gmail.com*
16. Longjam Lilashwori Devi, Research Scholar, Department of Commerce, Manipur University; *Email:leelalongjam@gmail.com*
17. L.S. Sharma (Dr.) Associate Professor, Department of Management, Mizoram University, Aizawl; *Email:lsksharma@yahoo.co.in*
18. M. Vasan (Dr.) Assistant Professor of Commerce K.S. Rangasamy College of Arts & Science (Autonomous), Tiruchengode, Tamil Nadu - 215; *Email:m.vasan@yahoo.com*
19. N. Dhaneshwar Singh, Assistant General Manager, North Eastern Development Finance Corporation Ltd., Guwahati, Assam; *Email: nepramdhane@yahoo.co.in*
20. Neelanjan Konwar (Dr.) President, Orchid Foundation for Development, Guwahati, Assam; *Email: neelpsy@yahoo.com*
21. Nicas Nibengo, Assistant Lecturer, Accounting and Finance, Faculty of Business Administration, St. Augustine University of Tanzania, P.O. BOX 6369, Mwanza Tanzania; *Email:nnibengo@hotmail.com*
22. O. Deepak Kumar Singh, Research Scholar, Department of Commerce, Manipur University; *Email:oinamdeepak@gmail.com*
23. Padmini Jindal, Research Scholar, National Institute of Financial Management, An Autonomous Institute of the Ministry of Finance, Faridabad, Haryana, India; *Email: padminijindal864@gmail.com*
24. P. Debnath (Dr.) Professor, Department of Commerce, Tripura University, Suryamani Nagar, Agartala; *Email: pralladdebnath@gmail.com*

25. Purnashree Das (Dr.) Faculty Member, Department of Commerce, Gauhati University; *Email: daspurnashree@yahoo.com*
26. Ratan Borman (Dr.) Associate Professor and Head, Department of Commerce, Assam University, Diphu Campus, Diphu, Karbi Anglong, Assam; *Email: rborman62@gmail.com*
27. R.K.P.G. Singha (Dr.) Head, Department of Commerce Pachhunga University College, Aizawl, Mizoram; *Email:pgsingha@yahoo.com*
28. Rohit Garg (Dr.) Associate Professor and H.O.D., Department of Management Studies, Hindu Institute of Management, Sonepat, Haryana; *Email: rohit.teacher@gmail.com.*
29. Rudra P. Pradhan (Dr.)Vinod Gupta School of Management Indian Institute of Technology, Kharagpur, India; *Email:rudrap@vgsom.iitkgp.ernet.in*
30. Sankar Sarma (Dr.), Department of Commerce, Shillong College, Shillong; *Email: shankar.s.sharma@gmail.com*
31. Siva Prasad Sarmah, Branch Manager, State Bank of India, Manipur University Branch, Canchipur; *Email: siva.sarmah@sbi.co.in*
32. Sreemoyee Guha Roy, Faculty Member, Department of Commerce, Shri Shikshayatan College, Kolkata; *Email:sreemoyeeguharoy@gmail.com*
33. S.S. Mahapatra (Dr.) Associate Professor, Department of Commerce, Sikkim Government College, Tadong, Gangtok; *Email: ssm_gangtok@yahoo.co.in*
34. Sujit Sikidar, (Dr.) Professor, Department of Commerce, Gauhati University; *Email: sujitsikidar@sify.com*
35. Th. Chouba Singh, Lecturer, Allsaintf Diocesan, Hr. Secondary School, Shillong, Meghalaya; *Email:thchaobasingh@yahoo.co.*
36. Thiyam Surjit Meitei, Research Scholar, Department of Commerce, Manipur University; *Email:surthiyam@gmail.com*
37. W.C. Singh (Dr.) Associate Professor, MIMS, Manipur University; *Email: drwcsingh@gmail.com*

List of Tables and Figures

Tables

Figures

List of Abbreviations

ABHA : Axis Bank Holistic Assistance
AGVB : Assam Grameen Vikas Bank
AIDIS : All India Debt and Investment Survey
APMACS : Andhra Pradesh Mutually Aided Cooperative Societies
APPBO : Average Population Per Bank Office
ASA : Activist for Social Alternatives
ASD : Association of Social Development
ATM : Automated Teller Machine
BARC : Bangladesh Rural Advancement Committee
BBA : Basic Bank Account/Bachelor of Business Administration
BC/BF : Business Correspondent / Business Facilitator
BIRD : Bankers Institute of Rural Development
BKCC : Baroda Kisan Credit Card
BPL/APL : Below Poverty Line/ Above Poverty Line
BRAC : Bangladesh Rural Advancement Committee
BRI : Bank Rakyat Indonesia
BSVS : Baroda Swarojgar Vikas Sansthan
CB : Commercial Bank
CD : Credit Deposit
CBOs : Community Base Organisation
CBR : Crude Birth Rate
CDA : Cluster Development Association
CDF : Credit and Development Forum
CDFIs : Community Development Financial Institutions
CD-Ratio : Credit to Deposit Ratio
CDR : Crude Death Rate/ Credit Deposit Ratio
CFLIs : Community Finance Learning Initiatives
CFSR : Committee on Financial Sector Reform
CGAP : Consultative Group to Assist the Poor
CGFSI : Credit Guarantee Fund Scheme for Small Industries

CMF : Centre for Micro Finance
CPP : Consumer Protection Principle
CRA : Community Reinvestment Act
CRAR : Capital to Risk-Weighted Assets Ratio
CSC : Common Service Centre
CSO : Civil Society Organisation
CSP : Customer Service Point
CSR : Corporate Social Responsibility
DCGR : Decennial Compound Growth Rate
DLCC : District Level Consultative Committee
DNBS : Department of Non-Banking Supervision of RBI
EBT : Electronic Benefit Transfer
ECS : Electronic Clearing System
EGS : Employment Guarantee Scheme
EMI : Equated Monthly Instalment
FFI : Full Financial Inclusion
FIC : Financial Included Customer
FIF : Financial Inclusion Fund
FIPB : Foreign Investment Promotion Board
FIPF : Financial Inclusion Plan Fund
FITF : Financial Inclusion Technology Fund
FSC : Farmers' Service Centre
FTTF : Farmers Technology Transfer Funds
GB : Grameen Bank
GCC/KCC : General Credit Card / Kisan Credit Card
GDP : Gross Domestic Product
GoI : Government of India
GSM : Global System for Mobile Communications
GVK : Gram Vikas Kendra
IAY : Indira Awas Yojana
ICE : Information, Communication and Entertainment
ICT : Information and Communication Technology
IHDS : India Human Development Survey
IDBI : Industrial Development Bank of India
IIBM : Indian Institute of Bank Management
IMR : Infant Mortality Rate
IRDA : Insurance Regulatory and Development Authority

JLG : Joint Liability Group
KYC : Know Your Customer
LDRB : Langpi Dehangi Rural Bank
LIC : Life Insurance Company of India
MDG : Millennium Development Goals
MFBs : Micro Finance Banks
MFDEF : Micro Finance Development and Equity Fund
MFI : Micro Finance Institution
MF-NBFC : Microfinance – Non-Banking Financial Company
MFS : Mobile Financial Services
MoRD : Ministry of Rural Development
MRP : Mixed Recall Period
MRRU : Microfinance Research and Reference Unit
NABARD : National Bank for Agriculture and Rural Development
NAFSCOB : The National Federation of State Cooperative Banks
NaMFI : National Mission on Financial Inclusion
NBFC : Non-Banking Financial Company
NDP : Net Domestic Product
NEC/NER : North Eastern Council/ North Eastern Region
NEFIS : Nationwide Electronic Financial Inclusion System
NEFT : National Electronic Funds Transfer
NGO : Non-Government Organisation
NIBM : National Institute of Bank Management
NIRD : National Institute of Rural Development
NRFIP : National Rural Financial Inclusion Plan
NREGA : National Rural Employment Guarantee Act
NSDP : Net State Domestic Product
NSSO : National Sample Survey Organisation
OTC : Over The Counter
OTS : One Time Settlement
PACS : Primary Agricultural Credit Society
PAIS : Personal Accident Insurance Scheme
PCARDB : Primary Cooperative Agriculture and Rural Development Bank
PCI : Per Capita Income
PKI : Public Key Infrastructure (for Digital Signatures)
POCA : Post Office Card Account

POS	: Point of Sale
PSLC	: Priority Sector Lending Certificate
RFA	: Revolving Fund Assistance (Related to SGSY)
RFI	: Rural Financial Institution
RIDF	: Rural Infrastructure Development Fund of NABARD
RUDSETI	: Rural Development and Self Employment Training Institute
SAA	: Service Area Approach
SBI	: State Bank of India
SCARDB	: State Cooperative Agriculture and Rural Development Bank
SCB	: State Cooperative Bank
SEBI	: Securities and Exchange Board of India
SERP	: Society for Elimination of Rural Poverty
SEWA	: Self Employed Women's Association
SGRY	: Swarojgar Gramin Rojgar Yojana
SGSY	: Swarnajayanti Gram Swarojgar Yojana
SHG	: Self-Help Group
SHPI	: Self-Help Promotion Institution
SLBC	: State Level Bankers' Committee
SLRFIP	: State Level Rural Financial Inclusion Plan
SLSMC	: State Level Sanctioning and Monitoring Committee
SSI	: Small-Scale Industries
TFFI	: Technology Fund for Financial Inclusion
UBI	: United Bank of India
UFI	: Universal Financial Inclusion
UIBs	: Un-Incorporated Financial Bodies
UIN	: Unique Identity Number
URP	: Uniform Recall Period
UTI	: Unit Trust of India
VDB	: Village Development Board

1

Introduction

A. RAJMANI SINGHA

"Financial inclusion is not an option, but a compulsion"

Financial Inclusion is one of the buzz words of the world financial system today. Inclusion is the term used to delineate the extent to which all sections of the society have access to the formal financial system. The Norwegian Nobel Committee has given a substantial fillip to the objective of financial inclusion by awarding the 2006 Nobel Peace Prize to Prof Md. Yunus and his Grameen Bank. Worldwide, Yunus and *grameen* are acknowledged as have made the most path breaking impact on the access of the world's marginalized families to formal financial services. Awarding them the Nobel is a dramatic reiteration for the general public of the role played by them in promoting financial inclusion in today's world. (Sanjay Sinha 24th October, 2006 ET)

Inclusive growth as a strategy of economic development has received renewed attention in recent years owing to rising concerns that the benefits of economic growth have not been equitably shared. Growth is inclusive when there is an equality of economic opportunity. Financial inclusion makes growth broad based and sustainable by progressively encompassing the hitherto excluded population. Financial inclusion is no longer a policy choice but a policy compulsion *(RBI Annual Report 2010-11).*

International Experiences in promoting Financial Inclusion

Before studying the financial inclusion from Indian context, it may be worthwhile to have a look at the global experiences in tackling the problem of financial exclusion *vis-à-vis* financial inclusion so that we can learn from the international experience. The problem of financial exclusion is not concentrated to underdeveloped countries but it also spread to the developing and developed countries of the world. However, the degree and magnitude of exclusion or inclusion differ from one country to another country and one region to another region.

Therefore, emphasis has been on empowerment of the disadvantaged groups for access to public goods and services including banking services in the developed countries. The UN General Assembly had designated the year 2005 as the "International Year of Microcredit" stating that the year will be an important opportunity to give impetus to micro finance programmes throughout the world. Thus, the "International Year of Microcredit 2005" aimed at "Building Inclusive Financial Sectors to Achieve the Millennium Development Goals". A brief account of the experiences in promoting financial inclusion in few select countries is also discussed in the paragraphs below.

Levels of financial inclusion (defined as access to formal financial services) are still very low in a number of APEC economies. World Bank data for around 2000 suggest inclusion rates of below 10 per cent in Papua New Guinea, less than 30 per cent in Vietnam and the Philippines, and around 40 per cent in China and Indonesia. APEC should be applauded for deciding to tackle the problem of high levels of financial "exclusion" in some member economies.

The Financial Inclusion Task Force in **UK** has identified three priority areas for the purpose of financial inclusion, viz., access to banking, access to affordable credit and access to free face-to-face money advice. A Financial Inclusion Fund has been established to promote financial inclusion and assign responsibility to banks and credit unions in removing financial exclusion. Basic no frills accounts have been introduced. A Post Office Current Account (POCA) has been created for those who are unable or unwilling to access a basic bank account. The concept of a Savings Gateway has been introduced for those on low income employment. This offers a sum of £1 to those on low-income employment from the state for every £1 they invest, up to a maximum of £25 per month.

In **USA**, 9 to 20 per cent of the households lack a bank account and 22 per cent of low income families earning less than US$ 25,000 per annum do not have either a current or savings account. The government has taken various measures to deal with the problem of financial exclusion. The Community Development Financial Institutions (CDFIs) have been servicing the financial needs of the unorganised sector in USA, with the mission of "promoting access to capital and local economic growth by directly investing in and supporting CDFIs and expanding financial service organisations" lending, investment and services within under-served markets.

In **Brazil,** banking correspondents are allowed to provide all financial services, with the formally licensed banks taking full responsibility for the conduct of the correspondents linked to them. Bolsa Familia is a conditional cash transfer programme that delivers monthly allowances to the poorest 12 million Brazilian families, including indigenous people in extremely remote areas. For more than a year, the Ministry of Development has been planning to add financial inclusion to the cash transfer programme, not only to give the beneficiaries an opportunity to access services (financial access is considered a right in Brazil), but they believe that financial access could somehow work as an "exit tool", i.e., help the beneficiaries build up assets through savings and access to credit and reach a point where they don't need the cash transfer anymore. The financial inclusion programme intends to reach 12 million beneficiaries, their families (45 million people), but also the other 15 million people that are identified, mapped and classified as "poor" by the Ministry of Development, but who, at the moment, are not part of Bolsa Familia.

TERA Bank in **South Africa** uses wireless connections at grocery shops and provides debit cards to its members for accessing banking services. These shops are located around mines and other underprivileged areas and are connected to more than 10,000 ATMs using the Saswitch network. It uses satellite connectivity between its branches for real time transaction processing. On the other hand in 2004, the four large commercial banks in South Africa introduced entry-level "mzansi" accounts to comply with their obligations under the financial sector charter, which aimed to improve access to banking services. In terms of adoption, the initiative was a striking success, i.e., 6 million new accounts were opened, including 4 million by people who were previously unbanked.

In **Bangladesh,** Grameen Bank, ASD (Association for Social Development) and BARC (Bangladesh Rural Advancement Committee) are the three largest MFIs serving around 4 million customers each. The Grameen Bank is the only formal financial institution and the others are registered as NGOs. The micro credit approach has diversified into wider range of financial services. From vanilla credit products, they moved towards product differentiation by end use and target segments.

In **Indonesia,** there are several types of MFIs like commercial banks including Bank Rakyat Indonesia (BRI) owned by Government with a large "Unit Desa" network operating at sub-district level, privately owned rural BPRs (Bank Perkreditan Rakyat), credit cooperatives, etc. After the financial reforms of 1983, BRI transformed its Unit Desa network from loss making agents to commercial micro finance intermediaries.

Table 1.1 : Percentage of Population with a Bank Account Percentage

Sl. No.	*Country*	*%*	*Sl. No.*	*Country*	*%*
1.	Botswana	47.0	9.	Mexico City	21.3
2.	Brazil (urban)	43.0	10.	Namibia	28.4
3.	Colombia (Bogotá)	39.0	11.	South Africa	31.7
4.	Denmark	99.1	12.	Swaziland	35.3
5.	Djibouti	24.8	13.	Sweden	98.0
6.	India	59.0	14.	Tanzania	6.4
7.	Italy	70.4	15.	UK	87.7
8.	Lesotho	17.0	16.	USA	91.0

Source : Emerging Market Economics, Ltd. (2005), p. 20.

Peachey and Roe (2004), p. 13, United Nations (2006), p. 2.

Fedbank Hormis Memorial Foundation Inaugural Address by V. Leeladhar, Deputy Governor, Reserve Bank of India, December 2, 2005.

Note : In Botswana, Lesotho, Namibia and Swaziland, this is the percentage who says that they have a savings/transaction account from a bank. In India, this is the percentage of the adult population who has access to either savings or current account.

It may be observed that even in the developed countries, the State has accepted financial inclusion as an important measure for the empowerment of poor and disadvantaged sections of the society. However, it is difficult to assess what percentage of the population living in developing countries has access to savings account since information regarding small deposits and borrowings is not readily available. Table 1.1 demonstrates the striking disparities between access to savings accounts of undeveloped and developing countries with the information we currently have. While in developed nations, almost everyone has access to banking services, in less developed countries, access to banking services is often limited to a small section of the population. Increasingly, access to finance in developing countries is now being considered as a vital well which is as important and fundamental as access to safe water or primary education (Peachy & Roe, 2006; Beck & Dela Torre, 2006; Leeladhar, 2005).

Among the listed countries, Denmark and Sweden accounts the highest percentage of population included with having their bank account with 99.1 per cent and 98 per cent respectively. Only .09 per cent and 2 per cent of the population are financially excluded. On the other hand country like Tanzania has only 6.4 per cent of their population having bank account and rest 93.6 per cent of population were financially excluded. It is a great concern for the government and policy maker of Tanzania, if they are really thinking for the development of the country.

In developed countries on the other hand, financial inclusions generally related to issues about social exclusion and welfare. The levels of inequality (as measured by Gini coefficients for the respective countries) are negatively correlated to levels of financial inclusion (Kempson, 2006). Thus, Denmark and Sweden have extremely high levels of financial inclusion. Middle-level Gini coefficient countries like the USA and the UK show an exclusion level of between 9 per cent and 12 per cent against the inclusion level of 91 per cent and 88 per cent. Similarly, high levels of inequality, such as those persisting in South Africa, Namibia, Djibouti, Mexico city, Lesotho and Tanzania correspond to higher levels of exclusion. It is important to note that while the figures above pertain to having access to any kind of savings account altogether, one must also consider that section of the population which has access to some kind of savings account but is still removed from banking services that are prevalent in that country. For instance, in Sweden, internet banking is extremely common. Thus, not having access to internet banking may be serious impediment to conducting financial transactions such as making payments. It may be one of the reasons why the level of financial inclusion is very high in the Sweden. In France, cheques are the most common form of payment and as such, not having access to cheques would pose financial roadblocks.

Providing financial services to the poor has now become a matter of concern for almost all the developing countries of the world. Main factor that differentiate developed countries from that of developing countries is the existence of poor, unemployment and low standard of living. But the policies that are applicable for developed countries may not be practically applied on developing countries, e.g., like in developed countries banks savings are attached with tax incentives but this is not so in developing nations, here even if a person opens an account he does not uses the services just because of the distance, bad infrastructure facilities or laziness. Therefore, the problem that developing countries faces are common to all. Keeping in mind their problems all the countries have some what the common policies, KYC, No Frills Account, Post Office Banking, specialized financial institutions and different business models. Success of the financial inclusion depends on the interest of the government and not on any policies. For example documentation that are required for opening a bank account is least in developed countries, what required is just the ID, but in developing nations lots of legal formalities are to be first completed. Therefore, simplification of the norms can give positive results for more inclusion of people within the ambit of finance and inclusive growth.

Now if we considered the success of Grameen Bank Model in Bangladesh, then it would be found that it had achieved the height of success in just 34 years. How Mohd. Younus made it possible? The focus of GB is basically on providing finance to the poorest of the poor and further a special emphasis is given on women. Most important aspect of GB is that it provides loans to poor people without any collateral, what is required is only that a person belongs to a group of five members. For this the individual have organized themselves into a group of five persons and on the first instance only two members are allowed to take the loan. Once they repay the amount the next two are then allowed to take the loan. Even if a person does not repay the loan the burden does not fall on the other members and no legal action is taken against the defaulters, the success of this approach has proved that the poor can be provided with credit and interesting 97 per cent of the total customers are women. Most important factor that differentiate GB from others banks of the world is the principle of banking under one roof, i.e., all the services right from opening a bank account moving to insurance and pension are provided by it; secondly apart from general loan other types of loans such as housing, education and loan for almost every purpose are provided and they have not left even the beggars whom banks never targets as dream.

Today, China is poised to begin another era of financial innovation. In October 2010, state-owned China Mobile—the world's largest mobile network operator—stake in the Shanghai Pudong Development Bank, also government controlled. The operator is expected to launch a range of mobile financial services (MFS) nationally, and industry watchers predict a dramatic take-off in mobile payments in the near-term. Given that progress in mobile banking across markets is often stifled by inefficiencies between regulator, operator, and service provider, China's integration of the three is intriguing and opens up new possibilities. In addition, with mobile penetration high (64 per cent and growing) and bank card penetration relatively low, as well as accumulated experience from various recent pilots, 2011 indeed looks promising for MFS growth in China.

Indian Experience

Historically, the Reserve Bank of India (RBI) and the Government of India (GoI) have been making efforts to increase banking penetration in the country. Some of these measures include the creation of State Bank of India in 1955; nationalization of commercial banks in 1969 and further in1980; initiating the Lead Bank Scheme in 1970; establishing Regional Rural Banks (RRBs) in 1975; introducing a Self-Help Group (SHG)-Bank Linkage Programme in 1992 and formulating the Kisan Credit Card (KCC) scheme in 2001. In 2005, banks were advised to make available a basic banking "no-frills" account with low or nil minimum stipulated balances as well as charges to expand the outreach of such accounts to vast sections of the population. Many regulations have been amended from time to time with the new aspirations and demand from the market. In January 2006, banks were permitted to utilize the services of non-governmental organizations (NGOs/SHGs), micro-finance institutions and other civil society organizations as intermediaries in providing financial and banking services through the use of business facilitator (BF) and business correspondent (BC) models. To extend hassle-free credit to bank customers in rural areas, the guidelines on General Credit Card (GCC) schemes were simplified to enable customers' access credit on simplified terms and conditions, without insistence on security, purpose or end-use of credit. With a view of providing hassle-free credit to customers, banks were allowed to issue general credit cards akin to Kisan Credit Cards.

Moreover, the Government of India has also expressed its explicit concern on the issue of overall inclusion in the development process through its various initiatives such as the Rural Employment Guarantee Scheme, the Bharat Nirman Programme, the Sarva Shiksha Abhiyan, and the like. A Committee on Financial Inclusion, with Dr. C. Rangarajan as Chairman, has also been constituted by the Government of India in June 2006, to recommend a strategy to achieve 100 per cent financial inclusion in the country.

The banking industry has shown a tremendous growth in volume and complexity during the last few decades in India. The branches of commercial banks (CBs) and the regional rural banks (RRBs) have increased from 8,321 in the year 1969 to 69,170 branches at the end of 31st March 2004 and further rose to 82,794 and 87,768 at the end of 31st March 2009 and 2010 respectively. The average population per branch office has decreased from 64,000 in 1969 to 14,000 as on 31st March 2010. Despite making significant improvements in all the areas relating to financial viability, profitability and competitiveness, there are concerns that banks have not been able to include vast segment of the population, especially the underprivileged sections of the society, into the fold of basic banking services. There are approximately 400 million people in nearly six million villages and semi-urban areas are waiting for small loans and other banking services. There is scope for lending Rs 45,000 crore to these vast people. Against this potential, only 5 per cent or about 20 million have been served so far by the organized financial sector, with total disbursements of about Rs 3,900 crore which is only 8.67 per cent of the scope of lending.

Thus, there is a growing demand for financial inclusion of these segments of population who are considered as financially excluded groups. The then union Finance Ministers Budget speech covered *"Banks will be encouraged to embrace the concept of Total Financial Inclusion. Government will request all scheduled commercial banks to follow the example set by some public sector banks and meet the entire credit requirements of SHG members, namely (a) income generation activities, (b) social needs like housing, education, marriage, etc.; and (c) debt swapping"* (extract of Budget Announcement, 2008-09 Para No. 93)

The term financial inclusion needs to be interpreted in a relative dimension. Depending on the stage of development, the degree of financial inclusion differs among countries. For example, in a developed country non-payment of utility bills through banks may be considered as a case of financial exclusion, however, the same may not (and need not) be considered as financial exclusion in an underdeveloped nation as the financial system is not yet developed to provide sophisticated services. Hence, while making any cross country comparisons due care needs to be taken. A World Bank report states, "Financial inclusion, or broad access to financial services, is defined as an absence of price or non price barriers in the use of financial services."

Financial inclusion is delivery of banking services at an affordable cost to the vast sections of underprivileged and low income groups. By financial inclusion we mean the provision of affordable financial services, viz., access to payments and remittance facilities, savings, loans and insurance services by the formal financial system to those who tend to be excluded. It is important to recognize that in the policy framework for development of the formal financial system in India, the need for financial inclusion and covering more and more of the excluded population by the formal financial system has always been consciously emphasized.

Rangarajan's Committee on financial inclusion defines it as, "*Financial inclusion may be defined as the process of ensuring access to financial services and timely and adequate credit where needed by vulnerable groups such as weaker sections and low income groups at an affordable cost.*"

The essence of financial inclusion is in trying to ensure that a range of appropriate financial services is available to every individual and enabling them to understand and access those services. Apart from the regular form of financial intermediation, it may include a basic no frill banking account for making and receiving payments, a savings product suited to the pattern of cash flows of a poor household, money transfer facilities, small loans and overdrafts for productive, personal and other purposes, insurance of both life and non life etc. while financial inclusion in the narrow sense, may be achieved to some extent by offering any one of these services, the objectives of "Comprehensive Financial Inclusion" would be to provide a holistic set of services encompassing all of the above. (NABARD August 2008)

The new policy also places a lot of emphasis on the efforts made by the Bank to achieve, *inter alia*, financial inclusion and other policy objectives. But the study of distribution of Commercial Bank Branches-Region/State/Union Territory—shows that, there are certain under-banked States such as Bihar, Orissa, Rajasthan, Uttar Pradesh, Chhattisgarh, Jharkhand, West Bengal and a large number of North Eastern states such as Assam, Manipur and Nagaland, where the average population per branch office continues to be quite high compared to the national average of 14,000 people per bank branches as on 31st March 2010.

Within the country, there is a wide variation of population excluded from the coverage of banking services. The ratio of deposit accounts to the total adult population in the State of Kerala is as high as 89 per cent while Bihar is marked by a low coverage of 33 per cent. In the North Eastern States like Nagaland and Manipur, the coverage was a meager 21 per cent and 27 per cent respectively. The Northern Region, comprising the States of Haryana, Chandigarh and Delhi, has a high coverage ratio of 84 per cent.

The Distribution of Commercial Bank Branches in India–Bank Group and Population Group-wise clearly shows the dispersion of branches among rural, semi-urban, urban and metropolitan areas, by the various bank groups. It is evident that RRBs (80 per cent) and Local banks (66.6 per cent) branches are in rural and semi-urban areas, they are followed by State Bank group (67 per cent); other nationalized banks (59 per cent); private banks (42.8 per cent), whereas the foreign banks seem to be concentrating only on urban and metropolitan areas (99.6 per cent) and just have 0.4 per cent branches in rural and semi-urban areas. These reiterate the need to sensitize the private banks and the foreign banks to open branches in semi-urban and rural areas especially less financially included States of India.

Major Roadblocks to Financial Inclusion

From the previous discussion, it has been observed that many people across the globe are excluded from mainstream banking. They range from people with low income to people with low information and accessibility to people with no social security or insurance cover. The interaction with the NGOs, SHGs, BC and BFs brought to light underpinning problems of financial inclusion, which are briefly stated as under:

Lack of Information: Lack of information about the role and function of banks, banking services and products, interest rates, process and procedures, etc., stop people from including themselves in mainstream banking.

Insufficient Documentation: Many people (even in metropolis and urban areas) are unable to show their self identification documents during the opening of a bank account or while seeking loan from the banks.

Lack of Awareness: Many people including literate group are unaware of the banking terms and conditions laid down from time to time. For example floating rate of interest charges at the time of giving loan to the customers varies the rate of interest on increasing trend which is not aware by the customer. Only at the time of final settlement of account they understand the situation.

High Transaction Charges: Various commercial banks across the country and globe levy transaction charges on credit or debit transactions, on over usage of banking services, on cheque book issuance, etc.

Environment: Accessibility is a problem from all those people who live in geopolitically isolated regions. Moreover, as most of the commercial banks are located in the vicinity of cities, people living in rural areas have a geographical barrier in accessing banks.

Illiteracy: Because of illiteracy, a substantial number of people are unable to take recourse to banking services. For example in India all the bank documents were printed either in English or Hindi or both which is not easily understood by the people in rural areas or even the people living in semi urban areas.

Poverty: Those people who are living below poverty, especially out of work and in search of work never think of opening an account. Instead they are looking for two meals for him and his dependents.

Cultural and Psychological Barriers: Cultural and psychological barriers are another roadblock to financial inclusion in remote areas of the country. .

Why does Financial Inclusion Necessary?

Financial inclusion is an important national goal for a multitude of reasons. It has the potential to make an important contribution to the national economy while at the same time reducing social inequality. Most fundamentally, financial services enhance the quality of life and economic productivity of the low income households and small/microenterprises that gain access to them. These households and enterprises benefit in several distinct ways

1. Facilitate Economic Transactions: The financial transactions through financial inclusion have improved the economic transactions among the small and micro enterprises. It facilitate to those people who are living below poverty too through accessing financial services to them.

2. Manage day-to-day Resources: Low income families and people who are living below poverty line have small and unpredictable incomes, often seasonal. They can use credit and savings to tap into past or future income. The availability of savings and credit also prevents consumption needs from crowding out investments.

3. Improve Standard of Living: Families use financial services to gain access to education, health care, and other necessities that improve their standard of living. Home improvement loans, school fee loans, and health insurance can help make major differences in daily well-being.

4. Protect Against Vulnerability: Low income people face much vulnerability, from illness, to theft, to unemployment. Savings, credit, insurance, and even remittances provide sustainable and low-cost coping strategies. If a household loses a source of income, it might not have to withdraw a daughter from school, sell a valuable asset, or fall deeper into poverty.

5. Make Productivity-Enhancing Investments: In a household survey in India, about one-third of respondents reported that they are self-employed or entrepreneurs. These enterprises may use credit or savings to make investments in assets like a sewing machine, food processing machines, knitting and embroidery machines and other farm implements.

6. Leveraging Assets: The poor own assets, both social and physical. As Hernando De Soto has argued, without recognition by the formal sector, they cannot leverage these assets to build for the future. Borrowing against assets can help households capture the financial value of their assets at once, facilitating long-term investments.

7. Build Economic Citizenship: Financial services foster independence, giving people greater ability to manage their resources. For example, microfinance impact studies from Bolivia reported that microfinance clients were more self-confident, more actively involved in local governments, and more respected within their communities.

Achievement of full financial inclusion would give millions of poor people the financial tools to better manage their lives and economic activities. It is also possible that full inclusion could help reduce government welfare expenditures.

Model for Financial Inclusion

The model discussed below will be instrumental in bringing hundred per cent financial inclusion in our country.

Stage I: Create Awareness and Financial Literacy

Intensive awareness, education and promotion drive to create an in-depth impact on the masses.

- Government should promote introduction of basic banking in all educational institutions.
- Government sponsored publicity campaigns through all Medias.
- Banks should design and organize aggressive education-cum-promotion campaigns in unbanked areas to enhance financial literacy and awareness.
- Banks should involve the knowledgeable and well-informed local inhabitants in such activities.
- Banks should gather support from the NGOs, retired bank personnel, and academic institutions, to reach the desired numbers within a limited span of time.

Stage II: Basic Banking

The banks need to adopt a considerate approach towards this new clientele in the following ways that,—

- All banks should allow no frill accounts, i.e., savings accounts which can be opened with a nominal amount of Rs. 5 or even with zero balance.
- RBI along with banks should toil hard to reduce the amount of paper work in relation to the opening of an account as well as in getting small credits.
- Banks should make sure that local people are positioned in the front offices, so that the general public does not have to endure with language problem and does not have to suffer perceived/actual racial discrimination.
- Despite the risk, financing of first time entrepreneurs is a must for financial inclusion and growth. Banks should arrange and provide technical advice for these entrepreneurs.
- Banks should give free financial counsel to low-income households and small entrepreneurs.
- The pricing of the product should be also done keeping in mind the pockets of the potential clientele. The cost burden should proportionately be shifted to high potential sectors, who can afford a little upswing in their banking cost.

Stage III: Innovative Strategies

Basic banking itself needs to be supported by innovative strategies, such as,—

- Infrastructure sharing amongst banks and other organizations will help in lowering the operating cost and thus the cost benefit can be transferred to customers.
- Bank should open small extension counters at organization providing public utility services such as local schools, primary health care centres, village *mandies* and farmers' associations, etc.
- This should simultaneously be supplemented by mobile banks.
- Greater use of technology should be made by the banks to improve their reach, speed of processing, as well as to cut down the operating cost.

Commercial Banks and Financial Inclusion

Commercial bank plays an important role in making hundred per cent financial inclusion of rural India. Below given Table 1.2 depicts the region-wise distribution of commercial bank branches in India.

Table 1.2 : Region-wise Distribution of Commercial Bank Branches in India

Region	*No. of branches as on June 30th*				
	2005	*2006*	*2008*	*2009*	*2010**
1	*2*	*3*	*4*	*5*	*6*
Northern	11,359	11,634	13,530	14,240	15,221
N E India	1,953	1,969	2,098	2,191	2,292
Eastern	11,928	12,018	13,267	13,782	14,479
Central	13,765	13,879	15,586	16,391	17,417
Western	10,606	10,738	12,246	12,922	13,701
Southern	18.938	19,179	22,070	23,268	24,658
All India	68,549	69,417	78,797	82,794	87,768

Sources : 1. Indian Institute of Banking and Finance.

2. Report on Trend and Progress of Banking in India 2008-09.

3. State and population group-wise distribution of offices opened by Commercial Banks 2009-2010.

* Data for 2010 are provisional.

As on 30th June 2009, the total number of commercial bank branches in the country accounts 82,794 against 68,549 bank branches as on 30th June 2005. During July 2004 to 30th June 2009 there were 11,820 new bank branches have opened in the country. Among the different region of the country, Southern region comprises of Andhra Pradesh, Karnataka, Kerala, Pondicherry, Lakshadweep and Tamil Nadu accounts the highest number of bank branches as on 30th June 2009 with a total number of 22,563. Andhra Pradesh accounts the highest number of bank branches with 6,601 followed by Tamil Nadu with 5,937 bank branches. Also seen from the Table 1.3 that Southern region and Northern region are having the least number of people serve by per bank branch with 11,000 and highest is north eastern region with 21,000 average populations per bank branch.

Table 1.3 : Region-wise Average Population (in'000) per Commercial Bank Branches in India as on June 30th

Region	*2005*	*2006*	*2008*	*2009*
1	*2*	*3*	*4*	*5*
Northern	13	13	12	11
NE India	22	22	21	21
Eastern	20	20	19	19
Central	20	20	19	19
Western	15	15	14	14
Southern	12	12	11	11
All India	16	16	15	15

Source : Branch Banking Statistics, Vol. 4, 2009.

Region-wise average population per Commercial Bank Branches (APPBO) in India has been discussed in the above table. Of the different regions, southern and northern regions of India have the least number of populations covered by banks with 11,000 each as on 30th June 2009. Of these two regions, northern region has improved the average population per bank branch from 13,000 in 2005 to 11,000 in 2009 against the southern region having 12,000 in 2005 to 11,000 in 2009.

Table 1.4 also describes the region-wise coverage of banking services in India classifying number of current account holders, saving account holders, total number of accounts holders and also number of accounts per 100 of population. Northern region of India is having the better performance of coverage of banking services with 43 account holders out of 100 of population, followed by southern and western with 39 holders and 35 holders respectively. Unfortunately, North East India covers the least services of bank with 19 account holders against 31 holders out of 100 populations in the country. Thus, there were 81 persons out of 100 populations are financially excluded against the 69 persons in an average in the country.

Table 1.4 : Region-wise Coverage of Banking Services in India

Region	*Current Account*	*Savings Account*	*Total Number of Accounts*	*Total Population*	*No of a/c per 100 of population*
1	*2*	*3*	*4*	*5*	*6*
Northern	42,15,701	5,24,16,125	5,66,31,826	13,26,76,462	43
NE India	4,80,700	70,16,446	74,97,146	3,90,35,582	19
Eastern	18,10,122	4,77,50,775	4,95,60,897	22,70,72,580	22
Central	22,02,217	6,42,54,189	6,64,56,406	25,57,13,495	26
Western	31,78,102	4,95,25,101	5,27,03,203	14,90,71,747	35
Southern	46,66,014	8,33,86,898	8,80,52,912	22,34,45,381	39
All India	1,65,52,856	30,43,49,534	32,09,02,390	1,02,70,15,247	31

Sources : 1. Indian Institute of Banking and Finance.
2. Census of India 2001.

Below given Table 1.5 shows the number of "no frills" accounts opened in India for magnifying the volume of financial inclusion. Public sector bank accounts the highest number of opening accounts under no frills. Private sector banks stood the second position followed by foreign banks. Further, it is also observed that the number of accounts has increased all over India during the overdo of study.

Financial access points in India are highlighted in Table 1.6. There are 87,768 bank branches opened in the country. Despite having such a large bank branches the number of average population per bank office was 14,000. The population per ATM machine has improved significantly. It was 15,900 per ATM in 2007 but it has come down to 8,100 populations per ATM in 2010. Number of Kisan Credit Cards and General Credit Card issued in the country were 76 million and 1, 52,842 respectively.

Table 1.5 : Number of "no-frills" accounts opened in India (as on 31st March)

Sl.No.	Category of banks	2006	2007	2008	2009
1.	Public sector	3,32,878	58,65,419	1,10,26,619	2,98,59,178
2.	Private sector	1,56,388	8,56,495	15,60,518	31,24,101
3.	Foreign	231	2,753	30,260	41,482
	Total	4,89,497	67,24,667	1,26,17,397	3,30,24,761

Source : RBI.

Table 1.6 : Financial Access Points in India

Sl.No	Areas	Status
1	Total No: of no-frills accounts	33.02 million as on March 30th, 2009
2	Total No. of Bank Branches	87,768 as on 2010 (Prov.)
	Average Population Per Bank	64,000 in 1969 to 14,000 in 2009
3	Total No. of Rural Branches	31,727
4	Total No. of ATMs	47,953
	Population per ATM	8,100 in 2010 from 15,900 in 2007
5	No. of PoS machines	5,22,148
6	No. of Kisan Credit Cards	76 million (CMIE2008-09)
7	No. of GCC issued by PSBs	1,52,842 (March 31st, 2009)
8	No. of SHGs	69,53,000 (March 2010)

Source : RBI.

The given Table 1.7 represents the distribution of States according to extent of financial exclusion in terms of four ranges of exclusion. Andhra Pradesh is the only State in the country having the highest degree of financial inclusion or lesser degree of financial exclusion with less than 25 per cent exclusion or more than 75 per cent of financial inclusion. Karnataka, Kerala, Madhya Pradesh, Maharashtra, Punjab, Rajasthan, Tamil Nadu and West Bengal also having the second highest degree of financial inclusion in the country with the range of 25 per cent to 50 per cent financial exclusion. Nagaland, Sikkim, Tripura, Bihar, Chhattisgarh, Himachal Pradesh, Jammu & Kashmir, Orissa and Uttar Pradesh have a moderate rate of 50 per cent to 75 per cent of financial exclusion. On the other hand, Arunachal Pradesh, Assam, Manipur,

Meghalaya, and Mizoram States are having the highest rate of financial exclusion not only among the eight sister States of North East India but within the country including Jharkhand and Uttaranchal.

Table 1.7 : Distribution of States according to extent of estimated Financial Exclusion

Extent of Financial Exclusion	*States*
Above 75%	Arunachal Pradesh, Assam, Manipur, Meghalaya, Mizoram, Jharkhand and Uttaranchal
50% to 75%	Nagaland, Sikkim, Tripura, Bihar, Chhattisgarh, Himachal Pradesh, Jammu & Kashmir, Orissa and Uttar Pradesh
25% to 50%	Karnataka, Kerala, Madhya Pradesh, Maharashtra, Punjab, Rajasthan, Tamilnadu and West Bengal
Below 25%	Andhra Pradesh

Source : Report of the Committee on Financial Inclusion, January 2008.

National Rural Employment Guarantee Act, a rural development scheme implementing throughout the country is also directly encouraging financial inclusion in the country. For making payment to all the workers working under NREGS should have their account either in the bank or in the post office account. Table 1.8 represents the information in connection with the opening of accounts under bank and post office throughout the country as on November 2010. The percentage of accounts against the total population will not represent the total financial inclusion of the States or country. However, it is an attempt to know the information of financial inclusion State-wise under NREGA scheme. Among the 31 States and Union Territories, Tamil Nadu State accounts the highest percentage with 22.06 per cent against the total population as per Census 2011, followed by Chhattisgarh with 21.08 per cent. Table 1.8 depicts the details of percentage of accounts against the total population of the State or Union Territories.

Another strategy for enhancing financial inclusion is Credit Card issued under Kisan Credit Card and General Credit Card.

Table 1.8 : Population covered under Financial Inclusion through NREGA (up to November 2010)

Sl.No.	State/UT	No. of bank A/c	No. of Post Office A/c	Total A/c opened	Population as per 2011 census (prov)	% of A/c against total population
1.	Andhra Pradesh	19,57,469	1,19,82,641	1,39,40,110	8,46,65,533	16.46
2.	Arunachal Pradesh	16,512	6,598	23,110	13,82,611	1.67
3.	Assam	14,83,481	13,40,683	28,24,164	3,11,69,272	9.06
4.	Bihar	16,44,246	52,46,477	68,90,723	10,38,04,637	6.64
5.	Chhattisgarh	23,95,973	29,87,469	53,83,442	2,55,40,196	21.08
6.	Gujarat	10,10,054	21,42,391	31,52,445	6,03,83,628	5.22
7.	Haryana	2,64,962	15,264	2,80,226	2,53,53,081	1.11
8.	Himachal Pradesh	7,22,460	56,981	7,79,441	68,56,509	11.37
9.	Jammu & Kashmir	2,64,535	805	2,65,340	1,25,48,926	2.11
10.	Jharkhand	11,77,219	22,70,318	34,47,537	3,29,66,238	10.46
11.	Karnataka	35,05,564	9,85,980	44,91,544	6,11,30,704	7.35
12.	Kerala	12,15,237	1,09,463	13,24,700	3,33,87,677	3.97
13.	Madhya Pradesh	62,62,342	9,69,848	72,32,190	7,25,97,565	9.96
14.	Maharashtra	6,41,981	10,96,445	17,38,426	11,23,72,972	1.55
15.	Manipur	1,01,750	1,43,921	2,45,671	27,21,756	9.03
16.	Meghalaya	21,892	27,394	49,286	29,64,007	1.66
17.	Mizoram	23,515	58,842	82,357	10,91,014	7.55

contd...

Table 1.8 contd...

18.	Nagaland	1,161	0	1,161	19,80,602	0.06
19.	Orissa	38,61,411	15,24,622	53,86,033	4,19,47,358	12.84
20.	Punjab	3,88,622	1,19,557	5,08,179	2,77,04,236	1.83
21.	Rajasthan	46,41,539	50,86,261	97,27,800	6,86,21,012	14.18
22.	Sikkim	36,809	23,245	60,054	6,07,688	9.88
23.	Tamil Nadu	1,57,45,470	1,66,065	1,59,11,535	7,21,38,958	22.06
24.	Tripura	4,24,832	1,88,566	6,13,398	36,71,032	16.71
25.	Uttar Pradesh	71,41,394	1,19,346	72,60,740	19,95,81,477	3.64
26.	Uttarakhand	7,49,656	1,60,234	9,09,890	1,01,16,752	8.99
27.	West Bengal	33,01,085	41,58,694	74,59,779	9,13,47,736	8.17
28.	Andaman & Nicobar	38,689	670	39,359	3,79,944	10.36
29.	D & N Haveli	13,776	0	13,776	3,42,853	4.02
30.	Goa	8,938	0	8,938	14,57,723	0.61
31.	Pondicherry	16,409	0	16,409	12,44,464	1.32
	Total	5,90,78,983	4,09,88,780	10,00,67,763	1,19,20,78,161	8.39

Note : Chandigarh, Daman & Diu, Delhi and Lakshadweep data are not available.

Source : 1. www, nrega.nic.in

2. Census of India 2011.

Table 1.9 : Kisan Credit Card Scheme—State-wise Progress
(As at the end of March 2010) (Amount in crore and Number of Cards issued in '000)

Sl. No	State/UT	Cooperative Banks		Regional Rural Banks		Commercial Banks		Total	
		Cards Issued	Amount Sanctioned	Cards Issued	Amount Sanctioned	Cards Issued	Amount Sanctioned	Cards Issued	Amount Sanctioned
1	2	3	4	5	6	7	8	9	10
1.	Andhra Pradesh	3,594	6,751	2,068	4,405	9,919	32,880	15,582	44,036
2.	Assam	14	18	154	513	399	795	568	1,326
3.	Arunachal Pradesh #	1	1	3	5	19	42	23	48
4.	Bihar	833	1,008	1,110	4,067	1,862	8,181	3,805	13,256
5.	Gujarat	1,206	18,457	248	2,644	1,543	22,622	2,997	43,723
6.	Goa $	4	19	—	—	12	139	17	158
7.	Haryana	1,259	7,833	372	3,363	861	9,319	2,492	20,516
8.	Himachal Pradesh	192	513	55	273	256	1,461	503	2,247
9.	Jammu & Kashmir	53	78	24	173	15	101	93	353
10.	Karnataka	1,867	7,197	1,255	6,135	2,543	15,476	5,665	28,808
11.	Kerala	1,482	4,087	473	1,687	1,512	5,468	3,466	11,241
12.	Madhya Pradesh	3,389	14,262	575	3,041	1,813	14,906	5,777	32,209
13.	Maharashtra	5,395	32,157	330	1,180	2,972	13,859	8,697	47,197
14.	Meghalaya #	11	15	22	40	46	120	79	174
15.	Mizoram #	2	1	9	56	15	34	26	92
16.	Manipur #	14	34	2	3	28	76	44	113
17.	Nagaland #	3	2	2	4	23	44	28	49
18.	Orissa	3, 592	10,323	705	1,523	1,257	3,804	5,553	15,649
19.	Punjab	904	6,370	140	1,719	1,353	16,979	2,398	25,068

contd...

Table 1.9 contd...

20. Rajasthan	2,960	8,915	499	4,735	1,762	20,647	5,220	34,298
21. Sikkim #$	3	8	—	—	8	32	11	40
22. Tamil Nadu ##	1,638	5,481	294	675	4,224	14,592	6,156	20,748
23. Tripura #	4	6	53	94	64	147	121	248
24. Uttar Pradesh**	6,280	7,578	3,916	14,320	6,917	39,731	17,113	61,629
25. West Bengal	1,535	5,782	375	1,814	1,535	4,756	[illegible],445	12,352
26. Andaman & Nicobar #$	4	10	—	—	3	10	7	20
27. Chandigarh $	—	—	—	—	3	20	3	20
28. Daman & Diu @$					2	14	2	14
29. New Delhi #$	2	9	—	—	22	295	24	304
30. D & N Haveli @$	—	—	—	—	3	29	3	29
31. Lakshadweep @$					1	3	1	3
32. Pondicherry #	7	34	—	—	60	232	67	267
33. Jharkhand**	279	544	387	496	503	1,555	1,168	2,596
34. Chhattisgarh	1,046	2,413	301	779	317	1,718	1,663	4,910
35. Uttarakhand	314	689	50	220	304	2,835	668	3,744
Total	37,888	1,40,594	13,421	53,964	42,176	2,32,923	93,485	4,27,481

'—' : Nil/Negligible.

StCB functions as Central Financing Agencies. @ No Cooperative Banks in these UTs. $ No RRBs in these States/UTs.

** Data under reconciliation.

No. of cards issued by Cooperatives in Tamil Nadu during the year is 95,089 and amount sanctioned Rs. 25,174 lakhs. However, the same is nullified to reflect the reduction of 237,432 in cumulative number of cards issued by Tiruchirapally DCCB, affected during the year.

Source : Report of Trends and Progress of Banking in India.

Table 1.9 represents the State-wise progress of Kisan Credit Card issued throughout the country as on 31st March, 2010. Kisan Credit Card is issued through three forms of banks such as Cooperative bank, Regional rural bank and Commercial bank. Uttar Pradesh accounts the highest number of cards issued in cooperative bank and regional rural bank respectively. On the other hand Andhra Pradesh stands the highest number of card issued under commercial banks.

Table 1.10 : State and Population Group-wise Distribution of Offices opened by Commercial Banks in North East India

Sl. No	*States*	*As on March 31st 2008*	*As on March 31st 2009*	*As on March 31st 2010*	*Absolute growth from 2008-2010*
1.	Arunachal Pradesh	74	77	81	7 (9.46)
2.	Assam	1,370	1425	1493	123 (8.98)
3.	Manipur	76	81	81	5(6.58)
4.	Meghalaya	194	206	213	19 (9.79)
5.	Mizoram	92	95	99	7 (7.61)
6.	Nagaland	83	87	91	8 (9.64)
7.	Sikkim	71	71	74	3 (4.22)
8.	Tripura	209	220	234	25 (11.96)
9.	NE India	2,169	2,262	2,366	197 (9.08)
	All India*	78,797	82,794	87,768	8,971 (11.38)

Source : http//www.rbi.org.in/ publication view.aspx id=13085

Financial Inclusion in North East India

North East India is one of the most backward regions in the country not only in terms of both industrially and economically but also in terms of financial inclusion too. More than 70 per cent of the populations depend on the agriculture as their livelihood and more than 80 per cent are living in rural areas. On the other hand more than 80 per cent of the populations are financially excluded in the region. Geographically, the region is isolated from the rest of the country and majority of the area is covered by the hilly areas. In the

NER, the level of financial inclusion is not related to the poor alone but also related with many other factors. Gauged by any measure, financial penetration and financial inclusion is very low in the region. Many indicators could be used to measure banking penetration and financial inclusion of the region. Table 1.10 depicts the State and population group-wise distribution of offices opened by commercial banks in North East India.

Population Per Branch and Area Per Branch

The Average Population per Bank Office (APPBO) of 18,833 in NER is markedly higher than the all-India figure and is particularly high in the rural areas of Assam, Manipur and Nagaland. Non-functional bank branches in Manipur (12 RRB branches) and Nagaland (2 branches) have raised the APPBO in Manipur above 30,000 and in Nagaland above 24,000. The geographical area per branch in the region is also much larger than the national average and this negates the advantage of lower APPBO in Arunachal Pradesh, Meghalaya and Mizoram. The data represents in Table 1.11 indicate that the area per branch in the States of Arunachal Pradesh (1,232 square km), Meghalaya (121 square km) and Mizoram (276 square km), is much higher than the national average of 47 square km. The scenario is the same in other States, except in Assam and Tripura. The extra distance and time required for travel to the branch is compounded by the poor road connectivity in the region, indicating an effectively lower degree of penetration of banking than would be indicated by this measure alone.

The State-wise distribution of commercial bank branches in North Eastern region is also shown in Table 1.11. Among the eight sister States Assam State is having the highest number of bank branches with 1,340 as on 30th June, 2006, followed by Tripura with 231 and Meghalaya with 224 respectively. Manipur State is having the highest number of population covered by per bank branches with 26,518 and least one is shown in Mizoram with 10,406 only which is less than the all-India average of 15,726.

Ratio of Bank Accounts Per 100 Adult Populations

A narrow measure of financial inclusion examines the ratio of current and savings accounts of scheduled commercial banks per

Table 1.11 : Bank Branch Network and Average Population Per Bank Office in North East India

States	*Total Branches*	*Share of SCBs in %*	*Share of Coop in %*	*Share of Rural SCB in %*	*Share of total Rural branch in %*	*Total APPBO*	*Rural APPBO*	*Area per SCB branch sq. km*
Arunachal Pradesh	99	68.7	31.3	77.9	73.7	11,632	12,556	1,232
Assam	1,340	94.9	5.1	62.0	60.4	20,697	29,883	62
Manipur	93	83.9	16.1	51.3	48.4	26,518	41,717	286
Meghalaya	224	82.6	17.4	70.8	65.6	11,304	13,845	121
Mizoram	90	88.9	11.1	75.0	70.0	10,406	7,508	276
Nagaland	94	77.7	22.3	50.7	52.1	23,577	37,206	227
Sikkim	NA	NA	NA	NA	NA	NA	NA	NA
Tripura	231	80.5	19.5	64.0	61.0	14,714	20,003	56
NE India	2,147	90.5	10.7	63.3	61.9	18,833	25,724	131
All India*	69,969	—	—	45.7	—	15,726	24,856	47

* Pertains to only SCB branches.

Source : Compiled from various issues of BSR, RBI, Basic Statistics, NEC and CSO.

Note : Population figures implicitly are obtained from the NSDP and per capita NSDP reported by the respective Directorate of Economic and Statistics, and for the most recent years, they are extrapolated assuming an unchanged population growth.

100 adult populations. Data given in Table 1.12 shows that as on March 31, 2005, the ratio ranged from 19.5 in Manipur to 40.9 in Meghalaya, with a regional average of 37.3, distinctly lower than the national average of 59.2.

Table 1.12 : Current and Savings Accounts Per 100 of Adult Population in NE India

States	*2001*	*2002*	*2003*	*2004*	*2005*
Arunachal Pradesh	45.9	46.5	44.2	38.8	37.75
Assam	39.4	38.1	38.1	37.7	39.08
Manipur	20.1	18.7	18.6	17.3	19.50
Meghalaya	44.3	43.1	43.5	41.5	40.93
Mizoram	25.8	23.4	25.0	24.5	28.97
Nagaland	22.3	20.5	20.4	19.4	19.74
Sikkim	NA	NA	NA	NA	NA
Tripura	37.0	36.3	35.8	35.9	36.67
NE India	38.2	36.9	36.8	36.2	37.32
All India	55.0	54.4	54.4	56.3	59.25

Source : Compiled from various issues of BSR, RBI, Basic Statistics, NEC and CSO.

Note : Population figures implicitly are obtained from the NSDP and per capita NSDP reported by the respective Directorate of Economic and Statistics, and for the most recent years, they are extrapolated assuming an unchanged population growth. The share of adult population is assumed to have remained unchanged from the 2001 Census.

Against the marginal improvement at the national level between 2001 and 2005 from 55 to 59.2, the ratios declined in all the States of the region, barring Mizoram. The maximum decline of 8 percentage points to 37.8 was observed in Arunachal Pradesh. The same ratios for rural and urban areas in the region show that for rural areas they were above the national average only in Arunachal Pradesh. The ratios were very low in Manipur and Nagaland with over 90 per cent of the rural adult population being financially excluded. For the urban areas, the ratio was above the national average in Assam only. In the rest, they were much lower, particularly in

Manipur, Mizoram and Nagaland. The ratio declined in both rural and urban centres or at least in one of them in all the States.

Indebtedness to Formal Financial Institutions

The All-India Debt and Investment Surveys (AIDIS), show the indebtedness of households to formal financial institutions in Table 1.13. Barring rural households in Tripura, the percentage of indebted households in the region is significantly lower than the national average. The percentage of total indebtedness ranges from 1.5 (Meghalaya) to 30.7 (Tripura), as against the national average of 42.7. The share of households indebted to non-institutional sources is also significantly lower than the national average, barring in Arunachal Pradesh and Manipur. Within the institutional sources, government is the most important source of institutional credit in many States, and its share in the total debt is higher than the national average in all the States. Further, credit to Net State Domestic Product (NSDP) ratio is another measure of banking penetration. The credit to NSDP ratio of all the States in the region is not only lower than the national average, but, barring Meghalaya, is also lower than any other State / Union Territory of India.

Table 1.14 shows the State-wise Kisan Credit Card scheme in North East India as on 31st March, 2010 under three separate banks, i.e., cooperative banks, regional rural banks and commercial banks. Commercial banks accounts the highest number of card issued with 42,364 followed by cooperative banks with 37,888 in the country. However, in North East India Commercial banks accounts the highest which is followed by regional rural banks with total cards of 6,02,000 and 2,45,000 respectively.

A sum of Rs 1,593.9 crore have been sanctioned for opening of Kisan Credit card in North Eastern States covering all the eight States. Among the North Eastern States, Assam plays the important role contributing two-third of the amount sanctioned as well as number of credit cards issued to farmers, followed by Tripura, Meghalaya, Manipur and Mizoram respectively.

Table 1.13 : Indebtedness of Households (percentage reporting cash loan outstanding), Institutional Sources of Indebtedness and Credit to Income ratio in 1991

States	Indebtedness			Sources Rural %			Sources urban %			Credit/
	Rural	Urban	Total	Banks	Govt	Money lender	Banks	Govt	Money lender	NSDP ratio
Arunachal Pradesh	2.7	1.6	4.3	19.3	41.6	8.7	22.6	0	0	17
Assam	6.2	6.2	12.4	42.8	17.9	4	73.8	17.7	0.1	26
Manipur	3.7	3.2	6.9	31.5	9.2	2.3	17.4	11.6	1	11
Meghalaya	0.4	1.1	1.5	23.2	67.4	0	98.6	0.4	0	41
Mizoram	3.9.	6.3	10.2	0.06	97.6	0	30.2	68.3	0.3	N.A
Nagaland	3.1	5	8.1	34.3	21	3.3	6.4	83.1	0	9
Sikkim	NA	NA	NA	NA	NA	NA	NA	NA	NA	NA
Tripura	23.6	7.1	30.7	62.7	26.5	1.9	27.2	24.6	0	18
All India	23.4	19.3	42.7	55.3	6.1	17.6	38.8	11.1	10.2	62

Source : AIDIS, 1991, BSR, 2004 and Handbook of Statistics of Indian Economy, 2004-05.

Table 1.14 : State-wise Kisan Credit Card Scheme in North East India (As at the end of March 2010)
(Amount in crore and Number of cards issued in '000)

Sl.No	State/UT	Cooperative Banks		Regional Rural Banks		Commercial Banks		Total	
		Cards Issued	Amount Sanctioned	Cards Issued	Amount Sanctioned	Cards Issued	Amount Sanctioned	Cards Issued	Amount Sanctioned
1.	Arunachal Pradesh	1	1	3	5	19	42	23	48
2.	Assam	14	18	154	513	399	795	567	1,326
3.	Manipur	14	34	2	3	28	76	44	113
4.	Meghalaya	11	15	22	40	46	120	79	174
5.	Mizoram	2	1	9	56	15	34	26	92
6.	Nagaland	3	2	2	4	23	44	28	49
7.	Sikkim	3	8	—	—	8	32	11	40
8.	Tripura	4	6	53	94	64	147	121	248
	North East Total	52	85	245	715	602	1,290	899	2,090
	All India Total	37,888	1,40,594	13,421	53,964	42,364	2,33,190	93,673	4,27,748

Source : NABARD.

Suggestive Measures for 100 per cent Financial Inclusion in North East India

The path towards 100 per cent financial inclusion faces several issues. Some of the concerns in this endeavour are as follows:

Coverage: North East India is difficult for any programme to reach out to every one of outreach people due to hilly terrain. The inclusion efforts especially in the rural areas are difficult because of geographical location and transport bottleneck. Hence, the remittances of money by these people are often dependent on informal channels.

Infrastructure: Poor infrastructural facilities in many parts of the region inhibit the development process. It is important that there must be adequate road, rail, digital connectivity and adequate power and infrastructure facilities which are important prerequisites for operation of a banking outlet *vis-à-vis* socio-economic development of the region.

Financial Products: It is imperative that products that cater to the needs of the masses are available in different forms as per the needs and requirements of the clients. Simple products rather than sophisticated instruments are required at affordable cost for the people. Flexibility is an important criterion and the products and services available should be flexible.

Delivery Models: Efforts need to be taken to identify best delivery models/ business models for financial inclusion. The typical brick and mortar bank branches may not be feasible in all villages because of viability and other reasons. Banks have to adopt/ experiment with all delivery models like satellite branches, mobile branches, business correspondents/POS, and mobile telephony services. Near about 8,000 post offices and 2,000 odd bank branches must be used for achieving the ultimate target of 100 per cent financial inclusion in the region.

Technology: Despite significant technological advancements there are issues of standardization, interoperability and costs that inhibit smooth technology solutions. The financial services offered with the help of ICT should ideally be standardized, interoperable and cost effective. One of the major reasons for the slow progress in providing banking services in the hinterland is the high transaction costs associated with the low value large volume transactions. Technology to a great extent can reduce the cost of transactions.

Role of Financial Intermediaries: The banks are not uniformly geared up for financial inclusion. While the commercial banks have taken significant steps to facilitate inclusion, the RRBs and the cooperative banks need to gear up their efforts in this area. Insurance and capital market products should be an integral component of any package on financial inclusion.

Participative Efforts: It is important that all the participative stakeholders work together to achieve the goal of financial inclusion. Banks, State Governments, technology providers, regulators and other developmental agencies need to work together in tandem to drive the efforts towards achieving total financial inclusion.

Branch Expansion: While in any plan for financial sector development the physical presence of a bank branch is important, the topography of the region, the dispersal of population, transport bottlenecks and law and order conditions in some areas inhibit further branch expansion other than in certain commercial centres. Further, given the unique cultural and language barriers which banks have to cross to connect with people in the NER, banks would be well advised to use the larger community to build bridges.

Linkage with SHGs: It is suggested that banks together with NABARD may actively engage themselves with facilitation of group formation and group linkage for savings and deposits as also for providing other financial services like insurance. NABARD may review its guidelines for this purpose if required and also allow refinance for banks financing MFIs in the NER.

Forex Facilities: There are very few branches where forex facilities even of the most basic type are available. Despite there being so many international borders, even basic money changing facilities are not available at branches near the borders. Further at certain land custom centres identified as having large export transactions, the banks do not provide expeditious facilities such as LCs, etc. Reserve Bank, Guwahati may allocate specific responsibility to the different branches (including RRB branches) for providing need based forex facilities at these centres and arrange for special training for the branch staff.

Training and Sensitization Workshops: In order to sensitize all stakeholders and ensure their commitment for implementing the plan for financial inclusion, the IIBM may design and conduct a series of workshops starting from the apex level for bank CEOs and senior State level functionaries down to the district level and even Block level where felt necessary. Local CBOs, NGOs as also those identified as relationship managers also need to be provided specific sensitization and training.

Publicity Drive and Media Campaign: In its interaction with the NGOs and other local people, the Committee observed that there is very little awareness of the facilities that are available from the banks. It is, therefore, paramount that a massive awareness campaign is launched in NER for promoting financial inclusion. A massive awareness campaign may be launched in the NER for promoting financial inclusion.

To conclude, a broader definition of financial inclusion is the need of the hour. Instead of starting with bank accounts and working out how we can deliver them to the poor, a more pragmatic approach is to start by understanding their financial needs and requirement so that an enabling environment for products that meet them can be established. One of the extraordinary developments over the last several years has been the new appetite shown by non-banks to help meet these needs, for example, by developing new payment instruments. This is a trend worthy of the support of financial regulators throughout the world, and these new services should be understood as being very much a part of financial inclusion.

Financial inclusion will strengthen financial deepening and provide resources to the banks to expand credit delivery. Thus, financial inclusion will lead to eradicate the poverty of rural masses by encouraging economic generated activities through small loans and overdrafts and brings them into the orbit of financial inclusion. This will help in streamlining and accelerate the economic growth of the country. A joint effort of the people in mass, SHGs, SHPI, Commercial banks, Regional Rural banks, NABARD and Ministry of Finance, Government of India are need of the hour. With their full cooperation and support the dream of 100 per cent financial inclusion can be achieved in another ten to fifteen years in North East India in particular and India in general. The day is not far from now when all the Indians will have bank account and everybody will take part in financial inclusion.

Review of the Papers

There are thirty research papers contributed by scholars from within and outside the country. Of the total papers following seven broad areas have been divided and placed them as per the content of the papers under different sub headings

A: Financial Inclusion and Inclusive Growth
B: Financial Inclusion and Microfinance
C: Financial Inclusion and Commercial Banks
D: Financial Inclusion and ICT
E: Financial Inclusion and Micro Insurance
F: Financial Inclusion and Rural Development
G: Financial Inclusion and Entrepreneurship Development

There are eleven research papers under the sub theme **Financial Inclusion and Inclusive Growth**, they are:

"Financial Inclusion: An Impact Analysis on Institutional Effort for Outreach" was the title of the paper jointly contributed by **Purnashree Das and Sujit Sikidar**. The present experimental study has been conducted by the researchers by undertaking a field visit to the Kukurmara village of Kamrup District and Parakuchi village in the same district. The two villages have been selected for the purpose of the present study because they have been adopted as model villages for the purpose of financial inclusion by financial institutions; and in both the villages the RBI officials had conducted a massive campaign on financial literacy for financial outreach and financial inclusion. They tried to access the outcome of the campaign and also tried to ascertain the extent of financial inclusion and the penetration of banking services in the selected villages under study.

On the basis of survey conducted by the researchers it is found that the bank's efforts have yielded 88.59 per cent financial inclusion in the Kukurmara village and 80 per cent in Parakuchi village of Kamrup district of Assam. The survey also revealed that such financial exclusion could be mainly attributed to: (i) Illiteracy; (ii) Shyness of the villagers to come to the Bank premises; (iii) Lack of substantial income to open an account; (iv) Inability to meet the expense of making a photograph; and (v) Inability to comply with KYC norms of the banks.

Further it is also found the extent of credit facilities and approximately 72 per cent of the total population. The different types of credit facilities offered by the bank are: (i) Loans under SGRY; (ii) Piggery Loan; (iii) Weaving Activity Loan; (iv) General Credit Card (AGVBGCC); (v) Kisan Credit Cards; (vi) Retail Trade Loans; (vii) Loans to Joint Liability Groups (JLGs); and (viii) Handloom Loan, etc.

In the similar line the disbursement of loans extended to the population of the Parakuchi village include: Kisan Credit Card (KCC), Self Help Group (SHG) loans, agriculture and allied activities loan like piggery, horticulture, weaving loan, etc. To enable to make a comparative study of similar efforts made in two other pockets of the country such as Andhra Pradesh and West Bengal have been selected by the researchers highlighting the various efforts undertaken by these two pockets State of the country.

In the concluding remarks, the researchers arrive at the inference that launching of a financial inclusion campaign in the villages creates a widespread awareness especially among the members of the village who are outside the banking service network. The categories of such persons are housewives, petty shop owners, traders, farmers, etc.

To make the programme of 100 per cent financial inclusion successful, it is necessary to have the participation of some voluntary organizations, clubs, charitable institutions, teachers and other institutions. They may act as an agent to fill up the gap between banks and mass people to implement Financial Inclusion scheme at grassroots level.

Prallad Debnath contributed a paper entitled *"Contours of Financial inclusion in India—A Quest."* In his paper it is highlighted that the financial inclusion is now a common objective for many central banks among the developing nations along with India. In India the basic concept of financial inclusion is having a saving or current account with any bank. In reality it includes loans, insurance services and much more. The first ever index of financial inclusion to find out the extent of the reach of banking services among 100 countries, India has been ranked 50. Only 34 per cent of Indian individuals have access to or receive banking services. In order to increase this number the Reserve Bank of India and the Government of India take innovative steps. One of the reasons for opening new branches of Regional Rural Banks was to make sure that the banking service is accessible to the poorer sections of the society as a whole. With the directives from RBI, our banks are now offering "No Frill" accounts to low income groups of the society. These accounts either have a low minimum or nil balance with some restrictions in transactions between the people and the banks. The individual bank has the authority to decide whether the account should have zero or minimum balance. With the combined effort of financial institutions, six million new "No Frill" accounts were opened world-wide in the period between March 2006-2007.

Banks are now considering to a large extent financial inclusion as business opportunity in an overall economic environment that facilitates the growth and development of the country. Taking into account their inflow of income from agricultural operations, migration from one place to another, seasonal and irregular work availability and income; the existing financial system needs to be redesigned to suit their requirements. Security and safety of deposits, low transaction cost, convenient operating time, minimum paper work, frequent deposits, speedy and easy access and products suitable to income and consumption are to be reckoned at the same time. In the path of super power we the Indians need to achieve the growth of our country with equal opportunity. It will be achieved only when the inclusive finance system available in the country are fully implemented.

"Financial Inclusion: An Indian Perspective" was the paper contributed by **W.C. Singh**. Financial Inclusion in the Indian context implies the provision of affordable financial services. viz., access to payments and remittance facilities, savings, loans and insurance services by the formal financial system to those who tend to be excluded. In order to be financially included, a wide network of financial institutions has been established over the past years. The organized financial system comprising of commercial banks (CB), regional rural banks (RRB), cooperative banks, primary agricultural credit societies (PACS), post offices, MFIs, NBFC, and NGOs cater

the needs of financial service requirements of the poorer people and all the sections of the society. In order to promote the financial inclusion plan, specific financial instruments/products have also developed from time to time. The trends of financial inclusion in India has been improving continuously in terms of expansion in the number of bank branches throughout and at the same time declining the number of population per office due to increase in the number of bank branches.

He also emphasizes the issues on Financial Inclusion in real terms where ability of the citizen to access appropriate financial services and products. The identification of the right kind of financial services or product on the basis of a single individual cannot be generalized here as an appropriate financial inclusion strategy for all. Individuals have varied opinion of their like and dislikes and so varied opinion on the financial inclusion. Some of the thoughts are religious belief; Gender issues; Poverty; Structural problems; Legal identity; Exclusion due to disability; Self exclusion; Attitude of the bankers; Bank Charges; Income level and Challenge of the politica rocess.

In his concluding remarks he summarises that the financial inclusion alone cannot prevent poverty, it can help reduce its worst effects and help provide routes into work, enterprise, and good standard of living. There has been great improvement in terms of financial inclusion since independence but an effective government strategy to combat financial exclusion has a crucial role to play in enabling those on low income and others who are financially excluded to take their own steps away from poverty. Constant innovations and changes in this sector push regulators to react with dynamism to new challenges and opportunities in the market. The present stage of development in our country demands lot of deepening in the financial inclusion by increasing its breadth and coverage of formal finance. The strategy for financial inclusion will lead to financial development in our country which will help to accelerate economic growth.

K. Gyanendra Singh contributed a paper entitled, *"Inclusive Growth: Trends in India"*. In India, the Eleventh Five Year Plan has outlined several inter-related components like rapid growth that reduces poverty and creates employment opportunities, access to essential services in health and education especially for the poor, equality of opportunity, empowerment through education and skill development, employment opportunities underpinned by the National Rural Employment Guarantee, environment sustainability, recognition of women's agency and good governance. The need for such vision and plan arose from the fact that India's success growth story has left far behind a significant portion of the population. As such it is required to analyze the various growth and development indicators on an all India basis as well as on regional basis so that a suitable policy framework can be drawn to bridge the growth and development gaps to those significant portion of the population and foster inclusive growth.

Over the years the contribution of primary sector to the total GDP has declined and the share of tertiary sector to the total GDP increased significantly while the share of secondary sector increased marginally and remained more or less constant over the years. The share of primary sector to total GDP which was above 50 per cent during 1950s and 1960s declined to a low of about 18 per cent in 2009. The share of secondary sector increased from about 10 per cent during the 1950s to about 25 per cent during the 2009. However, the share of tertiary sector has increased tremendously and its share has almost doubled since the 1950s. Its share was about 30 per cent during the 1950s and 1960s and in 2009 its share is about 56 per cent. Thus the Indian economy underwent structural transformation from primary sector towards tertiary sector bypassing the secondary. However, this service sector led growth is concentrated in cities like Bangalore, Chennai, Delhi, Kolkata, Mumbai, Pune, etc. and thus widened regional disparity.

Further, it is also found that though the all India poverty declined over the years, there is a huge variance across the regions and this inter-regional differences need to be addressed. While poverty still remains a major area of concern for India, the overall performance of the health sector is also not very optimistic though there is overall development over the years. The distribution in rural areas shows that 63 per cent of the male usual status workers were engaged in agriculture and 19 per cent and 18 per cent in secondary and tertiary sectors respectively.

In his concluding remarks he opined that India will be emerging as a global power in the present century. It is also one of the largest and fastest growing economies of the world and it is expected that she will emerge as an Asian giant in a period of 10 to 15 years from now even bypassing China. While we are optimistic about the growth prospects and marching towards a new era, we should not forget to engage our people in this process. Inclusive growth is all about expanding opportunities and capability enhancement at the economy level.

Another joint paper contributed by **Elangbam Nixon Singh and C. Vanlalkulhpuia** on the topic *"Financial Inclusion through Derivatives Market: An Indian Experience"*. Financial services play a vital role in the economic growth of a country. For the welfare of the society, two aspects of financial services are highly important: first, financial options, viz., banks, insurance companies and stock markets and second, easy accessibility to such financial options for all the citizens of the country. In this perspective, development in derivatives market in India can be seen as means of providing accessibility to derivatives to all the citizens of the country. In this regard, the Committee of Financial Inclusion, National Bank for Agriculture and Rural Development (NABARD) has defined financial inclusion as "the process of ensuring access to financial services and timely and adequate where needed by the weaker sections and low income groups at an affordable cost".

The financial sector development can broadly pursued four objectives; efficiency, stability to mitigate and manage their own risks, transparency and financial inclusion through resource mobilization and risk management. Both OTC and Exchange traded derivatives products have been increasing steadily over the years. These instruments are important components of the overall financial sector strategy and the broad regulatory objective is required to ensure their potential usage, consistent with both financial development and the contribution of financial markets to economic growth.

Concerted efforts need to be made to drive the agenda of inclusive growth, encouraging more investors to access capital markets. Regulators and other industry stakeholders are driving this single-point agenda to tap the potential in smaller towns and cities. In this regard, development of derivatives market in India can go a long way for financial inclusion for the society, particularly the rural farmers.

In terms of the growth of derivatives markets, and the variety of derivatives users, the Indian market has equalled or exceeded many other regional markets. While the growth is being spearheaded mainly by retail investors, private sector institutions and large corporations, smaller companies and State-owned institutions are gradually getting into the act. The variety of derivatives instruments available for trading is also expanding.

There remain major areas of concern for Indian derivatives users. Large gaps exist in the range of derivatives products that are traded actively. In equity derivatives, NSE figures show that almost 90 per cent of activity is due to stock futures or index futures, whereas trading in options is limited to a few stocks, partly because they are settled in cash and not the underlying stocks. Exchange-traded derivatives based on interest rates and currencies are virtually absent.

K. Aparna highlights about the working of financial inclusion in a paper *"Working of Financial Inclusion in Nizamabad District, Andhra Pradesh"*. The study is based on primary data carried out in Nizamabad district in Andhra Pradesh. A sample of 80 households (HHs) were taken. Twenty households from four different income groups were surveyed. It is evidenced that the occupation has no relation with the concept of financial inclusion. Out of total 204 adults, 132 adults were engaged in different types of work. Rests of them are idle due to their age factor, few are pursuing their studies and most of the females are house wives.

It is also observed that most of the low-income holders of bank accounts, hardly ever use them. Further, most of the HHs took loan from informal sector. They could not get loan from formal sector mainly because of lack of formal employment besides low and irregular monthly income sources. This segment is of the opinion that, when we are trustworthy to a moneylender why not to the Government? To overcome this, bank must develop dedicated organizations and pursue the activities through partnership with them.

Another joint paper contributed by **Clifford G. Machogu, Jairus B. Amayi and Nicas Nibengo** on the issue *"Credit Drivers Towards Poverty Reduction in Tanzania: Customers of Financial Institutions*

Perceptions". In their study, they have analyzed perceptions of financial institutions "customers" regarding financial capital towards income poverty reduction. The level of Public awareness on financial capital services, as the driving force in Mwanza Tanzania. It also discusses the constraints for demand and supply of financial capital and the level of magnitude of financial capital contributions on income poverty reduction in Tanzania.

The study established that over 50 per cent of the respondents believed that financial capital contributes to the growth of economic activities and social well-being is high, or conversely, less than half the respondents believes that financial capital's contribution to economic growth and social well-being is positive. Positive economic contributions were attributed to growth of business sales revenue and profit by averagely 32.57 per cent, and 25.71 per cent respectively. On account of expansion in business assets, 15.43 per cent was recorded while provision of employment recorded 8.57 per cent. The 9.71 per cent attributed positive contribution to social well-being was due to commitment and accountability to personal development, improved education, land and housing, acquisition of household items, food and health accessibility, and health improvement.

It is also highlighted that finance is an important component of development, including poor people. Indeed, evidence from their study has shown that more than half the population perceived financial capital to have reduced income poverty and lowered income inequality. In addition to facilitating overall economic growth, financial capital had helped individuals smooth their income, insure against risks, and broaden investment opportunities. Testimonies have been evidenced in promoting individuals education, facilitated trade and commerce and improved individual accessibility to food and good health.

Despite this positive contribution, productive sectors such as industrial and agriculture have been perceived to have low accessibility to financial capital, hence less contribution to GDP. Therefore, the most important factor for a prosperous future of contribution of financial capital on income poverty reduction lies in honesty and mutual concern by financing industrial, agricultural, infrastructural and construction sectors.

Finance Development, Growth, and Inflation: The Trilateral Analysis in India is the title of the paper contributed by **Rudra P. Pradhan.** The paper investigates the finance- growth nexus in India in a Trivariate framework by incorporating inflation. It finds that financial development has substantial impact on both economic growth and inflation. While financial development and economic growth are bidirectional, financial development and inflation are unidirectional.

The main innovations in this paper, compared to existing literature on finance-growth nexus, are twofold. First, the use of Trivariate framework in which, in addition to growth and finance development, we incorporate inflation, particularly in the context of India. This marries the Granger causality literatures on the finance-growth nexus and inflation-growth nexus. The inclusion of inflation in the finance-growth nexus is very relevant, as it will highlight the issue of macroeconomic stability in the economy. The direct link between inflation and growth has been widely studied, particularly because control of inflation is often seen as the single most important goal to which monetary policy can aspire in the pursuit of macroeconomic stability. On the contrary, the lack of control has been increasingly linked to banking and financial crises.

Second, to investigate the issue in the globalization era of 1990s, India all through followed a closed economy policies since her independence. It was only after 1985, a shift towards globalization was started. The attempts were, however, seems to be considered as half-hearted, self-contradictory and often self-reversing in nature. In contrast, globalization in the 1990s had been much wider and much deeper and decidedly marked a U-turn in many ways in the direction of economic policy followed by India during the last fifty-eight years of centralized economic planning.

The globalization of 1990s were undertaken in many ways such as devaluation of rupee, dismantling import license system, full convertibility on trade account, fiscal retrenchment and credit squeeze, abolition of export subsidies, introduction of import entitlement scheme for exporters, unification of the exchange rates, removal of the quantitative restrictions, massive reduction in the tariff rates and protection rates, easing the restrictions on foreign investments and so forth. The impact of globalization is, however, multidimensional and can be judged in many ways in the direction of socio-economic development. That involves both benefits and failures in the Indian economy.

In his concluding remarks the authors suggests that financial development is considered as a policy variable to forecast economic growth and inflation in India, especially in the globalization era of 1990s. That means the proper linkage between the three will ensure macroeconomic stability in the Indian economy.

"100% Financial Inclusion: The Road Map Ahead" is the title of another paper contributed by **S.P. Sarmah** discussing about the present status of financial inclusion of north eastern India in particular and whole country in general, different strategies for 100 per cent financial inclusion . It is also highlight that the Union Finance Minister Shri Pranab Mukherjee while reviewing the status of financial inclusion in the North Eastern States on 8th November, 2011 at Kolkata remarks that banks have achieved only 46 per cent of their Financial Inclusion goal in West Bengal and eight North Eastern States, viz., Assam, Arunachal Pradesh, Manipur, Mizoram, Nagaland, Meghalaya, Sikkim and Tripura and 100 per cent to be completed by March 2012. Of the 10,721 unbanked villages having population of 2,000 and above identified for Financial Inclusion in the region under the first phase, banks have already covered 4,969 villages either by opening brick and mortar branch or through business correspondence model.

In order to have focused attention for the Financial Inclusion efforts, the State Level Bankers Committee (SLBC) has been advised to identify one or more district for 100 per cent FI. Responsibility is given to the banks in the area for ensuring that all those who desire to have a bank account are provided with one by allocating the village among different banks. The 100 per cent FI drive is progressing all over the country. So far, 431 districts have been identified by SLBCs for 100 per cent FI out of which 204 districts in 18 States and 5 Union Territories achieved the target of 100 per cent Financial Inclusion so far.

He also gave more emphasis on the challenges ahead for 100 per cent financial inclusion of India such as Infrastructure; Financial Products; Delivery Models; Technology; Role of Financial Intermediaries, etc. Further, recommendation of Committee on Financial Sector Reform for 100 per cent Financial Inclusion is also highlighted in the present paper.

In his concluding remarks summarized that India is a vast country with 1.20 billion populations. Its GDP growth rate is attractive at 8-9 per cent over the years despite the fact the world economy is passing through a trying phase of recession, inflation and uncertainty. India's growth story will be a futile growth story if the growth can not encompass all sections of people and inclusive growth is the *mantra* of the policy makers of the country. For inclusive growth that is uniform development of people and place is to be achieved through Financial Inclusion. All the villages, all the Blocks should have access to formal Banking system so that they can avail the facilities offered by this formal channel. Despite the vastness of our country we have no dearth of talents, resources, network to reach out to those poor and under privileged section of the society. 100 per cent financial inclusion can be a reality as per our commitment.

Ksh. Ranjan Singh also contributed a paper on "A Road to Financial Inclusion through the Activities of UIBs (Registered Money Lenders) in Manipur". He emphasized that despite of having a strong banking network consisting of Scheduled commercial banks— public sector banks—State Bank group, Nationalized banks; private sector banks—old private banks, new private banks; Foreign banks, Regional rural banks, Non-scheduled commercial banks and Cooperative banks along with a number of term lending national and State level financial institutions and investment institutions, India still a larger population remained excluded from basic banking and credit facilities which is also known as financial exclusion. This gap is being filled by the credit purveyors in the informal (unorganized) financial system. In the State of Manipur, unincorporated financial bodies are taking a vital role in order to fill the credit gap as well as in the socio-economic development of the State. It is an agreed fact that UIBs have been contributing to the efforts to make financial inclusion a dream to come true.

Even these efforts, still the way to successful financial inclusion is very far. Along with the efforts from the organized sector of the financial system, there is also need for equal effort and contribution from the players in the unorganized sector of the Indian Financial System. Unincorporated financial bodies in the State are also providing financial services and credit facilities to various customers from various backgrounds. Many of the customers of these UIBs are excluded customers of the formal banking system in the State. They are unable to access to the banking services in the State due to various reasons. Many of them are women vegetable vendors and unemployed poor trying to provide themselves self employment. They have denied by the banking services of the State. Due to lack of number of bank branches in the State, there is high density of customers in these banks and many State Bank branches are found to be overcrowded and there are long queue in front of the banks and ATM booths in the State. In such situation initiative of banks to make financial inclusion successful in the State is not found to be quite positive. There are 61 UIBs (registered money lenders) in the State operating mainly in different parts of Imphal east and west districts of the State. These UIBs are having 300-500 customers at an average which are enjoying credit facilities. It clearly shows the role of UIBs to make financial inclusion a dream comes true in the State. Their contribution in this effort cannot be ignored at all and recognition should be given to them on their credit.

To sum up he concluded that UIBs are playing an important role in the financial inclusion and socio-economic development of the State in particular and the whole country in general. Along with the measures to regulate UIBs and to protect the interest of public depositors, certain measures should also be taken by the RBI and the State governments in order to develop these UIBs.

"Business Correspondent (BC)/Business Facilitator (BF) Model: A way forward to bring Financial Inclusion" is the title of the paper contributed by **Longjam Lilashwori Devi**. To achieve the 100 per cent financial inclusion, role of business correspondence (BCs) and business facilitator (BFs) have been covered up in the present study. BCs/BFS are agents who can be hired by banks to provide a subset of banking services in places where it is not commercially or physically viable to set up branches in the present condition. The model is an innovative medium of achieving some significant results in the field of financial inclusion. The BC and BF model ensures a closer relationship between poor people and the organized financial system. The Reserve Bank permitted commercial banks to make use of the services of non-governmental organizations (NGOs/SHGs), micro-finance institutions and other civil society organizations, insurance agents, retired government servants like postmasters,

school teachers, ex-servicemen and ex-bank staff as intermediaries for providing financial and banking services. These intermediaries could be used as business facilitators (BF) or business correspondents (BC) by commercial banks.

In her concluding remarks, she says that BC/BF model has not yet grounded fully in India and yet to be grounded in the North Eastern region. The model had the potential to be very successful; nevertheless, much still needed to be done to validate its inclusion in the sector. RBI and GoI with commercial banks have been trying many experimental projects to make the model a viable and feasible instrument of expanding financial services outreach. Restraints coming out of regulatory norms should be removed. There is a consensus that the viability issue needs to be addressed with a great sense of urgency. Otherwise, with the possible folding up of some BCs would create unmanageable bottleneck in the country.

Technology plays central role in making the model viable by providing connectivity between financial service provider and the customer. Model which is successful in some States does not means to succeed in the other States. Innovation in the model is needed to suit the diverse work culture and social milieu. In the North East State bank should establish relationship with mobile service provider to serve as business correspondent. BCs are required to play a major role for creating awareness, selling the product at the point of service to those customers with full care and responsibility. Young business correspondents having background of finance, commerce, business and economics must be recruited to launch a campaign of innovative business, banking and corporate in Manipur. The business correspondents should play a great role in this mammoth campaign launched for promoting the banking sector with a social outlook. The key success of the BF/BC model lies in the intertwine activities of technology, regulatory bodies and the player.

There are seven papers on the sub theme **Financial Inclusion and Microfinance.** They are given below:

Rohit Garg has also contributed a paper on *"Microfinance and Financial Inclusion"*. In this paper he has highlighted that the emergence of the Grameen Bank in Bangladesh drew attention to the role of "micro-credit" as a source of finance for micro entrepreneurs from the late 1980s. Lack of access to credit was seen as a binding constraint on the economic activities of the poor. Micro-loans delivered to groups of poor women seemed to offer a simple and direct remedy and the connection between providing credit and removing poverty was intuitively appealing. Resources could be made available through the political process, while government sponsorship of mass credit bought vote banks. Less well understood was the need for micro-credit to be financially sustainable.

For the past decade or more the idea of *micro-credit* as a panacea for poverty has lost ground to a more holistic notion of *microfinance,* seen as encompassing a range of financial services needed by the poor. It was ironic that by 2006, the year in which Muhammad Yunus and Grameen Bank were awarded the Nobel Peace Prize for their pioneering work in "micro-credit", the term itself had been eclipsed and retained virtually no currency in professional circles. Nonetheless, Yunus's Nobel Prize has served to cement "micro-credit" ever more firmly into the popular, journalistic and political vocabularies. This is unfortunate in that it impedes a full understanding of the financial service needs of the poor and how they might best be satisfied.

More recently, the term "Financial inclusion" focuses attention on the need to bring previously excluded people under the umbrella of financial institutions. Financial inclusion is the most useful frame of reference for considering how poverty might be reduced through provision of financial services. And microfinance remains the most potent weapon available for reducing financial exclusion. Financial exclusion in developing member economies reflects the fact that the "informal" or "un enumerated" economy is of major importance as a source of livelihood for the poor, while for them the household is the primary unit of both production and consumption. A number of considerations impede the access of households to financial services. These include geographic isolation, low population densities and gender, which lead to unequal access in economies where financial sector development is limited. Particular sectors, notably small holder and peasant agriculture, with their associated post-harvest and off farm economic activities, pose special challenges for financial service provision. A general problem in the developing member economies is the inability of many lower income households to meet lenders' requirements for formal physical collateral.

Microfinance is considered to be a valuable tool for the alleviation of poverty around the globe. In order for microfinance to realize its full potential, however, it must be sustainable and capable of expansion beyond the limitations imposed by a reliance on development assistance. Both developing and developed nations are key actors in this regard. Developed-country bilateral aid programmes and multilateral institutions should focus efforts on defining common standards by which to measure the effectiveness of microfinance in reducing poverty.

This chapter recommends exploring means to leverage additional capital for MFIs. One interesting area is remittances. Aggravated, these are large transfers and represent significant cash flows from developed to developing economies. Linking these funds to microfinance would help to channel these resources to the formal, productive sector. Furthermore, using microfinance institutions to link remittance flows to asset accumulation—such as purchasing a home or financing micro and small businesses—would represent a significant step forward in using remittances to contribute to sustainable microfinance. These issues and research agenda items provide a particularly rich opportunity to measure the impact of microfinance on urban poverty reduction in Latin America. This should lead to valuable conclusions regarding donor programmes and national policies in this sector.

"Predatory Microfinance" is the title of the paper contributed by **Kristiano Raccanello.** To begin, he has started with the performance of the Grameen Bank (Yunus, 2003) highlighting microfinance as one of the most important tools to combat poverty through financing microenterprises start-up capital. This strategy, coupled with greater economic development at community level and through women empowerment, has been endorsed by the World Bank and other international organizations that directly or indirectly support microfinance institutions (MFIs). The merit of the microfinance schemes is to provide an avenue to credit and savings services to those people whose have no access to the formal financial sector.

Further it is also present the recent studies (Ditcher and Harper, 2007) critique MFIs commercial lending and point out the limitations of these schemes because of their large-scale implementation that seems to respond to an inertial phenomenon rather than being based on rigorous evidence. Also, MFIs when seeking their financial sustainability through services' commercialization can end up harming clients, because of the spillover effects and aggressive marketing techniques (Bateman, 2010). Thus, even though microfinance at its inception represented a financial alternative to moneylenders for a significant part of the population, little has been done to avoid that (some of) these institutions providing financial services with a marketing-tailored-social-label would replace them. That is to say, predatory lending practices implemented by some MFIs have led clients to a debt trap, sometimes with tragic consequences which has been witnessing in different parts of world in recent past.

In most countries of the world, predatory practices have not been addressed from a legal point of view; this is why the lack of regulations is probably the most important element that contributes to the proliferation of such practices (Stark, 2005). Predatory lenders exploit the gaps in financial legislation through tailoring credit contracts. Accordingly, predatory lending characteristics modify continuously; a situation that hampers establishing a definition of these (predatory) practices that have been mostly acknowledged in mortgage market, payday loans, money lending, pawn broking and credit sales (US-HUD, 2001). The most common practices in credit contracts consist of: (i) structuring loans that result in a seriously disproportionate net harm to borrowers; (ii) charging excessive interest rates and fees compared to the risk of the borrower; (iii) loans involve fraud; (iv) lack of transparency; (v) loans involving waiving legal redress; (vi) lending discrimination; and (vii) servicing abuses (Drury, 2009, pp. 139-140). Often, predatory loans are granted without an appropriate check of the credit quality of the potential borrower, and by using different methods to persuade consumers to underwrite the loan (Reiss, 2009). Additionally, those borrowers with a poor financial education cannot anticipate the costly financial consequences of the debt (Carr and Kolluri, 2001, Carrand Schuetz, 2001, Leslie and Hood, 2009).

Research on predatory loans has focused on developed countries that, paradoxically, are those equipped with a legislative framework that allow for greater consumer protection. Thus, in developing countries it should be expected that the proliferation of these practices may find a fertile soil where to grow. In these countries, limited financial inclusion forced people to rely to informal finance schemes; so, MFIs turned out to be an alternative to loan sharks.

"Microfinance in India: Various Policy Measures and their Implementation" contributed by **Kompalli Sasi Kumar**. In this twenty-first century, we must take along an active people-centred and growth-oriented poverty alleviation strategy—a strategy which seems to incorporate women's aspirations, dynamism and involvement. It is envisaged that self-help groups will play a vital role in such strategy. But there is a need for structural orientation of the groups to suit the requirements of new business.

Micro credit movement has to be viewed from a long-term perspective under SHG framework, which underlines the need for deliberate policy implications in favour of assurance in terms of technology back-up, product market and human resource development. Hence, there is a need for the development of an innovative and diversified micro-finance sector, which will make a real contribution to women empowerment.

He also emphasized on the major hindrances to Financial Inclusion such as Poverty; Ignorance; lack of access to financial services; geographic access to bank branches or remote banking facilities; affordability of products such as insurance, where premiums often price out those living in the most deprived and risky areas; suitability of products like current accounts, which offer an overdraft and an easy route to debt; Cultural and psychological barriers.

The lack of access by certain segments of the society to appropriate, low-cost, fair and safe financial products and services from mainstream providers actually results in *Financial Exclusion*. This is a critical policy concern, because the options for operating a household budget, or a micro / small enterprise, without mainstream financial services can often be expensive. This process becomes self-reinforcing and can often be an important factor in social exclusion, especially for communities with limited access to financial products, particularly in rural areas.

To conclude, that with increasing liberalization and higher economic growth, the role of banking sector is poised to increase in the financing pattern of economic activities within the country. To meet the growing credit demand, the banks need to mobilize resources from a wider deposit base and extend credit to activities hitherto not financed by banks. The trend of increasing commercialization of agriculture and rural activities should generate greener pastures, and banks should examine the benefits of increasing penetration therein. Financial inclusion will strengthen financial deepening and provide resources to the banks to expand credit delivery.

"Regulating Microfinance: A Step Ahead for the Betterment of Financial Inclusion" is the title of the paper contributed by **Padmini Jindal**. The paper is highlighted the need to regulate different legal forms of MFIs using different models for the disbursement of loans to the poor under a uniform regulatory framework in order to create a level playing space and obstruct regulatory arbitrage.

With different legal entities in the microfinance sector, MFIs expanding their spectrum of services and products like addition of insurance and pension products, and new commercial entrants in the sector, there is a calling for the development of a uniform regulatory framework, which will turn out to be a progressive step ahead towards the goal of financial inclusion. The regulation is required to enable MFIs to offer deposit services to the poor, the lack of which is a major shortcoming of the sector. The regulation is required for the customers' benefit as they have poor financial literacy and bargaining power, they are easily exploitable and vulnerable. The regulation is also required as the players in the sector are getting increasingly competitive due to the affirmed establishment of the sector. It is quoted in the Malegam Sub-Committee report 2011 that the Government of Andhra Pradesh, in its representation, has argued that the MFIs are riding "piggy-back" on the SHG infrastructure created by the programme and the JLGs are being formed by poaching members from existing SHGs.

The paper concludes that the Reserve Bank of India (RBI) should be regarded as the sole authority to uniformly supervise different legal forms of MFIs with respect to both prudential and non-prudential regulations. The paper proposes that the RBI should convert MFIs into Microfinance Banks (MFBs), one by one or a bunch, and permit them to offer deposit services to the poor, whose operations are transparent and matured and financial statements are reliable and strong.

R.K.P.G. Singh contributes a paper entitled, *"Financial Inclusion through Self Help Group: A North East India Perspective"*. Financial Inclusion has become the burning issue in academic research, public policy meeting, seminars and many other forums. Micro financing as an alternative means of financing for the poor has emerged strongly in many countries. In most of the Indian States; banks, NGOs and SHGs are engaged in this business. Although the main objective behind this financing has been the empowerment of the poor through financial support, several road blocks are there to achieve this noble objective.

Since both the outreach and sustainability are important for the success of this programme it is important to ponder over the experience of similar economies before experimenting in ours. Previously focus of development was given importance on labour, capital, institutions, etc., as the concern for growth and development. The leading works hardly include finance as factor of growth. The major contribution of finance to economic growth has also often been overlooked by economists. But at the present context there has been a lot of works done analyzing how financial system help in developing economies. The work done in this field just not looked at how finance facilitates economic activity but also social aspects like poverty, food shortage, hunger, etc. Like any research on a particular field, the outcomes have been diverse and the agreement is that finance helps but the degree of impact vary.

In North Eastern States, this scheme has got slow momentum due to many reasons, e.g., lack of awareness due to illiteracy, lack of good NGOs, lack of motivation for formation of NGOs, lack of proper training to banks, NGOs and government officials, lack of cooperation between bank and Block officials, lack of sound credit structure of banks and lack of follow up programmes which must be sort out very soon with the help of different agencies of SHGs and government machinery.

Thus, the overall progress of micro finance is at a snail pace due to various constraints discussed above comparing to other parts of the country. At the same time, the SHG movement in North East India has started late comparing to other parts of the country. Very few social entrepreneurs are coming forward to take micro finance as an alternative. So, rigorous effort should be made to promote the social entrepreneur to take initiative to make success the venture.

"Status of Microfinance in Nagaland" is the title of the paper contributed by **Gautam Patikar.** Micro finance in Nagaland is of recent origin. Unlike other parts of the country and general practice followed worldwide, the Microfinance programme in Nagaland is unique. Though, the programme is under the Department of Rural Development yet the approach is two fold, viz., Microfinance through Self Help Groups (SHGs) and Microfinance through Village Development Board (VDB).

Realizing the growing importance of SHG bank linkage programme and as per the recommendations of the NABARD Working Group, the RBI decided to extend SHG-bank linkage programme beyond the pilot phase and advised the banks to make it a part of their mainstream banking function. As an effect, micro finance through SHGs has gradually emerged in Nagaland. The State Governments and NABARD are playing a more proactive role in this area by identifying various NGOs/MFIs, organizing training programme for capacity building, etc.

Considering the plight of the State the adoption and implementation of Microfinance Programme is noteworthy. Despite of making some headway, micro finance in Nagaland is still in its nascent stages. Microfinance yet remains a powerful tool for development. It may not be a panacea, but it has brought a sea of change in the lives of many. By reaching the unreached poor in the rural areas micro finance innovations are yielding results and giving hope to the large number of poor through providing credit.

The emergence of Microfinance and Self Help Groups in the State is a revolution and if properly managed can bring about further positive change not only in the economy but also in the quality of life of the large (general) masses. But in order to make the approaches more useful means for poverty alleviation and sustainable rural development, there is a need for sincere intervention by the promotional agencies particularly the banks and Block authority in the areas of awareness building, skill development and training. Considering the number of clients, range of services and the increase involvement of both formal and informal sector institutions, there is tremendous scope for the sustaining of micro finance development in Nagaland.

Thiyam Surjit Meitei is the author of the paper *"Microfinance A Tool for Accelerating Financial Inclusion: A Case Study in Manipur"*. Microfinance refers to a broad range of financial services, primarily credit, made available to people who do not have access to formal banking services. Normally, these services would be required in areas with small population and "ticket-size" entailed would also be relatively smaller (factors making banks' presence unviable). Therefore, Micro-financial institutions (MFIs) facilitate the reach of financial services at a more "micro" level. Microfinance takes an integral role to develop economic condition of the rural poor. It also gives the financial services to those who cannot access formal financial services. The poor skilled people who have no collateral security can also access microfinance loan easily for running their small business. Now-a-day the commercial bank knows the importance of microfinance and they introduced the microfinance as a part of their activities. They form the SHGs with no-frills account and give the micro loan through their account. It gives a great impact to the financial inclusion

From this study it is found that the number of bank branches in the State is least compared with its population (i.e., as on March 2009 population per bank branch is 33,000) and it is necessary to open more number of bank branches in the State so that to reach the banking facilities to the maximum population of the State. Again the number of SHGs bank linked and number of no-frill account open in different nine districts of the State are positively correlated it means if the number of SHGs is increased then the number of no-frill account open in nine different districts are also increased. In all over India there are around 6.9 million SHGs are linked with bank that is those members who are in this group have been getting banking services. Last but not the least it is also cleared that after joining to microfinance the members of the SHGs get the formal banking facilities in the simple and easy way. Therefore it can be concluded that microfinance is the one of the best tool for accelerating the financial inclusion.

Four papers were contributed in the sub-theme Financial **Inclusion and Commercial Banks.** They are:

"Initiatives of Commercial Banks for Financial Inclusion: A Case of Selected Nationalized Banks in India" was the title of the first paper contributed by **M. Vasan** highlighting the role and initiation taken by the nationalized commercial banks for financial inclusion in India. Despite of having around 87,000 bank branches operating all over he country, the average population per bank office is about 14,000 with high rate of more than 30,000 in the North East India and less than 10,000 in southern States of India.

In India, the focus of the financial inclusion at present is confined to ensuring a bare minimum access to a savings bank account without frills, to all. Internationally, the financial inclusion has been viewed in a much wider perspective. Having a current account/savings account on its own, is not regarded as an accurate indicator of financial inclusion. "Financial Inclusion" efforts should offer at a minimum, access to a range of financial services including savings, long and short term credit, insurance, pensions, mortgages, money transfers, etc., and all this at a reasonable cost.

He also emphasizes the initiative taken by the selected nationalized commercial banks such as State Bank of India, Bank of Baroda, Canara Bank, Corporation Banks, Punjab and National Banks in different States and region of the country along with different schemes, fact and figures. Challenges ahead while implementing financial inclusion such as lack of proper model; risk management; cash management; lack of viable programme, etc., were also highlighted which need immediate attention from the stakeholders, government, business correspondents.

The success of financial inclusion lies with the joint efforts of government, banks, business correspondence, business facilitators and clients. In his concluding remarks he says that financial inclusion is not a onetime effort, but it is an ongoing process.

It is concluded that the financial inclusion is not a onetime effort; it is an ongoing process. It is a huge project which requires concerted and team efforts from all the stakeholders such as the Government, financial institutions, the regulators, the private sector and the community at large. From the sporadic attempts of today dispersed across the nation, it should gather momentum and grow in geometric proportions and develop into a focused and effective movement. If this is to be achieved, it requires the passionate involvement, dedication and commitment of all stake holders. It requires a major mindset change in the minds of every individual involved—banker, bureaucrat, regulator *et. al.*, and, therefore, creating awareness at all levels. At the same time, the role of technology in the whole scenario cannot be undermined either. It has to be admitted that today, more than even before, technology plays a vital role in bringing about integration in society of all social and economic classes. Accessibility, affordability, appropriateness and benefits determine how deep financial inclusion penetrates the social fabric of the village. Financial inclusion can empower even the poorest person and bring about a dramatic change in his fate.

Another joint paper contributed by **Ratan Borman and Ayekpam Ibemcha Chanu** on *"Role of RRBs in Financial Inclusion in Tribal Areas : A Case study of Langpi Dehangi Rural Bank in Assam Hills"*. A case study on the Langpi Dehangi Rural Bank (LDRB), a regional rural bank of Assam, is the core area of their study to assess the bank's contribution towards the struggle of financial inclusion. The LDRB, which has been working in Assam Hills since 1982 to bring more and more population within the fold of banking services by extension of bank offices in rural and remote areas, providing access to basic banking services, facilitating bank accounts, savings, credit and other banking services in order to achieve inclusive growth is the only regional rural bank that covers entire two hill districts of Assam. This paper examines the role of LDRB in delivering banking/financial services with regard to financial inclusion in Assam hills and problems faced by the bank in rendering such services.

Consequences of financial exclusion will vary depending on the nature and extent of services denied. Financial exclusion complicates day-to-day cash flow management—being financially excluded the low-income households as well as the micro and small enterprises deal entirely in cash and are susceptible to irregular cash flows. In case of low-income households, the absence of access to bank accounts and other saving opportunities will lead to lack of savings; low investments; lack of financial planning and security for old age; difficulties in gaining access to credit or getting credit from informal sources at exorbitant rates; increased unemployment due to lack of self-employment opportunities; higher incidence of crime, etc. The small business may suffer due to loss of access to middle class and higher-income consumers, higher cash handling costs, delays in remittances of money, lots of reliance on private money lenders for small credits. It may thus be advocated that financial exclusion not only widens the *"Rich-Poor divide "*, it also lead to *"Social Exclusion"*. Hence, inclusive financial system is required because it enhances efficiency and welfare by providing avenues for secure and safe saving practices and by facilitating a whole range of efficient financial services

Financial inclusion is a win-win opportunity for the poor, for the banks and for the nation (Subbarao, 2009). In such a situation, the Regional Rural banks can play a significant role. The case study of LDRB easily shows about its performance and wide prospect of financial inclusion in the future. It is also fact that most of the financially excluded groups are from the rural areas. As RRBs are mainly concentrated in the rural areas of the country, a special focus may be given to RRBs with regard to financial inclusion. In the conclusion, it is also suggested that the government should take strong initiative for financial inclusion by formulating pro-poor people policy and programmes.

"Banking Service and Financial Inclusion in Mizoram : Special Reference to NABARD Activity" is the title of the paper contributed by Chanambam **Nalini Devi.** In India out of 100 persons, only 31 persons hold a bank account in a bank. While in the North Eastern Region it is just 19 persons out of 100 that hold a bank account. This finding is based on the assumption that one person has only one account, theoretically speaking while this assumption may not be correct as many persons could have more than one bank account. We find that on an all India basis 59 per cent of adult population in the country has bank accounts in other words, 41 per cent of the population is un-banked. In rural areas the coverage is 39 per cent against 60 per cent in the urban area. The un-banked population is higher in the North Eastern region and the Eastern Region. Generally in North Eastern region credit deposit ratio (CDR) is low as compared to the other parts of India. In case of Tripura, the CD ratio is 33 per cent against the national average of 73 per cent as on 31st March, 2011. When compared to Tripura, Mizoram is a little bit higher that is 46.34 per cent.

For development of any nation, the role of banking is very important, without the proper functioning in the banking sector there is difficult to setting development target. So, banking performance and developmental activities go hand in hand. Today, banks are already offering services over mobile to communities that have been historically unbanked. In rural areas, where accessibility is a problem, banks are using the micro-finance network and business correspondents and facilitators to bring more people under the ambit of banking services. Capitalizing on the huge untapped potential in smaller towns and cities and rendering financial services to this segment of people poses a big challenge, few banks have explored technology solutions to increase the scale of their micro-finance portfolios, with the use of smart cards and core banking solution. However often a multitude of operational issues and quoted as reasons for lagging behind in financial inclusion targets. Till such time complete technology integration takes place on all fronts, there are bound to be areas where intermediate brick-and-mortar structures need to be in place. Even with Business Correspondents (BCs) issues arise regarding their supervision and customer grievance redressed. Certain accounting issues in this regard also needed to be addressed. All these operational issues and many more can be resolved if banks begin to look at financial inclusion as business opportunity rather than an obligation to fulfil their corporate social responsibility.

North-Eastern Region of India is lacking behind in almost all the sectors like infrastructural facilities, industrial sector and service sector which include under this sector mainly hospital facilities and banking facilities. For all round development we need to develop proper facilities for banking service in different areas in this region. Recently, D. Subbarao has stressed that "Credit Flow" in North East as a major challenge and said that the RBI would prioritise this as a major task to stimulate growth of industry, trade and commerce in the region". Low credit deposit ratio in the region is an area of concern.

"Regional Rural Bank and its Role in Financial Inclusion–A Case Study of Meghalaya" is a joint paper contributed by **S. Sarma and Th. Chaoba Singh.** The major segment of Indian population lives in the rural area and most of them are not availing benefits of

financial institution, only 41per cent of the adult population of the country has access to the benefits of financial institution. In other words we can say that 59 per cent of the population is outside the purview of the financial inclusion. Our nation has introduced several reforms to inculcate the formal financial habit of the excluded people. In the Eleventh Plan idea of financial inclusion has received a deep attention of financial regulators, government and the banking sector, like many other nations.

In India, rural credit policy was framed in keeping two main objectives in mined (i) To include a large number of population within the formal financial system; and (ii) By using credit instrument for poverty eradication. To achieve these goals Government of India and RBI had introduced series of measures but failed to achieve the goals. A working group was constituted in the year 1975 by Government of India under the chairmanship of M. Narasimham to explore the possibilities of an alternative rural credit agency. Following the recommendation of the above said committee RBI were set up first on 2nd October, 1975. As on 31st March 2010 there were 82 RRBs with a network of 15,475 branches spread over 619 districts in 26 states and 1 union territory.

It has derived a conclusion that the volume of deposit, the volume of loans and advances disbursed, number of account opened has shown an upward trend and the growth rate of increase was marginal as compared to our neighbouring States. The branch expansion was almost stagnant except in the last two years. Therefore, it is very much necessary to explore the ways and means to provide financial services to the rural and poor people as rural development has direct bearing in the overall economic development of the country.

Financial Inclusion and ICT is another sub theme of the book. Two papers are contributed in this area by the researchers:

"Information Technology Application Models for Financial Inclusion" is a paper based on information technology contributed by **L. S. Sharma.** Financial access is necessary as it enables access to financial savings, credit, remittance, insurance, pensions from formal financial institutions at cheaper cost. Taken together this enables movement from the margin to mainstream. It allows a paper

trail of transactions effected through the banking system and thus curbs illegal transactions. The inhibitors to this process are the small character of loans. Low value, high volume nature of transactions in the penny economy makes administrations of loans and recoveries costly. Once appropriate technological solutions are in place, then technology can be leveraged effectively to overcome the barriers of geography. RBI emphasizes a bank led model of financial inclusion relying on information technology solution.

Technological developments in the form of telecommunications and internet technology have helped to extend the banking services in the remote areas. Technology has able to reach out to the customers and instead of making customers approach towards banks, with the development of technology using hand held devices connection through GPRS/GSM/CDMA/landline networks. Technology will have to play a vital role if financial inclusion has to be successful. Lack of adequate number of bank branches and service delivery models has been one of the hurdles in catering to the financial services of the underprivileged. A branch-based delivery mechanism is not feasible as it entails huge costs. Hence, there arises the need as well as demand for trying out with new types of technology based delivery mechanisms.

The study highlights the importance of financial inclusion and discusses the various technological experiments which have been adopted to reduce the gap of financial exclusion. It has been seen that an overwhelming majority of rural India do not avail the financial services from banks. Although most of them are aware of the benefits of the basic financial services, they are not able to reap the benefits as the transactions cost and necessary requirements for opening an account cannot be fulfilled easily. So the financial institutions have to tailor made the services for the beneficiaries. Once the transactions cost is brought down to a minimum, the services can be provided by bringing down the price of the services. Opening an account requires documents relating to the identity of the person, income statement, age proof, residence proof, etc. The vulnerable section of the population does not possess and properly keep evidences of such documents. The Unique Identity Number (UIN) is expected to be a major breakthrough and it may be used as the documentation proof for access to financial services.

"Microfinance and ICT Infrastructure in Rural India: Accelerating Financial Inclusion through Innovative Technologies and Alternative Channels" is the title of a joint paper contributed by **H. Ramananda Singh and N. Dhaneshwar Singh.** The microfinance sector in India has made tremendous progress in terms of size and magnitude, outreach and dimensions of socio-economic impact in the recent years. From mere 500 SHG under pilot phase by NABARD in 1992, SHG-Bank Linkage programmes of NABARD has now achieved the spectacular growth in as much as 6.1 million SHGs with outstanding saving of Rs. 54,556.2, million and loan outstanding of Rs.2,26,798.5 million as on 31 March, 2009. Moreover, many MFIs of different legal forms have also contributed for exponential growth of this sector through innovative technology driven financial products and services.

One of the key challenges in extending access to financial services in under-served rural markets has been the high 'cost to serve'. This includes the costs associated with origination; supervision and continuous monitoring that are incurred in these markets. Increasingly, technology is being viewed as key to a low-cost banking strategy foı the rural market.

If the current structure of the bank branches were to be used to cater to the need and requirement of the rural population, it would mean setting up a bank branch in virtually every village. The cost of such a large network would not justify the revenues generated from it, given the nature of transactions. Thus, the challenge for banks/ MFIs is to innovate a low-cost network/delivery channel with a high outreach and flexibility with respect to the timing of its operation.

Information and Communication Technology (ICT) can address both of the above challenges. ICTs will continue to impact microfinance operations worldwide. As prices of relevant technology like ATMs, biometrics, voice recognition, smart-cards, and PDAs continue to fall, more MFIs will be able to take advantage of the benefits they offer. New technologies and applications are constantly being developed aimed at increasing the reach and efficiency of microfinance organizations. Improvement will make operations more secure, increase transparency (and thus scalability), reduce repetitive tasks, and provide data mining capabilities that will allow MFIs to compete effectively and better manage their operations. While mobile money is now in its emerging stages, it is rapidly moving toward consolidation and growth.

To conclude, the active participations and collaborative efforts of various agencies like banks, MFIs, corporate houses, telecoms, Government, regulators, etc., are needed for systematic integrations and harmonic synchronization between microfinance and ICT infrastructure for accelerating financial inclusion in the coming years. It will create the necessary atmosphere to create wealth and enable rural India. We now need to build on this and work towards empowering India.

There are two papers on the sub theme **Financial Inclusions and Micro Insurance.** They are:

Sreemoye Guha Roy contributed a chapter on *"Micro Insurance-Tailor Made for the Poor"*. Micro Insurance, the subject matter of this paper, is the most recent in the wave of micro movements that have been sweeping international development thinking and practice in recent years. Founded on the basic principles of the micro credit revolution, micro insurance extends social security mechanisms and insurance products to groups that are in dire needs but have been historically bypassed by these services. Recognizing the poor as willing and capable agents in their own socio-economic change, micro insurance seeks to incorporate marginalized and low income groups in the main stream capitalist economy by providing them with insurance products that address their security needs and purchasing capacities.

Micro-insurance is a key element in the financial services package for people at the bottom of the pyramid. The poor face more risks than the well-off, but more importantly they are more vulnerable to the same risk. Usually, the poor face two types of risks—idiosyncratic (specific to the household) and covariate (common, e.g., drought, epidemic, etc.). To combat these risks, the poor do pro-active risk management—grain storage, savings, asset accumulation (especially bullocks), loans from friends and relatives, etc. However, the prevalent forms of risk management (in kind savings, self-insurance, mutual insurance) which were appropriate earlier are no longer adequate. Poverty is not just a state of deprivation but has latent vulnerability. Micro insurance should, therefore, provide greater economic and psychological security to the poor as it reduces exposure to multiple risks and cushions the impact of a disaster. There is an overwhelming demand for social protection among the poor. Micro insurance in conjunction with micro savings and micro credit could, therefore, go a long way in keeping this segment away from the poverty trap and would truly be an integral component of financial inclusion.

Micro insurance is the key component of poverty alleviation. But, the penetration of insurance products among the poor is very low. This is mainly because of lack of awareness about the benefits of insurance and reluctance of insurers to sell insurance to the poor due to high delivery costs. Keeping this in view, insurance companies should go beyond devising new products to improving their processes for building awareness, marketing enrolment, premium collection, claim settlement and renewal among the hitherto unreached. Micro insurance will also require a regulatory framework that is flexible enough to allow Insurers, NGOs, and Self Help Groups to innovate in product design and delivery models to make insurance affordable to the poor and still be economically viable. In the golden words of C.K. Prahlad, "Improving the lives of the billons of people at the bottom of the pyramid is a noble endeavour. It can also be lucrative."

"Micro Insurance for Micro Entrepreneurs of Manipur—The Way Forward" is another paper on Micro insurance contributed by **A. Rajmani Singha.** Of late, the micro credit-microfinance-microenterprise movement has been making a silent revolution in the upliftment of rural India through the emergence of vibrant Self Help Groups (SHGs) and it has become an effective tool to address the problem of poverty and empowerment. These provisions have enabled the poor households to increase their income and build their own assets, employment and empowerment. But, still they are vulnerable to withstand unexpected events and remain exposed to multiple risks, which take away the gains made due to their association with the SHGs. Besides, the poor living in risk prone area (floods and drought), are not willing to invest further for their enterprise development fearing that their business assets are exposed to risks. To overcome such unexpected risks micro insurance (MI)

will be the best option to ensure them a social and economic security. MI is the provision of insurance cover to the low income households.

As the Micro insurance sector in Manipur is in its infancy stage, all the stakeholders, viz., government agencies, regulator, insurers, banks, MFIs, SHPIs, and NGOs and SHGs have to put in their concerted efforts in building the sector into a new height. The significant and important of this sector and linkage with other sectors such as micro lending, micro credit, and micro finance and micro enterprise should be made aware to all the stakeholders. Here, government both central and State shall launch a Micro Insurance pilot project in a few selected subdivision or district level to demonstrate to the mainstream insurers that micro insurance can be profitably delivered to the poor in a sustainable manner provided needed flexibilities are inbuilt in the products and processes customized for the target market. Government shall dedicate a Special Fund for innovations which will assist the pioneering stakeholders, to experiment with the innovative products, flexible processes.

Even though the recent IRDA guidelines on micro insurance have recognized the SHGs working for at least 3 years, as micro insurance agents, it has not recognized the SHGs as an eligible entity to take the insurance cover in its name. IRDA has to recognize all SHGs / CBOs as an informal entity and allow the insurers to transact business with the SHGs / CBOs as done by the RBI in case of SHG Bank linkage programme. IRDA shall revise its guidelines and bring the Community managed insurance programmes, under regulation, as they are real innovators. IRDA shall prescribe a lower capital requirement as in Uganda and Sri Lanka, so that the international micro insurers will be attracted into India and they will bring their expertise to take the sector forward. IRDA shall designate selected institutions as Resource Institutions on MI and they may be given the responsibility of nurturing the small NGOs and help them in putting the systems and procedures in place for effective management of the MI programme.

Micro insurance is now only NGO/ MFI driven. The alternate channels like bank branches of commercial banks, RRBs, co-operatives, in the rural areas, Post offices, Agro input dealer networks, SHG marketers shall be developed to increase the outreach. For the poor to make it affordable, the premium should be as low as possible.

Financial Inclusion and Rural Development is the six sub theme of the book and there are two papers contributed by the researchers:

O. Deepak Kumar Singh wrote a paper on *"Financial Inclusion: Its Need in Rural Development of Manipur"*. The present paper highlights the different points to the importance of financial inclusion in the State of Manipur. Further, it is also found that the spirit of financial inclusion among the people of the State. A few commentators have also pointed to the similarity between sub-prime crisis and financial inclusion. The sub-prime market was originated to provide finance to people with weak credit histories (financial inclusion).

The majority of the population of the State is largely excluded from financial services and it needs to be more careful. Therefore, it is necessary to cover all the villages by Bank after making an accurate household survey. The need of the time is to properly assess the products of various financial inclusions. Never yet experience facility of the financial products in the State includes No Frill SB Account, Small over Draft Facility for General Consumption, General Credit Card for Income based activity, micro insurance life and disability cover health insurance cover, mutual fund, etc. But these financial products available in the rural people of the State are limited only to the private sector and cannot be easily afforded by rural poor.

Financial Inclusion has far reaching consequences, which can help many people come out of adverse poverty conditions. The financial markets must act responsibly and ensure that the spirit of financial inclusion is not breached in the future.

S.S. Mahapatra contributed a paper on *"SRDA and Inclusive growth in Sikkim"*. This is a noble attempt made by the author. Sikkim Rural Development Agency (S.R.D.A.) is an organization. The main objective of establishment of this organization is to involve the development of rural poor (BPL) in the developmental process, which is based on the philosophy that all the people should equally share the benefit of development. This organization is making all out effort to identify the local needs and resources. The organization is implementing a number of poverty alleviation schemes under ***Swarnajayanti Gram Swarojgar Yojana*** (SGSY).

The SGSY is a holistic programme covering all aspects of self employment such as organization of the poor into self–help groups, training, credit, technology, infrastructure, marketing, etc. The SGSY gives emphasis on group financing for poverty alleviation by organizing the rural poor living under BPL category into self help groups (SHGs). Accordingly the bulk of assistance under SGSY is expected to be provided to SHGs for supporting the group level micro enterprises and individual enterprises established by their members. The SGSY seeks to promote self employment opportunities to rural people through promotion of micro enterprises in clusters which would facilitate proper implementation and monitoring of the activities effectively. The objective of SGSY is to bring the ***Swarozgaris*** above the poverty line by providing them with income generating assets through mix of Bank credit and Government subsidy by ensuring appreciable sustained level of income over a period of time.

The last sub theme of the book is **Financial Inclusions and Entrepreneurship Development**. A lone chapter is presented below:

"Entrepreneurship Development and Financial Inclusion in North East India: Past, Present and Future Challenges" is the last chapter contributed jointly by **Konwar N. and Felix. M.J.** Cultivating an entrepreneurship spirit among the masses is a very important strategy for economic development of a country. It is a mean to empower the poor societies. Entrepreneurs are the main agents to create a robust economic activity between nations, societies. When nations, societies, individuals are actively trade with each other, there will be less thought of "involvement of unwanted activities" towards each other. We realize we are interdependent. War is pointless. If I kill you, I in turn kill my own self. You and I are one. We need each other like the activities in North East India

Recently we came across the works of Andrew Bernstein, Dr. Edward Younkins and Michael Novak that documents how entrepreneurship brings peace, create wealth and help in the moral development of the ethical entrepreneur. A poster boy for ethical entrepreneurship in India is Narayana Murthy and Azim Premji. Imagine if 100 Narayana Murthys and Azim Premji is created in India. How much change could that bring to a billion Indians?

More Financial literacy outreach should be organized by financial institutions both public as well as private. To develop awareness on different schemes of government, subsidies and loans, microcredit and finance, rigorous efforts of the government is the need of the hour. One of the authors has been involved with the rural planning and credit department of Reserve Bank of India (RBI-NE) in these exercises. RBI had opened 6 new sub-offices in the 6 States of North East India, except Assam which has its regional office in Guwahati since 1949. Agartala in Tripura has inaugurated its office on 18th May, 2011.This is to encourage the other public and private banks to be operational so as to include the 70 per cent population who are financially excluded in North East India.

SECTION - I

Financial Inclusion and Inclusive Growth

2

Financial Inclusion: An Impact Analysis on Institutional Effort for Outreach

PURNASHREE DAS AND SUJIT SIKIDAR

Introduction

A country's progress cannot be measured only by its number of institutions, size of population, per capita income and its GDP. While a country like India has made significant progress in many fronts but a large segment of its populace still remains excluded from the country's formal financial system with limited access to financial services. The country has long realized the significance of financial inclusion and has made commendable efforts to realize the same, but it still has a long way to go.

Financial inclusion is an all embracing strategy encompassing several issues such as:

- Opening a bank account for those who so far remain excluded and bringing banking to unbanked areas;
- Provide access to credit;
- Provide affordable insurance and remittance facilities; and
- Credit counselling and financial education.

In 2003, the then Secretary General of the United Nations (UN), Dr. Kofi Annan had said: "The stark reality is that most poor people in the work still lack access to *sustainable financial services*, whether it is *savings, credit or insurance*. The great challenge before us is to address the constraints that exclude people from full participation in the financial sector. Together we can and must build inclusive financial sectors that help people improve their lives".

It may be noted that in India, the present focus of financial inclusion is confined to ensuring every citizen a bare minimum access to a savings bank account without frills, i.e., hassle-free. However, when considered from an international perspective, financial inclusion is a much wider concept; simply having and operating a savings account is not an indicator of financial inclusion.

In its platinum jubilee year, the RBI's vision is to connect every Indian to the country's banking system. In tune with this objective, it has permitted commercial banks to make provisions for 'no-frills' account as well as to use the services of NGOs/SHGs, micro-finance institutions and other civil society organizations as intermediaries for providing financial and banking services from January 2006. Moreover, it has also asked the commercial banks in different regions to start a 100 per cent financial inclusion campaign on a pilot basis as a result of which States or U.T.s like Pondicherry, Himachal Pradesh and Kerala have already announced 100 per cent financial inclusion in all their districts.

India is an agrarian economy with almost two-thirds of the population living in the rural and semi-urban areas, and directly or indirectly dependent on agriculture as a means of sustenance. And this lot of the population is bereft of institutional support, most notably of institutional financial access. The role of financial institutions in bringing about balanced inclusive growth cannot be over emphasized.

Having considered the issues cited above, we have undertaken a research enquiry to ascertain by way of an experimental study on the extent of financial inclusion that has been achieved in a given select part of a State. The present research enquiry has been undertaken with the following objectives.

Objectives

1. To ascertain the institutional efforts made towards financial inclusion.
2. To conduct a field survey over select pockets of Kamrup district where institutional effort has been made to launch a programme of financial outreach and inclusion.
3. To make a comparative study of similar efforts made in two other pockets of the country.

Methodology Adopted

The present study has been conducted by the researchers by undertaking a field visit to the Kukurmara village of Kamrup District on 10th of November, 2010 and Parakuchi village in Kamrup district on 3rd August, 2011. In the Kukurmara village in the Kamrup District, the researchers had visited the Assam Gramin Vikas Bank (AGVB) which is located in the Kukurmara Market, to gather primary information of the extent of financial inclusion in the village and the role of the AGVB in this context.

In the Parakuchi village in the Kamrup District, the research investigators had visited the Assam Gramin Vikas Bank, Jarubari Branch which covers a portion of the village; the United Bank of India, Kulshi Branch which covers the rest of the village. Both these branches were visited with an aim to gather primary information on the Financial Inclusion campaign and the outcomes thereof.

Rationale for Selecting the Selected Villages

The selected villages of Kukurmara and Parakuchi have been selected for the purpose of the present study because they have been adopted as model villages for the purpose of financial inclusion by financial institutions; and in both the villages the RBI officials had conducted a massive campaign for financial outreach and inclusion. The present researchers tried to access the outcome of the campaign. For this purpose they tried to ascertain the extent of financial inclusion and the penetration of banking services in the selected villages under study.

Having discussed the rationale of the study, we now propose to present the outcomes of the field surveys carried out in the village of Kukurmara in Kamrup District on the 10th of November, 2010; and on the village of Parakuchi in Kamrup District on 3rd of August, 2011 which have been discussed hereunder.

Outcome of Field Survey Conducted in Kukurmara Village, Kamrup District

A survey was conducted by the present paper writers jointly on the 10th of November, 2010 in the Kukurmara village of Kamrup District which has been adopted as a model village for financial inclusion by the Assam Gramin Vikas Bank (AGVB) under the aegis of the RBI. The outcome of our survey has been deliberated hereunder.

Coverage among the Villagers

The survey revealed that the village has a total population of 552 households. Up to September, 2010, the bank's efforts have yielded 88.59 per cent financial inclusion in the village. To be more precise, a total of 489 families have been financially included, whereas only 63 families (11.41%) have been excluded from the purview of banking services. By financial inclusion it is meant the number of families (at least one person from each family) having account with AGVB, Kukurmara. The survey also revealed that such financial exclusion could be mainly attributed to:

- Illiteracy,
- Shyness of the villagers to come to the Bank premises,
- Lack of substantial income to open an account,
- Inability to meet the expense of making a photograph,
- Inability to comply with KYC norms.

Even though the bank offers 'no-frills' account, the excluded population has not shown much eagerness to open accounts with the Bank. However, for the purpose of making a photograph, a digital camera was provided to the Local Gaon Panchayat, but still it could not be utilized for the purpose.

The Bank is currently pursuing the Business Facilitator (BF) Model, whereby the BF acts as middleman for mobilizing deposits and opening accounts for the villagers who are relieved from the duty to personally come to the Bank branch for opening accounts or depositing money. Thus, their valuable time and conveyance cost is saved. However, the RBI has directed all the banks to adopt the Business Correspondent (BC) model and the AGVB hopes to get the BC model streamlined by 2012 which would go a long way in mobilizing more resources and extending more credit services to the village of Kukurmara, thereby guaranteeing it 100 per cent financial inclusion in the near future.

Extension of Credit Facilities

The credit delivery system adopted by AGVB as observed by the present researchers has been deliberated hereunder. The AGVB has done an excellent work in the village by extending credit facilities to around 400 families, constituting approximately 72 per cent of the population. The different types of credit facilities offered by the bank are:

(*a*) **Loans under SGRY:** ?5 Self Help Groups (SHGs) have been identified and given credit under the Swarojgar Gramin Rojgar Yojana (SGRY) whereby Rs. 10,000-20,000 is initially given to them as direct loan, and after its repayment another sum of Rs. 25,000 is given as credit. Out of this, Rs. 10,000 is a subsidy on which on interest is also required to be paid. It is basically a Revolving Fund loan where interest is charged at 8.5 per cent per annum on the balance Rs. 15,000.

(*b*) **Piggery Loan:** A total number of 13 persons have been given loans for raising piggery which is quite an attractive business in the locality. An amount of Rs. 20,000 is given to each person getting credit under this scheme.

(*c*) **Weaving Activity Loan:** 3 SHG groups have been identified and given credit under this scheme of DRDA whereby an amount of Rs. 2,50,000 is released in a span of 3 years. Here, again, Rs. 1,25,000 is subsidy.

The village essentially being a Scheduled Caste village is eligible for 50 per cent subsidy for all forms of financial accommodations.

(*d*) **General Credit Card (AGVBGCC):** Such credit cards have been distributed to 42 people in the said village. These cards have been issued under Government of India's instruction to the Bank. The landless farmers or those villagers, who do not have any property to keep as mortgage so as to obtain loans, qualify for this scheme of the AGVB, whereby up to Rs. 25,000 credit limit is given to the assisted persons on no security basis.

(*e*) **Kisan Credit Cards:** 8 Kisan Credit Cards have been distributed till date by the bank, whereby a total of Rs. 1,48,800 has been disbursed.

(*f*) **Retail Trade Loans:** Such loans have been given for starting retail shops, etc., to a total of 7 persons amounting to a total of Rs. 40,000.

(*g*) **Loans to Joint Liability Groups (JLGs):** Such loans have been given to 3 groups for raising Piggery. A total of Rs. 3,00,000 have been provided under this scheme.

(*h*) **Overdraft:** The overdraft facility has been given against "no-frills" account also whereby the customers enjoy a zero balance account. An overdraft of Rs. 500 has been given to 11 persons each for miscellaneous small activities. This is, indeed, an innovative credit arrangement by the Bank.

(*i*) **Handloom Loan:** 1 Handloom Weaver Group has been identified constituting 5 weavers and an assistance of Rs. 1,00,000 has been extended without any form of security. However, this loan does not qualify for any subsidy.

We also visited the Ziakur village under the same survey. It may be mentioned here that Ziakur village has also been adopted by the AGVB. The Bank is also actively performing similar work in the Ziakur village, but not with so much success. The level of financial inclusion achieved in Ziakur village is much less than that of Kukurmara village. In course of our survey, we met the officials of AGVB, including the Branch Manager, Sri Bratajit Das who furnished us with all the relevant information necessary for our survey. We are beholden to the people in the branch of the AGVB. It has also been revealed during our survey that Ziakur village is also under the coverage of the AGVB, Kukurmara Branch.

Outcome of Field Survey Conducted in Parakuchi Village

The present authors had undertaken a field visit on 3rd August, 2011 in order to do a research investigation to examine the extent of financial inclusion and outreach achieved under the Financial Inclusion campaign in Parakuchi village in Kamrup district under Chayani Borduar Block which is located around 40 km away from Guwahati city.

On the date of our visit to Parakuchi village on 3rd August, 2011, there is no bank branch located at Parakuchi; instead bank branches from other neighbouring villages serve the banking needs of the village. Agriculture is the main source of income for the village. The village has a total of around 500 households, of which nearly 80 per cent have been brought under the banking network.

The Parakuchi village came into limelight in the month of December 2010 when the RBI Deputy Governor had visited the village on the 12th December, 2010 to launch a massive Financial Outreach campaign. The financial outreach camp was organized by the Parakuchi Boys United Club on 12th December, 2010 which mobilized its members to take advantage of banking services made available under the scheme.

The banking needs of the Parakuchi village are met by the Assam Gramin Vikas Bank, Jarubari, United Bank of India, Kushi Branch and the State Bank of India, Mirza Branch. Interestingly, a portion of the village is covered by the AGVB, Jarubari and the remaining portion by the UBI, Kushi Branch; but since the State government's salaries and pensions are paid through the SBI, therefore, the SBI has an overall presence in the village, although the distance of the SBI, Mirza Branch is substantial than the other branches serving the village. All of these banks participated in the financial outreach camp.

The nearest bank to the Parakuchi village is AGVB, Jarubari branch and UBI, Kulshi branch. More than 60 per cent of the villagers, who attended this financial outreach camp on the 12th of December, 2010 have opened their bank account with these two banks.

As a first step, we had visited the Assam Gramin Vikas Bank located at Jarubari. We contacted Mr. Jiten Kumar, the Branch Manager and other officials of the bank from whom we could gather the primary information relating to the efforts made by the bank towards financial inclusion. On the day of the financial outreach camp, a total of 239 zero balance bank accounts were opened by the AGVB, Jarubari branch. Subsequently, the number of bank accounts opened rose to 255.

After gathering the pertinent information from AGVB, Jarubari, the present researchers visited the UBI, Kulshi Branch which was also a participant of the Financial Inclusion campaign on 12th December, 2010. Our research investigation revealed that on the very day of the financial outreach camp, around 300 no-frills accounts were opened by the UBI, Kulshi branch.

To encourage the development of banking habits among the villagers, an amount of Rs. 100 have been collected on the day of opening the bank account in the financial outreach camp so that a Pass Book could be given.

As a mark of incentive for financial outreach, the RBI has gifted certain pairs of desk and benches to the Parakuchi Uccha Buniyadi Bidyalaya in the month of December 2010. Besides, the RBI has also provided a TV set and a computer during the same period. The idea behind this move was to bring the teachers, students and officials attracted towards the banking services. This will, at the same time, make them a potential stakeholder of financial services and at the same time bring unbanked into the banking network.

Fortunately, the teachers and officials of the school who were outside the banking network had also opened their account on the same day.

The research investigation also revealed that the financial outreach camp that was launched in Parakuchi on 12th December, 2010 has encouraged women members to open bank accounts. On the date of our field survey, we have ascertained that around 300 women members of different households at Parakuchi village have opened their bank accounts spread over the three bank branches namely the AGVB, Jarubar; the UBI, Kulshi; and the SBI, Mirza branch. This testifies the improvement of banking habits, savings behaviour and enhancement of financial awareness.

Our research investigation has revealed that the remittances from the Indira Awas Yojana (IAY), Job Cards, Pension, etc., are made through the bank accounts, which is why the villagers are now keener on opening a no-frills bank account.

Disbursement of loans under different heads also constitutes a kind of financial inclusion and empowerment of the rural populace. Different kinds of loans extended to the population of the village include: Kisan Credit Card (KCC), Self Help Group (SHG) loans, agriculture and allied activities loan like piggery, horticulture, weaving, etc.

With reference to the Objective No. 3 as stated above, we now focus our attention on two other locations, viz., one in Andhra Pradesh and the other in West Bengal. The extent of innovation undertaken by financial institutions in respect of financial inclusion in those locations is discussed hereunder.

Institutional Efforts Undertaken in Andhra Pradesh

- Andhra Pradesh has prominent MFIs, viz., SKS, Spandana Spoorthy Financial Services, Share Microfin and Asmitha Microfin has proposed in 2011 to merge their business. Mergers and consolidation was considered to be an alternative proposition in order to reduce operational costs and achieve scale of operation. This alternative was tested owing to Andhra Pradesh curbed lending and loan recovery practices.

- MFIs are an improvement over money lenders charging 60 per cent interest and using forcc to seize assets. Unlike banks, MFIs lend without any collaterals. Till 2010, they charged interest rates up to 30 per cent to cover high operational costs. Business grew relatively at a higher rate largely because of the absence of collateral; and the peer pressure among borrower groups kept defaults below 2 per cent.
- There are lots of contradictions and counter repercussions regarding regulation of MFIs. The suggested measure may be to lay prudential norms by the RBI, and the State government to monitor over the activities of MFIs.
- It will be pertinent in this context to mention the extent of business created by the MFIs as indicated below:

Table 2.1 : Performance Appraisal of MFIs in Andhra Pradesh

Name of MFIs	*Net Worth Rs. (in crores)*	*Asset Under Management (AUM)*
SKS	1,800	4,300
Spandana Spoorthy Financial Services	500	3400
Share & Asmitha	450	3200
Basix	350-400	1100

Source : *The Economic Times*, dated 13th August, 2011.

- The Draft Micro financial Sector (Developmental Regulation) Bill 2011 says the RBI will regulate the MFIs and will enjoy the power to frame policies for the sector.
- The RBI is not fully empowered to regulate the MFIs. To give loans to MFIs is a bank's job. Banking is always a risk-taking business and banking can never be done in complacency.
- Asset quality under management of an MFI can be a concern. This is more so as interest rate is hardening. As a general rule, when interest rates rise probability of NPA becomes high.*

---

* *The Economic Times*, dated 13th August, 2011.

Institutional Efforts Undertaken in West Bengal

- In Baruipur in West Bengal, the RBI launched on August 13, 2011, the Axis Bank Bandhan Holistic Assistance (ABHA), a Financial Inclusion programme of Axis Bank in association with MFI Bandhan. It is one effort to make more people credit-worthy as part of the Financial Inclusion programme. By making people credit-worthy, it benefits banks because as a long term strategy of the banks, their credit off-take increases.
- ABHA will have a Rs. 100 crore corpus. While Axis Bank foundation, the Corporate Social Responsibility (CSR) arm of the bank, will provide Rs. 75 crores, and Bandhan will contribute the rest.
- As a pilot initiative, 500 low-income families are targeted. Gradually 50,000 families from the two districts of Murshidabad and South 24 Paragana will be covered under the initiative. Axis Bank shall contribute 1 per cent of their total profits as part of their CSR initiative to the Axis Bank foundation, ABF. The focus is on creating sustainable livelihood.

Our research investigation lends us to arrive at the inference that launching of a Financial Inclusion campaign creates a widespread awareness especially among the members of the village who are outside the banking service network. The categories of such persons are housewives, petty shop owners, traders, farmers, etc.

To make the programme of Financial Inclusion successful, it is necessary to have the participation of some voluntary organisations, clubs, charitable institutions, school teachers, high schools and other institutions. They may act as an agent to implement Financial Inclusion scheme at grassroots level.

Existing banks, post offices located in those pockets may also be converted into change agents because they are in close contact with the people offering semi-financial services.

Our research investigation suggest that India had the world's largest postal network with over 1.55 lakhs post offices, out of which 1.40 lakhs are in rural areas as in August 2011. If RBI allows India Post to start its own banking operations, it will have the potential to emerge as one of the biggest banks in the country and also ensure inclusive growth.

India Post has 23.70 crore savings accounts having deposits worth Rs.56,369 crore. Access to banking as well as credit facilities remains a far cry with only 10 per cent of the population availing of credit facilities.

The Expert Committee Report of 2011 makes a strong case for harnessing the Post Office savings bank for achieving financial inclusion as the reach of Post Offices is twice as extensive as that of all commercial banks together.

REFERENCES

R. Kamath, A. Mukherji, M. Sandstorm, Accessing Institutional Finance: "A demand Side Story for Rural India", *Economic and Political Weekly*, Vol. XLV, No. 37, September 11, 2010, Mumbai, pp. 56-58.

Rana Kapoor, Frugal Innovations for Financial Inclusion, *The Economic Times*, dated 31st May, 2010.

Speech by Dr. Duvvuri Subbarao, Governor, Reserve Bank of India at the Bankers' Club in Kolkata on December 9, 2009.

V. Leeladhar, "Taking Banking Services to the Common Man—Financial Inclusion", *RBI Bulletin*, January, pp. 73-77.

www.iibf.org.in

www.rbi.org

3

Contours of Financial Inclusion in India—A Quest

P. DEBNATH

Introduction

In order to achieve the objective of growth with equity in India, it is imperative that financial products and services are developed with financial inclusion. Financial inclusion is the delivery of financial services at an affordable cost to sections of disadvantaged and low income segment of the society. Unrestrained access to public goods and services is the *sine qua non* of an open and efficient society. It is argued that as the banking services are in the nature of public good, it is essential that availability of banking and payment services to the entire population without discrimination is the prime objective of public policy. The term "financial inclusion" has gained importance since the early, 2000s, and is a result of findings about financial inclusion and its direct correlation to poverty. Financial inclusion is now a common objective for many central banks among the developing nations along with India. In India, the basic concept of financial inclusion is having a saving or current account with any bank. In reality it includes loans, insurance services and much more. The first ever index of financial inclusion to find out the extent of the reach of banking services among 100 countries, India has been ranked 50. Only 34 per cent of Indian individuals have access to or receive banking services. In order to increase this number the Reserve Bank of India and the Government of India take innovative steps. One of the reasons for opening new branches of Regional Rural Banks was to make sure that the banking service is accessible to the poorer sections of the society as a whole. With the directives from RBI, our banks are now offering "No Frill" accounts to low income groups of the society. These accounts either have a low minimum or nil balance with some restrictions in transactions between the people and the banks. The individual bank has the authority to decide whether the account should have zero or minimum balance. With the combined effort of financial institutions, six million new "No Frill" accounts were opened worldwide in the period between March 2006-2007. In India too Banks are now considering to a large extent financial inclusion as business opportunity in an overall economic environment that facilitates the growth and development of the country. On 29 December, 2003, Former UN Secretary-General Kofi Annan said, "*The stark reality is that most poor people in the world still lack access to sustainable financial services, whether it is savings, credit or insurance. The great challenge before us is to address the constraints that exclude people from full participations in the financial sector. Together we can and must build inclusive financial sectors that help people improve their lives.*" The United Kingdom was one of the first countries to realize the importance of financial inclusion. It published its strategy of financial inclusion in its report *Promoting Financial Inclusion* which was published alongside the Pre-Budget Report of 2004. The UK Government also set up the Financial Inclusion Fund of £120 million to help bring about Financial Inclusion. The Financial Inclusion Task force was formally launched on 21 February, 2005 to monitor progress on financial inclusion and to make suitable recommendations. According to United Nations the main goals of inclusive finance are as follows:

- Access at a reasonable cost of all households and enterprises to the range of financial services for which they are "bankable," including savings, short and long-term credit, leasing and factoring, mortgages, insurance, pensions, payments, local money transfers and international remittances.
- Sound institutions, guided by appropriate internal management system, industry performance standards, and performance monitoring by the market, as well as by sound prudential regulation where required.

- Financial and institutional sustainability as a means of providing access to financial services over time.
- Multiple providers of financial services, wherever feasible, so as to bring cost-effective and a wide variety of alternatives to customers (which could include any number of combinations of sound private, non-profit and public providers).

Nature of Financial Inclusion in India

A commission (Khan Commission) was set up by the Reserve Bank of India in 2004 to look into financial inclusion and the recommendations of the Commission were incorporated into the mid-term review of the policy (2005-06). In the report RBI exhorted the banks with a view of achieving greater financial inclusion to make available a basic "no-frills" banking account. In India, Financial inclusion first featured in 2005, when it was introduced, that, too, from a pilot project in UT of Pondicherry, by K.C. Chakraborty, the Chairman of Indian Bank. Mangalam village became the first village in India where all households were provided banking facilities. In addition to this KYC (Know Your Customer) norms were relaxed for people intending to open accounts with annual deposits of less than Rs. 50,000. The General Credit Cards (GCC) was issued to the poor and the disadvantaged people of the village with a view to help them access easy credits. In January, 2006 the Reserve Bank of India permitted commercial banks to make use of the services of non-governmental organization (NGOs/SHGs), micro-finance institutions and other civil society organizations as intermediaries for providing financial and banking services to them. These intermediaries could be used as business facilitators (BF) or business correspondents (BC) by commercial banks. The bank asked the commercial banks in different regions to start a 100 per cent financial inclusion campaign on a pilot basis. As a result of the campaign, States or U.T.s like Pondicherry, Himachal Pradesh and Kerala have announced 100 per cent financial inclusion in all their districts. Reserve Bank of India's vision for 2020 is to open nearly 600 million new customers' accounts and service them through a variety of channels by leveraging on it. Despite of all these efforts, illiteracy and the low income followed by low savings and lack of bank branches in rural areas of India continue to be a road block to financial inclusion in many States. Apart from this there are certain in current model which is followed. There is inadequate legal and financial structure. India, being a mostly agrarian economy, hardly has schemes which lend for agriculture. Along with microfinance it is thus necessary to focus on micro insurance to help bracket the situation as a whole.

According to UN, "A financial sector that provides access to credit for all "bankable" people and firms and to savings and payments services for everyone. The plethora of FI is that the inclusive finance does not require that everyone who is eligible use each of the services, but they should be able to choose and use them if desired. As per the report of the C. Rangarajan Committee in 2008 as "the process of ensuring access to financial services and timely and adequate credit where needed by vulnerable groups such as weaker section and low income groups at an affordable cost. " On the other hand, as per treasury committee, House of Commons, UK (2005) "Ability of individuals to access appropriate financial products and services." The main reason for financial inclusion is the lack of a regular or substantial income. In most of the cases people with low income do not qualify for loan. The proximity of the financial service is another fact. The loss is not only the transportation cost but also the loss of daily wages for a low income individual. Most of the excluded consumers are not aware of the bank's products, which are beneficial for them. Getting money for financial requirements from a local money lender is easier than getting a loan from the bank. Most of the banks need collateral for their loans. It is very difficult for a low income individual to find collateral for a bank loan. Moreover, banks give more importance to meeting their financial targets. So they focus on larger accounts. It is not profitable for banks to provide small loans and make a profit. Three Major Aspects of Financial Inclusion make people to access financial markets, access credit markets, Learn financial matters along with financial education. The Reserve Bank of India, in its platinum jubilee year, wants to connect every Indian to the country's banking system. RBI is currently working on a three-year financial inclusion plan and is discussing this with each bank to see how to take this forward, K.C. Chakrabarty, Deputy Governor, RBI said.

"Nearly forty years after nationalization of banks, 60 per cent of the country's population does not have bank accounts and nearly 90 per cent do not get loans," he pointed out. Despite heightened focus on financial inclusion, Indian banks still somewhat failed to bring the under-and un-banked people into the mainstream banking fold. India has currently the second highest number of financially excluded in the world. Approximately, 40 per cent of India's population have bank accounts, and only about 10 per cent have any kind of Life Insurance coverage, while a meagre 0.6 per cent has non-life insurance coverage. The main reason for financial inclusion is the lack of a regular or substantial income. In most the cases people with low income do not qualify for loan. The proximity of the financial service is another fact. The loss is not only the transaction cost but also the loss of daily wages for a low income individual. Most of the excluded consumers are not aware of the bank's products, which are beneficial for them. Moreover, banks give more importance to meeting their financial targets. So they focus on larger accounts. It is not profitable for banks to provide small loans and make a profit.

Financial inclusion mainly focuses on the poor who do not have formal financial institutional support and getting them out of the clutches of the local money lenders. As a first step towards this, some of our banks have now come forwarded with general purpose for issuing credit cards and artisan credit cards which offer without collateral and free small loans. The RBI has simplified the KYC (Know Your Customer) norms for opening a "no frill" account. This will help the low income individual to open a "No Frill" account without identity proof and address proof. In such cases banks can take the individual's introduction from an existing customer whose full KYC norm procedure has been completed. And the introducer must have a satisfactory transaction with the bank for at least 6 months. This simplified procedure is available to those who intend to keep a balance not exceeding Rs. 50, 000 in all accounts taken together. With this facility we can channel the untapped, considerable amount of money from the low income group to the formal economy. Banks are now permitted to utilize the service of NGOs, SHGs and other civil society organizations as intermediaries in providing financial and banking services through the use of business facilitator and business correspondent models.

Self-Help Groups and Financial Inclusion

Self Help Groups are playing a very important role in the process of financial inclusion. SHGs are usually groups of women who get together and pool money from their savings and lend money among them. Usually they are working with the support of NGOs. The SHG is given loans against the group members' guarantee. Peer pressure within the group helps in improving recoveries. Through SHGs nearly 40 million households are linking with the banks. Micro finance is another tool which links low income groups to the banks. Yet, banks are fighting to fulfil the financial inclusion dream. The main reason is that the products designed by the banks are not satisfying the low income families. The provision of uncomplicated, small, affordable products will help to bring the low income families into the formal financial sector as the objective. Banks have limitations to reach directly to the low income consumers. Correspondents can be considered to be an excellent channel which banks can use to distribute their products information. Educating the consumers about the financial benefits and products of banks which are beneficial to low income groups will be a great step to tap their potentials. Banks are now using new technologies like mobile phones to reach low income consumers. These are possible that the telephone providers themselves will start basic banking services like savings and payments. Indian telecom consumers have few links to financial institutions. So without much difficulty telecom providers can win the battle with banks. Banks should, therefore, be proactive about transferring this technology into an opportunity. The Government of India has long history of working to expand financial inclusion. Nationalization of the major private sector banks in 1969 was a big step. In 1975 GoI established RRBs with the same aim. It encouraged branch expansion of bank branches especially in rural areas. The RBI guidelines to banks show that 40 per cent of their net bank credit should be lent out to the priority sector. This mainly consists of agriculture, small scale industries, retail trade, etc. More than 80 per cent of our population depends directly or indirectly on agriculture. So 18 per cent of net bank credit should go to agriculture lending. Recent implication of KYC norms are another milestone. Financial inclusion is a great step to alleviate poverty in India. But to achieve this, the government should provide a less perspective environment in which banks are free to pursue the innovations necessary to reach low income consumers and still make a profit. Financial service providers should learn more about the consumers and new business models to reach them. In Indian financial inclusion will be a good business ground in which the majority of her people will decide the winners and losers.

Survey of Related Literature

Financial inclusion is an integral part to the inclusive growth process and sustainable development of the country. However, the financial inclusion models that banks come up with should be replicable and viable across the country. Stating this in his special address at the Financial inclusion summit, organized by Confederation of Indian Industry (CII) in New Delhi, Mr. Pranab Mukherjee, Minister of Finance, Government of India, said that although the banking network has rapidly expanded over the years, the key challenge would be to extend the banking coverage to include the large population living in 6 lakh villages in the country. Expressing his immense confidence in the Indian banking system to deliver on the plan for financial inclusion, Mr. Mukherjee said the system, which demonstrated its resilience in the face of the recent global financial crisis, should adopt strong and urgent measures to reach the unbanked segment of society and unlock their savings and investment potentials. Turning to the private sector banks, he urged the players to build in the financial inclusion plans in their respective business strategies. He added that while 80 per cent of the public sector banks (PSBs) have already adopted the core banking solutions (CBS), steps are being taken to persuade the remaining 20 per cent PSBs to adopt CBS. Finance Minister said that interventions and initiatives like the UID project will go a long way to ease the bank's concerns pertaining to know Your Customers (KYC) criteria when dealing with a large segment of potential and existing customers. Mr. Mukherjee laid particular emphasis on the adoption of new and appropriate technologies for promoting financial inclusion. He took the example of the Mahatma Gandhi National Rural Employment Guarantee Act scheme to highlight how wage payments can be channelled through the banking system.

This will lend new meaning to financial inclusion, he said, and added that banks need to come up with a definite financial inclusion plan. To tap the fortune at the bottom of the pyramid, he recommended robust electronic transfers between bank branches located in the rural hinterland. This will facilitate the rural customers to transfer their income and conduct financial transactions seamlessly. Talking about an enabling environment, Mr. Mukherjee has very rightfully urged the private sector to support the designing of physical products including devices, software and financial services, training and capacity building so as to create a large manpower pool including business correspondents, and develop a business plan to tap the local talent that exists in the rural areas, on the lines of the e-choupal model.

Earlier, Dr Janmejaya Sinha, Chairman, CII Taskforce on Financial inclusion and Chairman (Asia Pacific), The Boston consulting group, said in his address that 135 million of the 204 million households in the country face financial inclusion. Now, with 570 million people in the country being in the 0-25 age group, a very large segment would be entering the workforce in the coming years. Their financial inclusion at this stage would be of crucial importance in the context of inclusive growth process and sustainable development.

Mr. Sinha said that financial illiteracy is a key stumbling block in furthering financial inclusion. This has led to the financial illiterate segment making negative savings in many cases. He added that banks need to view the situation as not an obligation to be met but an opportunity that is to be weaved into their business strategies. He felt that a proactive approach will see the banking network expanding in an all-inclusive manner like the telecom sector did. Mr. Sinha set a five-point agenda for financial inclusion, which called for: (*a*) increasing overall consciousness of the need for financial inclusion; (*b*) increase in wireless and broadband connectivity in the rural areas to support rural banking; (*c*) spread of financial literacy programmes; (*d*) greater experimentation for financial inclusion through business correspondents, self-help groups, etc., and (*e*) greater collaboration between the key stakeholders in the banking system are of immensely important to financial inclusion.

Ms Chanda Kochhar, Chairperson, CII National Committee on Banking and Managing Director and CEO, ICICI Bank, in her address, very eloquently said with a low ratio of 1 bank branch for 16,000 people, financial inclusion is far-fetched today. But, the idea of financial inclusion should be broad based, such that people are able to not only access credit, but also fetch various financial services and products through the banking access point.

She said that at the micro-level, the financial services providers should aim for a holistic approach that meets the different financial needs of the target customers, address not just rural but also large urban excluded segments, reduce cost of transactions with proper technology adoption, and support the development of support infrastructure.

Ms Kochhar further said that at the macro-level, there should be an eco-system that binds the different facets of banking and financial systems to deliver financial inclusion. She urged the banking and technology players to collaborate more firmly to strengthen financial inclusion, while adding that building financial habits among a large section of society will be just as important an objective to be focused upon.

Mr. Haris Bhartia, President, CII, in his opening remarks, said that CII's theme of "Business for Livelihood" is aligned to the objective of financial inclusion for sustainable high growth and development of the priority sectors.

He again said that financial inclusion will lead to the surplus rural income being converted into a pool of liquid funds for the economy. In this, the private sector has a key role to cut out, by way of designing appropriate products and services, adoption of new and innovative technologies, and reduction of cost of banking and financial transactions as well.

Mr. Chandrajit Banerjee, Director General, CII, in his closing remarks enlightened that CII is bringing financial and technology players to work closely to realize the goal of financial inclusion in true sense.

Biggest achievement of P. Chidambaram as Home Minister is that he restored to a great extent the confidence of the people who had lost in country's security establishment in the aftermath of 26/11. The term inclusion takes a peek into an improved security environment in India.

Strategy and Techniques for accessing of Financial Products and Services

Financial Products refer to instruments that help you to save, invest, get insurance or get a mortgage. These are issued by various banks, financial institutions, stock brokerages, insurance providers, credit card agencies and government sponsored entities. Financial products are categorized in terms of their type or fundamental asset class and volatility of risk and return. Further, financial services refer to services which are provided by the finance industry. The finance industry encompasses a broad range of organizations that deal with the management of money. Among these organizations are credit unions, banks, credit card companies, consumer finance companies, stock brokerages, investment funds and some government sponsored enterprises. As of 2004, the financial services industry represented 20 per cent of the market capitalization of the S&P 500 in the United States. The term "financial services" became more prevalent in the United States partly as a result of the Gramm Leach-Bliley Act of the late 1990s, which enabled different types of companies operating in the U.S financial services industry at that time to merge. Companies usually have two distinct approaches to this type of business. One approach would be a bank which simply buys an insurance company or an investment bank, keeps the original brands of the acquired firm, and adds the acquisition to its holding company simply to diversify its earnings. Outside the U.S (e.g., in Japan), non-financial services companies are permitted within the holding company. In this scenario, each company still looks independent, and has its own customers, etc. In other style, a bank would simply create its own brokerage division or insurance division and attempt to sell those products to its own existing customers, with incentives for combining all things with one company. These are Savings facility, Credit and Debit cards access, Electronic fund transfer, all kinds of commercial loans, Overdraft facility, Cheque facility, Payment and remittance services, Low cost financial services, Insurance (medical insurance),Financial advice, Pension for old age and investment schemes, Access to financial markets, Micro credit during emergency and Entrepreneurial credit and so on.

Profile of Financially Excluded People and Barriers

In India, the financially excluded people are largely comprise of Marginal farmers, Landless labourers, Oral lessees, Self employed and unorganized sector enterprises, Urban slum dwellers, Migrants, Ethnic minorities and socially excluded groups, senior citizens, women. The North East, eastern and central regions of India contain most of the financially excluded population. Lack of legal entity like voter ID, driving licence, birth certificates, employment identity card etc., particularly financial literacy and lack of basic education prevent people to have access to financial services. Level of income too decides to have financial access. Low income people generally have the attitude of thinking that banks are only for rich. While getting loans or at the time of opening accounts banks places many conditions, so the uneducated and poor people find it very difficult to access financial services. Due to lack of financial literacy and basic education, it is very difficult for those people who lack of both to read terms and conditions and account filling forms. Many people voluntarily excluded themselves due to psychological barriers and they think that they are excluded from accessing financial services. As the name suggests that commercial banks operate only in commercially profitable areas and they set up branches and main offices only in that areas. People who lived in under developed areas find it very difficult to go to areas in which banks are generally resided. Finally, people who lack basic education do not know the importance of the financial products like insurance, Finance, Bank accounts, Cheque facility, etc. In the absence of finance, people who are not connected with formal financial system lack opportunities to grow due to vast unutilized resources that are in the form of money in the hands of people who lack financial inclusive services. At the same time, if this condition persists, banks will lose business for ever due to lack of opening of bank accounts. And the people, who lack financial services, presumed that they are excluded from mainstream of the society at large. Further, people who do not have bank accounts may not go to bank as far as possible. In turn, they lack basic financial auxiliary services like DD, Insurance coverage and other emergency need loans transactions, etc.

Conclusion

In order to address the issues of financial inclusion, the Government of India constituted a "Committee on Financial Inclusion" under the Chairmanship of Dr. C. Rangarajan. The Committee submitted its final report to Hon'ble Union Finance Minister on 4 January, 2008. Economic growth follows financial inclusion. In order to achieve the objective of growth with equity, it is imperative that infrastructure is developed with financial inclusion. In fine, despite of benefits went on to the people leading to Indian economy in general and banking services in particular have made rapid strides in the recent past. However, a sizeable section of the population, particularly the vulnerable groups, such as weaker sections of the society and low income groups, continue to remain excluded from even the most basic opportunities and services provided by the financial sector. To address the issue of such financial inclusion in a holistic manner, it is essential to ensure that a range of financial services is available to every individual. The main reason for financial exclusion is the lack of a regular or substantial income. In most of the cases people with low income do not qualify for loan. The proximity of the financial service is another fact. The loss is not only the transportation cost but also the loss of daily wages for a low income individual. Most of the excluded customers are not aware of the bank's products, which are beneficial for them. Getting money for their financial requirements from a local money lender is easier than getting loan from the bank. Most of the banks need collateral for their loans. It is very difficult for a low income individual to find collateral for a bank loan. Moreover, banks give more importance to meeting their financial targets. So they focus on larger accounts instead of small ones. It is not profitable for banks to provide small loans and make profit. These barriers as much as possible will have to curve so that these people are included in the main stream of development of the country like India. Taking into account their inflow of income from agricultural operations, migration from one place to another, seasonal and irregular work availability and income; the existing financial system needs to be redesigned to suit their requirements. Security and safety of deposits, low transaction cost, convenient operating time, minimum paper work, frequent deposits, speedy and easy access and products suitable to income and consumption are to be reckoned at the same time. In the path of super power we the Indians need to achieve the growth of our country with equal opportunity. It is thus provided by inclusive finance system available in the country.

REFERENCES

A. Bishnoi, *Managing and Marketing Financial Services.*

D.M. Mithani, *Money, Banking, International Trade and Public Finance.*

H.C. Machiraju, *Indian Financial System.*

L.W. Chandler, *An Introduction to Monetary Theory.*

N.P. Mahapatra, *Towards Financial Inclusion in India.*

Oliver Schmidt, *Micro-Finance Perspectives and operations.*

R.C. Machiraju, *Indian Financial System.*

RBI: *Hand Book of Monetary Statistics of India.*

RBI: *Report of the Committee on Rural Banks.*

RBI: *Report of the Second Working Group on Money Supply in India.*

RBI's Review

Readings in Financial Inclusion—Indian Institute of Banking and Finance.

Reports of Syndicate Bank, Karnataka.

Sameer Kochhar, R. Chandrasekhar, K. C. Chakraborty, Deepak B. Pathak *Financial Inclusion.*

Sharon Collard, Elaine Kempson, Nicoladomini—*Promoting Financial Inclusion.*

Usha Thorat, *Financial Inclusion—The Indian Experience.*

V.A. Avadhani, *Marketing of Financial Services.*

V.K. Balla, *Indian Financial System and Risk Management.*

Vasant Desai, *Indian Financial System and Development.*

Wadhva C.D., *Rural Banks for Rural Developments.*

Woodworth, G.W., *The Money Market and Monetary Management.*

4

Financial Inclusion : An Indian Perspective

W. C. SINGH

Introduction

Financial inclusion means the access of banking services to the low income and disadvantaged people in the society. The access of these people to the formal financial system is of critical importance for the economic upliftment. In India the basic concept of financial inclusion is having a saving or current account with any bank and availing the facilities of deposits, loans, insurance, credits, payments and other possible services. In a developed country these facilities have become a common requirement of each and every individual. Despite rapid expansion of the banking services and its network in India, there is a vast majority of people which do not have access to basic banking services resulting in the financial exclusion. Dr. C. Rangarajan Committee on financial inclusion defines it as:

> Financial inclusion may be defined as the process of ensuring access to financial services and timely and adequate credit where needed by vulnerable groups such as weaker sections and low income groups at an affordable cost.

The definitional emphasis of financial inclusion varies across countries and geographies, depending on the level of social, economic and financial development; the structure of the stake holding in the financial structure; the socio-economic characteristics of the financially excluded segments; and also the extent of the recognition of the problem by the authorities or governments. Broadly, financial exclusion is construed as the inability to access necessary financial services in an appropriate form due to problems associated with access, conditions, prices, marketing or self-exclusion in response to discouraging experiences or perception of individuals/entities.

The importance of an inclusive financial system is widely recognized by the governments of many countries of the world. It has become a means for a systematic growth and development of a country as every citizen of the country improves their future financial status. In India, the RBI (Reserve Bank of India) has adopted many schemes to increase the access of the poorer segments of the society. It encourages the expansion of bank branches, especially in rural areas, resulting in multifold increase in branch network from around 8,000 in 1969 to more than 89,000 today. Despite all these effort, a significant proportion of our population still remained outside the coverage of the formal banking system. It is estimated that about 40 per cent of Indians lack access even to the simplest kind of formal financial services.

Need for Financial Inclusion

The growth trend of the Indian economy has experienced the new phase of higher growth over the last few years. Earlier there were hardly 6 per cent growth for the last many years but the growth rate has accelerated to about 8 per cent over the last few years. One of the important elements for such a higher level of growth in the last few years is the progress in the financial sector. It means financial development spurs economic growth. Now the policy makers are on their toes as any problem in the financial sector could freeze the entire economy and can even lead to a contagion. Research supports the view that development of financial system contribute to economic growth (Rajan and Zingales, 2003). Evidence also indicates that various measures of financial development are robustly and positively related to economic growth (King and Levine, 1993; Levine and Zervos, 1998). Other studies establish a positive relationship between financial development and growth at the industry level (Rajan and Zingales, 1998). World Bank has also done a study on this subject for rural India and found that about 40 per cent of households have deposit accounts, 20 per cent have outstanding loans and only 15 per cent have any insurance (Basu, 2006).

Financial exclusion is broadly defined as the lack of access by certain segments of the society to suitable, low cost, fair and safe financial products and services from the mainstream providers. Thus the essence of financial inclusion is to ensure that a range of appropriate financial services is available to every individual and enable them to understand and access those services. The anatomy of various financial products or services and the institutional structure can be presented as follows:

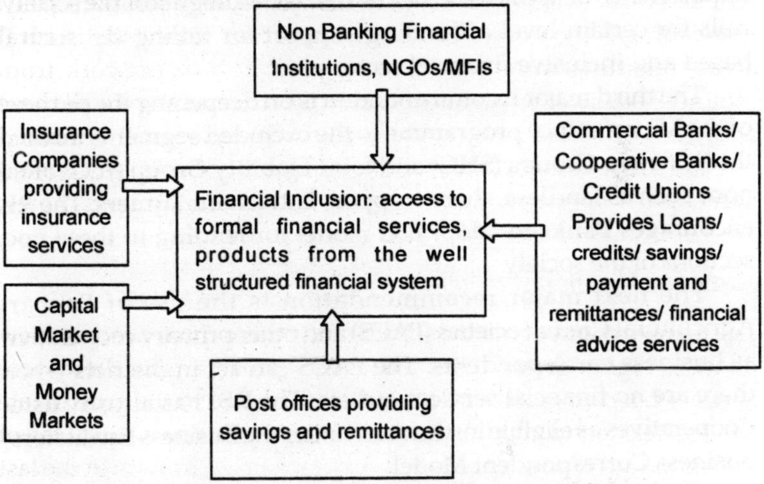

Fig. 4.1 : Anatomy of a Structure of Financial Inclusion

Major Recommendations of Committee on Financial Inclusion

The first major recommendation of the Financial Inclusion Plan is launching the National Rural Financial Inclusion Plan (NRFIP) with a clear target to provide access to comprehensive financial services to at least 50 per cent of the excluded rural cultivators and non cultivator households, across different States of India by 2012 through rural and semi-urban branches of Commercial Banks and Regional Rural Banks. The remaining households have to be covered by 2015.

The second major recommendation is to set up two funds—the Financial Inclusion Promotion & Development Fund (FIPF), and the Financial Inclusion Technology Fund (FITF) with a corpus fund of Rs. 500 crore each to be contributed equally by the Government of India, Reserve Bank of India, and National Bank for Agriculture and Rural Development (NABARD). The FIPF will focus on many intervention programmes like Farmers' Service Centres, Promoting Rural Entrepreneurship, Self Help Groups, Developing Human Resources through Training, Establishing Resource Centres, and Capacity Building of Business Facilitators and Business Correspondents. The FITF focuses on extending outreach to the requirements of application of low cost technology solutions which calls for certain level of funding support for rolling out such IT based and inclusive financial sector plan.

The third major recommendation is on deepening the outreach of the Microfinance programme to the excluded segments through the Self Help Groups (SHG) and Joint Liability Group (JLG) of the poor such as landless, share croppers and tenant farmers. The RBI encourages Banks to adopt JLG model for lending to these poor sections of the society.

The next major recommendation is the use of Primary Agricultural Credit Societies (PACS) and other primary cooperatives as business correspondents. The PACS can act in districts where there are no financial services outlets. The RBI has already listed Cooperatives as eligible institutions under the Business Facilitators/ Business Correspondent Model.

The fifth recommendation of the Committee is the promotion of the Micro Finance Institutions (MFIs). The Micro Finance-Non Banking Finance Companies (MF-NBFC) could be permitted to provide thrift, credit, micro insurance, remittances and other financial services up to a specified amount to the poor in rural, semi-urban, and urban areas. The MF-NBFCs may also be recognized as Business Correspondents of banks for only providing savings and remittances services. The IRDA Micro Insurance Guidelines, 2005 may also permit MF-NBFCs to offer micro insurance services as agents of regulated life and non life insurance companies.

The next recommendation is on the opening of specialized branches of microfinance in potential urban centres for exclusively catering microfinance and SHG-Bank Linkage requirements of the urban poor. The NABARD has made a provision in its Act to provide microfinance services to the urban poor.

These recommendations of Dr. C. Rangarajan Committee on Financial Inclusion could bring lots of improvement in the inclusive growth of the country.

Measurement of Financial Inclusion/Exclusion

The published literature on financial inclusion so far lacks comprehensive measures that can be used to indicate the extent of financial inclusion or exclusion across countries. Lack of information is much more conspicuous in developing countries where there is little information on who is served by the formal financial sector, which financial institutions or services are the most effective at supporting access by the people or what barrier may be hindering the accessibility. The access to finance can be measured in terms of access to certain institutions such as banks, insurance companies, MFIs, etc., and to the services that these institutions provide. Such an access to financial services or institutions may range from the more formal to a less formal system.

As per the RBI Reports (2008), the core and headline indicators place a given population along a continuum of access, depending on its usage of formal, semi formal, and informal financial services, and those excluded from the use of financial services. The access to finance could be divided into four segments (*i*) the proportion of the population that uses a bank or bank like institution; (*ii*) the population which uses service from non-bank "other formal" financial institutions, but does not use bank services; (*iii*) the population which only uses services from the informal financial service providers; (*iv*) percentage of population transecting regularly through formal financial instruments; and (*v*) the population which uses no financial services.

As per the report, the second group of core indicators looks in greater detail at the kinds on financial services offered. The financial service functions identified to be used as the basis for indicators are: (*i*) transactions or payment services; (*ii*) savings and investment services; and (*iii*) loan or credit services. In fact, there is no single comprehensive measure that can be used as indicator of financial inclusion across countries and across economies of the world.

Financial Inclusion in India

Financial Inclusion in the Indian context implies the provision of affordable financial services, viz., access to payments and remittance facilities, savings, loans and insurance services by the formal financial system to those who tend to be excluded. In order to be financially included, a wide network of financial institutions has been established over the past years. The organized financial system comprising of commercial banks (CB), regional rural banks (RRB), cooperative banks, primary agricultural credit societies (PACS), post offices, MFIs, NBFC, and NGOs cater the needs of financial service requirements of the poorer people and all the sections of the society. In order to promote the financial inclusion plan, specific financial instruments/products have also developed from time to time.

The recent changes in India in terms of financial inclusion are highly appreciable. Table 4.1 shows the growth of Bank Offices in India during 2006- 2010.

Table 4.1 : Offices of Commercial Banks in India 2006-2010
(as on 31st March)

Bank Group	*2006*	*2007*	*2008*	*2009*	*2010*
State Bank of India and its Associates	14,310	14,673	15,846	16,878	18,114
Nationalized Banks $	35,858	37,431	39,234	40,854	43,187
Public Sector Banks	50,168	52,104	55,080	57,732	61,301
Old Private Sector Banks	4,819	4,826	4,690	4,908	5,174
New Private Sector Banks	2,016	2,598	3,632	4,328	5,213
Private Sector Banks	6,835	7,424	8,322	9,236	10,387
Foreign Banks	259	272	279	295	310
Regional Rural Banks	14,807	14,843	15,070	15,485	15,723
Non-Scheduled Commercial Banks	41	46	46	46	47
All Commercial Banks	72,110	74,689	78,797	82,794	87,768

Note : 1. Data on number of offices include administrative offices.
2. Data for 2006 to 2009 have been revised and data for 2010 are provisional.
3. $ includes IDBI Bank Ltd.

Source : RBI Publication (4th March 2011)

Table 4.2 : Statistics relating to Scheduled Commercial Banks at a Glance (as on 31st March)

Indicators	*2006*	*2007*	*2008*	*2009*	*2010*
Number of Commercial Banks	222	182	173	170	167
Scheduled Commercial Banks	218	178	169	166	163
Of which Regional Rural Banks	133	96	90	86	82
Non-Scheduled Commercial Banks	4	4	4	4	4
Number of Bank Offices in India	71,685	74,346	78,666	82,794	87,768
Rural	30,436	30,575	31,105	31,676	32,528
Semi-Urban	15,811	16,620	17,897	19,213	20,771
Urban	13,034	14,049	15,530	16,693	18,171
Metropolitan	14,204	13,102	14,134	15,212	16,279
Population per office (in Thousands)	16	15	15	15	14
Aggregate deposits of Scheduled Commercial Banks in India (Rs. In crores)	21,09,049	26,11,934	31,96,940	38,34,110	44,92,826
Demand Deposits	3,64,640	4,29,731	5,24,310	5,23,085	6,45,610
Time Deposits	17,44,409	21,82,203	26,72,630	33,11,025	38,47,216
Per capita deposits of Scheduled Commercial Banks (Rs.)	19,130	23,382	28,610	33,919	39,107

(contd...)

Table 4.2 contd...

Per Capita Credit of Scheduled Commercial Banks (Rs.)	13,869	17,541	21,218	24,617	28,431
Banks' Advances to priority sector (Rs. In crores)	5,12,790	6,55,317	7,81,476	9,08,929	10,91,57,429
Share of priority sector advances in Scheduled Commercial Banks (per cent)	33.8	33.1	31.6	30.3	31.2

Note: 1. Number of Bank Branches includes Administrative Offices.
2. Classification of offices as per population census of 2001.
3. Population per office, per capita, deposits, and per capita credit are based on March 01, supplied by the Office of the Registrar General, India.

Source : RBI Publication (04 March, 2011).

From Table 4.1 it is seen that there has been an increase of 21.71 per cent in the number of banks in the five years time. It is a great positive change in the direction of financial inclusion.

Table 4.2 shows statistics relating to scheduled commercial banks at a glance. This data also explains very clearly the number of bank offices population-wise (on the basis of Rural, Semi Urban, Urban, and Metropolitan) along with the number of population per bank office/branch from 2006 to 2010. The details of per capita deposits and bank credits are also given clearly.

Table 4.3 : Region-wise Distribution of Scheduled Commercial Banks and Population Per Office Region-wise

as on 31st March

Region	*No. of Reporting Office*		*No. of Population per Office*	
	2009	*2010*	*2009*	*2010*
Northern Region	13575	14480	11352	10824
North Eastern Region	2114	2210	20193	19557
Eastern Region	13333	13962	19093	18448,
Central Region	15767	16795	18831	17985
Western Region	12118	12964	13963	13241
Southern Region	22149	23586	10986	10409
All India	79056	83997	14683	14009

Source : Compiled from the Quarterly Statistics on Deposits and Credit of Scheduled Commercial Banks, March 2009 and 2010, RBI.

Table 4.3 shows the region-wise distribution of scheduled commercial banks during 2009 and 2010 and the average population per office region-wise. It shows that there has been an increase in the widening of financial inclusion during this period.

The trends of financial inclusion in India has been improving continuously in terms of expansion in the number of bank branches throughout and at the same time declining the number of population per office due to increase in the number of bank branches.

Some Issues on Financial Inclusion

The financial inclusion in real terms should be the ability of the citizen to access appropriate financial services and products. The identification of the right kind of financial services or product on the basis of a single individual cannot be generalized here as an appropriate financial inclusion strategy for all. Individuals have varied opinion of their like and dislikes and so varied opinion on the financial inclusion. Some of the thoughts are highlighted as follows:

Religious Belief: The idea of financial services or products may not comply with the Islamic Law, which generally talks against charging of interest from the people.

Gender Issues: Access to financial services is limited to a society like India where the male dominance still are in practices in many of the societies/communities. This tradition acts as a hindrance toward financial inclusion for all.

Poverty: Higher rate of population below poverty line results in lower demand for financial products and services.

Structural Problems: The process of financial inclusion is sometimes deferred due to unavailability of suitable services or products, stringent documentation, and collateral requirements.

Legal Identity: Lack of legal identity for a section of people in the society in terms of their records to the local/district/State authority leads to financial exclusion too.

Exclusion due to Disability: Physically challenged people might find it difficult to access the facilities of financial services or products visiting the premises.

Self Exclusion: Some individuals feel that there is no point in applying for financial products because he/she expects to be refused by the officials of the financial institutions/industry. Such conclusions are drawn generally on the basis of past experience.

Attitude of the Bankers: The general attitude or perception of the bankers at large is that the poor are not credit worthy and they should be avoided from granting financial facilities. This attitude still prevails to most of the senior employees of the banks.

Bank Charges: The financial system has come up to a great height but there are very high financial charges to be borne by the customers. For some people it is still felt that they are paying high price for availing these facilities. This is a hindrance to financial inclusion.

Income Level: The income level of the people and their place of living have been a very important deciding factor for financial inclusion. Poor people living in remote areas find it difficult to access the financial services.

Challenge of the Political Process: Financial inclusion is perceived as a non-urgent issue by the policy makers of many States of India. They are not putting in the policy agenda of the State and it delays the progress of the economy.

Concluding Remarks: While financial inclusion alone cannot prevent poverty, it can help reduce its worst effects and help provide routes into work, enterprise, and good standard of living. There has been great improvement in terms of financial inclusion since independence but an effective government strategy to combat financial exclusion has a crucial role to play in enabling those on low income and others who are financially excluded to take their own steps away from poverty. The Reserve Bank of India has introduced many programmes and policies for the appropriate financial inclusion. Constant innovations and changes in this sector push regulators to react with dynamism to new challenges and opportunities in the market. The present stage of development in our country demands lot of deepening in the financial inclusion by increasing its breadth and coverage of formal finance. The strategy for financial inclusion will lead to financial development in our country which will help to accelerate economic growth.

REFERENCES

Basu, P. (2006), *Improving Access to Finance for India's Poor*, Washington DC: The World Bank.

Government of India, 2008, *Report of the Committee on Financial Inclusion in India* (Chairman Dr. C. Rangarajan).

In Developed Economies: Lessons for Developing Countries. University of Bristol.

Kempson, E.; A. Atkinson; and O. Pilley. 2004, *Policy Level Response to Financial Exclusion*.

King, R.G. and R. Levine (1993), Finance and Growth: Schumpeter Might Be Right, *Quarterly Journal of Economics*, 108, 717-37.

Levine, R. and S. Zervos (1998), Stock Markets, Banks, and Economic Growth, *American Economic Review*, 88, 537-58.

Rajan, R.G. and L. Zingales (1998), Financial Development and Growth, *American Economic Review*, 88, 559-86.

Rajan, R.G. and L. Zingales (2003), Saving Capitalism from Capitalists, Crown Business, New York.

World Bank, 2008. *Finance for All—Policy and Pitfalls in Expanding Access.* The World Bank, Washington, DC.

5

Inclusive Growth : Trends in India

K. GYANENDRA SINGH

Introduction

The quest for inclusive growth has gained momentum in India since its incorporation as the main objective in the Eleventh Five Year Plan (2007-12). The approach to the Eleventh Plan clearly states that "the Eleventh Plan provides an opportunity to restructure policies to achieve a new vision based on faster, more broad-based and inclusive growth. It is designed to reduce poverty and focus on bridging the various divides that continue to fragment our society" (Government of India, 2006). This quest also finds its roots from the declaration of Millennium Development Goals (MDG) by the United Nations (UN) in 2000 following the three-day Millennium Summit held in its headquarters where the world leaders have agreed to achieve eight international development goals, viz., (*i*) eradicate extreme hunger and poverty; (*ii*) achieve universal primary education; (*iii*) promote gender equity and empower women; (*iv*) reduce child mortality; (*v*) improve maternal health; (*vi*) combat HIV/AIDS, malaria and other diseases; (*vii*) ensure environmental sustainability; and (*viii*) develop a global partnership for development by the year 2015 (UNDP). In India, the Eleventh Five Year Plan has outlined several inter-related components like rapid growth that reduces poverty and creates employment opportunities, access to essential services in health and education especially for the poor, equality of opportunity, empowerment through education and skill development, employment opportunities underpinned by the National Rural Employment Guarantee, environment sustainability, recognition of women's agency and good governance (Planning Commission). The need for such vision and plan arose from the fact that India's success growth story has left far behind a significant portion of the population. As such it is required to analyze the various growth and development indicators on an all India basis as well as on regional basis so that a suitable policy framework can be drawn to bridge the growth and development gaps and foster inclusive growth.

Performance of the Economy and Regional Dimension

In terms of Net Domestic Product (NDP) and Per Capita Income (PCI), the two most important and widely used measure of growth and performance of an economy, the growth rate has been increasing with the passage of time. The decennial compound growth rate (DCGR) of NDP in India has increased from 3.23 per cent in 1971-80 to 5.97 per cent and 7.31 per cent in 1991-2000 and 2001-07 respectively. The DCGR of PCI in India has also increased from 0.93 per cent in 1971-80 to 3.90 per cent and 5.62 per cent in 1991-2000 and 2001-07 respectively (Singh, 2011: 158). *The Economic Survey 2010-11* gives an optimistic picture of the growth of the Indian economy as presented by Table 5.1.

Table 5.1 : Growth Rate of GDP and Per Capita NNP (Per Cent)

Year	*GDP at factor cost (2004-05 price)*	*Per Capita NNP (1999-00 price)*
2005-06	9.52	7.8
2006-07	9.58	7.9
2007-08	9.34	8.1
2008-09PE	6.76	4.8
2009-10QE	7.96	6.1
2010-11AE	8.58	—

Source : *Economic Survey 2010-11*.
PE = Provisional Estimates; QE = Quick Estimates;
AE = Advanced Estimates.

It can be observed from the above table that the growth prospects of the Indian economy is optimistic and she has also proved her resilience during the global meltdown of 2008 which originated in the United States. While the overall growth rate of the Indian economy is increasing the economy underwent a massive structural transformation. Over the years the contribution of primary sector to the total GDP declined and the share of tertiary sector to the total GDP increased significantly while the share of secondary sector increased marginally and remained more or less constant over the years. The share of primary sector to total GDP which was above 50 per cent during 1950s and 1960s declined to a low of about 18 per cent in 2009. The share of secondary sector increased from about 10 per cent during the 1950s to about 25 per cent during the 2009. However, the share of tertiary sector has increased tremendously and its share has almost doubled since the 1950s. Its share was about 30 per cent during the 1950s and 1960s and in 2009 its share is about 56 per cent.

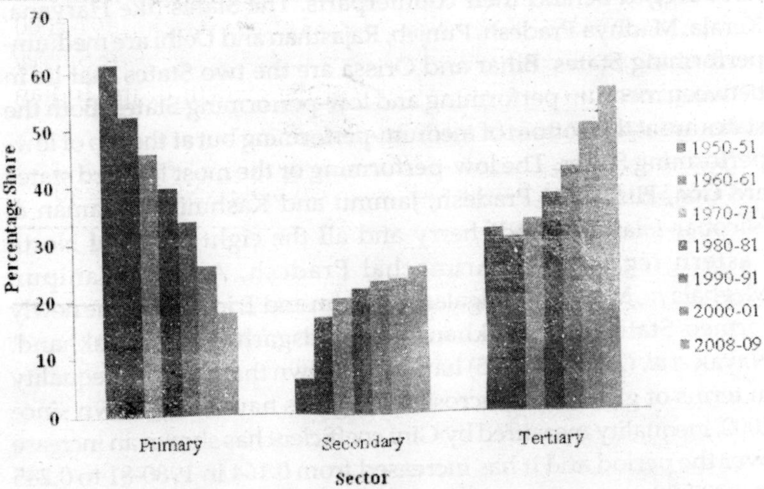

Figure 5.1 : GDP by Activity (Percentage Share)

Source : Calculated from Central Statistics Office.

Note : 1950-51 to 2000-01 is based on 1999-00 price and 2008-09 is based on 2004-05 price.

Thus the Indian economy underwent structural transformation from primary sector towards tertiary sector bypassing the secondary. However, this service sector led growth is concentrated in cities like Bangalore, Chennai, Delhi, Kolkata, Mumbai, Pune, etc. and thus widened regional disparity. The studies by Ahluwalia (2000, 2003), Bhanumurthy and Mitra (2004) and Bhattacharya and Sakthivel (2004) have indicated that economic reforms initiated since 1991 to boost our economy has widened the income inequality between the rich and poor States further widening regional disparity. However, these studies have not taken into consideration the peripheral hilly regions of North Eastern India which are largely left behind by the new process of market-led growth which we adopted since liberalization. The regions of India, as evident from Table 5.2, can be classified into high-performing, medium-performing and low-performing States. The high-performing States are Andhra Pradesh, Gujarat, Karnataka, Maharashtra, Tamil Nadu, Uttar Pradesh and West Bengal. All these States are coastal States except Uttar Pradesh.

However, Kerala and Orissa are the two coastal States which have lagged behind their counterparts. The States like Haryana, Kerala, Madhya Pradesh, Punjab, Rajasthan and Delhi are medium-performing States. Bihar and Orissa are the two States that lie in between medium performing and low-performing States. Both the states are at the bottom of medium-performing but at the top of low-performing States. The low-performing or the most laggard states are Goa, Himachal Pradesh, Jammu and Kashmir, Andaman & Nicobar Islands, Pondicherry and all the eight States of North Eastern region, viz., Arunachal Pradesh, Assam, Manipur, Meghalaya, Mizoram, Nagaland, Sikkim and Tripura and the newly formed States like Jharkhand, Chhattisgarh and Uttarakhand. Nayak *et al.* (2010: 104-105) have also shown that though inequality in terms of growth rate across the regions have come down since 2000, inequality measured by Gini coefficient has shown an increase over the period and it has increased from 0.164 in 1980-81 to 0.245 in 2007-08.

Thus we see that after liberalization the service sector led growth has transformed the Indian economy from the "Hindu Rate of Growth" and placed it among the largest and fastest growing economies of the world in the present century along with China.

Table 5.2 : Percentage Share of NDP by Region

State/UT	*1999-00*	*2004-05*	*2005-06*	*2006-07*	*2007-08*	*2008-09*	*2009-10*
Andhra Pradesh	7.63	8.20	8.19	8.11	8.26	8.52	9.43
Arunachal Pradesh	0.10	0.11	0.10	0.10	0.10	0.10	NA
Assam	2.10	2.05	2.00	1.91	1.82	1.79	2.02
Bihar	3.02	2.85	2.70	2.94	2.91	3.24	3.59
Jharkhand	1.98	1.92	1.81	1.79	1.69	1.64	NA
Goa	0.37	0.43	0.44	0.44	0.47	NA	NA
Gujarat	6.07	6.69	7.16	7.18	7.23	7.07	NA
Haryana	3.11	3.69	3.70	3.91	4.00	4.23	4.95
Himachal Pradesh	0.82	0.88	0.86	0.81	0.78	0.78	0.89
Jammu and Kashmir	0.89	0.89	0.87	0.81	0.77	NA	NA
Karnataka	5.94	5.90	6.15	5.89	5.99	6.04	6.77
Kerala	4.03	4.12	4.19	4.16	4.11	4.21	NA
Madhya Pradesh	4.77	4.04	3.93	3.80	3.70	3.78	4.36
Chhattisgarh	1.56	1.63	1.69	1.87	1.99	2.09	24.14
Maharashtra	14.25	14.32	14.36	14.58	14.89	15.01	18.35
Manipur	0.19	0.18	0.17	0.16	0.15	0.14	NA
Meghalaya	0.21	0.22	0.22	0.22	0.21	0.22	NA
Mizoram	0.09	0.09	0.09	0.09	0.08	0.08	NA
Nagaland	0.17	0.21	0.19	0.18	NA	NA	NA
Orissa	2.52	2.70	2.60	2.73	2.98	2.96	3.40
Punjab	4.01	3.70	3.67	3.53	3.63	3.72	4.45
Rajasthan	4.87	4.42	4.26	4.38	4.35	4.42	4.90
Sikkim	0.05	0.06	0.06	0.06	0.06	0.06	NA
Tamil Nadu	7.85	7.64	7.86	7.98	7.60	7.52	NA
Tripura	0.30	0.33	0.33	0.31	0.28	NA	NA
Uttar Pradesh	10.29	9.39	9.25	8.90	8.78	9.04	10.96
Uttarakhand	0.73	0.90	0.87	0.90	0.89	0.88	1.05
West Bengal	8.22	8.21	7.93	7.85	7.86	7.99	NA
A & N Islands	0.05	0.06	0.06	0.06	0.06	NA	NA
Chandigarh	0.25	0.35	0.37	0.37	0.37	0.38	0.45
Delhi	3.36	3.62	3.69	3.75	3.73	3.83	NA
Pondicherry	0.19	0.19	0.21	0.25	0.26	0.26	0.30
India	100	100	100	100	100	100	100

Source : Calculated from *Economic Survey, 2010-11.*

Though the growth was unevenly distributed and concentrated only in few regions the overall performance of the economy can be appreciated. While India emerges as the largest and fastest growing economy of the world, an altogether different policy framework is required to bridge the gaps and reduce regional disparity. Another important dimension of this success growth story is that this growth has not transformed into the overall development of the country.

Socio-economic Dimension of Growth

If we go by the human development index (HDI, *the average achievements in three dimensions of human development: a long and healthy life, access to knowledge and a decent standard of living*), India is in medium human development with a value of 0.519 and her rank is 119 out of 169 countries in the world in 2010. Since 2005, the ranking of HDI of India has just moved by 1 (one) positive point. In terms of Inequality-adjusted HDI (IHDI, *adjusts the HDI for inequality in distribution of each dimension across the population*) the value is 0.365. The difference between HDI and IHDI is 0.154 or 15.4 per cent and this is the loss in potential human development due to inequality. The Multidimensional Poverty Index (MPI, *multiple deprivations at individual level in health, education and standard of living*) of India in 2000-2008 is 0.296. For the period 2000-08, the percentage of population below income poverty line in terms of Purchasing Power Parity (PPP) $1.25 a day is 41.6 per cent and 28.6 per cent according to the national poverty line of Rs. 356.03 per capita per month in rural area and Rs. 538.30 per capita per month in urban area (Human Development Report 2010).

According to the Planning Commission of India, the percentage of population below poverty line using Uniform Recall Period (URP, *in which the consumer expenditure data for all the items are collected from 30-day recall period*) is 27.5 per cent and the number of persons is 3017.20 lakhs in 2004-05. However, using Mixed Recall Period (MRP, *in which the consumer expenditure data for five non-food items, viz., clothing, footwear, durable goods, education and institutional medical expenses are collected from 365-day recall period and the consumption data for the remaining items are collected from 30-day recall period*) the percentage of population below poverty line is 21.8 per cent and the number of persons is 2384.99 lakhs in 2004-05. In terms of poverty in India there is no significant difference between rural and urban areas. The URP estimation of poverty is 28.3 per cent in rural and 25.7 per cent in urban in 2004-05. Accordir.g to MRP, the poverty estimate is 21.8 per cent in rural and 21.7 per cent in urban in 2004-05 [Planning Commission (*a*)].

The poverty estimate of India Human Development Survey (IHDS) 2005 is also quite close to that of Planning Commission. The national poverty estimate as per IHDS is 25.7 per cent with rural poverty at 26.5 per cent and urban poverty at 23.7 per cent (Desai *et al*, 2010: 20). The region wise poverty estimates also shows that there is a huge variance among the states of India. The level of poverty according to URP is as high as 46 per cent in Orissa, 41 per cent in Bihar, Chhattisgarh and Jharkhand and as low as 5 per cent in Jammu and Kashmir, 7 per cent in Chandigarh and 8 per cent in Punjab. As per MRP, the poverty level is as high as 40 per cent in Orissa, 32 per cent in Bihar, Chhattisgarh and Jharkhand and as low as 4 per cent in Chandigarh and Jammu and Kashmir, 5 per cent in Punjab and 6 per cent in Himachal Pradesh (Table 5.3).

Thus we see that though the all India poverty declined over the years, there is a huge variance across the regions and this inter-regional differences need to be addressed. While poverty still remains a major area of concern for India, the overall performance of the health sector is also not very optimistic though there is overall development over the years.

The indicators on health show that there is improvement in the overall performance of the health sector. The life expectancy at birth and Infant Mortality Rate (IMR) has improved as compared to the previous years. The IMR is 50 in 2009 compared to 110 and 80 in 1981 and 1991 respectively. In 2009 IMR for female is 52 while that of male is 49. The life expectancy at birth is around 63 years in 2002-06 compared to 55 years and 60 years in 1981-85 and 1989-93 respectively. There is no significant difference among male and female in terms of life expectancy at birth.

Table 5.3 : Number and Percentage of Population below Poverty Line, 2004-05

State/UT	URP		MRP	
	No. of Persons (lakhs)	Percentage	No. of Persons (lakhs)	Percentage
Andhra Pradesh	126.10	15.8	88.71	11.1
Arunachal Pradesh	2.03	17.6	1.54	13.4
Assam	55.77	19.7	42.39	15.0
Bihar	369.15	41.4	290.01	32.5
Chhattisgarh	90.96	40.9	71.11	32.0
Delhi	22.93	14.7	15.83	10.2
Goa	2.01	13.8	1.74	12.0
Gujarat	90.69	16.8	67.43	12.5
Haryana	32.10	14.0	22.56	9.9
Himachal Pradesh	6.36	10.0	4.27	6.7
Jammu and Kashmir	5.85	5.4	4.54	4.2
Jharkhand	116.39	40.3	100.39	34.8
Karnataka	138.89	25.0	96.60	17.4
Kerala	49.60	15.0	37.51	11.4
Madhya Pradesh	249.68	38.3	210.97	32.4
Maharashtra	317.38	30.7	259.83	25.2
Manipur	3.95	17.3	3.00	13.2
Meghalaya	4.52	18.5	3.43	14.1
Mizoram	1.18	12.6	0.89	9.5
Nagaland	3.99	19.0	3.03	14.5
Orissa	178.49	46.4	153.59	39.9
Punjab	21.63	8.4	13.30	5.2
Rajasthan	134.89	22.1	107.18	17.5
Sikkim	1.14	20.1	0.87	15.2
Tamil Nadu	145.62	22.5	115.10	17.8
Tripura	6.38	18.9	4.85	14.4
Uttar Pradesh	590.03	32.8	458.15	25.5
Uttarakhand	35.96	39.6	28.86	31.8
West Bengal	208.36	24.7	173.23	20.6
A & N Islands	0.92	22.6	0.71	17.6
Chandigarh	0.74	7.1	0.40	3.8
Dadra & Nagar Haveli	0.84	33.2	0.77	30.6
Daman & Diu	0.21	10.5	0.16	8.0
Lakshadweep	0.11	16.0	0.09	12.3
Pondicherry	2.37	22.4	1.92	18.2
All India	3017.20	27.5	2384.99	21.8

Source : Planning Commission (*a*).

Table 5.4 : Selected Health Indicators of India

Parameter	*1981*	*1991*	*Current level*
Crude Birth Rate (CBR) (per 1000 population)	33.9	29.5	22.5 (2009)
Crude Death Rate (CDR) (per 1000 population)	12.5	9.8	7.3 (2009)
Infant Mortality Rate (IMR) (per 1000 live births)	110	80	50 (2009)
Male			49
Female			52
Child (0-4 years) Mortality Rate (per1000 children)	41.2	26.5	15.2 (2008)
Life expectancy at Birth	*1981-85*	*1989-93*	*2002-06*
Total	55.4	59.9	63.5
Male	55.4	59.0	62.6
Female	55.7	59.7	64.2

Source : *Economic Survey, 2010-11.*

In 1981-85 and 1989-93, the life expectancy at birth for both male and female was 55 years and 59 years respectively. In 2002-06 it is 62 years for male and 64 years for female. Though this indicates a healthy environment, it is still far behind countries like Japan and Hong Kong (China) where the life expectancy at birth is above 80 years. Across the regions in India, there is huge variance in terms of IMR. The IMR in the year 2008 is as high as 70 in the State of Madhya Pradesh, 69 in Orissa, 67 in Uttar Pradesh and 64 in Assam and as low as 10 in Goa, 12 in Kerala and 14 in Manipur (*Economic Survey, 2010-11*).

Here also we observe the more or less same phenomenon where the difference across the regions in terms of health indicators is high in magnitude and this remains another area where policy framework should be to reduce the regional differences.

As far as unemployment is concerned, the National Sample Survey (NSS) 66th round quinquennial survey 2009-10 has shown that unemployment rate (*number of persons/person-days unemployed per 1000 persons/person-days in the labour force which includes both employed and unemployed*) is 6.6 per cent although it has decreased since the last survey, i.e., 61st round 2004-05. The unemployment rate as per Current Daily Status (CDS, *unemployed during each day of the reference week*) declined from 8.2 per cent in 2004-05 to 6.6 per cent in 2009-10. In rural areas, the unemployment rate declined from 8.2 per cent in 2004-05 to 6.8 per cent and in case of urban it was from 8.3 per cent in 2004-05 to 5.8 per cent in 2009-10. The rural-urban divide is clearly visible as the unemployment rate in rural is 6.8 per cent in 2009-10 while it is 5.8 per cent in urban areas. However, the gender-wise unemployment rate is skewed towards female. The male unemployment rate in 2009-10 is 6.1 per cent while that of the female is 8.2 per cent. The situation in urban areas is worse as the female unemployment rate is 9.1 per cent in 2009-10 compared to male unemployment rate of 5.1 per cent. The rural scenario is relatively better as the female unemployment rate is 8 per cent compared to male unemployment rate of 6.4 per cent (Government of India, 2011). However, a greater concern is for the female unemployment which is high both in case of urban and rural.

The distribution of working population in India also gives us a very interesting trend. While the share of agriculture to total GDP is continuously declining over the years (Figure 5.1), a majority of our working population is still engaged in agriculture.

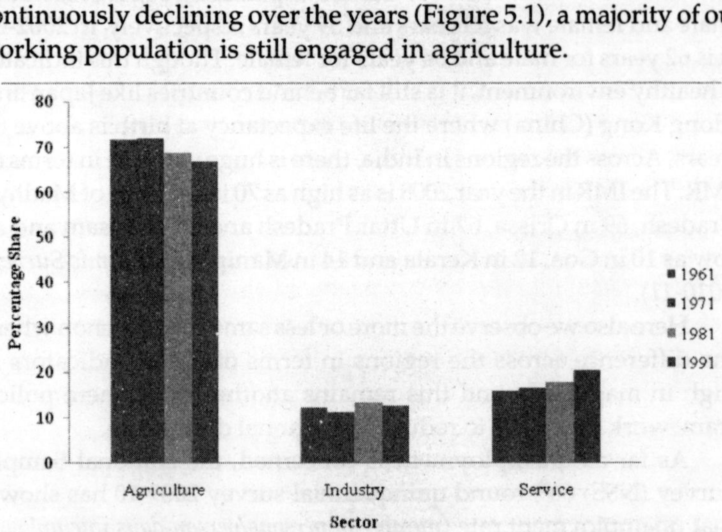

Figure 5.2 : Occupational Distribution of Working Population (Percentage Share)

Source : Calculated from various Census Reports.

Employment in agriculture sector declined by 5 percentage points from 71.8 per cent in Census year 1961 to 66.8 per cent in Census year 1991. While the employment in the industrial sector more or less remained constant at 12 per cent since 1961 to 1991, the employment in service sector increased marginally from 16 per cent in 1961 to 20.5 per cent in 1991. As per 2001 Census, out of the total workers 31.65 per cent were cultivators and 26.55 were agricultural labours. The distribution of usual status (*principal status + subsidiary status*) workers in 2009-10 as per NIC 2004 classification for collection of information on industry of employed shows that 53.2 per cent were engaged in agriculture and 21.5 per cent and 25.3 per cent in secondary and tertiary sector respectively (Calculated from Government of India, 2011).

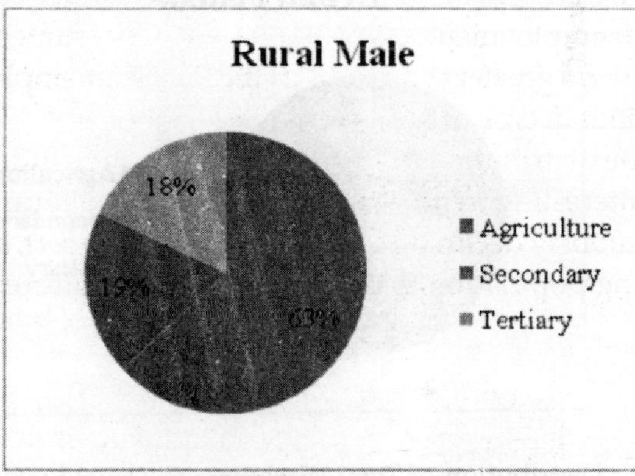

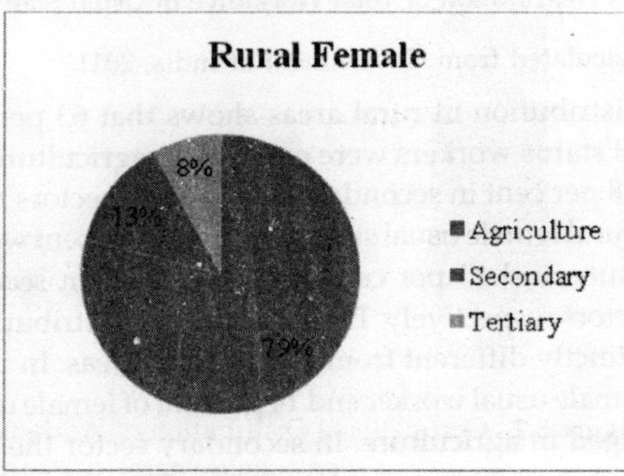

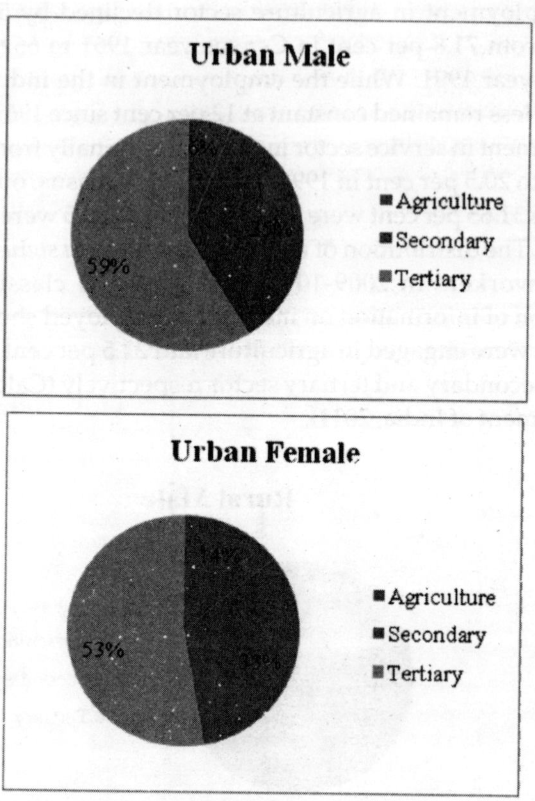

Figure 5.3 : Distribution of Total Workforce in Usual Status (% Share).

Source : Calculated from Government of India, 2011.

The distribution in rural areas shows that 63 per cent of the male usual status workers were engaged in agriculture and 19 per cent and 18 per cent in secondary and tertiary sectors respectively. In case of rural female usual status worker 79 per cent were engaged in agriculture and 13 per cent and 8 per cent in secondary and tertiary sectors respectively. The occupational distribution in urban area is distinctly different from that of rural areas. In urban area 6 per cent of male usual worker and 14 per cent of female usual worker were engaged in agriculture. In secondary sector the rate was 35 per cent male and 33 per cent female usual workers. A maximum share to the tune of 59 per cent male and 53 per cent female usual workers were engaged in tertiary sector (Figure 5.3).

The discrepancy in service sector led growth is also clearly visible in case of distribution of the working population. Majority of the working population are engaged in agriculture in rural area whereas in the urban area majority of them are engaged in the tertiary sector. This is another impediment towards inclusive growth.

Conclusion

India is emerging as a global power in the present century. It is also one of the largest and fastest growing economies of the world and it is expected that she will emerge as an Asian giant in a period of 10 to 15 years from now even bypassing China. While we are optimistic about the growth prospects and marching towards a new era, we should not forget to engage our people in this process. Inclusive growth is all about expanding opportunities and capability enhancement at the economy wide and household levels. It is not only about entitlement but empowerment (Ali, 2007). Inclusion is including the excluded in the development process and not simply a target of development programmes (Planning Commission, 2007).

The above analysis shows that our growth process has left out a significant portion of our population. Naturally the question arises as to how to make this growth more inclusive. The optimistic growth rate mainly led by service sector has created a rural-urban divide and widened regional disparity. There is a high degree of inter-State imbalance in the growth of the economy. Human development, poverty and health still remain a challenge to growth. A large section of the population is still engaged in agriculture and this is a widely prevalent phenomenon in rural areas. This is a serious issue and an area of concern and imperative towards inclusive growth.

Given this context, there is a need to design and implement policies and schemes which are specifically targeted towards the excluded. While the economic logic behind the underdevelopment of the peripheral regions is understandable, a policy framework for the development of these backward regions needs to be formulated. Identifying the local resources available and setting up industries accordingly is the first and foremost step towards upliftment of these regions. A strong resource-industry linkage needs to be established. A strong dyadic linkage between the local resources and industries to be set up will help in the long run sustainability of the new industries while providing raw materials and at the same time reducing transportation costs on both the raw materials as well as finished products (had it not been produced locally). Regarding the peripheral regions of the North East, the promotion of border trade will come in handy as the present service sector led growth is more successful in areas with better infrastructure. As these regions are quite far in terms of distance and lack in infrastructure, border trade as a strategy for frontier development may be promoted through mobilizing cross border synergies. This can be realized through establishing better political and economic ties with neighbouring countries like Bangladesh, China and Myanmar.

As has been observed above, a majority of our population is still engaged in unorganized sectors like agriculture and as such there is an urgent need to address this issue. If growth is associated with faster growth in agriculture and absorption of surplus labour in industry, the objective of inclusive growth can be achieved. Creating job opportunities in organized sector and shifting the surplus labour from agriculture towards industry requires skill development along with rapid expansion of the industrial sector. This again requires better infrastructure and social overhead capital which can be brought about by better planning and central government assistance. Here the financial institutions will have to play a very crucial role especially in infrastructure development. They are the major source of infrastructure financing especially in rural areas which is the need of the hour. This can be realized by adopting a more balanced growth approach, i.e., simultaneous investments in all the sectors.

Besides, a well designed scheme should be put forward especially targeted towards the excluded. Though there are many schemes which are already implemented, a reality check on whether these schemes reach our target group or not are very much necessary. The main problem is that our development schemes are hijacked in the middle by corrupt officials who include politicians and they hardly reach the target group. The government delivery mechanism needs to be redesigned. Here, community based organizations may be encouraged and these organizations may be given the authority and powers towards implementation of a scheme or a development project in their respective areas. This will eliminate the middle man and in the process corruption can be checked and the benefits will reach the target group. Last but not the least, realizing our interdependencies of existence and peaceful co-existence among all the social groups is a must towards fostering inclusive growth.

REFERENCES

Ahluwalia, Montek S., 2000, Economic Performance of States in Post Reform s Period, *Economic and Political Weekly*, Vol. 35, No. 19, May 06-12.

Ahluwalia, Montek S., 2003, State-Level Performance under Economic Reforms in India, in Anne O. Kruegar (ed.), *Economic Policy Reforms and the Indian Economy*, Oxford University Press, New Delhi.

Ali, Ifzal, 2007, Inequality and the Imperative for Inclusive Growth in Asia, *Asian Development Review*, Vol. 24, No. 2.

Bhanumurthy, N. R. and Arup Mitra, 2004, Economic Growth, Poverty and Inequality in Indian States in the Pre-reform and Reform Periods, *Asian Development Review*, Vol. 21, No. 2.

Bhattacharya, B. B. and S. Sakthivel, 2004, Regional Growth and Disparity in India: A Comparison of Pre- and Post-Reform Decades, *Economic and Political Weekly*, Vol. 39, No. 10, March 06-12.

Census of India, censusindia.gov.in

Central Statistics Office, www.mospi.nic.in

Desai, Sonalde B., Amaresh Dubey, Brij Lal Joshi, Mitali Sen, Abusaleh Sharif and Reeve Vanneman, 2010, *Human Development in India: Challenges for a Society in Transition*, Oxford University Press, New York.

Economic Survey 2010-11, http://indiabudget.nic.in

Government of India, 2006, *Towards Faster and More Inclusive Growth: An Approach to the 11th Five Year Plan*, Planning Commission, New Delhi.

Government of India, 2011, *Key Indicators of Employment and Unemployment in India 2009-2010*, NSS 66th Round, National Sample Survey Office, Ministry of Statistics and Programme Implementation, New Delhi.

Human Development Report 2010, hdr.undp.org/en/reports/global/hdr2010

Nayak, P. K., Sadhan Kumar Chattopadhyay, Arun Vishnu Kumar and V. Dhanya, 2010, Inclusive Growth and Its Regional Dimension, *Reserve Bank of India Occasional Papers*, Vol. 31, No. 3.

Planning Commission, planningcommission.gov.in/plans/planrel/fiveyr/11th/11_v1_ch1.pdf

Planning Commission (*a*), planningcommission.nic.in/news/prmar07.pdf

Planning Commission, 2007, *Towards Inclusive Growth: The Gender Dimension*, Submitted to the Planning Commission by the Committee of Feminist Economists during the formulation of the 11th Five Year Plan, New Delhi.

Singh, K. Gyanendra, 2011, *Security and Development: The Political Economy of Insurgency in Manipur*, Akansha Publishing House, New Delhi.

UNDP, http://www.beta.undp.org/undp/en/home/mdgoverview.html

6

Financial Inclusion through Derivatives Market An Indian Experience

ELANGBAM NIXON SINGH AND
C. VANLALKULHPUIA

Introduction

The term *'financial inclusion'* assumes a varied significance for different financial institutions, whether banks or mutual funds. For banks, the term signifies bringing the un-banked population under the financial services net, while for mutual funds, financial inclusion aims to increase access to mutual fund products channelizing savings into appropriate product schemes based on risk profiles. Capital markets have immense potential to drive the agenda of financial inclusion by providing investors with the opportunity for wealth creation. Products and services need to be tailored to suit the requirements of the investor in terms of risk appetite and expected return. To design these products suitably, it is necessary to lay the foundation of financial literacy and draft proper customer segmentation. A low-cost distribution mechanism is required, ideally.

In this regard, development of derivatives market in India can go a long way for financial inclusion for the society, particularly the rural farmers. The term *'derivative'* indicates that it has no independent value, i.e. its value is entirely *'derived'* from the value of the underlying asset. The underlying asset can be securities, commodities, bullion, currency, livestock or anything else. In other words, Derivative means a forward, future, option or any other hybrid contract of pre-determined fixed duration, linked for the purpose of contract fulfilment to the value of a specified real or financial asset or to an index of securities. Financial markets are, by nature, extremely volatile and hence the risk factor is an important concern for financial agents. To reduce this risk, the concept of derivatives comes into the picture. The primary purpose behind investing in derivative instruments is to enable individual or corporate investors to either increase their exposure to certain specified risks in the hope that they will earn returns more than adequate to compensate them for bearing these added risks, known as *speculation*, or reduce their exposure to specific financial risks by transferring these risks to other parties who are willing to bear them at lower cost, known as *hedging* (John D. Finnerty & Mark S. Brown: 2000)[1].Derivatives are products whose values are derived from one or more basic variables called bases. These bases can be underlying assets (for example forex, equity, etc.), bases or reference rates. For example, *wheat farmers may wish to sell their harvest at a future date to eliminate the risk of a change in prices by that date. The transaction in this case would be the derivative, while the spot price of wheat would be the underlying asset* (NSE, 2001)[2].

Apart from being looked upon as a social responsibility, financial inclusion also presents a huge business opportunity, capable of spearheading growth in the financial services space. However, to turn this agenda of inclusive growth into a viable business model, it is imperative to make use of technology, without which increased participation from masses cannot be sought. Online banking, online distribution of mutual funds, mobile banking, etc., are some of the emerging areas in the financial services industry. These claim to increase efficiencies, speed of transaction and add to the customer's convenience. At the same time, NBFCs have the advantage of wide distribution networks in rural areas and are, therefore, well placed to secure mass participation in financial products. Therefore, the NBFC segment deserves more attention today. Apart from optimizing their strength in distribution, their ability to introduce innovation in products and then map a distribution model for it is quite immense. They also follow a focused approach to deal with the dedicated business model and ensure that it remains within the estimated budget. The technology platform with the capability to fast track financial inclusion is that of mobile communication and the internet. Internet stock trading is popular among retailers, with India reported to have 70 million to 80 million internet users and around 5.2 million broadband internet connections (Rawat, R. S., 2011)[3].

Literature Review

Financial services play a vital role in the economic growth of a country. For the welfare of the society, two aspects of financial services are highly important: first, financial options viz., banks, insurance companies and stock markets; and second, easy accessibility to such financial options for all the citizens of the country. In this perspective, development in derivatives market in India can be seen as means of providing accessibility to derivatives to all the citizens of the country. In this regard, the Committee of Financial Inclusion, National Bank for Agriculture and Rural Development (NABARD) has defined financial inclusion as "the process of ensuring access to financial services and timely and adequate where needed by the weaker sections and low income groups at an affordable cost".

The financial sector development can be broadly pursued four objectives; efficiency, stability to mitigate and manage their own risks, transparency and financial inclusion through resource mobilization and risk management (Gokarn, 2011)[4]. Both OTC and Exchange traded derivatives products have been increasing steadily over the years. These instruments are important components of the overall financial sector strategy and the broad regulatory objective is required to ensure their potential usage, consistent with both financial development and the contribution of financial markets to economic growth.

According to Usha Thorat, Director, Centre for Advanced Financial Research and Learning, access to microfinance by itself cannot be taken as financial inclusion, as the latter idea requires having an individual bank account which brings the account holder into the national payment system and insures her deposit. Addressing the valedictory of a three-day summit on microfinance, Thorat, who was a Deputy Governor of the Reserve Bank of India, had opined that "Financial inclusion has become a global buzz word, figuring on the agenda of G-20 meetings. We need to convince banks about the profitability of serving the poor" (Business Standard, 2011)[5].

Regarding the business houses of India also, the affiliation with (The Options Industry Council) OIC is an extension of (Financial Technologies India Limited) FTIL Group's efforts to increase awareness on trading of financial and listed derivatives products in India. "The association with OIC is a pioneering endeavour by the Group to increase its educational efforts and enable financial inclusion in India through financial literacy (Chagger, Sandeep, 2010)[6]. Apart from this, access to the full range of financial services including derivatives based on warehouse receipts, to enable farmers to get the best price for their produce is one of the seven desirables for Universal Financial Inclusion (UFI) being available to all adults in India, over a reasonable period of time, say by March 31, 2013 (Mahajan, Vijay, 2011)[7]. In addition to the physical risks which impact crop yields, farmers also suffer from price risks. In bumper years, their harvest fetches low prices. In order to hedge against such price risks the right instrument is commodity derivatives, particularly options in which a farmer can be assured of selling his produce at a certain price in future. The Committee also noted that the Indian farmer is highly attuned to dealing in spot markets, traditionally known as *Mandis*, where the commodity is exchanged for cash. The Committee, therefore, supports any initiatives towards improving the transactional efficiency of spot markets. However, the Committee noted the fact that a vast majority of financially excluded farmers have only small marketable surplus of any commodity and thus cannot benefit from the vibrant commodity exchanges, where the minimum traded lot is much larger than what the individual farmer has to offer. In order to extend the benefits of derivative exchanges to excluded farmers, aggregative mechanism such as cooperatives need to come up (NABARD, 2008)[8].

Objectives and Research Design

Derivatives are recognized as the best and most cost-efficient way of meeting the felt need for risk hedging in certain types of commercial and financial operations. Derivatives markets have been in existence in India in some form or the other for a long time. A series of reforms of the stock market between 1993 and 1996 paved the way for the development of exchange-traded equity derivatives markets in India.

This chapter traces the development of derivatives trading in India and its recent trends. Data for the study has been mainly based on secondary one collected from SEBI annual reports. NSE, RBI and BSE reports were also taken into consideration for the purpose of analyzing with an objective of observing how far derivatives market has penetrated into the Indian society. At the end, it comes up with some concrete measures to further develop the derivatives markets as a means of financial inclusion for the society, particularly the rural farmers of the country.

Development of Derivative Markets in India : A Background

Derivatives markets have been in existence in India in some form or the other for a long time. In the area of commodities, the Bombay Cotton Trade Association started futures trading in 1875, and by the early 1900s India had one of the world's largest futures' industries. In 1952, the government banned cash settlement and options trading and derivatives trading shifted to informal forwards markets. In recent years, government policy has changed, allowing for an increased role for market-based pricing and less suspicion of derivatives trading. The ban on futures trading of many commodities was lifted starting in the early 2000s, and national electronic commodity exchanges were created.

In the equity markets, a system of trading called *badla* involving some elements of forwards trading had been in existence for decades. However, the system led to a number of undesirable practices and it was prohibited off and on till the Securities and Exchange Board of India (SEBI) banned it for good in 2001. A series of reforms of the stock market between 1993 and 1996 paved the way for the development of exchange-traded equity derivatives markets in India. In 1993, the government created the NSE in collaboration with State-owned financial institutions. NSE improved the efficiency and transparency of the stock markets by offering a fully automated screen-based trading system and real-time price dissemination. In 1995, a prohibition on trading options was lifted. In 1996, the NSE sent a proposal to SEBI for listing exchange-traded derivatives. The report of the L. C. Gupta Committee (1998), set up by SEBI[9], recommended a phased introduction of derivative products and bi-level regulation (i.e., self-regulation by exchanges with SEBI providing a supervisory and advisory role). Another report, by the J.R. Varma Committee in 1998, worked out various operational details such as the margining systems. In 1999, the Securities Contracts (Regulation) Act of 1956, or SC(R)A, was amended so that derivatives could be declared "securities". This allowed the regulatory framework for trading securities to be extended to derivatives. The Act considers derivatives to be legal and valid, but only if they are traded on exchanges. Finally, a 30-year ban on forward trading was also lifted in 1999.

The economic liberalization of the early nineties facilitated the introduction of derivatives based on interest rates and foreign exchange. A system of market-determined exchange rates was adopted by India in March 1993. In August 1994, the rupee was made fully convertible on current account. These reforms allowed increased integration between domestic and international markets, and created a need to manage currency risk. Figure 6.1 shows how the volatility of the exchange rate between the Indian Rupee and the U.S. Dollar has increased since 1991. The easing of various restrictions on the free movement of interest rates resulted in the need to manage interest rate risk.

Thus, derivative products have been introduced in a phased manner starting with Index Futures Contracts in June 2000. Index Options and Stock Options were introduced in June 2001 and July 2001 followed by Stock Futures in November 2001 (N.L, Ahuja, 2005)[10]. Sectoral indices were permitted for derivatives trading in December 2002. Interest Rate Futures on a notional bond and T-bill priced off ZCYC have been introduced in June 2003 and exchange traded interest rate futures on a notional bond priced off a basket of Government Securities were permitted for trading in January 2004. During December 2007 SEBI permitted mini derivative (F&O) contract on Index (Sensex and Nifty). Further, in January 2008, longer tenure Index options contracts and Volatility Index and in April 2008, Bond Index was introduced. In addition to the above, during August 2008, SEBI permitted Exchange traded Currency Derivatives.

Trends in Derivative Market

Introduction of exchange traded derivatives is one of the significant developments in the history of India's securities market. In India, derivatives trading began with the launch of index futures in June 2000 followed by index options, single stock options and single stock futures in 2001. Interest rate futures were also launched in June 2003. The two premier stock exchanges, namely NSE and BSE provide trading platforms for derivative.

Over the years, turnover on the derivative market has grown exponentially in terms of the number of contracts and value. This trend continued in 2009-10 too. Presently, the derivatives market in India is dominated by NSE with its share of over 98 per cent in the total turnover as well as number of contracts. There had been revival of derivatives trading at BSE since 2006-07, which continued in

2009-10 also. The total turnover in the derivative segments surpassed the combined turnover in the cash segment of both BSE and NSE since early 2004. By the end of March 2010, the turnover of derivatives market was more than five times the combined cash market turnover of BSE and NSE (Figure 6.1).

The turnover in the derivatives segment at NSE recorded a mixed trend during 2009-10 (Table 6.1). The highest turnover was recorded in November 2009 (Rs. 16, 61,816 crores) followed by July 2009 (Rs. 15,73,509 crores) and February 2010 (Rs. 15,69,877 crores). Growth in the derivatives turnover at NSE was the highest in June 2009 when turnover rose by 24.8 per cent, followed November 2009 (10.1 per cent) and April 2009 (9.9 per cent). The average daily turnover at NSE in 2009-10 has increased by 59.1 per cent to Rs. 72,097 crores from Rs. 45,311 crores in 2008-09. The total number of contracts traded in the derivative segment of NSE rose marginally by 3.4 per cent to 67,92,93,922 in 2009-10 from 65,73,90,497 in 2008-09, whereas, at BSE, the number of contracts traded declined substantially from 4,96,502 in 2008-09 to 9,026 in 2009-10.

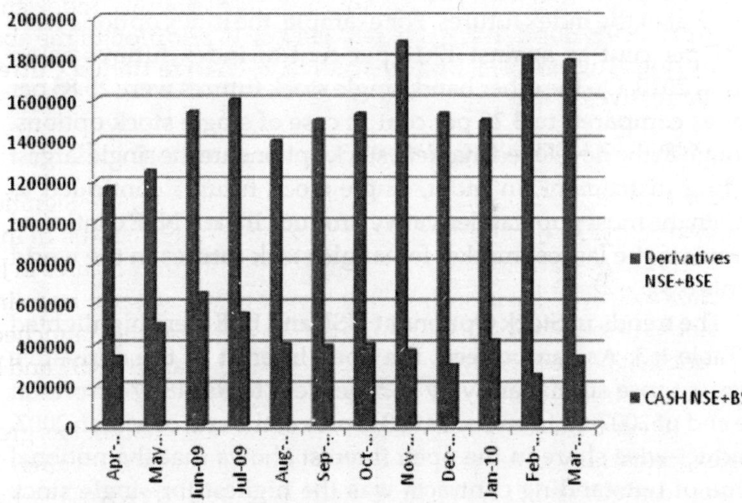

Figure 6.1 : Derivatives Turnover *vis-à-vis* Cash Market Turnover (2009-10)

Source : *NSE, BSE.*

The value of the contracts traded in the derivative segment of NSE increased by 60.4 per cent to Rs. 1,76,63,665 crores in 2009-10 from Rs. 1,10,10,468 crores in 2008-09, whereas the turnover at the derivatives segment of BSE declined to Rs. 234 crores in 2009-10 from Rs. 11,775 crores in 2008-09. The open interest in the derivative segment has increased by 69.8 per cent to Rs. 97,978 crores at the end of 2009-10 from Rs. 57,705 crores at the end of 2008-09.

A clear-cut change was seen in the product composition and turnover in the derivatives market in India (Table 6.2). Futures in general and single stock futures, in particular, used to dominate derivatives product in India with over 86 per cent share in total derivatives turnover every year. However, the picture has been changing in last couple of years in favour of Index Options. During 2009-10, the largest share in the total derivatives turnover has been contributed by Index options with 45.5 per cent share in it whereas the share of index options in the total turnover in 2008-09 was 33.9 per cent. In 2009-10, Index options were followed by Single Stock Futures (29.4 per cent) and Index Futures (22.3 per cent).

In the recent trend, the popularity of index options is increasing than that of the index futures. For example, the index options were 53.77 per cent as against 17.11 per cent of index futures as on March 2010. On the other hand, single stock futures were 25.85 per cent as compared to 3.28 per cent in case of single stock options. Though in the developed markets, stock options are the single largest trading instrument, in India, single stock futures continued to remain the most popular derivative product. In fact, NSE continued to remain the largest market for single stock futures in the world (Table 6.3).

The trends in Stock Options at NSE and BSE were highlighted at Table 6.3. As can be seen, the open interest in the derivative segment rose significantly by 26.5 per cent to Rs. 48,974 crores at the end of 2007-08 from Rs. 38,723 crores at the end of March 2007. Product-wise share in the open interest shows that the notional value of outstanding contracts was the highest for single stock futures (Rs. 21,143 crores), followed by index futures (Rs. 15,557 crores), index options (Rs. 11,636 crores) and stock options (Rs. 636 crores).

Table 6.1 Trends in Turnover and Open Interest in Derivatives at NSE and BSE

Year/ Month	No. of Contracts		Turnover (Rs. Crores)		Open interest at the End of the Year/Month			
					No. of Contracts		Notional Turnover (Rs. Crores)	
	NSE	BSE	NSE	BSE	NSE	BSE	NSE	BSE
1	2	3	4	5	6	7	8	9
2003-04	5,68,86,776	3,82,258	21,30,649	12,452	2,35,792	35	7,187	1
2004-05	7,70,17,185	5,31,719	25,47,053	16,112	5,92,646	0	21,052	0
2005-06	15,76,19,271	203	48,24,250	9	10,28,003	0	38,469	0
2006-07	21,68,83,573	17,81,220	73,56,271	59,007	17,91,389	408	38,710	13
2007-08	42,50,13,200	74,53,371	1,30,90,478	2,42,309	22,82,671	3,175	48,900	74
2008-09	65,73,90,497	4,96,502	1,10,10,482	11,775	32,27,759	22	57,705	0
2009-10	67,92,93,922	9,026	1,76,63,665	234	34,89,790	0	97,978	0
Apr-09	5,62,10,317	113	11,43,363	2	27,53,069	8	57,076	0.17
May-09	4,82,85,515	393	12,27,253	7.95	23,05,330	1	64,823	0.02
Jun-09	5,24,08,197	3	15,31,981	0	25,27,295	1	58,987	0.02
Jul-09	6,68,27,086	4	15,73,509	0.09	24,67,693	0	62	0
Aug-09	5,96,70,387	1	14,73,646	0	29,55,633	1	75,134	0.03

(contd...)

Table 6.1 (contd...)

Sep-09	5,25,01,332	1	13,88,378	0.03	32,39,338	1	88,791	0.02
Oct-09	57,09,794	0	15,10,418	0	33,36,784	0	83,327	0
Nov-09	6,27,65,075	1	16,61,816	0.03	33,90,368	0	91,419	0
Dec-09	5,54,24,003	147	15,24,982	4	23,56,002	25	77,760	0.61
Jan-10	5,31,01,821	7935	14,90,297	209.71	35,65,510	0	93,194	0
Feb-10	6,04,29,963	399	15,69,877	10	33,40,490	0	88,141	0
Mar-10	5,59,60,432	29	15,68,148	0.75	34,89,790	0	97,978	0

Source : *NSE, BSE.*

Table 6.2 : Product-wise Derivatives Turnover at NSE (Per Cent)

Year/ Month	Index Futures	Index Options	Single Stock Options	Single Stock Futures	Total
2003-04	26.02	2.48	10.19	61.29	100
2004-05	30.32	4.79	6.63	58.27	100
2005-06	31.38	7.02	3.74	57.87	100
2006-07	34.52	10.77	2.63	52.08	100
2007-08	29.19	10.41	2.74	57.66	100
2008-09	32.42	33.89	2.08	31.60	100
2009-10	22.27	45.45	2.86	29.41	100
Apr-09	26.39	39.69	2.72	31.17	100
May-09	25.86	35.08	2.54	36.52	100
Jun-09	2265	35.62	3.25	38.49	100
Jul-09	24.34	44.57	2.46	28.64	100
Aug-09	24.86	44.70	2.46	27.98	100
Sep-09	21.78	43.87	3.08	31.27	100
Oct-09	21.82	44.33	3.00	30.84	100
Nov-09	21.88	49.13	2.63	26.37	100
Dec-09	21.61	49.62	2.81	25.96	100
Jan-10	20.06	46.69	3.45	29.80	100
Feb-10	20.82	53.97	2.63	22.58	100
Mar-10	17.11	53.77	3.28	25.85	100

Source : *SEBI.*

Popularity among Investors for Derivatives

As investors embrace the use of derivatives-based strategies for minimizing risk exposures and enhancing performance, they have grown more comfortable with the contracts and pushed the derivatives market to new heights. The surge in popularity of derivatives-based strategies is in part due to the increasing need among investors to manage risk. For example, multinational corporations might be active in currency derivatives to hedge their exposure to exchange-rate volatility, while many pension funds are drawn to interest-rate swaps because they offset a significant amount of their interest-rate exposure.

There was a significant rise in registration of various types of membership for derivative segment at both NSE and BSE. The transactions undertaken by trading-cum-clearing members constituted 57.2 per cent of the total turnover of the F&O segment in 2009-10. The percentage share in the traded value by trading-cum-self clearing members and trading members was 28.9 per cent and 13.9 per cent, respectively (Table 6.4). Investors' desire to hedge various risks and to identify opportunities for higher investment returns will be the driving force behind the increased acceptance of, and comfort with, sophisticated derivatives-based investment strategies and should ensure the continued growth of the derivatives market thereby acting as a means of financial inclusion among the people in the country.

Conclusion and Suggestions

Concerted efforts need to be made to drive the agenda of inclusive growth, encouraging more investors to access capital markets. Regulators and other industry stakeholders are driving this single-point agenda to tap the potential in smaller towns and cities. In this regard, development of derivatives market in India can go a long way for financial inclusion for the society, particularly the rural farmers.

In terms of the growth of derivatives markets, and the variety of derivatives users, the Indian market has equalled or exceeded many other regional markets. While the growth is being spearheaded mainly by retail investors, private sector institutions and large corporations, smaller companies and State-owned institutions are gradually getting into the act. The variety of derivatives instruments available for trading is also expanding.

There remain major areas of concern for Indian derivatives users. Large gaps exist in the range of derivatives products that are traded actively. In equity derivatives, NSE figures show that almost 90 per cent of activity is due to stock futures or index futures, whereas trading in options is limited to a few stocks, partly because they are settled in cash and not the underlying stocks. Exchange-traded derivatives based on interest rates and currencies are virtually absent.

Liquidity and transparency are important properties of any developed market. Liquid markets require market makers who are willing to buy and sell, and be patient while doing so. In India,

Table 6.3 : Trends in Stock Options at NSE and BSE

Year/ Month	No. of stocks		No. of Contracts		Turnover (Rs. in Crores)		Open interest at the end of the Year /Month: No. of contracts		Open interest at the end of the Year /Month: Notional value (Rs. in Crores)	
	NSE	BSE	NSE	BSE	NSE	BSE	NSE	BSE	NSE	BSE
1	2	3	4	5	6	7	8	9	10	11
2003-04	53	44	5583071	7621	217212	332	29779	0	871	0
2004-05	53	46	5045112	89	168858	3	92497	0	3154	0
2005-06	116	76	5240776	2	180270	0.1	27108	0	1024	0
2006-07	155	89	5283310	6	193811	0.19	19204	0	447	0
2007-08	228	0	9460631	15	359137	0.3	34602	0	636	0
2008-09	250	0	1,32,95,970	0	2,29,227	0	78,573	0	2,521	0
2009-10	190	0	1,40,16,270	0	5,06,065	0	97,522	0	3,137	0
Apr-09	234	0	8,07,323	0	31,427	0	32,083	0	1,152	0
May-09	233	0	6,44,280	0	31,168	0	30,853	0	1,480	0
Jun-09	233	0	8,82,947	0	49,746	0	92,481	0	2,527	0
Jul-09	183	0	12,68,003	0	38,706	0	59,768	0	1,784	0
Aug-09	180	0	11,29,195	0	36,214	0	92,098	0	2,756	0
Sep-09	179	0	12,37,428	0	42,758	0	77,201	0	2,508	0

(contd...)

Table 6.3 (contd...)

Oct-09	179	0	13,78,569	0	45,387	0	74,399	0	1,957	0
Nov-09	179	0	13,60,703	0	43,666	0	89,504	0	2,677	0
Dec-09	179	1	12,52,898	0	42,855	0	41,012	0	1,328	0
Jan-10	179	0	14,14,178	0	51,454	0	83,872	0	2,492	0
Feb-10	190	0	12,23,627	0	41,285	0	72,915	0	2,274	0
Mar-10	190	0	14,17,119	0	51,398	0	97,522	0	3,137	0

Source : *BSE, NSE.*

market making is primarily the province of Indian private and foreign banks, with public sector banks lagging in this area. A lack of market liquidity may be responsible for inadequate trading in some markets. Transparency is achieved partly through financial disclosure.

Further regulatory reform will help the markets grow faster. For example, Indian commodity derivatives have great growth potential but government policies have resulted in the underlying spot/ physical market being fragmented (e.g., due to lack of free movement of commodities and differential taxation within India). Similarly, credit derivatives, the fastest growing segment of the market globally, are absent in India and require regulatory action if they are to develop.

As Indian derivatives markets grow more sophisticated, greater investor awareness will become essential. NSE has programmes to inform and educate brokers, dealers, traders, and market personnel. In addition, institutions will need to devote more resources to develop the business processes and technology necessary for derivatives trading. Further development of the market will hinge on adoption of international accounting standards and disclosure practices by all the market participants, including corporate (Gopinath, Shyamala: 2007)[11]

As the market activity pick-up and the volumes rise, the market will definitely need a strong and independent regular; similar to the Securities and Exchange Board of India (SEBI) that regulates the securities markets. Unlike SEBI which is an independent body, the Forwards Markets Commission (FMC) is under the Department of Consumer Affairs (Ministry of Consumer Affairs, Food and Public Distribution) and depends on it for funds. It is imperative that the Government should grant more powers to the FMC to ensure an orderly development of the commodity markets. The SEBI and FMC also need to work closely with each other due to the inter-relationship between the two markets (N. L. Ahuja: 2006)[12].

While the Indian regulatory framework for derivatives is mostly consistent with the international practices, some elements of financial infrastructure need to be strengthened. It is suggested that the bankruptcy and insolvency laws should clearly prescribe providing due concern to rights of securities holders on winding up or on insolvency of intermediaries and multilateral netting procedures innovation.

The Basel Committee on Banking Supervision and IOSCO Technical Committee have presented recommendations for public disclosure of trading and derivatives activities of banks and securities firms which could also be used by such non-financial companies that make material use of complex financial products. These recommendations need to be enforced which can emphasize the importance of transparency in promoting financial stability. It is observed that transparency based on meaningful public disclosure plays an important role in reinforcing the efforts of supervisory authorities in encouraging the sound risk management practices and promoting financial market stability (IOSCO: 1999)[13].

The report of the Bank for International Settlements (BIS: 1998)[14] on "*OTC Derivatives: Settlement Procedures and Counterparty Risk Management*" makes a series of recommendations for actions by derivatives counterparties, prudential supervisors and central banks that could reduce risks to the participants and to the financial system. The followings need to be flagged to the statutory regulators:

Both the derivatives counterparties and prudential supervisors should ensure that the "master agreements" and "confirmations" for OTC derivatives should always be executed in time. The backlogs and associated risks should always be strictly monitored, since some jurisdictions permit close-out netting upon counterparty's insolvency only if the parties had entered into a "master agreement". Thus, failure to sign a master agreement may jeopardize a dealer's ability to enforce close-out netting in the event of its counter party's default.

Further, since a clearing entity has the potential to mitigate each of the types of counterparty risks associated with OTC derivatives, the central banks and prudential supervisors of counterparties should ensure that there are no unnecessary legal or regulatory barriers to the establishment of clearing entities for OTC derivatives. It is observed that safeguards that have proved effective in clearing entities for exchange-traded derivatives appear likely to be effective for OTC derivatives as well.

Table 6.4 : Shares of Various Classes of Members in Derivatives Turnover at NSE and BSE

Year/ Month	Turnover (Rs. Crores)				Percentage Share		
	Trading member	Trading cum-Clearing Members	Trading cum-Self-Clearing Members	Total	Trading Members	Trading cum-Clearing Members	Trading cum-Self-Clearing Members
1 2	3	4	5	6	7	8	
2005-06	2494557	4980025	2173918	9648501	25.85	51.61	22.53
2006-07	3060253	7952147	3818532	14830932	20.63	53.62	25.75
2007-08	4550533	1,53,60,489	6756714	26667736	17.06	57.6	25.34
2008-09	33,99,848	1,24,60,554	61,84,083	2,20,44,486	15.42	56.52	28.05
2009-10	48,99,892	2,02,12,013	1,02,15,902	3,53,27,807	13.87	57.21	28.92
Apr-09	3,11,617	13,07,989	6,67,123	22,86,729	13.63	57.2	29.17
May-09	3,35,173	14,25,574	6,93,773	24,54,521	13.66	58.08	28.27
Jun-09	4,25,716	17,84,780	8,53,465	30,63,961	13.89	58.25	27.85
Jul-09	4,14,784	18,59,383	8,72,851	31,47,018	13.18	59.08	27.74
Aug-09	4,11,775	17,15,255	8,20,262	29,47,292	13.97	58.2	27.83
Sep-09	3,97,284	16,17,988	7,61,484	27,76,756	14.31	58.27	27.42

(contd...)

Table 6.4 (contd...)

Oct-09	4,47,173	17,28,262	8,45,035	30,20,835	14.8	57.22	27.97
Nov-09	4,76,271	18,63,460	9,83,901	33,23,632	14.33	56.07	29.6
Dec-09	4,31,298	17,16,852	9,01,823	30,49,972	14.14	56.29	29.57
Jan-10	3,88,140	17,02,573	8,90,310	29,81,023	13.02	57.11	29.87
Feb-10	4,29,623	17,55,387	9,54,763	31,39,772	13.68	55.91	30.41
Mar-10	4,31,038	17,34,147	9,71,111	31,36,296	13.74	55.29	30.96

Source : *BSE, NSE.*

REFERENCES

Bank for International Settlements (1998): Report by the Committee on Payment and Settlement Systems and the Euro-Currency Standing Committee of the Central Bank of the Group of Ten Countries. (1998), "OTC derivatives: Settlement procedures and counterparty risk management." *Bank for International Settlements*, September.

Business Standard (2011), "Financial inclusion is more than access to microfinance", June 24, Chennai.

Chagger, Sandeep, (2010), *"Financial Technologies"* a press release, accessed from www.ftindia.com.

Gokarn, Subir (2011), *"Regulatory Perspectives on Derivatives Markets in India"*, Address by the Deputy Governor, Reserve Bank of India at the International Options Market Association, World Federation of Exchanges Annual Conference organised by the National Stock Exchange at Mumbai on May 4.

Gopinath, Shyamala (2007), Keynote address delivered by Smt. Deputy Governor at the Euro money Inaugural India Derivatives Summit, 2007, Mumbai on October 24, 2007.

John D. Finnerty and Mark S. Brown (2000), *An Overview of Derivatives Litigation: 1994 to 2000*, 131, 132, 7 Fordham J. Corp. & Fin. L.

Mahajan, Vijay (2011), *Money Can Fly*, Civil Society (Special Edition), New Delhi, January.

N.L. Ahuja (2006), "Commodity Derivatives Market in India: Development, Regulation and Future Prospects", *International Research Journal of Finance and Economics*, Issue 2 (2006) © Euro Journals Publishing, Inc. 2006 http://www.eurojournals.com/finance.htm

N.L., Ahuja (2005), *Managing Foreign Exchange Risk with Derivatives*, paper presented at the International Conference of Asia-Pacific Association of Derivatives (APAD) held at IIM Bangalore, 27-30 July, 2005.

NABARD (2008), Report of the Committee on Financial inclusion January, chaired by C. Rangarajan (www.nabard.org)

National Stock Exchange of India Limited (2001). *"Indian Securities Market: A Review"*. National Stock Exchange of India Limited, Vol. IV, pp. 220-221.

Rawat, R. S. (2011), *Key to Double Digit Growth—Indian Capital Markets*, ASSOCHAM, India, accessed from www.pwc.com/india.

Report of Basel Committee on Banking Supervision and Technical Committee of IOSCO (1999), Recommendations for public disclosure of trading and derivatives activities of banks and securities firms. *International Organisation of Securities Commissions*, October 1999.

SEBI Annual Reports for 2009-10, 2009-08, 2007-08, 2006-07, 2005-06.

SEBI—L.C. Gupta Committee, Reports & Documents (1998)—India Finance & Investment Guide.htm.

7

Working of Financial Inclusion in Nizamabad District, Andhra Pradesh

K. APARNA

Introduction

Financial inclusion is a term which is commonly used in today for more inclusive growth. Despite of the significant improvements made in the Banking Industry specially in the areas relating to financial viability, profitability and competitiveness; they have not been able to cover vast section of disadvantages and low-income group people. There are still large number of unbanked centres and unreached populations, in spite of rigorous efforts made by banks in branch networking to cover whole of the country. To have a bank account accessible to vast section of the population, the Reserve Bank of India took various steps like opening of basic banking no-frills accounts either with nil or minimum balances as well as charges and relaxation of KYC (Know Your Customer) norms.

The committee on financial inclusion headed by C. Rangarajan defines as: "Financial Inclusion is the process of ensuring access to financial services and timely and adequate credit where needed by vulnerable groups such as weaker sections and low income groups at an affordable cost".

District Profile

Nizamabad is one out of ten districts of Andhra Pradesh located in the West by Maharashtra, Medak in the south, Karimnagar in the east and Adilabad in the north. It has a total Geographical Area

7,956 sq. km with 3 revenue divisions and 36 mandals. The district has a population of 25.52 lakhs of which 12.52 are males and remaining 13.00 lakhs are females as per 2011 Census (provisional). The district has a literacy rate of 62.25 per cent of which 72.66 per cent are male and 52.33 per cent are female.

As per the data presented by the State Level Bankers Committee (SLBC) reveals that Nizamabad district is 100 per cent financially included district in Andhra Pradesh. It means all the households have a bank account. The present study is taken up to know the factual data relating to financial inclusion in Nizamabad district.

Objectives of the Study

The objectives of the present study are:

- To assess the extent of inclusive growth in the district of Nizamabad after 100 per cent financial inclusion;
- To study the impact of income on financial inclusion; and
- To examine the impact of occupation after and before financial inclusion of the district of Nizamabad.

Methodology

The present study is based on primary data collected directly from the selected households of Nizamabad district, Andhra Pradesh. A sample of 80 households (HHs) was taken as base on the convenient method of sampling collected in the month of April 2011. Twenty households from four different income groups were selected for the study. Collected data were classified and tabulated as per the necessity of the study. The secondary data were also used for the present study from books, journal and website.

Limitations of the Study

The study has limitations such as:

- It is confined to Nizamabad city only and it cannot represent the entire State of Andhra Pradesh.
- Since it is based on primary data, the information given by the respondents can be away from limitations.

Findings of the Study

It is observed from Table 7.1 that the literacy rate is only 50 per cent, i.e., 102 adults are uneducated out of 204 total respondents. 20 per cent of adults are above 50 years and most of them are leading life without the support of their children and most of them are widows. This is the major reason for high level of financial exclusion in case of income group below Rs. 1,500 per month. It is very interesting to see that out of total respondents 106 are females and remaining 98 respondents are males which accounts more than 50 per cent of the total. Out of the total respondents 52 of them are having their ration cards, 50 households are having mobile phones, and number of female adults as members of SHGs are 44 and number of households taken loan other than banks are 46.

Table 7.1 : Profile of the Respondents of Nizamabad District

Particulars	*Households monthly income*				
	Above Rs. 10,000	*Rs. 5,000 to Rs. 10,000*	*Rs. 1,500 to Rs. 5,000*	*Less than Rs. 1,500*	*Total*
No. of HHs surveyed	20	20	20	20	80
No. of Adults	44	72	48	40	204
No. of Males	22	38	22	16	98
No. of Females	22	34	26	24	106
No. of HHs having ration cards	02	20	18	12	52
No. of HHs having Mobile Phone	20	14	16	Nil	50
No. of adults above the age of 50 years.	06	14	02	18	40
No. of adults uneducated	02	44	20	36	102
No. of Females adults as members of SHGs	04	16	18	06	44
No. of HHs taken loan from other than Banks	10	14	14	08	46

Source : Primary Survey, April 2011.

Table 7.2 clearly indicates the rate of financial exclusion is high in case of three income groups accept those whose monthly income is above Rs. 10,000. The households whose monthly income is in the range of Rs. 1,500 to Rs. 5,000,12 households have bank account out of 20 households surveyed. The main reason for opening the bank account was to credit either the salary or pension. 60 per cent are financially excluded and only 20 per cent are included in case of households whose monthly income group is Rs. 1,500. It clearly indicates that the income and financial inclusion are positively correlated. That is more the income the less is the rate of financial exclusion.

Table 7.2 : Purpose for Taking Bank Account

HHs Monthly Income	*Purpose*					*Total No. of Current and Savings Accounts*	*No. of Accounts regularly used*
	Business	*To credit salary*	*To take loan*	*To credit position*	*Other purpose*		
Above Rs. 10,000	16	22	20	08	18	84	60
Rs. 5,000 to Rs. 10,000	02	02	02	06	08	20	16
Rs. 1,500 to Rs. 5,000	—	04	04	04	—	12	06
Less than Rs. 1500	—	—	02	—	02	04	—
Total	18	28	28	18	28	120	82

Source : Primary Survey, April 2011.

From Table 7.3, it is evidenced that the occupation has no relation with the concept of financial inclusion. Out of total 204 adults, 132 adults were engaged in different types of work. Rests of them are idle due to their age factor, few are pursuing their studies and most of the females are house wives.

It is observed that most of the low-income holders of bank accounts, hardly ever use them. Further, most of the households took loan from informal sector. They could not get loan from formal sector mainly because of lack of formal employment besides low and irregular monthly income sources. This segment is of the opinion that, when we are trustworthy to a moneylender why not to the Government? To overcome this, bank must develop dedicated organizations and pursue the activities through partnership with them.

Reasons for not Opening a Bank Account

Following reasons were identified on interviewing the households who does not have a bank account:

1. 80 per cent of the households have reported that they could not find a person to introduce them about the opening of bank account. They are not aware about the operation of bank account, its merit and demerits.
2. 10 per cent of the respondents have reported that they never felt the need of an account. Because, whatever the amount of daily earning are not sufficient for opening an account.
3. It is also found that 2 per cent of the households have reported that they cannot trust banks (for instance, they deposited money in Charminar Bank, which they could not get back) which they had a bad experience with the banks.
4. Another 2 per cent of the respondents have reported and found that the interest rate offered by bank on deposit is less in comparison with lending in their locality in unorganised forms.
5. It is also observed that 85 per cent of the households have opined that there are number of formalities for opening a bank account which is unknown to them and difficult for them.
6. 60 per cent of them have reported that they do not have proof of residence like house number, ration card or election card. Without these, none of the banks are ready to open a bank account.

Suggestions

On the basis of above findings of the study, following suggestions have been proposed for achieving 100 per cent financial inclusion and inclusive growth of selected area of study, i.e., Nizamabad district of Andhra Pradesh:

1. Banks should offer free life insurance coverage for all the account holders under the Financial Inclusion so that

Table 7.3 : Occupation of Family Members

	Male				*Female*				*Total*
	Business	*Govt. Job*	*Private employee*	*Self Employee*	*Business*	*Govt. Job*	*Private employee*	*Self Employee*	
Above Rs. 10,000	08	04	02	06	-	08	08	-	36
Rs. 5,000 to Rs. 10,000	10	-	18	04	-	-	-	12	44
Rs. 1,500 to Rs. 5,000	4	-	10	02	-	-	-	12	28
Less than Rs. 1,500	-	-	-	08	-	-	-	16	24
Total	22	04	30	20	-	08	08	40	132

Source : Primary Survey, April 2011.

excluded segment can be encouraged to include and feel secured as a part of inclusive growth.

2. Most of the financially excluded segment is of the opinion that "they are not treated alive if they won't caste vote in the elections". On similar grounds, bank should take initiative to educate them financial literacy as to the ownership of a bank account, operation of bank account, merits and demerits of bank accounts etc.
3. Bidi Card or SHG membership card should be accepted as a proof for identity as security for opening an account as well as raising loan of smaller amounts. If not there must be easy process and procedure for opening election card, ration card and house number.
4. Facilities for access to banking services should be made easy. Business facilitators and business correspondence should be given a fixed place and address like fair price shops in each village so that the excluded segment can approach them easily and bring within the ambit of financial inclusion.
5. All government schemes for rural development must be tied up with the banks and post office in such a way that the percentage of financial inclusion can be increased and achieve 100 per cent financial inclusion target of the government.

REFERENCES

Conference papers, Bankers Conference 2006, 3-4 Nov., 2006, Hyderabad.

Leeladhar. V., "Taking banking services to the common man—financial inclusion", commemorative lecture at the Fedbank Hormis Memorial Foundation at Ernakulam, December 2, 2005.

Report of the Committee on Financial Inclusion (January 2008).

Situation assessment survey of farmers' indebtedness of farmer household – fifty-ninth round (2003), NSSO, New Delhi.

8

Credit Drivers towards Poverty Reduction in Tanzania : Customers of Financial Institutions Perceptions

CLIFFORD G. MACHOGU, JAIRUS B. AMAYI AND NICAS NIBENGO

Introduction

Since 1961, the Government of Tanzania has been adopting various measures for economic growth and poverty reduction through fiscal and monetary policies. In the 1990s, attention focused on economic growth as the means of achieving improvements in human welfare with the mind set of "trickle down effect of economic growth". However, Poverty and Human Development Reports of the years 2007 and 2008 which assessed the trend of poverty in 2007 based on Household Budget Surveys (HBS) of 2006-07 and 2007-08 revealed that despite the high economic growth of 6.8 per cent to 7.8 per cent, respectively, 36 per cent of Tanzanians were living below poverty line. In the year 2007-08, it was estimated that 19 per cent of Tanzanians lived below the food poverty line (Poverty and Human Development Report, 2008). The report indicated that the percentage of households below poverty line, by region, 2007-08 for Mwanza was 48 per cent (HBS: 2007-08).

Despite the financial system reforms initiated in 1990, the National Microfinance Policy of 2000 and Small and Medium Enterprises Development Policy of 2003 (URT: 2003), which enabled availability and access to financial capital (*Chijoriga: 2000*): credits, hire purchase, lease financing, agro-inputs loans, agro-input vouchers; saving schemes and insurance schemes, public perception on the contribution of financial capital on income poverty reduction was not known. Besides, income poverty remains high in Tanzania, a marvel that has not been known with the current financial capital paradigm?

The study, therefore, was an endeavour to determine the level of Public awareness on contribution of financial capital on income poverty reduction. The study analyzed the driving forces for demand and supply of financial capital and the magnitude of financial capital contributions on income poverty reduction.

Literature Review

The study was based on the concept that financial capital, if correctly perceived can play an important role in increasing efficiency and productivity. Although growth is not a sufficient condition for poverty alleviation, there is evidence that higher incomes in the community benefit the poor segments of the population proportionately (Ikara, 2003). Financial sector is a key element in generating growth, and thus, it is an important ingredient in poverty reduction. Dollar and Kraay (2000), indicated that on average the poor do benefit from growth, as an increase in the rate of GDP per capita leads to a one for one increase in the average income of the poorest. The Financial Sector provides the best alternative source of capital to poor population, especially through micro financing. According to Collins and Borthworth (1996), the use of factor productivity in growth diagnostics, assesses the relative contribution of the factors of production and Total Productivity (TFP). The production functions are mainly founded on econometric work of different levels of sophistication from standard two inputs case to multi-inputs case. Thus $Q = f(k, l)$ in the two input case, where Q = output, k = Capital, l = labour input and f = function. This model provides an incremental reasoning on the contribution of capital in economic development. The role of financial and non-financial institutions is to provide capital to deficit units which invest this capital in different economic activities.

Financial capital theory suggests that, as financial capital increases within networks of transacting partners, the average level of benefits increases and the disparity of benefits decreases. In part, this inverse relationship between disparity of income and average income results from terms of trade in financial capital-rich networks which favours transacting partners, from increased investment in real assets and ultimately provide opportunities independent of one's income.

Financial Capital and Poverty

The connections between financial capital and poverty are two fold: Financial capital and poverty reduction are connected in that financial capital is an important resource that if properly managed can be used to reduce poverty. Utilization of financial capital directly reduces poverty through spill-over-effects of investment. Attitude toward investment will direct individuals' life cycle (Eakins, 1999). The lesson of the past several decades is that the productivity of physical, social, human and natural forms of capital depends on financial capital.

Financial Capital Paradigm

A paradigm, Robison *et al.*; (2002), is a description of a subject that includes definitions, identification of and description of variables, and expected cause and effect relationships. As paradigm mature, the proposed view of the subject becomes generally accepted by experts in the field. A mature paradigm can facilitate cooperative action in a particular area, because it reduces conflict and cost of obtaining agreements. The financial capital paradigm describes the influence of relationships on financial goods, and economic transactions and contains concepts drawn from nearly all of the social sciences. The elements of financial capital paradigm, besides financial capital, include perceptions, financial systems, participants, financial institutions, financial markets, financial instruments, policies and regulations.

The Link between Financial Capital and Poverty Reduction ih Tanzania

Financial Capital schemes through financial institutions and markets delivery in Tanzania were initiated early 2000 to meet different objectives. The most commonly mentioned objectives included: poverty alleviation and improved living standards, offering financing to the poor (Harper *et al.*; 2009), women empowerment, and the development of business sector as a means of achieving high standards and reducing market failure (Chijoriga; 2000)

According to Blomström and Kokko, (2003) and Borenzstein, De Gregorio, and Lee (1998), the contributions of Financial capital to the development of a country are widely recognized as filling the gap between desired investment and domestically mobilized saving, increasing tax revenues, and improving management and technology, as well as labour skills. These could help the country to fight its way out of poverty.

Research Methodology

This was a survey study design. The study collected information from households, financial institutions, non-financial institutions, experts, opinion leaders, business community, and salaried workers from Nyamagana and Ilemela districts in Mwanza City Tanzania. The financial institutions' population was drawn from 8 commercial banks, 3 non-bank financial institutions, 3 foreign bureaus and 54 savings and credit cooperatives. The total population of financial institutions was 68. The business population was drawn from 4,570 registered trade/industrial businesses, which included wholesalers and retailers. The government sample was drawn from 1 branch of Bank of Tanzania and 2 district councils. The population of financial market was drawn from Dar es Salaam Stock Exchange Market since Mwanza has not its own registered stock exchange market. Total sample size studied was 175 of which 125 were households and 50 key informants. Households sample was extracted from individual lists, which was obtained from list of borrowers from financial institutions and markets. Primary data were obtained using interviews with key informants and individual households' members.

Data Analysis, Discussion and Findings.

Level of Awareness on Contribution of Financial Capital on Income Poverty Reduction

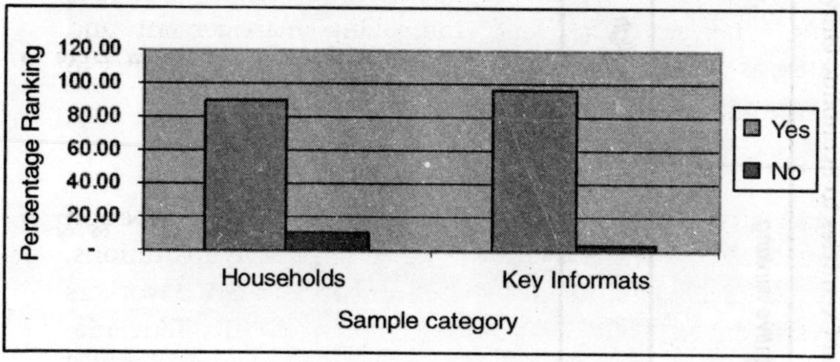

Figure 8.1 : Awareness on the meaning of Financial Capital

Source : Field Data (2009).

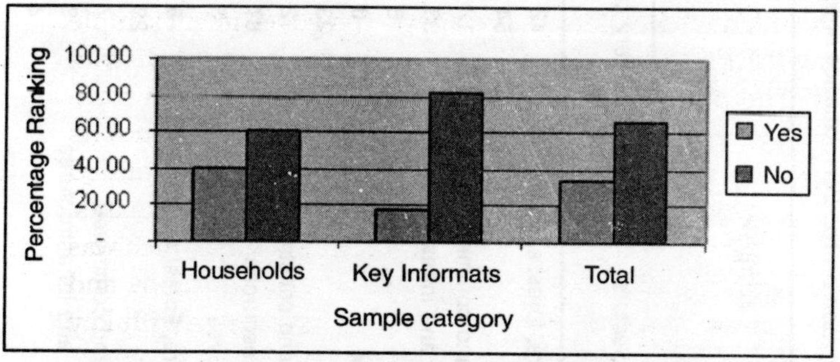

Figure 8.2 : Public Awareness on Uses and Accessibility of Financial Capital

Source : Field Data, (2010).

Driving Forces for Demand of Financial Capital in Mwanza City

Both Household and Key informant respondents mentioned nine reasons that drive people to seek financial capital assistance; financing working capital 25.71 per cent, education development 17.14 per cent, medical expenses 9.14 per cent, building and

Table 8.1 : Perception on the Performance of Financial Capital Countries to Economic Growth

Respondents ranking on contribution of financial capital to economic growth	Sectors	Qualitative ranking				
		Very Low	Low	High	Very High	Total
Households	Agriculture, forest and fishing	42	38	12	33	125
	Industry	54	45	16	10	125
	Trading and commerce	12	23	67	23	125
	Services and infrastructures	33	34	26	32	125
	Vending	6	52	67	0	125
	Education	0	23	98	4	125
	Health	23	34	43	25	125
	Building and constructions	12	44	56	13	125
	Natural resources	87	14	7	17	125
	cooperatives	3	56	54	12	125
Key respondents	Agriculture, Forest and fishing	8	16	23	3	50
	Industry	29	11	2	8	50
	Trading and commerce	7	6	37	0	50
	Services and infrastructures	8	17	23	2	50
	Vending	4	27	13	6	50

	Education	1	3	41	5	50
	Health	6	12	32	0	50
	Building and constructions	6	17	24	3	50
	Natural resources	18	7	19	6	50
	cooperatives	0	13	35	2	50
Combined key informants and Households	Agriculture, Forest and fishing	50	54	35	36	175
	Industry	83	56	18	18	175
	Trading and commerce	19	29	104	23	175
	Services and infrastructures	41	51	49	34	175
	Vending	10	79	80	6	175
	Education	1	26	139	9	175
	Health	29	46	75	25	175
	Building and constructions	18	61	80	16	175
	Natural resources	105	21	26	23	175
	Cooperatives	3	69	89	14	175

Source : Field Data (2010).

construction 10.29 per cent, purchasing machinery, tools and equipments 4.57 per cent, long term investment 5.14 per cent and purchasing motor vehicles 8 per cent. (Table 8.2)

Driving Forces for Supply of Financial Capital in Mwanza City

The forces that drive financial institutions to provide financial capital to the public include: Profit accounting 46 per cent, provision of capital to the public 39 per cent, pressure from political forces 29 per cent, financial institutions sustainability and growth 21 per cent and 9 per cent respectively, economic growth stimulation 17 per cent and public service provision 14 per cent.

Constraints for Demand of Financial Capital

Constraints for demand of financial capital as mentioned by respondents include: Public inadequate entrepreneurial and business management skills 18.29 per cent, High interest rates associated with financial capital 17.71 per cent, non formalization of business activities 17.14 per cent, unconducive business environment 13.14 per cent, unfavourable terms and conditions associated to financial capital 12.57 per cent, poor property regulation 12 per cent and little awareness of credit information 9.14 per cent (Table 8.4).

Constraints Facing Financial Institutions in Supply of Financial Capital to the Public

Constraints mentioned include Public inadequate entrepreneurial and managerial skills 22.29 per cent, poor regulatory environment 16.57 per cent, limited availability of reliable credit information from the public 13.71 per cent, high transaction costs for small volume 10.29 per cent, high costs for financial intermediation 9.14 per cent and high costs for establishing rural branches 7.43 per cent.

Providers of Financial Capital in Mwanza City

Eleven actors that provide financial capital to the public in Mwanza City include NMB Bank with 24.57 per cent, CRDB bank 20 per cent, NBC 8.57 per cent, Saving and Finance 5.71 per cent, Postal Bank 1.14 per cent, Azania Bank 8.57 per cent, Stanbic Bank 2.29 per cent,

Table 8.2 : Driving Forces for Demand for Financial Capital in Mwanza

Demand for financial capital	Driving force by percentage rating									
	Working Capital	Education development	Medical Express	Building and construction	Farming and livestock	Machinery tools and equipment	Long term investment	Home furniture	Car and motor vehicle	Total
Household	25.60	17.60	8.80	9.60	12.00	4.00	0.80	12.80	8.80	100
Key informants	26.00	16.00	10.00	12.00	4.00	6.00	16.00	4.00	6.00	100
Average	25.71	17.14	9.14	10.29	9.71	4.57	5.14	10.29	8.00	100

Source : Field Data (2010).

Table 8.3 : Perceived-Driving Forces for Institution Supply of Financial Capital

Supply for financial capital	Driving force or supply of financial capital							
	Profit making	Institution Sustainability	Institution Growth	Public Service Provision	Capital provision	Economic growth stimulation	Political forces	Total
Household	23.20	10.40	—	11.20	26.40	11.20	17.60	100
Key informants	34.00	16.00	18.00	—	12.00	6.00	14.00	100
Average	26.29	12.00	5.14	8.00	22.29	9.71	16.57	100

Source : Field Data (2010).

Bank of Africa 2.29 per cent, SACCOS 12.5 per cent, NGOs 4 per cent and TUNAKOPESHA 10.29 per cent.

Perceived Magnitude on the Contribution of Financial Capital on Business Activities

Respondents mentioned financial capital to contribute to growth of business sales revenue 32.57 per cent, profit increase 25.71 per cent, increase in business assets 15.43, opening new branches 8 per cent, provision of employment 8.57 per cent, and increase in business linkages and networking 9.71 per cent (Table 8.5).

Perceived Magnitude on the Contribution of Financial Capital on Personal Wellbeing

Perceived contribution were in terms of: increased personal commitment and accountability 9.71 per cent, improvement in education 37.71 per cent, improvement in shelter and housing 24 per cent, acquisition of household items and furniture 7.43 per cent, increased accessibility to food 12 per cent and improvement in general health 9.14 per cent.

Perceived Forms and Experiences of Financial Capital Services

The perceived forms and experiences in accessing and usage of financial capital as mentioned by respondents include: short term loans 85.14 per cent, long term loans 28 per cent, salaried workers loans 56 per cent, overdraft facilities 28 per cent, agricultural loans 31.43 per cent, livestock loan 13.71 per cent, Leasing 2.29 per cent and housing loans 29.14 per cent.

Qualitative Contribution of Financial Capital on Growth of Economic and Social Indicators

Respondents qualitatively ranked the contribution of financial capital to ten economic and social indicators. The low perception rating was as follows: industrial sector rated lowest by 81.71 per cent, agricultural sector 65.14 per cent, services and infrastructure 57.71 per cent, natural resources 51.43 per cent, health 50.86 per cent, building and construction 43.43 per cent, cooperatives 41.71 per cent and education 10.29 per cent. The highest perception rating

Table 8.4 : Constraints for Public Demand of Financial Capital

	Constraints for demand of financial capital							
Constraints for demand of financial capital	Inadequate entrepreneurial skills	Life awareness of credit information	Non-formalization of business activities	Poor property rights	Unfavourable credit terms and conditions	Unconducive business environment	High interest rates	Total
Household	11.20	7.20	20.00	9.60	16.80	12.80	22.40	100
Key informants	36.00	14.00	10.00	18.00	2.00	14.00	6.00	100
Average	18.29	9.14	12.00	12.00	12.57	13.14	17.71	100

Source : Field Data (2010).

Table 8.5 : Perceived Magnitude on the Contribution of Financial Capital on Business Activities

Contribution of financial capital to the business	Sales revenue increased	Profit increased	Business Assets Increased	Increase in business branches	Employ more staff	Business linkages and networking	Total
Household	36.00	26.40	14.40	9.60	8.00	5.60	100
Key Information	24.00	24.00	18.00	4.00	10.00	20.00	100
All respondents	32.57	25.71	15.43	8.00	8.57	9.71	100

Source : Field data, (2010).

was as follows: Education sector was rated highest with 89.71 per cent, trading and commerce 81.14 per cent, vending 69.71 per cent, cooperatives 58.29 per cent, building and construction 56.57 per cent, health 49.14 per cent, natural resources 48.57 per cent, services and infrastructure 42.29 per cent, agriculture 34.89 per cent and industrial sector 18.29 per cent.

Statistical Analysis and Description on the Findings

Using the median as measure of central tendency the results indicate that, over half of the population believes contribution of financial capital to growth of economic activities and social well-being is high. Conversely, less than half the population believes contribution of financial capital to economic growth and social wellbeing is low.

Conclusion

Finance is an important component of development, including poor people. Indeed, evidence from this study has shown that more than half the population perceived financial capital to have reduced income poverty and lowered income inequality. In addition to facilitating overall economic growth, financial capital had helped individuals smooth their income, insure against risks, and broaden investment opportunities. Testimonies have been evidenced in promoting individuals education, facilitated trade and commerce and improved individual accessibility to food and good health.

Despite this positive contribution, productive sectors such as industrial and agriculture have been perceived to have low accessibility to financial capital, hence less contribution to GDP. Therefore, the most important factor for a prosperous future of contribution of financial capital on income poverty reduction lies in honesty and mutual concern by financing industrial, agricultural, infrastructural and construction sectors.

Recommendations

Based on the findings above, the study makes the following recommendations to improve the contribution of financial capital on income poverty reduction.

The Financial System

The financial system should be at the service of man, systems, and governments, by allowing individuals and societies to come to their utmost fulfilment by assuming responsibility for their own development.

Supplier of Financial Capital

Supplier of financial capital, i.e., financial institutions and Markets should improve accessibility of financial capital services by : (1) Lowering interest rates that help to facilitate the growth of client businesses; (2) Financing industries, agricultural and construction sectors; (3) Offering training and couching their clients on entrepreneurship and business management skills; (4) Promote their financial capital services to the public to make them aware of the facility; and (5) be flexible and offer favourable credit terms and conditions.

Users of Financial Capital

Users of financial capital, i.e., the society should: (1) Formalize business activities to be able to attract financiers; (2) Formalize property rights and documentation; (3) Observe credit agreements, adhere to honesty and accountability; (4) Invest in most productive sectors, such as industry, agriculture and construction.

The Government

The government should: (1) establish entrepreneurship incubation centres to enable the community to acquire entrepreneurship skills and be competent in investment and business undertaking; and (2) Improve monetary system, fiscal policy and regulatory environment to protect both lenders and borrowers.

International Community

International Community should have a political will to stop World financial institutions such as World Bank and IMF from wasting productive capacity on financing the manufacture of arms and then selling the same to poor countries. Instead, they should finance production that is geared towards the satisfaction of real human needs.

Area for Further Research

This study recommends further research in Innovation and Inclusions in financial system issues, strategies and options in Developing Countries.

REFERENCES

Adam, R.H., (2004), *Economic Growth, Inequality and Poverty*: Estimating the Growth Elasticity of Poverty.

Albert, Ernest, (2008), The Disinherited of the Earth, ORDISEF Association, Kampala Uganda.

Atkinson, A.B. (1991), *Comparing Poverty Rates Internationally: Lessons from Recent Studies in Developed Countries*: The World Bank Economic Review, Vol. 5, No. 1, pp. 3-21.

Bagachwa, M.S.D. (1994), *Poverty Alleviation in Tanzania*: Dar es Salaam. Dar es Salaam University Press.

Bandera, O.M.S. (1997), *Micro and Small Enterprises Potentials for Development: General Considerations*: A paper presented to the workshop of Micro and Small Enterprises Research, November, Dar es Salaam.

Chijoriga, M.M. (2000), *The Performance and Sustainability of Microfinance Institutions in Tanzania*: Working Paper.

Collins, S. and B. Bosworth (1996), *The Empirics of Growth*: Brookings Institution.

Dorward, A; J. Kydd, J. Morrison and I. Urey (2004), *A Policy Agenda for Pro-poor Agricultural Growth*; World Development, Volume 33, Number 1, January, pp. 73-90.

Eele, G., J. Semboja, S.B. Likwelile and S. Ackroyd (2000), *Meeting International Poverty Targets in Tanzania*; Development Policy Review, Vol. 18, pp. 66-88.

Harper, V.L. *et al.*, (1999), *Measuring Transformation Assessing and Improving the Impact of Micro Credit*; Paper presented at Micro Credit Summit Meeting of Councils in Abidjan Cote de'Ivore, June.

Kothari, C.R. (1990), *Research Methodology: Methods and Techniques*; H.S. Poplai, 2nd Edition.

Kuzilwa, J.A. (2002), *The Role of Credit for Small Business Success*; A study of the National Entrepreneurship Development Fund in Tanzania, A paper presented at the 6th Annual International Conference on Entrepreneurship and Small Business Development (ICAESB), White Sand Hotel, Dar es Salaam.

Mbelle, Amon, (2006), *Prospects for achieving Broad-based and Equitable Growth in Tanzania:* A research report presented to eleventh REPOA Research Workshop White Sands Hotel, Dar es Salaam, Tanzania.

Pack, H.and C. Paxson (2001), "Is Africa Manufacturing Skill Constrained?"

Severine S.A. Kessy and Fratern M. Urion, (2006), *The Contribution of Microfinance Institutions to Poverty Reduction in Tanzania*; REPOA Research Report No. 06.3 Mkuki na Nyota, Dar es Salaam, Tanzania.

Szirimai, A. and Ranis, G; F. Stewart and A. Ramirez, (2000), "Economic Growth and Human Development" *World Development*, Vol. 28, No. 2, pp. 197-219.

9

Finance Development, Growth and Inflation : The Trilateral Analysis in India

RUDRA P. PRADHAN

Introduction

Finance development is considered as a key to economic growth. The relation between the two has attracted much attention in the literature, since the seminal work of Bagehot (1873) and Schumpeter (1911). The attention is mostly on the direction of causality between finance development and growth, as it has significantly different implications for development policy. There are studies for several countries including India (Pradhan, 2009). However, the existing studies have failed to reach the consensus confusion about the direction of causality.

There are at least three possible reasons for these inconclusive findings in the literature: the short spans of data, the use of different techniques, and the omitted variable bias. Different studies have different problems. For instance, a common view is that studies which focus on the two variable models may be biased due to the omission of relevant variables (see Narayan and Smyth, 2009; Clarke, 2005; Chang *et al.*, 2001; Stern, 2000; Hendry and Richard, 1982). Similarly for two cointegrated variables of I (1), if VAR is used against VECM, then the result may be spurious (see Granger, 1988; Engle and Granger, 1987).

In the light of various problems (methodological, omitted variables, and short span of data) that have plagued in various literatures in this area, further research on the casual relationship between finance growth nexus is important, given its implications for development policy. In this chapter, an attempt has been made to study the finance-growth nexus in India, especially during the globalization era of 1990s. The investigation on this period is very important in India, as it is one of the green phases of India's development.

The main innovations in this chapter, compared to existing literature on finance-growth nexus, are twofold. First, the use of Trivariate framework in which, in addition to growth and finance development, we incorporate inflation, particularly in the context of India. This marries the Granger causality literatures on the finance-growth nexus and inflation-growth nexus. The inclusion of inflation in the finance-growth nexus is very relevant, as it will highlight the issue of macroeconomic stability in the economy. The direct link between inflation and growth has been widely studied, particularly because control of inflation is often seen as the single most important goal to which monetary policy can aspire in the pursuit of macroeconomic stability (ECB, 2008). On the contrary, the lack of control has been increasingly linked to banking and financial crises (Duttagupta and Cashin, 2008).

Second, we investigate the issue in the globalization era of 1990s. India all through followed a closed economy policies since her independence. It was only after 1985, a shift towards globalization was started. The attempts were, however, seems to be considered as half-hearted, self-contradictory and often self-reversing in nature (Harris, 1987). In contrast, globalization in the 1990s had been much wider and much deeper and decidedly marked a U-turn in many ways in the direction of economic policy followed by India during the last fifty-eight years of centralized economic planning (Pradhan, 2010; Sachs *et al.*, 1991).

The globalization of 1990s were undertaken in many ways such as devaluation of rupee, dismantling import license system, full convertibility on trade account, fiscal retrenchment and credit squeeze, abolition of export subsidies, introduction of import entitlement scheme for exporters, unification of the exchange rates, removal of the quantitative restrictions, massive reduction in the tariff rates and protection rates, easing the restrictions on foreign investments and so forth (Ramakrishna, 2003). The impact of globalization is, however, multidimensional and can be judged in many ways in the direction of socio-economic development. That involves both benefits and failures in the Indian economy.

The major benefits that the country has been receiving during this globalization of 1990s are financial sector development and its link with growth and stability, measured by inflation. But the impact may be slightly affected by the recent global financial crisis, which hit in the world economy in the middle of 2008. Hence, the investigation will give some limelight on the nexus between finance-growth and inflation- growth in India. The residual of the paper is divided into three sections. Section 2 describes the methodology and discussions. Section 3 provides conclusion and policy implications.

Methodology and Discussions

The objective of this chapter is to study the direction of causality between financial development, economic growth and inflation in India during the post-globalization era of 1990s. The data are monthly observations from 1994 to 2010 and has been collected from Handbook of Statistics on Indian economy, Reserve Bank of India, Mumbai. The variables used under this study are broad money supply (M_3), use as a proxy to financial development and is measured as a percentage of GDP; Index of Industrial Production (IIP), used as a proxy to economic growth; Wholesale Price Index (WPI), used as a proxy to inflation. The investigation starts with studying the stationarity properties of time series variables and that is followed by cointegration analysis and Granger causality tests in a trivariate framework.

Testing for Integration

The Augmented Dickey Fuller (Dickey and Fuller, 1981) unit root test is usually applied to detect the order of integration. The estimation procedure of these two tests is described as follows:

$$\Delta Y_t = \alpha_0 + \alpha_1 Y_{t-1} + \sum_{i=1}^{p} \beta_i \Delta Y_{t-1} + \varepsilon_t \qquad ...(1)$$

Where Δ is the first difference operator; α_i (for $i = 0$ and 1) and β_i (for $i = 1, 2 \ldots p$) are constant parameters; and ε_t is an error term. The null hypothesis is H_0: $\alpha_1 = 0$ against H_1: $\alpha_1 \neq 0$. Though the

Augmented Dickey Fuller (ADF) test is very simple and frequent use in econometric analysis, it is not reliable in small samples, because of its poor size and power properties. That means ADF test can over-reject the null hypothesis when it is true and under reject it when it is false (see Dejong *et al.*, 1992; Harris and Sollis, 2003). The study, therefore, uses Dickey Fuller Generalized Least Squares (DFGLS) test (Elliot *et al.*, 1996) and Ng-Perron test (Ng and Perron, 2001) test to check the stationarity. DFLGS is an extension of ADF by detrending. Assuming that we need to test the order of integration of the variable Z_t, the DFGLS de-trending test is based testing H_0: $\varphi = 0$ in the regression.

$$\Delta Z_t^d = \varphi_0 + \varphi_0 + \varphi_1 + \varphi_1 \Delta Z_{t-1}^d + \varphi_2 Z_{t-2}^d + ... + \varphi_{p-1} \Delta Z_{t-p+1}^d + \varepsilon_{i,t} \quad ...(2)$$

Where, Z_t^d is the de-trended series. The null hypothesis of the test is that Z_t has a random walk trend, possibly with a drift, as follows:

$$Z_t^d = Z_t - \alpha - \beta t \quad ...(3)$$

The DFGLS proposes two alternative hypotheses: (1) Z_t is stationary about a linear trend; (2) it is stationary with a (possibly) non-zero mean, but with no linear time trend.

For the first hypothesis, the test is performed by estimating the intercept and trend using the GLS technique. The estimation is performed by generating the following variables.

$$\bar{Z} = [Z_1(1-\bar{\alpha}L)Z_2, ..., (1-\bar{\alpha}L)Z_T] \quad ...(4)$$

$$\bar{W} = [W_1(1-\bar{\alpha}L)W_2, ... (1-\bar{\alpha}L)W_T] \quad ...(5)$$

$$W_t = (1, t)'\bar{\alpha} = 1 + \frac{\bar{c}}{T} \quad ...(6)$$

Where T represents the number of observations for Z_t and $\bar{c}$ is fixed (see Elliot *et al.*, 1996). The OLS is performed on the following equation:

$$\bar{Z} = \mu_0 \bar{W} + \mu_1 W_t + \varepsilon_t \quad ...(7)$$

And the OLS estimators (μ_0 and μ_1) are utilized for the removal of trend from Z_t. The ADF test is then applied on the transformed variable by fitting the OLS regression.

$$\Delta Z_t^d = \alpha + \beta Z_{t-1}^d + \sum_{j=1}^{k} \gamma_j \Delta Z_{t-j}^d + \varepsilon_t \quad ...(8)$$

Where, the null hypothesis is to test whether β is equal to zero or not.

Now for second hypothesis, we take $\overline{c} = -7$ in the equation of $\overline{\alpha}$ and then compute $\Delta Z_t^d = Z_t - \mu_0$.

The ADF regression is fitted on new transformed variables and then null hypothesis is to test whether β is equal to zero or not. In both the cases, the tabulated variable is provided by Elliot *et al.* (1996). Though the DFGLS test is very impressive with power gains, the simulation shows that the test exhibits strong size distortion.

The study, therefore, uses Ng and Perron unit root test to determine the order of integration. The test purposes four test statistics based on the lines of GLS de-trended data. The modelling structure of Ng and Perron unit root test are as follows:

$$k = \sum_{t=2}^{T} (D_{t-1}^d)^2 / T^2 \qquad ...(9)$$

While de-trended GLS tailored statistics are given by

$$MZ_a^d = \lfloor T^{-1}(D_T^d)^2 - f_0 \rfloor / 2k \qquad ...(10)$$

$$MZ_t^d = MZ_a XMSB \qquad ...(11)$$

$$MSB^d = (k/f_0)^{0.5} \qquad ...(12)$$

$$MP_T^D = (\overline{c}^2 k - \overline{c} T^1)(D_T^d)^2 / f_0 \text{ if } x_t = \{1\} \text{ and}$$

$$MP_T^D = (\overline{c}^2 k + (1 - \overline{c} T^1)(D_T^d)^2 / f_0 \text{ where } \overline{c} = -7 \text{ if } x_t = \{1\}$$

and $\overline{c} = -13.5$ if $x_t = \{1, t\}$ ...(13)

Please note that the null hypothesis of unit root cannot be rejected, if the test statistic is higher than critical value. If the variable is stationary at the level data, it is integrated of order zero [I (0)]. Similarly, if the variable is stationary at the first difference, it is integrated of order one [I (1)] and if the variable is stationary at the second difference, it is integrated of order two [I (2)] and so on. The estimated results of unit root tests are reported in Table 9.1. It shows that all the variables (economic growth, financial development and economic growth) are non-stationary at the level data but found stationary at the first differences. That means the variables are integrated of order one, i.e. I [1]. This confirms the possibility of cointegration among these three variables.

Table 9.1 : Unit Root Test Results

Variables	*ADF Test*		*DFGLS Test*		*Conclusion*
	Level	*First Difference*	*Level*	*First Difference*	
FD	0.130	– 2.64*	0.93	– 1.66	1 (1)
EG	0.111	– 3.81*	1.56	– 1.12	1 (1)
INF	– 1.160	– 10.2*	1.43	– 15.9*	1 (1)
Ng—Perron Test					
At Level					
	MZ_a	MZ_t	MSB	MPT	
FD	1.083	0.861	0.794	47.40	
EG	1.542	2.803	1.817	239.8	
INF	1.362	1.539	1.131	93.88	
At First Difference					
FD	– 0.356	– 0.245	0.689	96.05*	1 (1)
EG	– 0.037	1.137	3.667*	672.8*	1 (1)
INF	– 87.78*	– 6.63*	0.075	0.279	1 (1)

Note : ADF: Augmented Dickey Fuller Test; PP: Phillips-Perron Test; LD: Level Data; FD: Financial Development; EG: Economic Growth; INF: Inflation; I (1): Integration of Order One; and *: Indicates Statistical Significance at 10%.

Testing for Cointegration

Cointegration is a technique to avoid spurious or nonsense regression and at the same time being able to recognize the existence of long run relations. Cointegration is a multivariate problem and can occur between two or more time series, if one or more linear combinations of different non-stationary time series produce stationary time series (Engle and Granger, 1987). The linear combination shows the long run relationship between different time series because it is a description of the lasting effects shared by the different time series (Johansen, 1995). The long run relationship, as a statistical point of view, means the variables move together over time so that short term disturbances from the long term trend will be

Table 9.2 : Johansen Long Run Results

DV	*FD*	*EG*	*INF*	*EC*	*Inferences*
FD	—	4.299*	0.339	– 4.78*	EG = > FD
EG	13.09*	—	26.81*	2.67*	FD = > EG INF = > EG
INF	3.739*	0.004	—	0.28	FD = > INF
Overall	Conclusion:				FD < = > EG FD = > INF

Note: DV: Dependent Variable; FD: Financial Development;EG: Economic Growth; INF: Inflation; ECT: Error Correction; F: F-statistics; *: Indicates Statistical Significance at 5% level.

corrected. A lack of cointegration suggests that such variable have no long run equilibrium relationship and in principle, they can wander arbitrarily far away from each other (Dickey *et al.*, 1991). Note that regression among integrated series is meaningful, if they involve cointegrated variables.

The Johansen (1988) maximum likelihood (ML) test is applied to examine the cointegration between the time series variables. The econometric procedures of these statistics are as follows:

Let X_t be a ($n \times 1$) vector of variables with a sample of *t*. Assuming X_t follows I(1) process, identifying the number of cointegrating vector involves estimation of the vector error correction representation (Johansen and Juselius, 1990):

$$\Delta X_t = A_0 + \prod X_{t-p} + \sum_{i=1}^{p-1} A_i \Delta X_{t-i} + \varepsilon_t \quad \text{...(14)}$$

Where, vector ΔX_t and ΔX_{t-1} are I (1) representation. The long run equilibrium relationship among X_t is determined by the rank of Π (say *r*) is zero, then equation (3) can be transferred to a VAR model of *p*th order and the variables in level do not have any cointegrating relationship. If $0 < r < n$, then there are $n \times r$ matrices of α and β such that

$$\Pi = \alpha \beta' \quad \text{...(15)}$$

Where, both α and β are ($n \times r$) matrices. The cointegrating vectors β have the property that $\beta' X_t$ is stationary [I (0)] even though X_t is non-stationary [I (1)]. Johansen likelihood ratio test looks for two statistics: trace statistics and maximum eigen value.

The likelihood ratio test statistic for the null hypothesis that there are at most *r* cointegrating vectors is the trace test and is computed as:

$$Trace = -T \sum_{t=r+1}^{n} \log(1-\hat{\lambda}_i) \qquad ...(16)$$

Where $\hat{\lambda}_{r+1}, ... \hat{\lambda}_n$ are $(n-r)$ smallest estimated eigen values.

The likelihood ratio test statistic for the null hypothesis of *r* cointegrating vectors against the alternative of *r* + 1 cointegrating vectors is the maximum eigen value test and is given by

$$\lambda_{max} = -T \log(1-\hat{\lambda}_{r+1}) \qquad ...(17)$$

Here, the null hypothesis of *r* cointegrating vectors is tested against the alternative hypothesis of *r* +1 cointegrating vectors. Hence, the null hypothesis $r = 0$ is tested against the alternative $r = 1$, $r = 1$ against the alternative $r = 2$, and so forth. It is well known that the cointegration tests are very to the choice of lag length. The Schwarz Bayesian Criterion (SBC) is used to select the number of lags required in the cointegration test. The estimated results of both the statistics are reported in Table 9.3. The obtained results confirm the existence of two cointegrating relations among the variables. This implies that there is the presence of long run equilibrium relationship between financial development, economic growth and inflation. The results give an indication that there is the possibility of causality between them.

Table 9.3 : Test of Cointegration

Hypothesized Cointegrating H_0	*Number of Relationships* H_A	*Test Statistics* λ-Max	λ-Tra	*Critical Values* λ-Max	λ-Tra
$r = 0$	$r > 0$	30.64*	47.22*	21.13	29.80
$r \leq 1$	$r > 1$	14.38*	16.57*	14.26	14.50
$r \leq 2$	$r > 2$	2.195	2.195	3.841	3.841

Note: *r* indicates the number of cointegrating relationships. The optimal lag structure of the VAR was selected by minimizing the Akaike Information criterion. The critical values are taken from Johansen and Juselius (1990). *: Indicates Statistical Significance at 5% level.

Granger Causality in the ECM-VAR

The presence of cointegration relation forms the basis of the vector error correction model (VECM) specification (Toda and Phillips, 1993). The systems we consider are equivalent to the following one, where the ECM must be seen as correcting towards an equilibrium subspace. The VECM is represented as follows:

$$\begin{bmatrix} \Delta \ln FD_t \\ \Delta \ln EG_t \\ \Delta \ln INF_t \end{bmatrix} = \begin{bmatrix} \alpha_1 \\ \alpha_2 \\ \alpha_3 \end{bmatrix} + \begin{bmatrix} \beta_{11,1} & \beta_{12,1} & \beta_{13,1} \\ \beta_{21,1} & \beta_{22,1} & \beta_{23,1} \\ \beta_{31,1} & \beta_{32,1} & \beta_{33,1} \end{bmatrix} \begin{bmatrix} \Delta \ln FD_{t-1} \\ \Delta \ln EG_{t-1} \\ \Delta \ln INF_{t-1} \end{bmatrix}$$

$$+ \begin{bmatrix} \beta_{11,2} & \beta_{12,2} & \beta_{13,2} \\ \beta_{21,2} & \beta_{22,2} & \beta_{12,2} \\ \beta_{31,2} & \beta_{32,2} & \beta_{33,2} \end{bmatrix} \begin{bmatrix} \Delta \ln FD_{t-2} \\ \Delta \ln EG_{t-2} \\ \Delta \ln INF_{t-2} \end{bmatrix} + \ldots.$$

$$+ \begin{bmatrix} \beta_{11,p} & \beta_{12,p} & \beta_{13,p} \\ \beta_{21,p} & \beta_{22,p} & \beta_{23,p} \\ \beta_{31,p} & \beta_{32,p} & \beta_{33,p} \end{bmatrix} \begin{bmatrix} \Delta \ln FD_{t-p} \\ \Delta \ln EG_{t-p} \\ \Delta \ln INF_{t-p} \end{bmatrix}$$

$$+ \begin{bmatrix} \lambda_1 \\ \lambda_2 \\ \lambda_3 \end{bmatrix} [ECT_{t-1}] + \begin{bmatrix} \zeta_{1t} \\ \zeta_{2t} \\ \zeta_{3t} \end{bmatrix}$$

Where ECT_{t-1} is the lagged error correct term, derived from the long run cointegration relationship? The F-statistics has been used for the joint significance of the lagged independent variables, while *t*-statistics has been used to test the significance of error correction term. The estimated results authenticate that there is bidirectional causality between financial development and economic growth. That means financial development causes economic growth and economic growth also causes financial development in the Indian economy during the period 1994-2010. We also find the presence of unidirectional causality from financial development to inflation and inflation to economic growth. That means financial development significantly causes inflation and inflation significantly influence economic growth. The integration of these results gives an indication that it is the financial development which is very instrumental to both financial development and economic growth.

The above results also verified through generalized impulse response functions (GIRFs). The GIRFs trace the effect of a one-time shock to one of the innovations on current and future values of endogenous variables. The generalized impulse responses provided more insight into how a shock to inflation has an effect on financial development and economic growth. The results of generalized impulse responses for all these variables are presented in Figure 9.1. The GIRFs are provided the support of causality status between financial development, economic growth and inflation in the multivariate VAR system. The overall finding is the inflation that causes economic growth. Moreover, inflation is caused by financial development in the economy.

Conclusion and Policy Implications

The study explores the cointegration and causality relationship between inflation (WPI), economic growth (IIP) and financial development (M3) in India during the period 1994 to 2010. The empirical investigation has been undertaken by Vector Error Correction Model (VECM) specification. It first explored the stationarity of the variables and their long run equilibrium relationship. The empirical investigations confirm the followings: First, the three time series variables (WPI, IIP and M3) are stationary at the first differences, indicating that they are integrated of order one; Second, there is presence of two cointegrating vectors, indicating the presence of long run equilibrium relationship between inflation, economic growth and financial development; Third, VECM specifies the unidirectional causality from inflation to economic growth, financial development to economic growth, and a bidirectional causality between financial development and economic growth. The policy implication of this study is that inflation and financial development should be considered as the policy variables to forecast economic growth in the Indian economy.

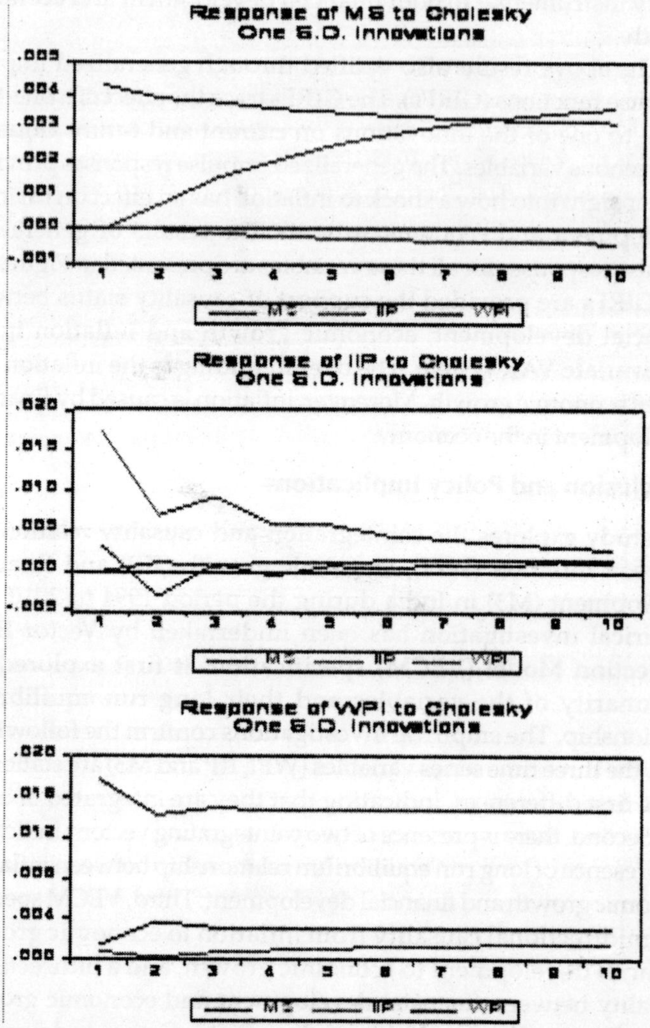

Figure 9.1 : Impulse Response Functions

REFERENCES

Bagehot, W., (1873), Lombard Street, Homewood, IL: Richard D. Irwin.

Chang, T., Fang, W and Wen, L.F. (2001), Energy Consumption, Employment, Output and Temporal Causality: Evidence from Taiwan Based on Cointegration and Error Correction Modelling Techniques, *Applied Economics*, 33, pp. 1045-1056.

Clarke, K.A., (2005), The Phantom Menace: Omitted Variable Bias in Econometric Research, *Conflict Management and Peace Science*, 22, pp. 341-352.

Dejong, D. N., Nankervis, J.C. and Savin, N. E., (1992), Integration *versus* Trend Stationarity in Time Series, *Econometrica*, 60, pp. 423-433.

Dickey, D.A. and Fuller, W.A., (1981), "Likelihood Ratio Statistics for Autoregressive Time Series with a Unit Root", *Econometrica*, 49 (4): pp. 1057-1072.

Dickey, D.A., Jansen, D.W., & Fuller, W.A., (1991), A Primer on Cointegration with an Application to Money and Income.*Review Federal Reserve Bank of St. Louis.* 73, pp. 58-78.

Duttagupta, R. and Cashin, P., (2008), *The Anatomy of Banking Crises*. IMF Working Paper, pp. 08-93.

ECB (2008), Price Stability and Growth. European Central Bank (ECB), *ECB Monthly Bulletin*, pp. 75-87.

Elliot, G., Rothenberg, T. J. and Stock, J. H., (1996), Efficient Tests for an Autoregressive Time Series with Unit Root. *Econometrica*, 64, pp. 813-836.

Engle, R. F. and Granger, C. W. J., (1987), "Cointegration and Error Correction: Representation, Estimation and Testing", *Econometrica*, 55 (2): pp. 251-276.

Harris, J. (1987). The State is Retreat? Why has India Experienced such Half-Hearted Liberalization in the 80's. *IDS Bulletin*, 18: pp. 28-36?

Harris, R. and Sollis, R., (2003), *Applied Time Series Modelling and Forecasting*.Wiley, West Sussex.

Hendry, D.F. and Richard, J.F., (1982), On the Formulation of Empirical Models in Dynamic Econometrics, *Journal of Econometrics*, 20, pp. 3-33.

Johansen, S. (1988), Statistical Analysis of Cointegrating Vectors, *Journal of Economics Dynamic and Control*, 12: pp. 231-254.

Johansen, S. (1991), Estimation and Hypothesis Testing of Cointegrating Vectors in Gaussian Vector Autoregressive Models, *Econometrica*, 59: pp. 1551-1580.

Johansen, S., (1995), *Likelihood-based Inference in Cointegrated Vector Autoregressive Models*, Oxford University Press, New York.

Johansen, S. and Juselius, K., (1990), Maximum Likelihood Estimation and Inference on Cointegration with Application to the Demand for Money, *Oxford Bulletin of Economics and Statistics*, 52: pp. 169-210.

Narayan, P. K. and Smyth, R. (2009), "Multivariate Granger Causality between Electricity Consumption, Exports and GDP: Evidence from a Panel of Middle Eastern Countries, *Energy Policy*, 37, pp. 229-236.

Ng, S and Perron, P. (2001), Lag Length Selection and the Construction of Unit Root Test with Good Size and Power, *Econometrica*, 69, pp. 1519-1554.

Pradhan, R.P. (2006), Globalization in India: Achievements and Failures, *South Asian Journal of Human Rights*, 12, pp. 1-24.

Pradhan, R.P. (2009), The Nexus between Financial Development and Economic Growth in India: Evidence from Multivariate VAR Model, *International Journal of Research and Reviews in Applied Sciences*, 1, pp. 141-151.

Ramakrishna, G., (2003), Globalization and Balance of Payments Experience of India, *Indian Development Review*, 1: pp. 27-46.

Sachs, J.D., Varshney, A. and Bajpai, N. (1991), *India in the Era of Economic Reforms*. New Delhi: Oxford University Press.

Schumpeter, J.A. (1911), *The Theory of Economic Development*, Cambridge, Mass: Harvard University Press.

Stern, D.I. (1993), A Multivariate Cointegration Analysis of the Role of Energy in the US Macroeconomy. *Energy Economics*, 22, pp. 267-283.

Toda, H.Y. and Phillips, P.C.B., (1993), Vector Autoregression and Causality, *Econometrica*, 61 (6): pp. 1367-1393.

10

Hundred Per Cent Financial Inclusion : The Road Map Ahead

SIVA PRASAD SARMAH

Introduction

India is the second most populous country in the world after China with 1.20 billion of population, whereas the world population has crossed the 7.00 billionth mark on 31st October, 2011. It is estimated that at the present rate of growth, India's population will surpass China's population by 2030, when it will have 1.60 billion of population. To feed and support this growing population our country is to face some of the threats and challenges which are daunting in nature but can be overcome with proper planning and foresight.

Financial Inclusion

In simple terms, Financial Inclusion means availability of basic banking service to all the people all across the country irrespective of location, time zone at affordable ease. Financial Inclusion is a prerequisite of inclusive growth which is aimed by our planners, government and policy makers. In India, the committee on financial inclusion headed by Dr. C. Rangarajan, former governor of Reserve Bank of India (RBI) and advisor to Prime Minister's Office on economic affairs, has suggested a National Mission on Financial Inclusion and observed that Financial Inclusion must be taken up in a mission mode. It enables people of unprivileged section to avail a range of transaction and payment services, access to affordable credit facility, insurance and safe saving products.

Why Financial Inclusion is Important?

The populations, who are underprivileged, are deprived of basic need of a noble livelihood like sanitation, square meal, health, banking facility and are vulnerable to different threats in the form of health problem, financial hardship, etc. Our policy makers have rightfully identified that because of lack of Financial Inclusion, the people who are not having access to formal banking services are more prone to be victim of indigenous money lender/banker who charge them exorbitantly whenever they are compelled to approach them in absence of formal banking system. Since they don't have a bank account, these people are deprived of simple credit products, making them more likely to turn to predatory or even illegal lenders leaving them in perpetual debt.

In India, despite of widespread expansion of banking sector, particularly after nationalization of major commercial banks in 1969 and 1980 (14 large commercial banks on 19th July 1969 and another 6 private sector banks on 15th April 1980 are nationalized) besides State Bank of India, a significant proportion of the households, especially in rural areas are still outside the coverage of the formal banking system. These households have been dependent upon the informal money lenders for their credit needs and have left a few avenues for keeping their savings.

What RBI is doing towards Financial Inclusion?

It has been the endeavour of Government of India and RBI to promote Financial Inclusion in the country through various channels. The following steps have been taken by RBI to bring the financially excluded people to the fold of the formal banking system. The steps include efforts like:

- Nationalization of Banks.
- Identifying priority sectors and setting up of targets for the same.
- Setting up of Regional Rural Banks (RRBs).
- Setting up of Local Area Banks (LABs).
- Credit delivery focus in rural areas through Service Area Approach (SAA).
- Enabling policy for micro finance by Banks.

- Simplified Know Your Customer (KYC) norms.
- No frills accounts.
- Kishan Credit Cards.
- General purpose credit cards.
- Small overdrafts in no-frill accounts.
- Permitting banks to use Business Correspondent (BC) and Business Facilitator (BF) models.
- It has been announced in the annual policy statement of RBI for 2005-06 that it would implement policies to encourage banks, which provide extensive services in unbanked areas while deincentivizing those banks which are not responsive to the banking needs of the community.

The Road Map Ahead for 100 per cent Financial Inclusion: With Special Reference to North Eastern States

The Union Finance Minister Shri Pranab Mukherjee while reviewing the status of financial inclusion in the North Eastern States on 8th November 2011 at Kolkata remarks that banks have achieved only 46 per cent of their Financial Inclusion goal in West Bengal and eight North Eastern States, viz., Assam, Arunachal Pradesh, Manipur, Mizoram, Nagaland, Meghalaya, Sikkim and Tripura and 100 per cent to be completed by March 2012. Of the 10,721 un-banked villages having population of 2,000 and above identified for Financial Inclusion in the region under the first phase, banks have already covered 4,969 villages either by opening brick and mortar branch or through business correspondence model.

The latest government guidelines mandate for setting up of a brick and mortar branch in villages having population of 5,000 and above by September 2012. Mr. Pratip Chaudhari, Chairman, State Bank of India, who is of the opinion that about 30 per cent of such branches would be opened by RRBs and rest 70 per cent by commercial banks for 100 per cent Financial Inclusion in the North Eastern States.

In order to have focused attention for the Financial Inclusion efforts, the State Level Banks Committee (SLBC) has been advised to identify one or more district for 100 per cent Financial Inclusion. Responsibility is given to the banks in the area for ensuring that all those who desire to have a bank account are provided with one by allocating the village among different banks. The 100 per cent Financial Inclusion drive is progressing all over the country. So far, 431 districts have been identified by SLBCs for 100per cent Financial Inclusion out of which 204 districts in 18 States and 5 Union Territories achieved the target of 100 per cent Financial Inclusion so far.

The Challenge Ahead: India's large size and population makes it difficult for any programme at a national level to reach out to everyone. The inclusion efforts in the urban centres and metros are difficult. Especially in case of migrant labourers who don't have identity particulars at their place of work. The remittance of money by these migrant workers to their home town is often dependent on informal channels.

Infrastructure: Adequate infrastructure like road, rail, digital connectivity, power and infrastructure facilities which are important pre-requisite for operation of banking outlet is not available in many parts of the country.

Financial Products: Simple, suitable products rather than sophisticated instruments are required at affordable cost for the people. Flexibility is an important criterion and the products and services available should be flexible.

Delivery Models: Delivery model/business model for financial inclusion plays a vital role in achieving 100 per cent Financial Inclusion. The typical brick and mortar bank branches may not be feasible in all villages because of viability and other reasons. Banks have to adopt/experiment alternate delivery channels like satellite branches, mobile branches, business correspondents/point of sale and mobile telephony services.

Technology: Despite significant technological advancements, there are issues of standardization, inter-operability and costs that inhibit smooth technology solutions. The financial services offered with the help of ICT should ideally be standardized. High transaction cost is another hindrance to provide banking services in hinterland associated with the low-value large volume transactions.

Role of Financial Intermediaries: The banks are not uniformly geared up for financial inclusion, while commercial banks have taken significant steps to facilitate inclusion but RRBs and cooperative banks need to gear up their efforts in this area. It is important that all the participative stakeholders work together to achieve the goal of Financial Inclusion. Banks, State government, technology providers, regulators and other developmental agencies need to be work together in tandem to drive the efforts towards achieving the 100 per cent Financial Inclusion.

Committee on Financial Sector Reform (CFSR): Recommendations with regard to Financial Inclusion

The committee on financial sector reform has come out with several recommendations to intensify the process of Financial Inclusion in the country. The committee opined that the most important financial services to the poor are vulnerable to reducing instruments. Thus access to safe and remunerative methods of savings, remittance, insurance and pensions needs to be expanded significantly.

The CFSR further recommended that an inclusive banking structure may be developed in an economy by creating and promoting small finance banks on the one hand and by creating strong linkage between large banks and small local entities. This linkage will facilitate the retailing of large bank's financial products to small clients. The CFSR reiterated the need to broaden the definition of Business Correspondent following the recommendations of Rangarajan Committee on Financial Inclusion.

The "no-frills" accounts may be promoted, further, to provide access to formal financial system to 90 per cent of the Indian population who are deprived of financial system. These accounts can be used for the disbursement of existing subsidies, disbursement of wages and allowances to beneficiaries of NREGS, etc. A Nationwide Electronic Financial Inclusion System (NEFIS) could also be created by linking the "no frills" accounts which will enable electronic transfer of funds to these accounts.

The following are some of the observations / recommendations of CFSR for hundred per cent Financial Inclusion:

- Priority sector lending requirements to be made uniform for both domestic and foreign banks,
- Introduction of Priority Sector Lending Certificate (PSLC) for equitable contribution of resources towards priority sector irrespective of location / positioning of Banks,

- Need to increase the commercial viability of reaching the unreached poor,
- Product innovation,
- Organizational flexibility, and
- Superior cost efficiency.

At the same time, the committee recognizes that greater commercial viability can't be truly achieved for all sections of the poor and, therefore, some kind of mandated coverage will always be required. Significant investment in financial literacy is required if the poor and under privileged are to make effective use of various initiatives to foster financial inclusion.

Conclusion

India is a vast country with 1.20 billion population. Its GDP growth rate is attractive at 8-9 per cent over the years despite the fact the world economy is passing through a trying phase of recession, inflation and uncertainty. India's growth story will be a futile growth story if the growth can't encompass all sections of people and inclusive growth is the *mantra* of the policy-makers of the country. For inclusive growth that is uniform development of people and place is to be achieved through Financial Inclusion. All the villages, all the Blocks should have access to formal Banking system so that they can avail the facilities offered by this formal channel. Despite the vastness of our country we have no dearth of talents, resources, network to reach out to those poor and under privileged section of the society. Hundred per cent financial inclusion can be a reality as per our commitment.

11

A Road to Financial Inclusion through the Activities of UIBs (Registered Money Lenders) in Manipur

KSH. RANJAN SINGH

Introduction

In the present monetized economy, people need financial services either from organized or unorganized sector. Credit and financial needs of the people of the State cannot be fulfilled only by the services of financial institutions in the organized financial sector. The role being played by unorganized financial sector in achieving financial inclusion in the State cannot be overlooked. Indian Financial System consists both these sectors/systems, i.e., formal (organized) financial system and the informal (unorganized) financial system. The formal financial system comes under the purview of the Ministry of Finance (MoF), the Reserve Bank of India (RBI), the Securities and Exchange Board of India (SEBI), and other regulatory bodies. The informal financial system consists of:

1. Individual money lenders such as neighbours, relatives, landlords, traders, and storeowners.
2. Groups of persons operating as "funds" or "associations". These groups function under a system of their own rules and use names such as "fixed fund", "association", and "saving club".
3. Partnership firms consisting of local brokers, pawnbrokers, and non-banking financial intermediaries such as finance, investment, and chit-fund companies.

Though our country, India, is proud of having a strong banking network consisting of Scheduled commercial banks – public sector banks—State Bank group, Nationalized banks; private sector banks—old private banks, new private banks; Foreign banks, Regional rural banks, Non-scheduled commercial banks and Cooperative banks along with a number of term lending national and State level financial institutions and investment institutions, still a larger population remained excluded from basic banking and credit facilities. This gap is being filled by the credit purveyors in the informal (unorganized) financial system. In the State of Manipur, unincorporated bodies engaged in financial services (registered moneylenders) are taking an important role in order to fill the credit gap as well as in the socio-economic development of the State. It is an agreed fact that UIBs have been contributing to the efforts to make financial inclusion a dream coming true.

Defining Unincorporated Bodies (UIBs)

According to Reserve Bank of India Act 1934 UIBs are individuals, firms or associations of individuals which are not incorporated/ registered under Companies Act 1956 whose business either wholly or partly includes any of the activities of financing, or acquisition of securities, letting or delivering of goods under hire-purchase agreement, managing, conducting or supervising, as foreman of chits or kuris or whose principal business is that of receiving deposits or lending in any manner.

"The UIBs are partnership concerns whose paid up capital is less than Rs. 1 lakh. Major source of their funds is fixed deposits from the public. Such UIBs are spread throughout the length and breadth of the country and their number is reported to be very large. They carry the name like "...... Finance and Investments" or "............ Finance Corporation" or "........... Pvt. Ltd." or "................& Co." and thus gives a picture of an incorporated body in the minds of the innocent depositors. Though these institutions were in existence since 1960s, they made rapid progress after 1991. The Banking Commission (1972) and all the subsequent committees have noticed that these institutions are heavily concentrated in States like Gujarat and Karnataka. These UIBs are registered with Registrar of Societies. In 1997 when the NBFIs started collapsing after the CRB fiasco, these UIBs also tumbled down. Most of these institutions were of the nature of "fly-by-night" operators.

The Unincorporated Bodies (UIBs) dealing with financial services which are also termed as "Petty Finance Corporations play a significant role in the economic development of our country by meeting the credit requirement of millions of people at the door steps on demand without insisting on procedural formalities unlike commercial banks, regional rural banks and co-operative banks. They are accessible at any time without any formalities according to the convenience of the needy of credit.

"There is a financial sector outside the banking sector generally known as the Non-Banking Financial Companies (NBFCs). NBFCs are the financial institutions that provide banking services, but do not hold banking licenses. Those Bodies that are not registered under the Companies Act are referred as the Unincorporated Bodies (UIBs). Since these Bodies have greater flexibility in their operations, they are able to reach small investors in attracting their surplus funds by way of public deposits and offering various incentives and better returns to them. Moreover, the constraints faced by the formal financial system in reaching rural/poor households and small business in a flexible and hassle free manner led almost as a natural consequence to emergence of various types of these bodies, which range from fairly sized NBFCs to much smaller Unincorporated Bodies. The UIBs have now become an important component of our financial sector. The easy procedure in their credit facilities and their offer of attractive rates of interest on public deposit enables their sharp growth over the years. The mushroom growth of these Bodies in the last decade brought about some unsavoury elements to the sector and fly by night operators started betraying the confidence of the depositors that had placed on them.

Registration of UIBs

After a series of collapse of UIBs and loss of deposits by the public, the Reserve Bank of India Act was amended in 1997. Section 45-S of the RBI Act 1934, relating to the acceptance of deposits by UIBs was amended. The amended provisions have come into effect from April 1, 1997. Thus, RBI, by prohibiting UIBs from accepting deposits from general public except from relatives has reduced their status to the money lender.

"Money lenders in India come under control of the Money Lenders Act, promulgated by each of the different States. The Act essentially sets out the appointment of a Registrar-General of Money Lenders who maintains a Register of Money-lenders in their jurisdiction. The Registrar provides for a license to money lenders to carry out their business, regulates the terms and conditions under which a loan is provided to borrowers, and arbitrates in disputes between money-lenders and borrowers in cases of default or other aspects. Compliance with the Act is rare, however, and majority of the money-lenders do not obtain such a license to operate.

To regulate and control the mushroom growth of UIBs (Money lenders), Finance Department, and Government of Manipur had introduced an Act under section 3 of the Bombay Money Lenders' Act 1946 as it is being extended to Manipur. The State Government had appointed the Registrar of Co-operative Societies, Manipur, Additional Registrar of Co-operative Societies, Manipur and Assistant Registrar of Co-operative Societies (G&B), Manipur as Registrar General of Money Lenders, Registrar of Money Lenders and Assistant Registrar of Money Lenders respectively. With the registration requirement under this Act, all the UIBs of the State must have to act as money lenders providing money lending or credit lending on various schemes with the interest rate ceiling of 3 per cent per month without accepting deposit from the public. A large range of people including government employees, businessmen, small vegetable vendors and security personnel are directly or indirectly benefiting from their financial services.

At present there are 61 such registered UIBs which are treated as money lenders under Bombay Money Lenders' Act 1946 in Manipur. Of these registered UIBs 17 of them were registered in 2005, 16 were in 2006, 9 of them were registered during the year 2007, 8 of them were registered during 2008 and 11 were registered during 2009 and there is no more registration till now.

Services of UIBs in Manipur

At the early stages of the establishment and development of these UIBs, they used to provide various services of varied nature. Some of them can be listed as follows – (*a*) Stop payment lottery in which the member who wins stop to pay further contribution; (*b*) Hire-

Purchase System, and (*c*) Instalment System. The most popular service of those days was the Stop Payment System which provides the members to win various items and assets of their choice.

During 1991 to 1993, when there was a stage of mushroom growth of UIBs, they have even started taking deposits from the general public through – (*a*) Savings Deposit, (*b*) Term/Fixed Deposit, and (*c*) Recurring Deposit. This was the stage when these UIBs started providing services of various financial institutions under one roof. But with the intervention of State government under the guidance of Reserve Bank, their functions have been restricted to a great extent and become very narrow and streamlined up to some extent.

At present, these UIBs provide very few services which are of money lending nature. They are being discussed below:

Business Loan

This particular type of service of lending nature is known by different names by different UIBs like Daily collection, Weekly collection, Monthly Collection, short-term loan, etc. As the name itself suggests, this business loan is given particularly to a wide range of business persons in the areas covered by their operation. These loans are given mainly to shopkeepers, vegetable vendors of Khwairamband Ima Keithels, workshops, other small retail shops and business persons.

The amount of loan given under this type of loan is at the range of Rs. 2,000 – Rs. 50,000. The rate of interest charged by the UIBs in such loans is 3 per cent per month. The period of maturity of these loans also differs from UIB to UIB, but most of them are at the range of 1-6 months. This amount of loan is collected daily, weekly, monthly, etc., in instalment system and at the end of the period, the UIBs can collect the whole amount of loan including the principal amount and interest on it.

Service Loan

It is also one of the most important and popular type of financial services provided by these UIBs. This type of loan is given only to the government employees. The amount of the loan is collected with interest every month at the time of receipt of salary by the employees from the Cashier or Drawing and Dispersing Officer (DDO) of the concerned department where the loanee is working. At present as the salaries are being paid in the bank accounts, the pass books of the loanees are kept in the custody of UIBs.

The rate of interest charged on this type of loan is 3 per cent per month. This type of loan is given mostly for longer period and the maturity period is 1-20 months. In most of the UIBs, the loan amount given to service loan is much greater than that of Business loan. The amount of loan of the service loan ranges from Rs. 10,000 to Rs. 1,00,000. These service loans are provided to the government employees for their various purposes.

Pension Loan

Pension loan is a type of loan provided by these UIBs particularly to the pensioners of government employees. In this type of loan, the pensioners have to surrender their pension passbooks for a certain period till the maturity of the period of the loan. The UIBs will collect the amount of pension monthly in the place of pensioners. After collecting the whole amount of the loan with the interest, the pension passbook will be handed over to the pensioners. The rate of interest charged by the UIBs on pension loan is 3 per cent per month as that of other types of loan. The period of maturity of this type of loan is 1-20 months.

Gold Mortgage

Gold Mortgage is another way of lending money by UIBs to its customers. Whenever any person wants to seek financial assistance from such financial institutions, they can keep their gold ornaments with the UIBs and can get financial assistance up to the amount allowed by the UIB in accordance with the value of the Gold ornament. The rate of interest charged for this is 3 per cent per month. Whenever the loanee does not repay back the loan amount with interest, the UIB will sell out the gold ornament and recover their amount of loan. In case, they return the loan amount with interest in time, the gold ornament kept with the UIB will be returned back to the loanee.

UIBs and Financial Inclusion

Financial inclusion is inclusion of those excluded from the payments system or from formal credit markets. Even after more than forty years of nationalization of banks in India, more than 40 per cent of the adult population in India has no access to formal banking and financial services. This exclusion could be on the grounds that the individual has either no savings/assets and hence no savings/current account in the bank. Besides, he also may not have access to any financial advice and perceives the cost of the financial services as not affordable.

Financial inclusion is to be undertaken in three steps – (*i*) providing access to financial products and services; (*ii*) availability of financial products and services in a fair and equitable manner; and (*iii*) credit counselling which includes providing sound services to arrest deterioration of incomes, restructuring of debt solution to overcome debt burden and improve money management skills.

In order to bring financial inclusion in India, Reserve Bank of India has asked the banks to (*i*) open "No frills" accounts through simplified know your customer (KYC) procedures and also to offer a small overdraft/General Credit Card not exceeding Rs. 25,000 to their customers. For self-help groups, a line of credit could be considered; (*ii*) provide other financial products like life/asset/health care insurance and mutual fund products; (*iii*) open accounts in villages/wards allocated to them; and (*iv*) provide financial counseling services and introduce a specific credit guarantee scheme under the DICGC Act for farmers.

In spite of these efforts, still the way to successful financial inclusion is very far. Along with the efforts from the organized sector of the financial system, there is also need for equal effort and contribution from the players in the unorganized sector of the Indian Financial System. Unincorporated bodies engaged in financial services in the State are also providing financial services and credit facilities to various customers from various backgrounds. Many of the customers of these UIBs are excluded customers of the formal banking system in the State. They are unable to access to the banking services in the State due to various reasons. Many of them are women vegetable vendors and unemployed poor trying to provide themselves self employment. They have denied by the banking services of the State. Due to lack of number of bank branches in the State, there is high density of customers in these banks and many State Bank branches are found to be overcrowded and there are long queues in front of the banks and ATM booths in the State. In such situation initiative of banks to make financial inclusion successful in the State is not found to be quite positive. There are 61 UIBs (registered money lenders) in the State operating mainly in different parts of Imphal east and west districts of the State. These UIBs are having 300-500 customers at an average which are enjoying credit facilities. It clearly shows the role of UIBs to make financial inclusion a dream coming true in the State. Their contribution in this effort cannot be ignored at all and recognition should be given to them on their credit.

Regulatory Initiative of State Government and RBI

The UIBs (registered Money Lenders) in India come under the control of the Money Lenders Act, promulgated by each of the different States. In Manipur also these UIBs are compelled to register under Bombay Money Lenders Act 1946 as extended to Manipur. At the time of issue of license to UIBs to work as money lender under Bombay Money Lenders' Act 1946, the State Government of Manipur put the following terms and conditions to UIBs through the Registrar of Money Lenders, Manipur:

1. This license shall be exhibited in prominent place on the premises where the business of money lending is carried on.
2. A signboard showing –
   (*a*) Name in which the business of money lending is carried on; and
   (*b*) The license number and date of registration shall also be exhibited.
3. The Cash Book, Ledger and Statement of Receipt and Expenditure shall be either in Form No. 4 and 7 or No. 5, 6, 7, 8, 9 and 10 respectively.
4. A Capital Account in Form No. 11 shall be opened.

5. The Statement of Account shall be furnished within 30 (thirty) days after closing the year for which the account of the money lending are ordinarily maintained.
6. Change of principal place of business shall be intimated within 7 (seven) days.
7. The rate of interest shall be limited at 3 per cent per month.

Under the guidance of Reserve Bank, State government has formed a specially dedicated police unit under the name Economic Offence Wing headed by an officer not less than the rank of a Police Commissioner so as to effectively investigate/deal with the cases relating to "non-banking financial companies and unincorporated financial institutions" which collected money on deposits and thereafter defaulted to repay the same on maturity.

Following the steps taken up by the Tamil Nadu government in order to protect the interest of depositors in financial establishments under the law "The Tamil Nadu Protection of Interests of Depositors (in Financial Establishments) Act, 1997", the State Finance Department has prepared "The Manipur Protection of Interest of Depositors (in Financial Establishment) Bill" and since it falls under the Concurrent List of Indian Constitution, it has been sent to Government of India for its prior approval in 2005 but still awaiting its approval.

With the amendment of RBI Act in 1997, the Section 45-S of the RBI Act 1934, relating to the acceptance of deposits by UIBs was amended and it came into effect from April 1, 1997. Thus, RBI, UIBs are prohibited from accepting deposits from the public except from relatives given under it. The UIBs which accept deposits in violation of the provisions of Chapter – III C of the RBI Act are liable to prosecution under the provisions of the Act. The State governments are being empowered concurrently to prosecute the offenders. The time limit for repayment of public deposits, except from those permitted sources (relatives) by the RBI Act 1934, held by all UIBs engaged in financial business expired on March 31, 2000. Accordingly, RBI cautioned UIBs engaged in the financial business to neither accept nor issue advertisements soliciting deposits. Concomitantly, members of the public were also cautioned about the risk of depositing money with such UIBs.

Besides the above initiatives, the Reserve Bank has conducted a number of seminars and awareness programmes in collaboration with the State Finance Department (institutional finance). Advertisement has also been put in the local newspapers cautioning the public from keeping deposits with the UIBs.

General Findings/Observations

1. UIBs work as a supplementary to the banks in Manipur. In Imphal West and East districts 61 UIBs have registered and operating along with 43 commercial bank branches.
2. Nature of services provided by UIBs are quite different from the banks operating in the State as they have daily collection, weekly collection and monthly collection loans along with service loan for government employees, gold mortgage loan, pension loan for the pensioners, etc.
3. Besides the credit facilities these UIBs are providing directly and indirectly employment opportunities to educated unemployed youths in the State.
4. Contribution from promoters, employees' contribution in the form of security deposits and winning amount of ROSCAs (Marup and Tender in local term) conducted by the UIBs are important sources of fund.
5. UIBs are investing capital at the range of rupees 10 to 50 lakh and some of them have the investment in terms of crores.
6. Some of the bankers felt that due to many reasons like easy accessibility, simpler documentation and procedure, absence of collateral securities and guarantor, etc. UIBs attract more customers to borrow.
7. Most of the beneficiaries of UIBs are government employees, businessmen and unemployed persons.
8. A large number of beneficiaries of UIBs are in association with them for a period of 1-5 years and very few of them are in association with UIBs for a period of more than 10 years.
9. Most of the customers of the UIBs are excluded poor from the formal banking system in the State.
10. Most of the UIBs are having customers at the range of 300-500. Their role in financial inclusion is inevitable.

Suggestions

The following few suggestions are being recommended to enhance the pace of financial inclusion through the activities and initiatives of UIBs in the State and for the growth of UIBs in the State.

1. Financial assistance should be provided to the UIBs by the financial institutions like SIDBI and NABARD and nationalized banks operating in the State similar to the financial assistance provided to Microfinance institutes.
2. State government should also be supportive to UIBs by making certain regulations to safeguard UIBs' interest and their depositors' interest equally.
3. UIBs should also be encouraged to merge themselves so that they can work competitively with nationalized, cooperative and rural banks and with sound financial strength and widely spread network of branches in the State.
4. These UIBs should also be compelled to get registered themselves under Companies Act and to come under the supervision and control of RBI as a Non-Banking Financial Company so that more financial discipline can be developed in themselves.
5. Training and awareness programmes should also be arranged for the staffs of UIBs and their customers so that mutual growth and benefit can be achieved.
6. Due to the financial assistance given to microfinance institutions in the State, many UIBs are intended to convert themselves into microfinance institutes.

Conclusion

It cannot be ignored that UIBs are playing an important role in the financial inclusion and socio-economic development of the State in particular and the whole country in general. Along with the measures to regulate UIBs and to protect the interest of public depositors, certain measures should also be taken by the RBI and the State governments in order to develop these UIBs.

REFERENCES

Bharati, V. Pathak. (2008), The Indian Financial System: Markets, Institutions and Services, Second Edition, Pearson Education, New Delhi, pp. 535-536.

Chakraborty, K. C. (2006), Financial Inclusion: Reaching the Unreached; *Chartered Financial Analyst*, November 2006, p. 56-57.

ICM, "A Typology of Informal Credit Suppliers: Money Lenders", http://www.gdrc.org/icm/suppliers/ml.html.

Krishna (2006), Impact of Non-Banking Financial Intermediaries on Commercial Banks, Mangalore University, Unpublished Ph.D. Thesis.

Ram Mohan, T.T. (2006), Inclusion: A Business Imperative; *The Economic Times*, November 30, 2006, p. 8.

Seminar's Handout on "Regulation for NBFCs and UIBs" organized by State Finance Department (Institutional Finance) and RBI, Guwahati at State Guest House, Imphal, Manipur, 16th November, 2009.

12

Business Correspondent (BC)/Business Facilitator (BF) Model : A Way Forward to bring Financial Inclusion

LONGJAM LILASHWORI DEVI

Introduction

"Financial inclusion with branchless banking" the term have gained page in every newspaper, journal, magazines, etc. The Reserve Bank of India (RBI) and the Government of India (GoI) have been making efforts to increase banking penetration in India. Committee after committee, have introduced various schemes to bring 100 per cent financial inclusion in India. Yet 50 per cent of India's 1.15 billion people do not have bank accounts; 95 per cent no general insurance; and 98 per cent no participation in the capital market; this despite 64,000 bank branches and 80,000 ATMs in the country (2011, Anil Bhasin). The RBI has taken up series of measures to bring financially excluded people into the structured financial system that include the creation of State Bank of India in 1955; nationalisation of commercial banks in 1969 and 1980; initiating the Lead Bank Scheme in 1970; establishing Regional Rural Banks (RRBs) in 1975; introducing a Self-Help Group (SHG)-Bank Linkage Programme in 1992 and formulating the Kisan Credit Card (KCC) scheme in 2001.In November 2005, banks were advised to make available a basic banking "no-frills" account with low or nil minimum stipulated balances as well as charges to expand the outreach of such accounts to vast sections of the population, simplified KYC norms, introduced General credit card (GCC) scheme. States Level Bankers Committee (SLBC) formed in each state was given the responsibility to ensure the implementation of the financial inclusion project by all banks, at least, one district of that State. Possibly the most important initiative of the Reserve Bank has been the Business Correspondent (BC) and Business Facilitators (BF) model.

The idea of BC model was first originated in Brazil. The model began in the 1990s as a way of controlling the 20 years of high inflation problem and to improve Brazil's social programmes. In Brazil, the BC model has become the most important channel to receive bill payments and services from the government. Speaking at the Skoch Mumbai conference, RBI Deputy Governor K.C. Chakrabarty at the outset said the banking correspondent or BC model is the most revolutionary reform which has taken place in the banking system. "No-frills account will not give any help to poor if he does not do banking transaction", he added. BCs/BFs are agents who can be hired by banks to provide a subset of banking services in places where it is not commercially or physically viable to set up branches in the present condition. The model is an innovative medium of achieving some significant results in the field of financial inclusion. The BC and BF model ensures a closer relationship between poor people and the organized financial system. The Reserve Bank permitted commercial banks to make use of the services of non-governmental organizations (NGOs/SHGs), micro-finance institutions and other civil society organizations, insurance agents, retired government servants like postmasters, school teachers, ex-servicemen and ex- bank staff as intermediaries for providing financial and banking services. These intermediaries could be used as business facilitators (BF) or business correspondents (BC) by commercial banks. The Union Finance Minister announced in the Budget 2010-11 that every village in the country with over 2000 population must have access to banking services by March 2012. In order to operationalise this process, commercial banks have prepared financial inclusion plans which have been submitted to the Reserve Bank. Operating a full-fledged branch is not a viable proposition considering the huge operational costs and limited business volumes. The business correspondents' (BCs) / business facilitators' (BFs) model is ideally the alternate viable business model in order to ensure greater coverage of hinterland clients in far-flung areas at reduced costs. This challenge will be better approach through the business correspondent (BC)/ Business Facilitator (BF) model by leveraging appropriate communication technology. Rangarajan also stressed the need for effective implementation of business facilitator and correspondent model for financial inclusion.

BC and BF Model of RBI

In January 2006, the Reserve Bank of India issued a new set of guidelines (circular of RBI) allowing banks to employ two categories of intermediaries (Models)—Business Correspondents (BCs) and Business Facilitators (BFs)—to expand their outreach. According to the guidelines, while the BCs are permitted to carry out transactions on behalf of the bank as agents, the BFs can refer clients, pursue the clients' proposal and facilitate the bank to carry out its transactions, but cannot transact on behalf of the bank.

Under the BF model, banks may use intermediaries such as NGOs, farmer's club, cooperatives, community base organizations IT-enabled rural outlets of cooperate entities, post offices, insurance agents, well- functioning Panchayats, village knowledge centres, agri-clinic/agri-business centres, Krishi Vigyan Kendras, and KVIC/KVIB units for providing facilitation services. The scope and activities to be undertaken by BF Model include:

- Identification of borrowers and fitment of activities;
- Collection and preliminary processing of loan application;
- Creation of awareness about saving and other products, education, and advice on managing money and debt counselling;
- Processing and submission of application to bank;
- Promotion and nurturing of SHGs/JLGs;
- Post-sanction monitoring;
- Monitoring and hand holding of SHGs/JLGs/credit groups/ others; and
- Follow-up for recovery.

Under the BC Model, NGOs/MFIs set-up under the Societies/ Trust Act, Societies registered under Mutually Aided Cooperative Societies Acts or the Cooperative Societies Acts of States' section 25 Companies, Registered NBFCs not accepting public deposits and

Post Offices may act as BCs. The scope and activities to be undertaken by BCs Model include:

- Identification of borrowers and fitment of activities;
- Collection and preliminary processing of loan application;
- Creation of awareness about saving and other products, education, and advice on Managing money and debt counselling;
- Processing and submission of application to bank;
- Promotion and nurturing of SHGs/JLGs;
- Post-sanction monitoring;
- Monitoring and hand holding of SHGs/JLGs/credit groups/others; and
- Follow up for recovery;
- Disbursal of small value credit;
- Recovery of principal/collection of interest;
- Collection of small value deposit;
- Sale of micro insurance/mutual fund product/pension products/other third party products; and
- Receipt and delivery of small value remittance/other payment instruments.

BC/BF model being unable to ground fully, financial inclusion committee formed under the chairmanship of Dr. C. Rangarajan (2008) has made some recommendations for the relaxation of norms for expanding the coverage of BC/BF:

1. In addition to institutions and individuals allowed by RBI to act as BC/BF, individuals like locally settled retired government employees like post masters, school teachers, ex-service men and ex-bank staff can act as BC/BF;
2. Further, MFs-NBFCs are also allowed to act as limited BCs of banks for only providing saving and remittance services;
3. The distance between the place of business of a retail outlet/sub-agent of a BC and base branch has been extended from 15–30 km in rural, semi-urban and urban areas; and
4. Technology has to be an integral part in sustaining outreach efforts through BC model.

Advantages of using BCs/BFs Model

Advantages of using the models by banks are listed down.

1. *A better alternative than bank branches:* Operating a full-fledged rural branch is not a viable proposition considering the huge operational costs and limited business volumes. The business correspondents' (BCs) / business facilitators' (BFs) model is ideally the alternate viable business model in order to ensure greater coverage of rural clients in far-flung areas at reduced costs. Under the set-up, banks are permitted by the Reserve Bank of India (RBI) to outsource selected banking services through BCs and their authorised agents. Customers have the freedom to use branch banking facilities even though the business correspondents are available in their locality or they are clients initially sponsored by BCs.
2. *Reaching the unreached:* The model enable banks to extend financial services to the unreached clients beyond their branch network as beneficiaries of the BCs are mostly located at unbanked and under banked areas. The model would be ideal for North Eastern States, the States full of terrains and scattered population, said Usha Thorat, RBI Deputy Governor.
3. *Doorstep banking:* Disbursement and loan recovery at the doorsteps of the beneficiary. Punjab National Bank is operating more than 3,800 business correspondents using handheld devices to increase its reach among unbanked areas to offer banking products at their doorstep.
4. *Better quality of assets:* NGOs, Post Offices, BDOs, social bodies and individuals engage as BC/BF know well about their target customer, thus loan facilitation by the NGOs/BCs (who are the promoter/builder of the groups) enhances quality of assets. "The key advantages of this channel are in terms of their local knowledge and ability to provide group loans". (O.P. Bhatt, Chairman, SBI).

Challenges faced by Banks in employing BCs/BFs Model

The engagement of BCs by banks for delivery of banking services exposes banks to multiple types of risks—credit risk, operational risk, legal risk, liquidity risk and reputational risk—to mitigate which banks need to take appropriate action challenges of banks in engaging BCs/BFs:

Operational Issues

Cash Handling: As almost all BC transactions are cash-based, the flow of cash with BCs has been highlighted as the biggest issue. Besides the logistics of handling large volumes of cash, it leads to increased costs and added operational risks. These assume greater importance in the context of the North Eastern region of the country, on account of higher security risks, vast and difficult terrain and poor connectivity. Allowing BCs to handle cash is the biggest challenge. Ninety-nine per cent of the financial transactions are in cash, warranting high-cost cash-handling operations and added operational risks. Moreover, clients tend to perceive that the BCs are the owners of the transactions and not facilitating them on the banks' behalf.

Irregular Accounting: Irregularities have been observed in accounting of clients' withdrawals and deposits by BCs and as a result there are delays in accounting the banking transactions with the Bank by the BC.

Gullible Client Profile: Beneficiaries of BC services are mostly illiterate and are susceptible to misguidance. Further, at times, clients tend to perceive the BCs themselves as banks. Lack of proper financial education of the clientele is a barrier to effective utilisation of the banking facility through the BC model. Recipients of BC services are mostly illiterate and unfamiliar with technology rendering them susceptible to misguidance by the BCs.

Fraud and Misappropriation: Since the BCs' staffs operate individually without any line supervision, the risk of fraud and misappropriation is higher. There have been instances noted of miscommunication by BCs. Failure to account for cash and falsification of records have been noticed and dealt with by banks.

Viability Issues

Inactive "No Frills Accounts": The majority of No Frill Accounts opened by BCs are not operational. In some locations that have achieved 100 per cent financial inclusion, the accounts in use have been less than 25 per cent. The average balances in savings accounts have been very low at unviable levels for banks.

Model Viability: There is a shortage of funding to BCs for meeting the group promotion costs in the case of SHG- Bank linkage models. In addition, there are financial constraints on the part of the BCs for capacity-building initiatives, such as investing in training for their staff.

BCs losing money: Initial losses are forcing many BCs to shut their operations. Business continuity risk in such cases is impacting banks adversely. It is time-consuming, costly and ineffective for banks to substitute these BCs with new entrants.

Regulatory Concerns

Interest Capping: Reaching unbanked areas warrants higher delivery costs and the rate cap does not allow much room for banks to recover the costs necessary to extend credit to hard-to-reach areas and in small amounts.

Distance Criteria: Banks do not always find it easy to get service area waivers from District-level Committees which are necessary to operate in certain areas. A number of requests are pending for approval and many requests have been rejected without any explanation.

Cash Settlement: Current regulations mandate BCs to complete accounting and settle cash with bank branches within 24 hours of transaction. Given the area of operation of BCs—rural areas with accessibility issues—making settlements within a prescribed timeframe have become a challenge.

Would BF/BC Model be an Appropriate Model for North East State Like Manipur?

The Centre has a roadmap to speed up financial inclusion and is trying to work through the branches of banks and otherwise. At present, there are 99 Blocks in the country, which do not have even a single bank branch. Of them, 86 are in the North East while 13 are in other parts of the country. Out of which 19 Blocks are in Manipur. Many diverse traditional system and even geographical condition make it difficult to replicate the model adopted elsewhere in the country into this region. In the case of the North East, it is found that the population in some Blocks is less than 10,000 raising the issue of financial viability of opening a bank branch there. In these

Table 12.1 : District-wise Branch Network of Banks in Manipur

Sl. No.	Name of the Bank	Imphal West	Imphal East	Thoubal	Bishnupur	Chandel	Chura-chandpur	Tamenglong	Senapati	Ukhrul	Total
1.	AXIS	2	—	—	—	—	—	—	—	—	2
2.	ALB	1	—	—	—	—	—	—	—	—	1
3.	BOB	3	—	—	—	—	—	—	—	—	3
4.	CBI	2	1	—	—	—	—	—	—	—	3
5.	HDFC	1	—	—	—	—	—	—	—	—	1
6.	ICICI	1	—	—	—	—	—	—	—	—	1
7.	IOB	1	—	—	—	—	—	—	—	—	1
8.	PNB	1	1	—	—	—	—	—	—	—	2
9.	PSB	1	1	—	—	—	—	—	—	—	2
10.	SBI	5	2	2	1	3	3	—	5	1	22
11.	UBI	4	3	2	1	1	1	2	1	2	17
12.	UCO	1	—	—	1	—	—	—	—	—	2
13.	VJB	1	—	—	—	—	—	—	1	—	2
ASCB TOTAL		24	8	4	3	4	4	2	7	3	59
14.	MRB	5	4	4	3	1	1	3	4	2	27
RRB TOTAL		5	4	4	3	1	1	3	4	2	27*

15. IUCB	5	3	—	—	—	—	—	—	—	8
16. MSCB	1	1	2	2	—	1	1	1	1	10
17. MPCB		—	—	1	—	—	—	—	—	1
18. MWCB	1	—	—	—	—	—	—	—	—	1
CO-OP TOTAL	7	4	2	3	1	1	1	1	1	20
TOTAL	36	16	10	9	5	6	6	12	6	106

Source : 27th Manipur state level bankers committee report

*Non-functioning branches of MRB: Senapati (4), Tamenglong (2), Ukhrul (1), Tamenglong (1) and Churachandpur (1)

areas, it is proposed to use the branchless banking with the help of technology to promote inclusion. The BC model would be ideal for North Eastern States, a region full of terrains and scattered population.

RBI has a scheme for viability gap funding, but banks do not seem very eager to go into these areas because of lack of business. Financial inclusion in the entire North East region has a long way to go. In the region there are areas which are completely unmotorable and in some parts only a strong four-wheeler can navigate. There are areas where there is no electricity, even if connected, it is not available most of the time. But despite all of this, there is mobile connectivity here and people use solar power extensively to charge their mobiles. Then, could mobile banking be the best model? The answer is no. Because there is always need for cash and mobile banking can only provide cashless banking transactions. Thus, here arise needs for the services of business correspondent/business facilitator. A potentially feasible inclusion model for the North Eastern region could be a combination of mobile and smart card-based and business correspondent-based solution that are supported by micropayment.

Banking Profile of Manipur

The State of Manipur has 9 districts in which there are 41 Blocks divided into 2,200 villages. Out of which 19 Blocks are unbanked and 189 villages are declared unbanked villages having population more than 2,000 as per 2001 Census. Organizational structure of banking sector in the State comprises of 13 commercial banks, 1 each RRB, SCB and SLDCB and few other co-operative banks, with a branch network of 106 branches. Of these, 71 branches are concentrated in the four valley districts, of as many as 36 branches are in Imphal west district alone which is identified for 100 per cent financial inclusion. The Manipur rural bank, the only RRB in the State, has 27 branches, of which 9 branches are non-functional. Manipur SCB's network comprises of 10 branches of which 5 rural, 3 semi-rural, 2 urban. Other banks in the cooperative fold account for 10 branches including MSLDCB with one branch. Per bank branch population in the State is placed at 23,648. Table 12.1 shows districts-wise bank branch network in the State. Of the 9 districts,

State Bank of India is the Lead Bank in 5 districts, viz., Imphal West, Thoubal, Chandel, Churachandpur and Senapati, and in the remaining 4 districts, viz., Imphal East, Bishnupur, Ukhrul and Tamenglong, the United Bank is the Lead bank. State Bank of India is the convener of State Level Banker Committee (SLBC) (Table 12.1).

The number of bank branches in Manipur is still very less. There is need for more branches to bring about maximum financial

Table 12.2 : Hub Bank Centres with Bidding Banks in Manipur

Centre No.	*Districts*	*Name of Bidding Bank*	*Hub–Bank location*	*Unbanked Blocks proposed to be linked*
1.	Senapati	(a) SBI	(I) Tadubi	(i) Paomata
				(ii) Purul
		(b) VJB	(I) Saikul	(i) Saikul
2.	Churachandpur	(a) CBI	(I) Singhat	(i) Singhat
				(ii) Saigaikot
		(b) SBI	(I) Thanlon	(i) Thanlon
				(ii) Tipaimuk
				(iii) Vangai Range
			(II) BSF Camp Pearsonmum	Nil
			(III) Tuibong*	(i) Tuibong
				(ii) Samulamlam
				(iii) Saikot
3.	Chandel	MRB	Tengnoupal	(i) Khengjoy
4.	Ukhrul	SBI	(I) Somsai*	(i) Lungchung Maphel
				(ii) Chingai
			(II) Kamjong	(i) Kamjong
				(ii) Kasom Khullen
5.	Tamenglong	(a) UBI	(I) Tamenglong*	(i) Tamei
				(ii) Tousem
		(b) SBI	(II) Noṇey	(i) Khoupum

Source : 27th Manipur State Level Bankers Committee Report.
*Branch opened

inclusion of the poorer sections of the society. The available branches are overcrowded killing lots of customers' time. There are always long queue of customers in almost every bank branches in the State.

At SLBC meeting December 2010, Smt. Surekha Marandi, Regional Director, RBI, Guwahati, pointed out that the main focus of the SLBC meeting held at Manipur was to increase the number of bank branches for extending banking facilities to the people of Manipur either by way of opening of new Bank Branch or utilizing the services of Business Correspondent (BC) model. However, she mentioned the BC alone cannot provide the banking facilities unless a link branch is established within the area of 30 Km. of radius from a CSP. So, she wanted to increase the bank branches which will not only provide the service to BC model but also increase the CD ratio of the State. The SLBC of Manipur has identified eleven centres as the agreed list for providing banking facilities by opening branches with support from Government of Manipur (GoM) and Reserve Bank under the special dispensation scheme of RBI. List of eleven Hub bank centres with bidding banks are given in Table 12.2. Out of the ten centres identified five branches are directed to be opened in 2010-2011 but only three branches are opened till July 2011,the remaining are to be opened by the end of 2011-2012. By the opening of these three branches the number of unbanked blocks without a single branch has been reduced to 12 blocks.

Role of BCs/BFs in Manipur

The then Union Finance Minister, Pranab Mukherjee in his Budget Speech 2010-11 directed all the banks to provide appropriate banking facilities to habitations having population in excess of 2000 by March 2012 using various models and technologies including branchless banking through business correspondents (BC). To address the direction SLBC Manipur has allotted 189 unbanked villages with population over 2,000 in Manipur to various bank branches as per "Service Area Approach" for financial inclusion by opening bank branches or using services of BCs/BFs model.

Table 12.3 : BCs/BFs engaged at Different Districts with the Coverage of Villages having Population of more than 2000

Sl. No.	*Name of district*	*No. of unbanked village with population of 2000 and above*	*No. of BC/BF engaged*	*No. of villages covered either by Bank branch or BC/BF*	*No. of villages uncovered either by Bank branch or BC/BF*	*% of covered village either by Bank branch or BC/BF*
1.	Imphal east	44	9	14 (1)	30	31.818
2.	Imphal west	46	11	22 (4)	24	47.826
3.	Thoubal	42	4	10 (3)	32	23.809
4.	Bishnupur	25	5	13	12	52.000
5.	Tamenglong	3	nil	1 (1)	2	33.000
6.	Senapati	5	nil	2 (2)	3	40.000
7.	Ukhrul	9	2	3 (1)	6	33.000
8.	Churachandpur	15	3	6 (1)	9	40.000
9.	Chandel	nil	nil	—	—	—
	Total	189	34	71 (13)	118	37.566

Source : Lead Bank Office, SBI

Note : # Figures in the bracket is number of villages covered by Bank branch.

Figure 12.1 : Financial Inclusion through different Agents

Table 12.3 shows district-wise engagement of BCs/BFs with their coverage of unbanked villages. Out of the 189 villages 13 villages are provided banking services by opening bank branches and 58 villages by BCs/BFs mode. According to Manipur SLBC, remaining 118 villages are to be covered by BCs/BFs mode. So BCs/BFs have a big role to play in connecting these villages to the formal financial sector. Here out of 34 BCs/BFs, one is for PNB, 3 for IUCB, 4 for MSCB and 26 for SBI. Besides BCs/BFs from SBI, no BCs/BFs from any other banks have started work. Till now SBI is the only Bank in Manipur that started functioning of BC/BF model. BFs in SBI in Manipur are appointed by SBI directly while appointed BCs are outsourced to Drishtee.

Figure 12.1 depicts that 7 per cent of the unbanked villages having population of more than 2,000 are providing banking services by bank branches, 31 per cent by BC/BF model and the remaining 62 per cent are to be facilitated by BC/BF model. It shows that BC/BF model is envisaged to play an important role in achieving total financial inclusion.

Table 12.4 : Number of Bank Accounts opened by BCs/BFs in Three Different Financial Years

Sl.No.	*Financial year*	*No. of BCs*	*No. of account opened by BCs/BFs*	*Credit deposit amt. in lacs*
1.	2009-10	19	1,1412	1573.63
2.	2010-11	37	2,434	155.53
3.	2011-12 (till July)	30	4,274	165.14
	Total	30	18,120	1894.3

Note : 1. Correlation between No. of BCs and No. of A/cs = – 0.9799

2. Correlation between No. of account and Credit deposit amt = 0.9821

Source : Progress Report for Channel Management Facilitator.

SBI has engaged 48 BCs for different villages of which 30 BCs are working in the financial inclusion of the various villages in and around their CSP (customer service point) for the last two years 18 BCs are found inactive as they are unable to bring a single customer for opening bank account. Out of the 30 BCs, only 3 are provided kiosk banking facilities with ICT devices and the remaining BCs are allotted villages for financial inclusion in the role of BF. For the complete process of financial inclusion of the villages, necessary ICT devices should be provided to open kiosk banking to BCs enabling them to assume their role as BC.

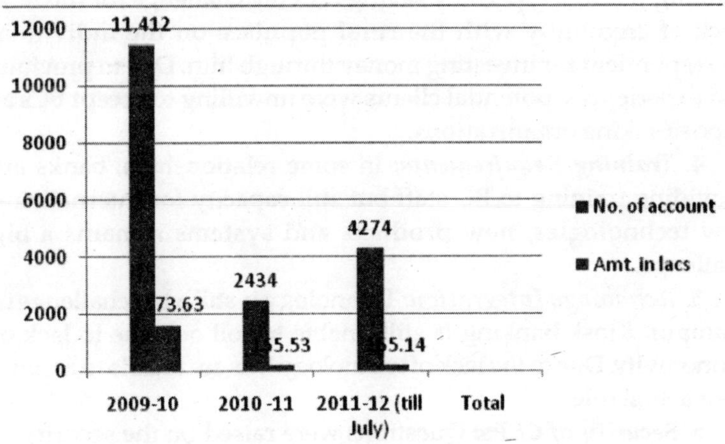

Figure 12.2 : Number of Accounts opened by BC/BF

From Table 12.4, it is found there is no correlation between number of BCs and number of accounts. Rather contrarily the highest number of BCs open the lowest number of accounts. It is seen that there were good performance in the initial stage but later it is declined. According to some of the BCs operated in Manipur, the declining result is due to the challenges (problems) faced by them in running the business.

Some of the issues/challenges in this model as listed out by various BCs are:

1. ***Dormant Accounts:*** BCs report that more than 80 per cent of no-frill accounts opened by clients are inactive, thus transactions after account opening have been minimal. End beneficiaries need to be financially literate to make appropriate use of banking services and services needed to be more specifically designed to meet demand.

2. ***Viability Problems:*** The commission paid by banks for BC services is not adequate to produce viable business models. There are costs involved in staff salaries and training and the current compensation structure does not cover costs. A majority of BCs reported significant losses and some have already suspended their operations.

3. *Community Mobilization:* Mobilizing communities for banking services especially savings is a big challenge for the BCs. Lack of credibility with the rural populace on the individual correspondent for investing money through him. Due to previous bad experiences, potential clients were unwilling to accept BCs as deposit-taking organizations.

4. *Training Requirements:* In some relationships, banks are providing training to BC staff but still capacity for internalizing new technologies, new products and systems remains a big challenge.

5. *Technology Integration:* Technology is still a big challenge in Manipur. Kiosk banking is still unable to roll out due to lack of connectivity. Due to the lack of technology BCs are unable to assume their actual role.

6. *Security of CSPs:* Questions were raised on the security of Customer Service Points; in Manipur CSPs in the remote areas is the big challenge of security again.

Suggestions for Strengthening BC/BF Model to be a Viable Model

1. Commission structure offer by the bank to the business correspondents need to be revised so that it could cover operational cost on a sustainable manner. Bank have to realise that for BC model to succeed the BCs who are the first level of contact for the customers have to be compensated adequately so that they too see this as a business opportunity.
2. Removal of the 10 per cent cap on the corporate holding in a BC, removal of BC as a not for profit company conditionality and use of Financial Inclusion Plan Fund (FIPF) to compensate BCs for the viability gap.
3. Initial security deposit asked by the banks from the BCs should be covered under the credit guarantee fund.
4. Linking of financial literacy and credit counselling centres with the BCs/BFs could fast tract the financial inclusion. BCs/BFs could act as service provider as well as counsellor for providing customized financial services.

5. For increasing the participation of disadvantaged sections of the society, RBI has to simplify the norms and facilitate more people participate as BCs.
6. RBI, GoM and banks should be ensured integration of technology to provide connectivity of BCs.

Conclusion

From the above discussion on the role of BC/BF model in financial inclusion, it is concluded that the model has not yet grounded fully in India and yet to be grounded in the North Eastern region. The model had the potential to be very successful; nevertheless, much still needed to be done to validate its inclusion in the sector. RBI and GoI with commercial banks have been trying many experimental projects to make the model a viable and feasible instrument of expanding financial services outreach. Restraints coming out of regulatory norms should be removed. There is a consensus that the viability issues need to be addressed with a great sense of urgency. Otherwise, with the possible folding up of some BCs would create unmanageable bottleneck in the country. Technology plays central role in making the model viable by providing connectivity between financial service provider and the customer. Model which is successful in some States does not mean to succeed in the other States. Innovation in the model is needed to suit the diverse work culture and social milieu. In the North East State Bank should establish relationship with mobile service provider to serve as business correspondent. BCs are required to play a role in creating awareness and shoulder all the responsibility in selling the product as a motto of service. Young business correspondents having background of finance, commerce, business and economics must be recruited to launch a campaign of innovative business, banking and corporate in Manipur. The business correspondents should play a great role in this mammoth campaign launched for promoting the banking sector with a social outlook. The key success of the BF/BC model lies in the intertwine activities of technology, regulatory bodies and the player.

REFERENCE

Agrawal, Reena (2011), "100% Financial Inclusion: A Challenging Task Ahead", http/in google.com.

Bhasan, Anil (2011), "Banking the Unbanked", *Business World*, 18th April.

Bhatt, O.P., (2011), "Successful Outreach Model", *Financial Express*, March.

Business Standard (2010), "Rangarajan against dilution of regulators autonomy", August 7.

CAB & ACCESS *Joint Report*, "Business Correspondents and Facilitators: Pathway to Financial Inclusion?".

Chakrabarty, K.C. (2011), "Financial Inclusion: India's New Mission", *Financial Express*, March.

Chitra Nayak, (2011), "Telecom and Organised Retail as Business Correspondent: An Analysis of BC Model, from CoFI", Monday, January 10.

Financial Inclusion Training Programme, "Building an Inclusive India", *www.cbiorg*

"Financial Inclusion and United Bank of India", (2011), http/ *www.ubiorg.nic.in.*

Karmakar, G. (2011), "Making BCs Viable", Inclusion Jan-Mar.

Kapoor, Rana (2011), "Enabling Financial Inclusion in North-East", *Economic Times*, 23rd May.

Kochhar, Sameer (2009), "Speeding Financial Inclusion", Skoch Publication. NABARD, (2011-12), "State Focus Paper", Manipur.

Nayak, Mahesh (2011), "Financial inclusion: For The People, By The People", *Business World*, 3rd January.

Rangarajan, C. (2008), "Financial Inclusion Committee Report".

Saha, Manojit (2011), "Mirage or Reality", *Business Standard*, January.

Sameer, Kochhar, R. Chandrashekhar, K.C. Chakrabarty, Deepak B. Phathak, (2009), *Financial Inclusion*, Skoch Publication.

Shinde Shivani & Manojit Saha (2010), "Providing Connectivity to Picking BCs, Tech Firm Do It All For Banks", *Business Standard*, Wednesday, 22nd December.

SLBC Meeting, "Agenda Notes and Background Papers for Manipur".

Thorat, Usha (2009), "RBI model to provide Banking Services in Remote Areas", *Business Line*, 6th Sept.

SECTION - II

Financial Inclusion and Microfinance

13

Microfinance and Financial Inclusion

ROHIT GARG

Introduction: Financial Inclusion and Microfinance

From the late 1980s, the emergence of the Grameen Bank in Bangladesh drew attention to the role of "micro-credit" as a source of finance for micro entrepreneurs. Lack of access to credit was seen as a binding constraint on the economic activities of the poor. Micro-loans delivered to groups of poor women seemed to offer a simple and direct remedy and the connection between providing credit and removing poverty was intuitively appealing. It was also politically attractive. Resources could be made available through the political process, while government sponsorship of mass credit bought vote banks. Less well understood was the need for micro-credit to be financially sustainable. Also, emphasis on credit to the exclusion of other financial services obscured the need to develop organic systems of financial intermediation, commencing with grassroots savings mobilization. Simplistic notions of micro-credit produced counter-reactions. For the past decade or more the idea of *micro-credit* as a panacea for poverty has lost ground to a more holistic notion of *microfinance*, seen as encompassing a range of financial services needed by the poor. It was ironic that by 2006, the year in which Muhammad Yunus and Grameen Bank were awarded the Nobel Peace Prize for their pioneering work in "micro-credit", the term itself had been eclipsed and retained virtually no currency in professional circles. Nonetheless, Yunus's Nobel Prize has served to cement "micro-credit" ever more firmly into the popular, journalistic and political vocabularies. This is unfortunate in that it impedes a full understanding of the financial service needs of the poor and how they might best be satisfied. More recently, the term *financial inclusion* has gained ground among professionals. "Financial inclusion" focuses attention on the need to bring previously excluded people under the umbrella of financial institutions. However, while "microfinance" has driven "micro-credit" out of the professional discourse, "financial inclusion" has not replaced "microfinance" as an operational concept. Financial inclusion is the most useful frame of reference for considering how poverty might be reduced through provision of financial services. And microfinance (using that term in a broad sense, explained below) remains the most potent weapon available for reducing financial exclusion. Financial exclusion in developing member economies reflects the fact that the "informal" or "unenumerated" economy is of major importance as a source of livelihood for the poor, while for them the household is the primary unit of both production and consumption. A number of considerations impede the access of households to financial services. These include geographic isolation, low population densities and gender, which lead to unequal access in economies where financial sector development is limited. Particular sectors, notably small holder and peasant agriculture, with their associated post-harvest and off farm economic activities, pose special challenges for financial service provision. A general problem in the developing member economies is the inability of many lower income households to meet lenders' requirements for formal physical collateral.

International development agencies and financial institutions have been active in developing new approaches to these problems. The UN Capital Development Fund (UNCDF) published an influential *Blue Book* on financial inclusion in 2005. The World Bank has devoted considerable resources to a research programme on "access to finance", within which attention is paid to financial exclusion of the poorest and to determining how access to financial services can be measured by governments. Also within the World Bank Group, the International Finance Corporation (IFC) supports private sector approaches to increasing access to financial services.

The Scope of Financial Inclusion

The scope of financial inclusion can be expanded in two ways :

(*a*) Through State-driven intervention by way of statutory enactments (for instance the US example, the Community Reinvestment Act and making it a statutory right to have bank account in France).

(*b*) Through voluntary effort by the banking community for evolving various strategies to bring within the ambit of the banking sectors the large strata of society.

When bankers do not give the desired attention to certain areas, the regulators have to step in to remedy the situation. This is the reason why the Reserve Bank of India is placing a lot of èmphasis on financial inclusion.

In India the focus of the financial inclusion at present is confined to ensuring a bare minimum access to a savings bank account without frills, to all. Internationally, the financial exclusion has been viewed in a much wider perspective. Having a current account/savings account on its own, is not regarded as an accurate indicator of financial inclusion. There could be multiple levels of financial inclusion and exclusion. At one extreme, it is possible to identify the "super-included", i.e., those customers who are actively and persistently courted by the financial services industry, and who have at their disposal a wide range of financial services and products. At the other extreme, we may have the financially excluded, who are denied access to even the most basic of financial products. In between are those who use the banking services only for deposits and withdrawals of money. But these persons may have only restricted access to the financial system, and may not enjoy the flexibility of access offered to more affluent customers.

Why is Financial Inclusion Important?

1. Why is financial inclusion important? It is important simply because it is a necessary condition for sustaining equitable growth. There are few, if any, instances of an economy transiting from an agrarian system to a post-industrial modern society without broad-based financial inclusion. As people having comfortable access to financial services, we all know

from personal experience that economic opportunity is strongly intertwined with financial access. Such access is especially powerful for the poor as it provides them opportunities to build savings make investments and avail credit. Importantly, access to financial services also helps the poor ensure themselves against income shocks and equips them to meet emergencies such as illness, death in the family or loss of employment. Needless to add, financial inclusion protects the poor from the clutches of the usurious money lenders.

2. There is another benefit of financial inclusion which we have yet to fully appreciate let alone exploit. Financial inclusion will make it possible for governments to make payment such as social security transfers, National Rural Employment Guarantee Programme (NREGA) wages into the bank accounts of beneficiaries through the "Electric Benefit Transfer" (EBT) method. This will minimize transaction costs including leakages. In parts of the country where such EBT has already taken off, the results are impressive and the experience of both payers and recipients extremely satisfying.
3. There are enormous benefits at the aggregate level too. The first and more obvious benefit is that financial inclusion provides an avenue for bringing the savings of the poor into the formal financial intermediation system and channels them into investment. Second, the large number of low cost deposits will offer banks an opportunity to reduce their dependence on bulk deposits and help them to better manage both liquidity risks and asset-liability mismatches.

Measuring Financial Inclusion

Closely related to financial inclusion is the idea of breadth of financial services. Breadth of financial services refers to the outreach of financial services in an economy. In other words, breadth measures how many people have access to financial services. Although financial inclusion should signify access to a range of different financial services, the percentage of people in a given area with access to a bank account is the typical measuring stick for breadth of financial services, (Beck & De la Torre, 2006). This approach assumes that a bank account enables poor households to perform important financial functions such as saving money safely outside the house, accessing credit, making loan or premium payments, and transferring money (Mohan, 2006). Thus, in this framework, a bank account *should* determine access to and usage of many other financial services (Littlefield *et al.*, 2006).

Unfortunately, it is difficult to discern access to savings accounts in developing countries as data on small deposits and borrowings is not readily available. Acknowledging such opacity and gaps in the data, Table 13.1 demonstrates the striking disparities in access to savings accounts between developed and developing countries. While in developed nations almost everyone has access to banking services, in less developed countries, access is often limited to small segments of the population.

Table 13.1 : Status of Financial Inclusion in Different Countries / Different States of India

Country/Location	*% with account*	*Country/Location*	*% with account*
Botswana	47	Nagaland	21
Brazil (urban)	43	Meghalaya	27
Colombia (Bogotá)	39	Bihar	33
Djibouti	24.8	Karnataka	66
Lesotho	17	Delhi, Haryana and Punjab	84
Mexico City	21.3	Kerala	89
Namibia	28.4		
South Africa	31.7		
Swaziland	35.3		
Tanzania	6.4		
Denmark	99.1		
Sweden	98		
Italy	70.4		
UK	87.7		
USA	91		

Source : Emerging Market Economics, Ltd. (2005), p. 20, Peachey and Roe (2004), p. 13, United Nations (2006), p. 2, Fedbank Hormis Memorial Foundation Inaugural Address by V. Leeladhar, Deputy Governor, Reserve Bank of India, December 2, 2000.

Note: In Botswana, Lesotho, Namibia and Swaziland, this is the percentage who says that they have a saving /transaction account from a bank. In India, this is the percentage of the adult population who has access to either a savings or current account.

International Experience in Promoting Financial Inclusion

An interesting feature which emerges from the international practice is that the more developed the society is, the greater the thrust on empowerment of the common person and low income groups. It may be worthwhile to have a look at the international experience in tackling the problem of financial exclusion so that we can learn from the international experience.

The Financial Inclusion Task Force in UK has identified three priority areas for the purpose of financial inclusion, viz., access to banking, access to affordable credit and access to free face-to-face money advice. UK has established a Financial Inclusion Fund to promote financial inclusion and assigned responsibility to banks and credit unions in removing financial exclusion. Basic bank no frills accounts have been introduced. An enhanced legislative environment for **credit unions** has been established, accompanied by tighter regulations to ensure greater protection for investors. A **Post Office Card Account (POCA)** has been created for those who are unable or unwilling to access a basic bank account. The concept of a **Savings Gateway** has been piloted. The concept of a Savings Gateway has been introduced for those on low income employment. This offers a sum of £1 to those on low-income employment from the state for every £1 they invest, up to a maximum of £25 per month. In addition the **Community Finance Learning Initiatives (CFLIs)** were also introduced with a view to promoting basic financial literacy among housing association tenants.

A civil rights law, namely Community Reinvestment Act (CRA) in the United States prohibits discrimination by banks against low and moderate income neighbourhoods. The CRA imposes an affirmative and continuing obligation on banks to serve the needs for credit and banking services of all the communities in which they are chartered. In fact, numerous studies conducted by Federal Reserve and Harvard University demonstrated that CRA lending is a win-win proposition and profitable to banks. In this context, it is also interesting to know the other initiative taken by a state in the United States. Apart from the CRA experiment, armed with the sanction of Banking Law, the State of New York Banking Department, with the objective of making available the low cost banking services to consumers, made mandatory that each banking institution shall offer *basic banking account* and in case of credit unions the *basic share draft account*, which is in the nature of low cost account with minimum facilities. Some key features of the basic banking account are worth-mentioning here.

- ✓ The initial deposit amount required to open the account shall not exceed US $ 25.
- ✓ The minimum balance, including any average balance, required to maintain such account shall not exceed US $ 0.10.
- ✓ The charge for periodic cycle for the maintenance of such accounts to be declared up front.
- ✓ The minimum number of withdrawal transactions which may be made during any periodic cycle at no charge to the account holder must at least be eight.
- ✓ A withdrawal shall be deemed to be made when recorded on the books of the account holder's banking institution.
- ✓ Except, as provided below, an account holder shall not be restricted as to the number of deposits which may be made to the account without incurring any additional charge.
- ✓ The banking institution may charge account holders for transaction at electronic facilities which are not operated by the account holder's banking institution as well as other fees and charges for specific banking services which are not covered under the basic banking account scheme.
- ✓ Every periodic statement issued for the basic banking account should invariably cover on it or by way of separate communiqué maximum number of withdrawals permitted during each periodic cycle without additional charge and the consequences of exceeding such maximum and the fee if any, for the use of electronic facilities which are not operated by the account holder's banking institution.

An interesting feature of basic banking account scheme is the element of transparency, i.e., the banking institution should, prior to opening the account, furnish a written disclosure to the account holder describing the main features of the scheme, i.e., the initial deposit amount required to open the account, minimum balance to be maintained, charge per periodic cycle for use of such account, maximum number of withdrawal transactions without any additional charge and other charges imposed on transactions for availing electronic facility not operated by the account holder's banking institution, etc.

Indian Scenario

Bank nationalization in India marked a paradigm shift in the focus of banking as it was intended to shift the focus from class banking to mass banking. The rationale for creating Regional Rural Banks was also to take the banking services to poor people. The branches of commercial banks and the RRBs have increased from 8,321 in the year 1969 to 68,282 branches as at the end of March 2005. The average population per branch office has decreased from 64,000 to 16,000 during the same period. However, there are certain under-banked States such as Bihar, Orissa, Rajasthan, Uttar Pradesh, Chhattisgarh, Jharkhand, West Bengal and a large number of North Eastern States, where the average population per branch office continues to be quite high compared to the national average. As you would be aware, the new branch authorization policy of Reserve Bank encourages banks to open branches in these under banked States and the under banked areas in other States. The new policy also places a lot of emphasis on the efforts made by the Bank to achieve, *inter alia*, financial inclusion and other policy objectives.

One of the benchmarks employed to assess the degree of reach of financial services to the population of the country, is the quantum of deposit accounts (current and savings) held as a ratio to the adult population. In the Indian context, taking into account the Census of 2001 (ignoring the incremental growth of population thereafter), the ratio of deposit accounts (data available as on March 31, 2004) to the total adult population was only 59 per cent (details furnished in Table 13.1). Within the country, there is a wide variation across States. For instance, the ratio for the State of Kerala is as high as 89 per cent while Bihar is marked by a low coverage of 33 per cent. In the North Eastern States like Nagaland and Manipur, the coverage was a meagre 21 per cent and 27 per cent, respectively. The Northern Region, comprising the States of Haryana,

Chandigarh and Delhi, has a high coverage ratio of 84 per cent. Compared to the developed world, the coverage of our financial services is quite low. For instance, as per a recent survey commissioned by British Bankers' Association, 92 to 94 per cent of the population of UK has either current or savings bank account.

Limitations of Microfinance

Microfinance is a highly attractive intervention for donors, because it offers the possibility of sustainable intervention with long-term impact on key economic and social indicators. Microfinance can be delivered in an institutional and financially sustainable manner that permits donors to withdraw after making relatively modest investments. However, microfinance is not a panacea or cure-all for all problems of development. Key areas where microfinance cannot make a contribution include: assisting the poorest through income transfers or subsidies or serving as a vehicle to provide health and education services. Microfinance also cannot be used as a substitute for investments in the infrastructure that is necessary to link more remote areas to markets. These areas necessarily require separate, specially designed interventions.

Conclusion

Microfinance is considered to be a valuable tool for the alleviation of poverty around the globe. In order for microfinance to realize its full potential, however, it must be sustainable and capable of expansion beyond the limitations imposed by reliance on development assistance. Both developing and developed nations are key actors in this regard. Developed-country bilateral aid programmes and multilateral institutions should focus efforts on defining common standards by which to measure the effectiveness of microfinance in reducing poverty. Donor policies should encourage sustainability by avoiding subsidies for lending and by using grants to help developing nations create a favourable policy and institutional infrastructure for microfinance; a key policy goal should be to ensure the safety and financial soundness of depository microfinance institutions. Donor programmes should meet the transparency test and use merit based frameworks for the allocation of scarce grant resources. Financial regulators and supervisors in developing countries should ensure prudent oversight by soliciting input from microfinance institutions and other civil society stakeholders. Several key questions require additional research and analysis to develop useful guidelines regarding micro lending as a means for reducing poverty in urban areas.

To address some of these issues, a comprehensive review of donor policies will be required. Bilateral and multilateral agencies should be surveyed to solicit the information directly Central investigative themes include: What is the aggregate amount of microfinance services offered by MFIs globally and in Latin America (broken down by urban and rural areas)? What is the total amount of development assistance to microfinance (with particular emphasis on aggregating bilateral and multilateral donor information)? What are the most appropriate matrices for determining the impact of microfinance on poverty reduction and the effectiveness of microfinance-oriented donor programmes (and what standardization methods are used)? What is the optimal national microfinance policy and regulatory framework that balances consumer protection with the need for "mystification"? This chapter recommends exploring means to leverage additional capital for MFIs. One interesting area is remittances. Aggregated, these are large transfers and represent significant cash flows from developed to developing economies. Linking these funds to microfinance would help to channel these resources to the formal, productive sector. Furthermore, using microfinance institutions to link remittance flows to asset accumulation—such as purchasing a home or financing micro and small businesses—would represent a significant step forward in using remittances to contribute to sustainable microfinance. These issues and research agenda items provide a particularly rich opportunity to measure the impact of microfinance on urban poverty reduction in Latin America. This should lead to valuable conclusions regarding donor programmes and national policies in this sector.

REFERENCES

Available for download athttp://www.uncdf.org/english/microfinance/pubs/bluebook/index.php

Commemorative Lecture by Shri V. Leeladhar, Deputy Governor Reserve Bank of India at the Fedbank Hormis Memorial Foundation at Ernakulam on December 2, 2005.

http://econ.worldbank.org/WBSITE/EXTERNAL/EXTDEC/EXTRESEARCH/0,,contentMDK:21285410~

PagePK: 64165401~piPK: 64165026~theSitePK: 469382, 00.html

The Peruvian scholar Hernando De Soto has shown that land tenure and land titling deficiencies prevent the poor from collateralizing the assets they have accumulated. See De Soto, *The Other Path* (1989).

Wright, *Microfinance: The Solution or a Problem?*, 1999.

www.ifc.org/ifcext/mekongpsdf.nsf/AttachmentsByTitle/FMDFactsheet/$FILE/A2FFactsheet Remarks by Dr. D. Subbarao, Governor, Reserve Bank of India at the Bankers' Club in Kolkata on December 9, 2009.

14

Predatory Microfinance

KRISTIANO RACCANELLO

"In the 1970s, when I began working here on what would eventually be called "microcredit", one of my goals was to eliminate the presence of loan sharks who grow rich by preying on the poor. At that time, I never imagined that one day microcredit would give rise to its own breed of loan sharks."

Muhammad Yunus (2011, p.A23)

Background

In most developing countries, the low penetration of the banking system and a limited financial inclusion are the main reasons that motivate vulnerable individuals to resort to high cost informal and semi-formal financial market (Leslie and Hood, 2009). During the last two decades, the performance of the Grameen Bank (Yunus, 2003) has promoted microfinance as one of the most important tools to combat poverty through financing micro-enterprises' start-up capital. This strategy, coupled with greater economic development at community level and through women empowerment, has been endorsed by the World Bank and other international organizations that directly or indirectly support microfinance institutions (MFIs). The merit of the microfinance schemes is to provide an avenue to credit and savings services to those people who have no access to the formal financial sector.

Some recent studies (Ditcher and Harper, 2007) critique MFIs commercial lending and point out the limitations of these schemes because of their large-scale implementation that seems to respond to an inertial phenomenon rather than being based on rigorous evidence. Also, MFIs when seeking their financial sustainability through services' commercialization can end up harming clients, because of the spillover effects and aggressive marketing techniques (Bateman, 2010). Thus, even though microfinance at its inception represented a financial alternative to moneylenders for a significant part of the population, little has been done to avoid that (some of) these institutions providing financial services with a marketing-tailored-social-label would replace them. That is to say, predatory lending practices implemented by some MFIs have led clients to a debt trap, sometimes with tragic consequences.

In most countries predatory practices have not been addressed from a legal point of view; this is why the lack of regulations is probably the most important element that contributes to the proliferation of such practices (Stark, 2005).

Due to the difficulty of framing these practices, since 2008 the Smart Campaign organized by the Consultative Group to Assist the Poor (CGAP, 2010, 2011a, 2011b) is intended to spread the Consumer Protection Principles (CPPs) to the MFIs. CPPs are a set of principles that MFIs should follow in order to improve ethics and transparency while offering microfinance products.

Predatory Lending and Microfinance

The term "predatory lending" refers to those practices that through manipulation or providing incomplete information provide benefits to the lender when exploiting the borrower's lack of knowledge regarding the loan terms. In this case, because the loan contract disproportionately favours the lender, the problems faced by the borrower to repay the debt significantly undermine his wealth and welfare (U.S. Department of Housing and Urban Development [US-HUD], 2001; Morgan, 2007).

Predatory lenders exploit the gaps in financial legislation through tailoring credit contracts. Accordingly, predatory lending characteristics modify continuously; a situation that hampers establishing a definition of these (predatory) practices that have been mostly acknowledged in mortgages market, payday loans, money lending, pawn broking and credit sales (US-HUD, 2001). The most common practices in credit contracts consist of:

(*i*) structuring loans that result in a seriously disproportionate net harm to borrowers; (*ii*) charging excessive interest rates and fees compared to the risk of the borrower; (*iii*) loans involve fraud; (*iv*) lack of transparency; (*v*) loans involving waiving legal redress; (*vi*) lending discrimination, and (*vii*) servicing abuses (Drury, 2009, pp.139-140). Often, predatory loans are granted without an appropriate check of the credit quality of the potential borrower, and by using different methods to persuade consumers to underwrite the loan (Reiss, 2009). Additionally, those borrowers with a poor financial education cannot anticipate the costly financial consequences of the debt (Carrand Kolluri, 2001, Carr and Schuetz, 2001, Leslie and Hood, 2009).

Because predatory practices can be performed during the process of granting credit, the concern that MFIs may resort to them for achieving a higher market share or higher benefits, is actually an important issue. According to the literature, even though a more competitive market advocates for a reduction of these practices (Bond, Musto, and Yilmaz, 2005), it is a fact that they have lasted through different institutional changes because of their characteristics. Additionally, competition may help to wipe out these practices when clients may also realize they are being implemented, but this will depend on people having specific knowledge and understanding about the financial products.

However, it is important to consider that often MFIs are providing their services in those regions where formal financial alternatives are scarce or where people cannot access them. As a consequence, the mix of borrowers' lack of knowledge, the need of funding and predatory lending practices might be leading people to a significant over-indebtedness posing a high debt burden on the personal or family financial budget.

The fact that competition might not be the ultimate solution to client over-indebtedness is represented by the recent news from Andhra Pradesh (India), one of the Indian States with a higher MFIs' density, where several suicides driven by debt owed to MFIs posed a caution note on MFIs' predatory/commercial behaviour. Apparently, despite the competition, the demand for financial services was still large enough to allow that the greed of some MFIs could be manifested.

A note of caution is needed; indeed, competition may help to reduce predatory practices, but it will not be enough to solve the problem.

Financial Education

According to the Organisation for Economic Cooperation and Development (OECD, 2005:13), financial education consists of:

> "(...) the processes, by which financial consumers/investors improve their understanding of financial products and concepts and, through information, instruction and/or objective advice, develop the skills and confidence to become more aware of financial risks and opportunities, to make informed choices, to know where to go for help, and to take other effective actions to improve their financial well-being."

The lack of financial education has been detected in several countries (OECD, 2005; Orton, 2007; Mendel, 2009), but this situation is particularly severe among women and people with low and middle education (Lusardi and Mitchell, 2006), among youths, elderly and low incomes sectors (Anderson, Zhan, and Scott, 2004; OECD, 2005, Lusardi, 2008; Agarwal, Driscoll, Gabaix, and Laibson, 2009). This is why governments established financial education programmes aimed at disseminating financial knowledge among the most vulnerable people (Vitt *et al.*, 2000), informing about the consequences of long-term indebtedness (Cohen and Sebstad, 2003), financing and investment options available to households (Maki, 2004) and providing information about predatory practices (Todd, 2002; Lucey and Giannangelo, 2006). Having financial knowledge has been associated with higher savings (Bernheim, Garrett, and Maki, 2001, Moore *et al.*, 2001) and lower outstanding debt (Elliehausen, Lundquist, and Staten, 2007).

Financial education can be easily confused with consumer protection because they both share the same goal: improving people's financial wellbeing. However, they are different concepts because consumer protection, through regulation and legislation, seeks to establish minimum standards of compliance in the financial sector, providing comprehensive, adequate and comparable information on prices, terms and conditions of financial products and services. It also achieves its purposes through providing mechanisms for addressing complaints and resolving disputes, and to respect the privacy in the handling of personal financial information. In contrast, financial education is intended, through education and counselling, to help consumers making informed decisions (OECD, 2005; Rutledge, 2010). In other words, the regulation related with consumer protection can avoid some wrong decisions, but it does not give them the faculty to make right decisions (H.M. Treasury, 2007); it follows that financial education and consumer protection complement each other.

Predatory Microfinance

Because predatory practices were widely known in financial markets under different kinds of fraudulent behaviours, it should have not been a surprise that they were spreading in the microfinance sector too. Since 2008, an organized effort at international level has been made in order to "[CPPs] promote ways for microfinance providers to (...) treat clients fairly and respectfully while avoiding practices that might harm them" (CGAP, 2010, p. 3). The seven CPPs* are summarized below:

Appropriate Product Design and Delivery: MFIs financial products should be designed and delivered according to the client characteristics and avoid harming clients because of their use.

Avoidance of Over-indebtedness: Interest payment on outstanding loan is the MFI's main source of income; thus, microfinance officers by increasing the amount lent will increase expected revenues. Of course, to the extent the debt increases, the default likelihood tends to grow too; so, it is imperative to carefully analyze customers' real repayment capacity, taking into account the existence of any undeclared debts. In order to avoid over-indebtedness customers also have the responsibility to develop their financial knowledge while carefully analyzing their financial needs.

---

* Readers may access the original document (CGAP, 2010, p. 3) and later various (CGAP, 2011a, 2011b) for a detailed discussion. The list is continuously updated and the one presented in this chapter refers to July 2011.

Transparency: All necessary informations needed by customers in order to understand the real cost of credit must be available. The data must be broken down properly and for any text-based-information an understandable language to customers must be used. MFIs should avoid providing important information and specific contract terms in small font size.

Responsible Pricing: The cost of services provided by the MFI should both allow the sustainability of the institution and being affordable to customers.

Responsible Treatment of Clients: Because some MFIs have implemented particularly aggressive selling practices, it is suggested that MFI's employees adhere to the company's ethical code. At the same time, the company will limit those compensation arrangements that may encourage employees' unethical behaviours.

Effective Complaint Resolution: MFIs looking to provide a better service according to customers' needs should implement mechanisms aimed at resolving users' problems and disagreements.

Privacy of Client Data: If each country, according to the institutional framework as well as the clients' will, MFIs can use and share clients' personal information within the established limits.

Most of the issues above suggest that some MFIs are performing several activities that might be very similar to predatory lending. Nevertheless, the CGAP paper as well as its subsequent revisions (CGAP, 2010, 2011a), do not mention the word "predatory" even once. Perhaps, the negative connotation of the term [predatory] could overshadow those brokering activities which have been extensively supported and financed by international organizations. If so, it could be embarrassing being jammed in the discussion about the meaning (and perception) of credit and debt as mentioned in Ditcher (2007). This is why it would be wise to avoid linking a negative adjective to an international approved strategy for poverty reduction. Nevertheless, it seems that the main poverty reduction tool certainly requires some adjustments to avoid previously unexpected (but actually detected and proved) spillover effects due to the incentives incompatibility.

The role and objectives of the relationship between MFIs and shareholders put forward two problems:

- A coordination problem among MFIs; and
- An incentive compatibility problem (between the MFIs and shareholders).

Coordination Problem

Which MFI is ready to take the first step toward transparency? Because those institutions that begin a process of information disclosure may be vulnerable to competitors, they will be discouraged to do so unilaterally, and no institution would opt to disclose its information (equilibrium without transparency). In this sense, the initiative of CGAP by setting up a critical mass of institutions who jointly implement information disclosure (i.e. a sort of policy) could reduce costs and making it viable, where reputation costs would push MFIs to adhere to it. Such change can trigger MFIs from a non-transparent equilibrium to a transparent equilibrium that ultimately benefits both institutions and clients.

Incentive Problems

Despite the pro-poor microfinance label, several MFIs are ultimately nothing more than a business seeking profit. In other words, MFIs are organizations that receive resources (primarily external funding: sometimes from donors but recently from shareholders and through IPOs , i.e., Banco Compartamos (Mexico in 2007) that after being packed as microloans are sold to clients who repay the debt through monthly payments.

Accordingly, MFIs must take into account that accessing funds is possible when they are able to offer an attractive rate of return to prospective shareholders. Undoubtedly, MFIs' portfolio management strategies reflect the financial results of the institution that, nevertheless, could benefit from implementing predatory practices. Indeed, shareholders' evaluation regarding MFIs potential growth rate takes place, besides quantitative ratios and forecasts, through analyzing qualitative market strategies. Aggressive market strategies may have volatile results but they may be also attractive to shareholders.

Predatory Lending *vs.* High Cost Lending

Although predatory lending usually charges high interest rates, high-cost credit is not necessarily predatory. Of course, even though MFIs provide credit at a lower rate than other informal lenders (i.e., loan sharks), this does not mean that MFI's loans are cheap. In fact, the interest rate charged by the MFI is based on its operating costs that are generally high due to the small size of the loans and in order to reach borrowers. In the absence of subsidized funding provided to the MFI, interest rates could be even higher but, from the clients' perspective, interest rates do not constitute a problem because of the profitability of business activities financed through loans.

Interest rates ceilings to prevent institutions charging high credit cost have not provided the expected effect because under these conditions MFIs have restricted microcredit supply or they have shown less transparency in lending with the purpose to increase the cost of the credit (Helms and Reille, 2004).

Consumers' Vulnerability

Since the 1960s, the literature reported that in the United States economically disadvantaged market segments were being discriminated through higher prices for lower quality products. Also, sellers adopted different price and financing strategies in order to elude the laws (for are view of the literature see Hill, 2002). Even though low income people, for its very same condition, have been vulnerable to being exploited, from a broader perspective, Baker, Gentry and Rustenburg (2005, pp. 129-131) indicate that the vulnerability is associated with individual characteristics (i.e., biophysical and psychosocial), situations that may temporary or permanently affect them (i.e., change in family structure), and other external conditions (i.e., stigmatization, discrimination). According to this view, any consumer can be considered as vulnerable because "[Consumer vulnerability] (...) arises from an imbalance in marketplace interactions (...) creating a dependence on external factors to create fairness in the marketplace" (Baker *et al.*, 2005, p. 134).

Ethics in Marketing Financial Products

Recently, some companies and corporations turned their attention to market segments that have been traditionally considered as vulnerable—women, children and the elderly—emphasizing the importance of ethics in marketing (Macchiette and Roy, 1994; Hill, 2002). In order to discern about the ethical implications of marketing strategies, Cui and Choudhury (2003) have proposed to combine three factors: market selection, the nature of the product and consumer characteristics. According to this framework, the loan—which is the most important product of the microfinance institution—is provided to a specific market target. Also, loans may be inherently harmful in case of misuse that may drive people to over-indebtedness, and clients can be vulnerable if demonstrating lower repayment likelihood. This combination is associated with predatory marketing practices that seek to promote credits that may affect customers' welfare (Carr and Kolluri, 2001). In this case, the lack of financial education, as well as low income and low savings levels, may be associated with over-indebtedness due to the overestimation of repayment capacity (Stegman and Faris, 2003; Peterson, 2004). Moreover, borrowers with these characteristics tend to underestimate the cost of credit in the short run (Stango and Zinman, 2007), a situation that can be strategically exploited by lenders and sellers who benefit by hiding relevant information or through price discrimination (Palmer and Conaty, 2002; Gabaix and Laibson, 2006; Stango and Zinman, 2011).

The predatory loan brokers' *modus operandi* is based on gaining the trust of the customers being courteous, available and by providing the resources quickly, but omitting the details and other contract terms. After signing the contract, when borrowers start asking additional information or when some payments are due, the lender reveals its predatory intentions (Hill and Kozup, 2007).

In order to eradicate these practices, that cannot be wiped off through the institutional framework only (Karpatkin, 1999), the implementation of an ethics code that make morally responsible those organizations that, even without violating the law, apply such marketing strategies (Laczniak, 1999; Delgadillo, Erickson, and Piercy, 2008; Laczniak, 2008), may largely benefit the market.

According to this view, the effort carried on by the CGAP to promote the CPP might have the success expected.

In Mexico, it has been recognized the vulnerability of consumers in the pre-contractual and contractual phase with financial institutions. Accordingly, some steps have been taken in order to reduce such exposure by modifying the Federal Consumer Protection Law that through the Law for the Protection and Defense of Financial Service Users, seeks to protect borrowers and financial sector users. From a policy perspective the implications are important, because financial intermediaries should respond for "(...) the explicit but also implicit [contract] terms when offering banking products and services, and (in case of) a lack of truthfulness in what has been promised (...) the satisfaction or dissatisfaction with the duty of pre-contractual information will be relevant to determine, according to the circumstances of each case, the extent of liability of the issuer (of the credit card)" (Cuarto Tribunal Colegiado en Materia Civil del Primer Circuito, 2010, pp. 2-3). Thus, lenders might be voluntarily using an unfair advantage over clients for their own benefit. In fact, as recognized by the same Mexican civil court: "(...) there is an imbalance (...) rooted in the position of the entrepreneur [lender] and the consumer [borrower] (...) the former is advantaged because of his organized seduction and control of information and the latter is doubly confused: because of the surprise [of being cheated](...) and his lack of information (...)"(Cuarto Tribunal Colegiado en Materia Civil del Primer Circuito, 2010, p. 2).

Again, the lack of financial education coupled with predatory lending strategies make people vulnerable to over-indebtedness, a situation that might be benefiting only financial intermediaries when loans are backed up by any financial collateral or joint liability.

Concluding Remarks

Research on predatory loans has focused on developed countries that, paradoxically, are those equipped with a legislative framework that allow for greater consumer protection. Thus, in developing countries it should be expected that the proliferation of these practices may find a fertile soil where to grow.

In these countries, limited financial inclusion forced people to rely to informal finance schemes; so, MFIs turned out to be an alternative to loan sharks.

Unfortunately, as Yunus (2011) recently referred to, MFIs are not immune from tantalizing profit-seeking practices. Indeed, the establishment and dissemination of the CPPs by the CGAP show that they are clearly carried out to the detriment of customers who can fall into a debt trap.

It is difficult to define predatory lending practices in legal terms because of their continuously changing features. However, in moral terms, the definition is linked to the intention to carrying out any fraudulent action intended to bias the outcome of the market to favour lender's profits. Accordingly, moral standards could be helpful to avoid that a poverty relief tool like microfinance being conducive to augment economic polarization.

REFERENCES

Agarwal, S.; Driscoll, J.C.; Gabaix, X.; and Laibson, D. (2009), *The Age of Reason: Financial Decisions over the Lifecycle*. Retrieved on April 2nd, 2010 from: http://ssrn.com/abstract=973790.

Anderson, S.G.; Zhan, M.; and Scott, J. (2004), Targeting Financial Management Training at Low-Income Audiences: Bits Briefs and Applications. *Journal of Consumer Affairs*, 38(1), pp. 167-177.

Baker, S.M.; Gentry, J.W.; and Rittenburg, T.L. (2005), Building Understanding of the Domain of Consumer Vulnerability.*Journal of Macromarketing*, 25(2), pp. 128-139.

Bateman, M. (2010), *Why Doesn't Microfinance Work?* London: Zed Books.

Bernheim, B.D.; Garrett, D.M.; and Maki, D.M. (2001), Education and Saving: The Long-Term Effects of High School Financial Curriculum Mandates. *Journal of Public Economics*, 80(3), pp. 435-465.

Bond, P.; Musto, D.K.; and Yilmaz, B. (2005), *Predatory Lending in a Rational World*. Working Paper No. 06, Federal Reserve Bank of Philadelphia.

Carr, J.H., and Kolluri, L. (2001), *Predatory Lending: An Overview*. Fannie Mae Foundation.

Carr, J.H., and Schuetz, J. (2001), Financial Services in Distressed Communities: Framing the Issue. *Finding Solutions*. Fannie Mae Foundation.

Cohen. M., and Sebstad, J. (2003), *Financial Education for the Poor*. (Working Paper No. 1). Washington, D.C.: Microfinance Opportunities.

Consultive Group to Assist the Poor [CGAP]. (2010), *Proposed Revised Client Protection Principles*. Washington, DC: CGAP/The World Bank.

Consultive Group to Assist the Poor [CGAP]. (2011a), *Implementing the*

Client Protection Principles. (Draft for Public Comment, March 2011), The Smart Campaign. Washington, DC: CGAP/The World Bank.

Consultive Group to Assist the Poor [CGAP]. (2011b), *The Smart Campaign Adds Seventh Client Protection Principle*. Press Release on July 20th, 2011.

Cuarto Tribunal Colegiado en Materia Civil del Primer Circuito (2010), Tarjetas de crédito. Aplicación de las teorías del contratante débil y de publicidad en fase precontractual para determinar la responsabilidad de la entidad emisora. *Semanario Judicial de la Federación y su Gaceta* XXXI (Enero), Tesis: I.4o.C.193.C, p. 2241.

Cui, G., and Choudhury, P. (2003), Consumer Interests and the Ethical Implications of Marketing: A Contingency Framework. *The Journal of Consumer Affairs*, 37(2), pp. 364-387.

Delgadillo, L.M.; Erickson, L.V.; and Piercy, K.W. (2008), Disentangling the Differences between Abusive and Predatory Lending: Professionals' Perspectives.*The Journal of Consumer Affairs*, 42(3), pp. 313-334.

Dichter, T. (2007), Can microcredit make an already slippery slope more slippery? Some lessons form the social meaning of debt. In: T. Dichter and M. Harper (Eds.). *What's Wrong with Microfinance?* (pp. 9-20). Bourton on Dunsmore: Practical Action Publishing.

Dichter, T., and Harper M. (Eds.).*What's Wrong with Microfinance?* Bourton on Dunsmore: Practical Action Publishing.

Drury, L.L. III. (2009), Predatory Lending and Its Impact on Consumer Credit. *Loyola Journal of Public Interest Law*, 10(2), pp. 137-148.

Elliehausen, G.; Lundquist E.C.; and Staten, M.E. (2007), The Impact of Credit Counselling on Subsequent Borrower Behaviour. *Journal of Consumer Affairs*, 41(1), pp. 1-28.

Gabaix, X., and Laibson, D. (2006), Shrouded Attributes, Consumer Myopia, and Information Suppression in Competitive Markets. *Quarterly Journal of Economics*, 121(2), pp. 505-540.

Helms, B. and Reille, X. (2004), Interest Rate Ceilings and Microfinance: The Story So Far (Occasional Paper No. 9), CGAP.

Hill, R.P. (2002), Stalking the Poverty Consumer: A Retrospective Examination of Modern Ethical Dilemmas, *Journal of Business Ethics*, 37(2), pp. 209-219.

Hill, R.P., and Kozup, J.C. (2007), Consumer Experiences with Predatory Lending Practices.*The Journal of Consumer Affairs*, 41(1), pp. 29-46.

H.M. Treasury. (2007), *Financial Capability: The Government's Long-Term Approach*. London: HMSO.

Karpatkin, R.H. (1999), Toward a Fair and Just Marketplace for All Consumers: The Responsibilities of Marketing Professionals. *Journal of Public Policy and Marketing*, 18(1), pp. 118-122.

Laczniak, G.R. (1999), Distributive Justice, Catholic Social Teaching, and the Moral Responsibility of Marketers. *Journal of Public Policy and Marketing*, 18(1), pp. 125-129.

Laczniak, G.R. (2008), Ethics of Marketing.In R.W. Kolb (Ed.) *Encyclopedia of Business Ethics and Society*. (pp.1336-1343). London: Sage Publications, Inc.

Leslie, C., and Hood, A. (2009), *Circling the Loan Shark*. London: New Local Government Network.

Lucey, T.A., and Giannangelo, D.M. (2006), Short Changed: The Importance of Facilitating Equitable Financial Education in Urban Society. *Education and Urban Society*, 38(3), pp. 268-287.

Lusardi, A. (2008), Financial Literacy: An Essential Tool for Informed Consumer Choice? (Working Paper UCC08-11). Joint Center for Housing Studies.Harvard University.

Lusardi, A., and Mitchell, O.S. (2006), Financial Literacy and Planning: Implications for Retirement Wellbeing. (Working Paper No. 2006-01).The Pension Research Council.The Wharton School of the University of Pennsylvania.

Macchiette, B., and Roy, A. (1994), Sensitive Groups and Social Issues. *Journal of Consumer Marketing*, 11(4), pp. 55-64.

Maki, D. (2004), Financial Education and Private Pensions. In W. Gale, J. Shoven, and M. Warshowsky (Eds.). *Private Pensions and Public Policies*. (pp. 126-139). Washington, D.C.: Brookings Institution Press.

Mandell, L. (2009), The Financial Literacy of Young American Adults—Results of the 2008 National Jump Start Coalition Survey of High School Seniors and College. University of Washington and the Aspen Institute.

Moore, A.; Beverly, S.; Schreiner, M.; Sherraden, M.; Lombe, M.; Cho, E.Y.N.; Johnson, L.; *et al.* (2001), Saving IDA Programmes and Effects of IDAs: A Survey of Participants Center for Social Development Washington University in St. Louis.

Morgan, D.P. (2007), Defining and Detecting Predatory Lending. (Staff Report No. 273). New York: Federal Reserve Bank of New York.

Organisation for Economic Cooperation and Development [OECD]. (2005), *Improving Financial Literacy—Analysis of Issues and Policies*. Paris: Organisation for Economic Cooperation and Development Publications.

Orton, L. (2007), *Financial Literacy: Lessons from International Experience*. Research Report. Ottawa: Canadian Policy Research Network.

Palmer, H., and Conaty, P. (2002), *Profiting from Poverty. Why Debt is a Big Business in Britain*. London: New Economics Foundation.

Peterson, C.L. (2004), *Taming the Sharks—Towards a Cure for the High-Cost Credit Market.* Akron, OH: The University of Akron Press.

Reiss, D.J. (2009), Regulation of Subprime and Predatory Lending. International Encyclopedia of Housing and Home, 2010; Brooklyn Law School, Legal Studies Paper No. 142. Retrieved on December 10th, 2010 from SSRN: http://ssrn.com/abstract=1371728

Rutledge, S.L. (2010), Consumer Protection and Financial Literacy: Lessons from Nine Country Studies. (*Policy Research Working Paper Series No. 5326*). Washington, D.C.: The World Bank.

Stango, V., and Zinman, J. (2007), Fuzzy Math and Red Ink: When the Opportunity Cost of Consumption is Not What it Seems. (Working Paper). Dartmouth College.

Stango, V., and Zinman, J. (2011), Fuzzy Math. Disclosure Regulation, and Credit Market Outcomes: Evidence from Truth-in-Lending Reform. *The Review of Financial Studies*, 24(2), 506-534.

Stark, D.P. (2005), Unmasking the predatory loan in Sheep's Clothing: Legislative Proposal. *Harvard BlackLetter Law Journal*, 21, 129-162.

Stegman, M.A., and Faris, R. (2003), Payday Lending: A Business Model that Encourages Chronic Borrowing. *Economic Development Quarterly*, 17(1), 8-32.

Todd, R.M. (2002), Financial Literacy Education: A Potential Tool for Reducing Predatory Lending? *The Region*, 16(4), 6-9. 34-36, Federal Reserve Bank of Minneapolis.

U.S. Department of Housing and Urban Development [US-HUD]. (2001), *Curbing Predatory Home Mortgage Lending*. Washington. D.C.: HUD-Treasury Task Force on Predatory Lending.

Vitt, L.A.; Anderson, C.; Kent, J.; Lyter, D.M.; Siegenthaler, J.K.; and Ward, J. (2000), Personal Finance and the Rush to Competence:Financial Literacy Education in the U.S.. Middleburg: Institute for Socio-Financial Studies for the Fannie Mae Foundation.

Yunus, M. (2003), *Banker to the Poor: Micro-Lending and the Battle Against World Poverty*. New York: Public Affairs.

Yunus, M. (2011), Sacrificing Microcredit for Megaprofits. *New York Times*, January 15th, 2011, page A23. Retrieved on September 8th, 2011 from: http://www.nytimes.com/2011/01/15/opinion/15yunus.html

15

Microfinance in India : Various Policy Measures and their Implementation

KOMPALLI SASI KUMAR

Introduction

In this twenty-first century, we must take along an active people-centred and growth-oriented poverty alleviation strategy—a strategy which seems to incorporate women's aspirations, dynamism and involvement. It is envisaged that self-help groups will play a vital role in such strategy. But there is a need for structural orientation of the groups to suit the requirements of new business.

Micro credit movement has to be viewed from a long-term perspective under SHG framework, which underlines the need for deliberate policy implications in favour of assurance in terms of technology back-up, product market and human resource development. Hence, there is a need for the development of an innovative and diversified micro-finance sector, which will make a real contribution to women empowerment.

Approaches of Financial Inclusion

A Committee on Financial Inclusion, with Dr. C. Rangarajan as Chairman, has also been constituted by the Government of India in June 2006, to recommend a strategy to achieve higher financial inclusion in the country.

According to C. Rangarajan there are six approaches in the system of Financial Inclusion, they are, as follows:

- ✓ First, credit to the farmer households is one of the important elements of Financial inclusion among them providing credit to the marginal and sub-marginal farmers as well as other small borrowers is crucial to the need of the hour.
- ✓ Second, rural branches must go beyond providing credit and extend a helping hand in terms of advice on a wide variety of matters relating to agriculture.
- ✓ Third, in district where population per branch is much higher than the national average commercial banks may be encouraged to open the branches.
- ✓ Fourth, there is need for the simplification of the procedures in relation to granting of loans to small borrowers.
- ✓ Fifth, the further strengthening the SHG-Bank Linkage Programme (BLP), as it has proved to be an effective way of providing credit to very small borrowers.
- ✓ Sixth, the business facilitator and correspondent model needs to be effectively implemented.

RBI and GoI move towards Financial Inclusion

Historically, the Reserve Bank of India (RBI) and the Government of India (GoI) have been making efforts to increase banking penetration in the country. Some of these measures include the creation of State Bank of India in 1955; nationalization of commercial banks in 1969 and 1980; initiating the Lead Bank Scheme in 1970; establishing Regional Rural Banks (RRBs) in 1975.

Introducing a Self-Help Group (SHG)-Bank Linkage Programme in 1992

In November 2005, banks were advised to make available a basic banking "no-frills" account with low or nil minimum stipulated balances as well as charges to expand the outreach of such accounts to vast sections of the population.

In order to ensure that persons belonging to low income group, both in urban and rural areas do not encounter difficulties in opening bank accounts owing to procedural hassles, to know your customer (KYC) procedures for opening accounts has been simplified. The Reserve Bank has directed banks to make available all printed material used by retail customers in English, Hindi and the concerned regional language.

More recently, in January 2006, banks were permitted to utilize the services of non-governmental organizations (NGOs/SHGs), micro-finance institutions and other civil society organizations as intermediaries in providing financial and banking services through the use of business facilitator and business correspondent models.

To extend hassle-free credit to bank customers in rural areas, the guidelines on General Credit Card (GCC) schemes were simplified to enable customers' access credit on simplified terms and conditions, without insistence on security, purpose or end-use of credit. With a view of providing hassle free credit to customers, banks were allowed to issue general credit cards.

A simplified mechanism for one-time settlement of loans with principal amount up to Rs. 25,000 which have become doubtful and loss assets as on September 30, 2005 was suggested for adoption. Banks have been specifically advised that borrowers with loans settled under the one time settlement scheme will be eligible to reassess the formal financial system for fresh credit.

The Reserve Bank has also been periodically issuing guidelines on public grievance redressal mechanism in banks, including constitution of Customer Service Centres for ensuring improvements in quality of service rendered. In the Reserve Bank, the Customer Service Department has recently been constituted to, *inter alia;* serve as the interface between customers and banks. Moreover, the Government of India has also expressed its explicit concern on the issue of overall inclusion in the development process through its various initiatives such as the *Rural Employment Guarantee* Scheme.

Current Indian Scenario

Bank nationalization in India marked a *paradigm shift* in the focus of banking as it was intended to shift the focus from class banking to mass banking. The rationale for creating Regional Rural Banks was also to take the banking services to poor people. The branches of commercial banks and the RRBs have increased from 8,321 in the year 1969 to 68,282 branches as at the end of March 2005.

The average population per branch office has decreased from 64,000 to 16,000 during the same period. The new Branch Authorization Policy of Reserve Bank encourages banks to open branches in these under banked States and the under banked areas in other States. The new policy also places a lot of emphasis on the efforts made by the Bank to achieve, *inter alia*, financial inclusion and other policy objectives. But the study of Distribution of Commercial Bank Branches—Region/State/Union Territory.

According to the information available with the Reserve Bank of India, about 5 lakh no-frill accounts, with and without value-added features, have been opened until March 31, 2006, of which about two-third are with the public sector and one-third with the private sector banks.

Though the RBI promoted no-frills savings bank account, had all the potential to revolutionize India's rural agricultural economy, as well as usher in the banking habit amongst a large number of the less privileged population. The product was lost among a myriad of financial offerings and most banks have shown little verve and vitality in marketing it and banking continues to remain an elitist to lower middle-class pursuit, restricted mainly to urban India. Population Group-wise Distribution of Deposits and Credits of Scheduled Commercial Banks shows that the percentage share of deposits is on the decline, in rural and semi-urban and urban areas. In contrast, the share in metropolitan areas has been rising continuously. The share of credit is lower than that of deposits in all regions except metropolitan, implying that resources get intermediated into metropolitan areas. This clearly brings out bank's 'aspiration to earn good margins by investing funds into high potential areas, instead of strictly abiding by the RBI norm of priority sector lending to under-developed and undeveloped areas. Even after RBI's emphasis to promote financial inclusion it is very surprising to see, that, rural area contributed only 10.8 per cent and semi-rural areas 14.4 per cent of the total deposits collected in March 2006. This reiterates the need to expand and consolidate the banking network and to adopt innovative measure to mobilize funds.

The Distribution of Commercial Bank Branches in India – Bank Group and Population Group-wise clearly shows the dispersion of branches among rural, semi-urban, urban and metropolitan areas, by the various bank groups. It is evident that RRBs (80 per cent) and Local banks (66.6 per cent) branches are in rural and semi-urban areas, they are followed by State Bank group (67 per cent); other nationalized banks (59 per cent); private banks (42.8 per cent), whereas the foreign banks seem to be concentrating only on urban and metropolitan areas (99.6 per cent) and just have 0.4 per cent branches in rural and semi-urban areas.

Major Hindrances to Financial Inclusion

The interaction with the NGOs and the SHGs brought to light underpinning problems of financial inclusion, which are briefly stated as under:

- **Poverty:** Being on a low income, especially out of work and on benefits.
- **Ignorance:** Low levels of awareness and understanding of products caused by lack of appropriate marketing or low levels of financial literacy.
- **Environment:** Lack of access to financial services caused by several factors, including geographic access to bank branches or remote banking facilities; affordability of products such as insurance, where premiums often price out those living in the most deprived and risky areas; suitability of products like current accounts, which offer an overdraft and an easy route to debt.
- Cultural and psychological barriers, such as language, perceived / actual racism and suspicion or fear of financial institutions.

The lack of access by certain segments of the society to appropriate, low-cost, fair and safe financial products and services from mainstream providers actually results in *Financial Exclusion*. This is a critical policy concern, because the options for operating a household budget, or a micro / small enterprise, without mainstream financial services can often be expensive. This process becomes self-reinforcing and can often be an important factor in social exclusion, especially for communities with limited access to financial products, particularly in rural areas.

The Model for Financial Inclusion

Deepening the financial system and widening its reach is crucial for both accelerating growth and for equitable distribution, given the present state of development of our country. After analyzing in depth the underpinning reasons of financial exclusion in India and going through the success stories of UK and USA, and interacting with NGOs mainly operating in different States of central India, it becomes obvious that we have to continue with our tireless endeavour to combat monsters like illiteracy, poverty, ignorance, cultural and psychological hurdles and simultaneously design innovative, lucrative and low cost banking products and services to lure public, to join the mainstream. Need was felt to reorient the attitudes of the operating staff to make them appreciate the benefits of extending the reach to wider sections of the society. The model discussed below will be instrumental in bringing hundred per cent financial inclusion in our country.

Awareness Camps for Masses

Intensive awareness, education and promotion drive to create an in-depth impact on the masses.

- Government should promote introduction of basic banking—relevance, services, merits as a topic in secondary and higher secondary classes in all education institutions.
- Government sponsored publicity campaigns through all medias—radio; television; newspapers; Rythu Bazaars (A.P. Government Initiative), Marketing Yards, Agricultural Farmers Meeting, e-choupal (ITC Limited initiative); village Panchayat; movies; local stage shows, etc.
- Banks should design and organize aggressive education-cum-promotion campaigns in unbanked parts of urban, semi-urban and rural areas to enhance financial literacy and awareness, as well as to remove the doubts and apprehensions that the masses have towards the banking sector.
- Banks should involve the knowledgeable and well-informed local inhabitants in such activities. This will help the banks to consolidate and ensure, prompt and extensive response from populace.
- Banks should gather support from the NGOs, retired bank personnels, and academic institutions, to reach the desired numbers within a limited span of time.

Once the fallacy is removed from the minds of the general public, they automatically will join the mainstream. The all-round awareness and education simulation will drive them to open savings and current accounts. This will mark the beginning of basic banking in true sense.

Inculcating Financial Discipline to Masses through Banking

The banks need to adopt a considerate approach towards this new clientele, to remove their qualms and disbeliefs. It is necessary that the basic banking should be comprehensive in scope and have attractive USPs that can lure people at large:

- All banks should allow no frill accounts, i.e., savings accounts which can be opened with a nominal amount of Rs. 5 or even with zero balance like State Bank of India initiative of Opening Savings Bank Account with Rs. 10.They should allow 6-7 withdrawals in the accounting period and should not restrict the number of deposits.
- RBI along with banks should toil hard to reduce the amount of paper work in relation to the opening of an account as well as in getting small credits. This would reduce the complexity and also speed up the processing at banks.
- Banks should make sure that local people are positioned in the front offices, so that the general public does not have to endure with language problem and does not have to suffer perceived/actual racial discrimination.
- It is all the more necessary for the banks that besides offering the conventional products and services they should set up teams who can understand the needs and requirements of the common man and design innovative products and services having greater suitability and desirability. Also banks should work as one stop store and offer diversified products in banking and insurance.
- Despite the risk, financing of first time entrepreneurs is a must for financial inclusion and growth. Banks should arrange and provide technical advice for these entrepreneurs. They will have to tone up their risk assessment and risk management capacities, and provide for these facilities.

- Banks should give free financial counsel to low-income households and small entrepreneurs.
- The pricing of the product should be also done keeping in mind the pockets of the potential clientele. The cost burden should proportionately be shifted to high potential sectors, who can afford a little upswing in their banking cost.

New Plans for Inclusion

Basic banking itself needs to be supported by innovative strategies, in order to improve the reach and reduce the operating cost of the banks. The aim of these strategies is to promote the banks in maintaining an arm's length relationship with this new clientele.

- Infrastructure sharing amongst banks and other organizations will help in lowering the operating cost and thus the cost benefit can be transferred to customers. And also, use of cloud computing techniques will help the banks extensively in sharing the networks and operations.
- Bank should open small extension counters at organization providing public utility services such as local schools, primary health care centres, village *mandies*, farmers' associations, cold storages and warehouses, railway stations, bus stations and bus stops, etc.
- This should simultaneously be supplemented by mobile banks. Wherever it is not economical to set up a branch, credit camps/loan *melas* must be organized on weekly basis, to disburse the funds.
- Greater use of technology should be made by the banks to improve their reach, speed of processing, as well as to cut down the operating cost.

Last but not the least the Government of India should initiate a "civil rights law" prohibiting discrimination by banks against low and moderate income neighbourhoods. This will create a pressure on banks to play an important role in bringing financial inclusion in the country.

This model will result in improved financial literacy; make banking enter into the daily routine of the masses; broaden the deposit base; wider disbursement of credits, larger number of transactions. Jointly it will lead to formalized and systematic banking; faster economic growth; new employment opportunities in the society and financial as well as social inclusion.

Conclusion

As poverty levels decline and households have greater levels of discretionary incomes, they will be first time financial savers. They will, therefore, need to have easy access to formal financial systems to get into the banking habit. Banks will need to innovate and devise newer methods of including such customers into their fold.

The micro-credit and the Self Help Group movements are in their infancy and they still need to gather force. Innovation in the form of business facilitators and correspondents will be needed for banks to increase their outreach for banks to ensure financial inclusion. New entrants to the banking system need households at their doorstep. There has been a burst of entrepreneurship across the country, spanning rural, semi-urban and urban areas. This has to be nurtured and financed. It is only through growth of enterprises across all sizes that competition will be fostered.

To conclude, that with increasing liberalization and higher economic growth, the role of banking sector is poised to increase in the financing pattern of economic activities within the country. To meet the growing credit demand, the banks need to mobilize resources from a wider deposit base and extend credit to activities hitherto not financed by banks. The trend of increasing commercialization of agriculture and rural activities should generate greener pastures, and banks should examine the benefits of increasing penetration therein. Financial inclusion will strengthen financial deepening and provide resources to the banks to expand credit delivery.

REFERENCES

Connolly, C., and K. Hajaj (2001), *"Financial Services and Social Exclusion"*, Financial Services Consumer Policy Center, University of New South Wales.

Economic Growth, *Financial Deepening and Financial Inclusion* by Dr. Rakish Mohan, Annual Bankers' Conference 2006, at Hyderabad on Nov., 2006.

Financial inclusion an abiding virtue, *The Hindu*, Monday, Jan. 16, 2006

Government of India: *Economic Survey* (various years), Government of India, New Delhi.

Inclusive Growth: The Role of Financial Education by Shyamala Gopinath, Deputy Governor, RBI

Kempson, E. (2006), Policy Level Response to Financial Exclusion in Developed Economies: Lessons for Developing Countries, paper presented at the conference, Access to Finance: Building Inclusive Financial Systems, World Bank, Washington, D.C.

No-frills bank accounts: Financial inclusion is good economics by C. J. Punnathara, Business Line, Thursday June 8, 2006

Taking Banking Services to the Common Man—Financial Inclusion by V Leeladhar.

16

Regulating Microfinance : A Step Ahead for the Betterment of Financial Inclusion

PADMINI JINDAL

Introduction

Since the 1980s, the microfinance sector worldwide, and more specifically in developing countries, has witnessed potent growth as the people and the financial institutions have dug and found the potential of microfinance to alleviate poverty among the marginalized population groups, especially the backward class and females in rural areas, by supporting self help groups (SHGs), joint liability groups (JLGs) and micro-enterprises growth. India accommodates the largest number of the world's poor containing 350-400 million poor or some 70-80 million families.[1] The country has discovered the potential market for the microfinance sector and lured funds from various sources. The MFIs in the country are still waiting to be permitted by the regulator to offer saving services or deposit services to the poor, which will be another good and apt source of funds to MFIs. This event will definitely endeavour the integration of financial products and services provided by the Indian MFIs to the poor and show a step ahead for the betterment of financial inclusion as poor people have the potential to save but could not realize it due to various reasons. Hence, regulation for the sector should be uniform and compatible as there are different legal forms of MFIs and different working models for the disbursement of loans

1. Human Development Report, 2006, New York: United Nations Development Programme (available at http://hdr.undp.org/hdr2006/).

to poor. The Malegam Sub-Committee report 2011 has recommended substantial codes of conduct to deal with the recent burning issues ranging from classification of NBFCs, MFIs charging exorbitant interest rates from the poor, to coercive methods of recovery.[2] The Microfinance (Development and Regulation) Bill 2007 was proposed to take NGO run MFIs and cooperatives under the umbrella of regulations, excluding NBFCs and Section 25 of the Companies Act. The NBFCs and NGOs converted into NBFCs in the sector are regulated by the central bank RBI under chapters III-B, III-C and V of the Reserve Bank of India Act. This chapter highlights need to regulate different legal forms of MFIs using different models for the disbursement of loans to the poor under a uniform regulatory ambit in order to create a level playing space and obstruct regulatory arbitrage.

Regulatory Needs and Challenges

With different legal entities in the microfinance sector, MFIs expanding their spectrum of services and products like addition of insurance and pension products, and new commercial entrants in the sector, there is a calling for the development of a uniform regulatory framework, which will turn out to be a progressive step ahead towards the goal of financial inclusion. The regulation is required to enable MFIs to offer deposit services to the poor, the lack of which is a major shortcoming of the sector. The regulation is required for the customers' benefit as they have poor financial literacy and bargaining power, they are easily exploitable and vulnerable. The regulation is also required as the players in the sector are getting increasingly competitive due to the affirmed establishment of the sector. It is quoted in the Malegam Sub-Committee Report 2011 that the Government of Andhra Pradesh, in its representation, has argued that the MFIs are riding "piggy-back" on the SHG infrastructure created by the programme and the JLGs are being formed by poaching members from existing SHGs.

2. Malegam Sub-Committee Report, 2011, New Delhi: Reserve Bank of India (available at http://rbidocs.rbi.org.in/rdocs/PublicationReport/Pdfs/YHMR190111.pdf).

With different lending models in the microfinance sector and their distinguishing mannerism, and collateral free microcredit loans, there lie certain unique challenges in front of the regulator. With high on-time repayments on microfinance loans in the recent past, though experience shows that once a loan is overdue, the ultimate collection of the loan is less likely, than in the case of loans that are backed by collateral (Rosenberg 2008). Shankar and Asher (2010) suggest that provisioning already delinquent loans needs to be more aggressive for microcredit loans as compared to other loans. The repayment of collateral free microfinance loans incentivizes borrowers to grab bulkier loans in the future. Whereas Shankar and Asher (2010) think that happen when stances like some members start consistently defaulting or rumours of MFIs failures start circulating in the sector, would endeavour MFIs to reduce future loan amounts extensively. They also recommend that it is the job of regulator to oversee that the MFIs are providing their customers with apt financial product and related financial knowledge and training. They advice the regulator should keep customers aware of the channels for dispute resolution, which are easily approachable, and the codes of conduct for MFIs besides devising and designing them. They also suggest that the cost of satisfying the regulations born by the MFIs should not impact their lending rates. The regulator should pay attention towards widely prevalent evidences of multiple-borrowing, over-borrowing and ghost borrowers, which are interlinked and are not healthy for flourishing growth of the sector and its members. If the regulator guides the conversion of MFIs into MFBs (Microfinance Banks), that means if the regulator permits existing MFIs to provide their customers with deposit services then the regulator will pass the biggest challenge.

Prudential and Non-Prudential Regulations

Prudential issues capture minimum capital limits, capital adequacy requirements and loan loss provisions (CGAP 2002).[3] The minimum capital limit, a rationing device, holds the number of MFIs within manageable limits of supervision (Rosenberg, 2008). Adequate

3. The Consultative Group to Assist the Poor is an international consortium of public and private development agencies.

capital cushions possible losses faced by the depositors and creditors of the MFIs, which sets as the base for the initialization of capital adequacy requirements. In order to tackle the possible losses due to delinquent microfinance loans faced by the MFIs loan loss provisions, serving as reserves, are built considering the peculiarities of MFI portfolios (Shankar and Asher, 2010).

Non-prudential rules cover transparent disclosure of interest rates, offering appropriate financial products and services, genuine selling practices and methods for collecting loans (CGAP 2002). The nature of the lending rates in the microfinance sector has attracted "margin caps" and caps on individual loans. The Malegam Sub-Committee Report 2011 has recommended the margin cap ranging from 10 per cent to 12 per cent and a cap of 24 per cent on individual loans. The doorstep delivery of microfinance loans generates higher transaction costs, calculated as a percentage of the small loan size, and hence results into higher lending rates as compared to the rates on most other loans. Capping can hinder the outreach to those customers whose profiles call for interest rates in excess of the cap. Also, MFIs could be incentivised and encouraged with a uniform interest rate cap for staying away from difficult and new territories where transaction costs are inevitably higher (Shankar and Asher, 2010). Demolition of the margin caps and the caps on individual loans would avoid inevitable and undesirable outcomes as noted by Shankar and Asher (2010) and presently improve outreach of the MFIs and hence lead to better financial inclusion.

The Malegam Sub-Committee Report 2011 has recommended only three components in the pricing of the loan, namely (*i*) a processing fee, not exceeding 1 per cent of the gross loan amount; (*ii*) the interest charge; and (*iii*) the insurance premium, for the fulfilment of transparent disclosure of interest rates by the MFIs. Porteous (2006) studied mature microfinance markets and highlighted the importance of requiring MFIs to unveil interest rates in a uniform manner in contributing to reduction of rates over time.

As banks are offering savings or deposit services to their customers, similarly the time has come that the MFIs should also be allowed to offer the same to their customers, which will fulfil the need to offer appropriate financial products and services. According to Shankar and Asher (2010) study, commercial banks, regional rural banks and post offices possess excellent geographical networks, but never tried to afford the doorstep collection of small and insignificant amount of deposits on a regular interval as needed by poor in actuality, amidst MFIs are very well adaptive to such a requirement, but not permitted by the regulator. The regulator may convert MFIs into MFBs, one by one or a bunch, and permit them to offer deposit services to the poor, whose operations are transparent and matured and financial statements are reliable and strong. There could be another way out for this issue, if the MFIs could be incentivised to collect deposits of poor in an economic manner and deliver all the deposits to the selected commercial banks and regional rural banks by the regulator. This way MFIs would be at par with the "business correspondent" and this model could successfully run in parallel to the new business correspondent model.

The non-prudential issue of coercive methods of recovery of microfinance loans was recently hyped as it was found that the practice of enforcing recovery by recovery agents is encouraged by visiting the residence of the borrowers. In this context, the Andhra Pradesh Micro Finance Institutions (Regulations of Money Lending) Act 2010 drafted by the State Government includes "frequenting the house or other place where such person resides or works, or carries on business, or happens to be". The Malegam Sub-Committee report 2011 suggests a solution for the issue in order to provide borrowers with their own privacy and maintain consistency in the repayments of loans. It is designating the Gram Panchayat office or a public place to be the meeting place for the collection of loans where all the members of the group and the recovery agent have to gather.

Regulatory Body for Prudential and Non-Prudential Rules

Shankar and Asher (2010) propose that the RBI would be an apt regulator for making MFIs adhere to the prudential norms, as the RBI supervises banks in India. Whereas a separate wing in the central bank named as "Wing of RBI for the Non-Prudential Regulations for the MFIs" should be established for accomplishing MFIs adhere to the non-prudential norms. Here MFIs relate to all different legal forms of MFIs such as NGO run MFIs, cooperatives, societies and trusts, NBFCs, NGOs converted into NBFCs, and Section 25 Companies established under companies act 1956. The Wing of RBI for the Non-Prudential Regulations for the MFIs should summon representatives from various organisations like Central and State governments, banks, MFIs, SHG federations, Sa-Dhan, NGOs and consumer forums in order to have requisite expertise as a group. The wing should consult with other financial sector regulators such as IRDA and PFRDA, for a potent supervision of insurance and pension services offered by MFIs. Hence, the RBI will be regarded as the sole authority to uniformly supervise different legal forms of MFIs with respect to both prudential and non-prudential regulations.

Conclusive Proposals

The RBI would be an apt regulator for making MFIs adhere to the prudential norms, whereas a separate wing in the central bank named as "Wing of RBI for the Non-Prudential Regulations for the MFIs" should be established for accomplishing MFIs adhere to the non-prudential norms. Hence, the RBI will be regarded as the sole authority to uniformly supervise different legal forms of MFIs with respect to both prudential and non-prudential regulations. The time has come the RBI should convert MFIs into MFBs, one by one or a bunch, and permit them to offer deposit services to the poor, whose operations are transparent and matured and financial statements are reliable and strong. There could be another way out for this issue, if the MFIs could be incentivised to collect deposits of poor in an economic manner and deliver all the deposits to the selected commercial banks and regional rural banks by the regulator.

REFERENCES

CGAP (2002), "Microfinance Consensus Guidelines", (http://www.cgap.org/gm/document. 9.2787/Guideline_RegSup.pdf).

Jindal, P.; Tiwari, R.; and Vidyarthi, H. (2010), *"Microfinance Institutions as Future Bankers to the Poor"*.

Malegam Sub-Committee Report (2011), "Report of the Sub-Committee of the Central Board of Directors of Reserve Bank of India to Study Issues and Concerns in the MFI Sector", (http://rbidocs.rbi.org.in/rdocs/PublicationReport/Pdfs/YHMR190111.pdf).

Porteous, D. (2006), "Competition and Microcredit Interest Rates", (http://www.cgap.org/).

Rosenberg, R. (2008), "How Should Governments Regulate Microfinance?" in S. Sundaresan (ed.), *Microfinance Emerging Trends and Challenges* (Cornwall: MPG Books), pp. 85-107.

Shankar, S. and Asher, M.G. (2010), "Regulating Microfinance: A Suggested Framework", *Economic and Political Weekly*, Vol. 45, No. 1, pp. 15-18.

Sinha, S.: "Microfinance Regulation for Financial Inclusion: The 'Street Child' Needs Nurturing", *Essays on Regulation and Supervision*, No. 22, (http://www.cgap.org/regulation).

17

Financial Inclusion through Self Help Group: A North East India Perspective

R.K.P.G. SINGHA

Introduction

Financial Inclusion has become the burning issue in academic research, public policy meeting, seminars and many other forums. Micro financing as an alternative means of financing for the poor has emerged strongly in many countries. In most of the Indian States; banks, NGOs and SHGs are engaged in this business. Although the main objective behind this financing has been the empowerment of the poor through financial support, several road blocks are there to achieve this noble objective. Since both the outreach and sustainability are important for the success of this programme it is important to ponder over the experience of similar economies before experimenting in ours. Previously focus of development was given importance on labour, capital, institutions, etc., as the concern for growth and development. The leading works hardly include finance as factor of growth. The major contribution of finance to economic growth has also often been overlooked by economists. But at the present context there has been a lot of works done analyzing how financial system help in developing economies. The work done in this field just not looked at how finance facilitates economic activity but also social aspects like poverty, food shortage, hunger, etc. Like any research on a particular field, the outcomes have been diverse and the agreement is that finance helps but the degree of impact vary.

The spread of banking facilities, though remarkable, has been uneven in the country, throwing up challenges for achieving financial inclusion. In fact, despite impressive growth of branch network in India, the vast sections of the society remain financially excluded and continue to remain away from the formal system and thereby access to affordable financial services including savings, credit and insurance. The banking industry in India has shown remarkable growth in volume and complexity during the last few decades. We have an exclusive banking infrastructure comprising 33,411 rural and semi-unban branches of commercial banks over 14,501 branches of RRBs, around 12,000 branches of DCCBs and nearly 1,00,000 cooperative credit societies at the village level. There is at least one retail credit outlet on an average for about 5,000 rural people, which translates into one outlet for every 1,000 households. This is a remarkable and extensive work. Given this network the moot question would be "Are the financial services needs of the rural poor comprehensively met its network?

NABARD has been instrumental in facilitating various activities under micro finance sector, involving all possible partners in the arena. It has been encouraging the voluntary agencies, bankers, and socially spirited individuals, other formal and informal entities and also government functionaries to promote and nurture SHGs. The focus in this direction has been on training and capacity building of partners, promotional grant assistance to Self-Help Promoting Institutions (SHPIs), Revolving Fund Assistance (RFA) to MFIs, equity/capital support to MFIs to supplement their financial resources and provision of 100 per cent refinance against bank loans provided by various banks for micro finance activities.

Research Methodology and Objectives of the Study

There are several forms of microfinance presently being practiced and available in the country. The present study tries to ànalyze the SHG-bank linkage model of microfinance in North East India based on secondary data taken from NABARD annual report and other sources like journal, publications, reports etc. SHG – bank linkage model has become very popular model in microfinance and thereby promoting financial inclusion in this part of the country.

The main objectives of the study are highlighted as under:

1. To study critically the importance of financial inclusion through SHGs in the present context.

2. To examine the SHG-Bank Linkages model and financial inclusion particularly in North East India.
3. To study critically the challenges encountered by SHGs in the way of financial inclusion.
4. To offer some suggestions for achieving financial inclusion through SHGs.

SHGs and Financial Inclusion

The Government of India formed a Committee on Financial Inclusion under the chairmanship of C. Rangarajan in June 2006. The Committee submitted its interim report in February 2007 and the final report in January 2008. On the basis of the recommendations of the Committee, Government of India announced the creation of two separate funds with an overall corpus of Rs. 500 crore each for financial inclusion. These are Financial Inclusion Fund (FIF), and Financial Inclusion Technology Fund (FITF). The Government has also declared its intention to convert the said Committee with suitable changes into a National Mission on Financial Inclusion (NaMFI), aiming at achieving universal financial inclusion within a specified time frame. The mission would aim at a target to provide comprehensive financial services, to at least 50 per cent of the financially excluded rural cultivator/non-cultivator households by 2012, and the remaining households to be covered by 2015. Based on the recommendations of the Committee, commercial banks including regional rural banks (RRBs) have been advised to add at least 250 rural household accounts every year at each of their rural and semi-urban branches, and also individuals such as retired bank officers, ex-servicemen, etc. to be appointed as business facilitators for business correspondents or credit counsellors. Furthermore, in order to strengthen the on-going financial inclusion, the Government advised all scheduled commercial banks to meet the entire credit requirements of SHG (self help group) members from 2007-08, namely (*a*) income generation activities, (*b*) social needs like housing, education, marriage, etc., and (*c*) debt swapping.

Micro Finance programmes are intended to reach poor segments of society as they lack access to financial services. It, therefore, holds greater promise to further the agenda of financial inclusion as it seeks to reach out to the excluded category of population from the banking system. The predominant micro finance programme namely SHG bank linkage programme has demonstrated across the country its effectiveness in linking banks with excluded category of poor segments of population. In this, process, the role of development NGOs is quite evident in providing the last mile connectivity as enables and catalyst between the SHG / village level co-operatives and the banks. This is also supplemented by the MFIs delivering credit.

The importance of financial literacy and financial counselling as essential components of the financial inclusion is also recognized. In pursuit of the financial inclusion, there are many issues and challenges both on the access and affordability—the two pillars of the financial inclusion, besides expanding reach to the triad of basic financial services savings, credit and insurance—payment system and the sustainability of the inclusion process are also essential.

Initiatives of Reserve Bank of India for Promotion of Financial Inclusion

The Reserve Bank of India in its annual policy Statement of April 2005 recognized the problem of financial exclusion and since then has initiated several policies aimed at promoting financial inclusion. To cite the major initiatives:

- Introduction of a basic "no frills" Banking account either with "nil" or low minimum balances as well as that would make such accounts accessible to vast sections of population. Several banks have already come out with their schemes.
- A simplified general purpose credit card (GCC) facility to be issued by the Banks without instance on collateral or purpose, with a revolving credit limit up to Rs. 25,000 based on cash flow of the household to enable hassle-free access to credit to rural households.
- Introduction of a Pilot Project for 100 per cent Financial Inclusion in the Union Territory of Pondicherry and one district each in all States / Union Territories. On the basis of the experience gained, the scope for providing 100 per cent financial inclusion in other areas / districts would be considered.

- Policy initiative on Business Correspondents and Business Facilitators model for last mile connectivity between the banks and the excluded segments of population.

In order to improve provision of financial services in the North Eastern region and prepare an appropriate State-specific monitorable action plan, RBI has set up a special committee to advance financial inclusion.

Models of Micro Finance Practice

There are varieties of delivery models of micro finance in India and the models are discussed below:

- **The SHG-Bank Linkage Model:** The popular model in the Indian micro finance context continues to be the SHG-bank linkage model that accounts for nearly 20 million clients. It started as an Action Research Project in 1989. Under this model, the self–help promoting institution (SHPI), usually a non-governmental organization (NGO), helps groups of 15-20 individuals through an incubation period after which time they are linked to banks. The bank lends to the groups after incubation period, and this linkage may be single or multiple period. Once the groups have been linked to the bank, the SHPI often supervises the loan portfolio. The financial needs of the SHGs are catered to by various financial institutions; the Commercial Banks, Co-operative Banks, Co-operative Credit Societies and Regional Rural Banks (RRB). There are around 94,000 Co-operative outlets, 14,000 branches of the RRBs and 33,000 suburban branches of the commercial banks in India.
- **The Grameen Model:** According to this model financial assistance, i.e., loans for productive purposes is provided by the MFIs/NGOs directly to the members of small groups (affinity groups consisting of about 5-7 members) on the strength of group assurance. It is often coupled with an obligation to save by the group members. This model is being followed in India by SHARE Microfinance Ltd., Activities for Social Alternatives (ASA) and CASHPOR Financial and Technical Services Ltd.

- **The Cooperative Model:** This has been initiated by Cooperative Development Forum (CDF), Hyderabad which has relied upon a "Credit Union" involving the "Savings First" strategy. It has built up a network of Women Thrift Groups (WTC) and Men Thrift Groups (MTGs). They are registered under Mutually Aided Cooperative Society Act (MACs) and mobilize savings resources from the members and access outside/supplementary resources from the institutional systems.
- **The Partnership Model:** The partnership model was conceived by ICICI Bank few years back. Later on, other bank like Housing Development Finance Corporation (HDFC) has followed the model. It involves lending money directly to an MFI's clients, while the MFI services the loan and charges a service fee to the client. Thus the effective interest rate to the client is higher than the ICICI Bank rate as stated on official bank documentation. To incentive the MFI to efficiently collect repayments, the MFI must repay all the defaulters up to a certain limit. Under the partnership model, loans are contracted directly between the bank and the final borrower, i.e., loans are not reflected on the balance sheet of the MFI. The MFI continues to originate, monitor and recover the loans until maturity in exchange for service fees. Additionally, the MFI must share the risk inherent in the portfolio generated by it.

SHGs in North East India

Financial exclusion is most acute in Central, Eastern and North Eastern regions having a concentration of 64 per cent of all financially excluded farmer household (from formal sources) in the country (415.61 lakh households out of 649.54 lakh households). Overall indebtedness to formal sources of finance alone is only 19.66 per cent in these three regions (4.09 per cent for North Eastern Region, 18.74 per cent for Eastern Region and 22.41 per cent for Central Region).

Another view point to measure the extent of Financial Exclusion would be: First, exclusion from the payment system, that is not having access to a bank account; Second, exclusion from formal credit markets, requiring the excluded to approach informal and exploitative markets. Going by the available data on the number of savings bank accounts assuming that one person has only one account, we find that on all India basis 59 per cent of adult population in the country have bank accounts—in other words 41 per cent of the population is unbanked. In rural areas the coverage of bank accounts is 39 per cent against 60 per cent in urban areas. The unbanked population is higher in the North Eastern and Eastern regions.

The extent of exclusion from credit markets are much more, as the number of loan accounts constituted only 14 per cent of adult population in rural areas, the coverage is 9.5 per cent against 14 per cent in urban areas. Regional differences are significant with the credit coverage at 25 per cent for the Southern Region and as low as 7, 8 and 9 per cent, respectively, in North Eastern, Eastern and Central Regions.

Table 17.1 highlights the achievement and progress made under micro-finance—savings of SHGs with banks during 2008-2009 in North East India. Just a cursory view of the table reveals the number of SHGs and savings amount under micro finance with various banks such as commercial banks, regional rural banks and cooperative banks operating in the region during the period of the study. It can be seen from the table, in terms of number of SHGs, Assam ranked the highest followed by Sikkim and Manipur respectively and Nagaland ranked the last. Again regarding savings of the SHGs with the banks in the North East region, Assam got highest position followed by Tripura and Sikkim respectively and Arunachal Pradesh ranked last.

Table 17.2 depicted the progress under Micro Finance – Bank Loan disbursed during 2008-09 in North Eastern Region. A perusal of Table 17.2 reveals that Assam ranked highest in terms of number of SHGs followed by Tripura and Meghalaya second and third respectively. Again in terms of loan disbursed Assam got highest rank followed by Tripura and Sikkim second and third respectively during the period of the study.

Problems of Micro Finance

Although micro finance has made substantial headway in India both in terms of coverage and outreach, however, there are some

Table 17.1 : Progress under Micro Finance – Savings of SHGs with Banks, 2008-09 in NER

(Rs. in lakhs)

State	Commercial Banks		Regional Rural Banks		Cooperative Banks		Total		Rank	
	No. of SHGs	Savings Amount	No. of SHGs	Savings Amount	No. of SHGs	Savings Amount	No. of SHGs	Savings Amount	No. of SHGs	Savings Amount
Assam	61122	3634.35	101239	2363.94	15635	298.63	180996	6296.92	1	1
Manipur	6067	173.61	1945	101.04	1613	53.04	9625	327.69	3	6
Meghalaya	4744	111.22	308	11.51	1005	34.92	6057	157.65	5	5
Sikkim	5697	262.12	15059	2506.20	2055	90.50	22811	2858.82	2	3
Tripura	4268	52.96	688	3767	192	3.00	5148	93.63	6	2
Nagaland	2266	35.83	1395	126.32	569	22.48	4230	184.63	7	8
A.P.	4803	121.71	4671	70.07	—	—	9474	191.78	4	7
Mizoram	1387	61.96	—	—	365	37.09	1752	99.05	8	4
Total	93354	445.75	125305	5216.75	21434	539.66	240093	10210.16	—	—

Source : Status of Micro Finance in India, 2008-09, NABARD.

Table 17.2 : Progress under Micro Finance—Bank Loan Disbursed during 2008-09 in NER

(Rs. in lakhs)

State	*Commercial Banks*		*Regional Rural Banks*		*Cooperative Banks*		*Total*		*Rank*	
	No. of SHGs	*Bank Loan*	*No. of SHGs*	*Bank Loan*	*No. of SHGs*	*Bank Loan*	*No. of SHGs*	*Bank Loan*	*No. of SHGs*	*Bank Loan*
Assam	11775	8300.78	13417	5647.83	1256	1747.59	26448	15696.20	1	1
Manipur	574	388.54	329	97.69	—	—	903	486.23	6	6
Meghalaya	396	293.39	408	177.42	199	38.62	1003	509.43	3	5
Sikkim	924	1189.81	—	—	58	62.86	982	1252.67	4	3
Tripura	1791	591.41	2799	4416.92	176	420.04	4766	5428.37	2	2
Nagaland	94	200.51	—	—	—	—	94	200.51	8	8
Andhra Pradesh	387	228.38	4	1.27	—	—	391	229.65	7	7
Mizoram	347	154.29	561	590.44	11	94.00	919	838.73	5	4
Total	16288	11347.11	17518	10931.57	1700	236.11	35506	24641.79	—	—

Source : Status of Micro Finance in India, 2008-09, NABARD.

certain major questions of concern which justify consideration. The coverage of poor families in SHG movement is yet to get impetus in some States like Bihar and North Eastern States. Another major worry is about uneven progression of micro finance which are shown by many studies. There are also many general problems which hamper the growth of SHGs in many States. The problems are highlighted as hereunder:

- Despite all the optimism surrounding micro finance, its impact has not yet been fully studied. There are many studies which reaches surprising inference that micro finance is more beneficial to borrowers living above the poverty line than the borrowers living below poverty line. The reason is that clients with more income are ready to take the risks like investing in new technologies which will give more income flows. On the other hand, poor borrowers, have an inclination to take out unadventurous loan which protect their subsistence, and hardly invest in new technology.
- Micro finance as pointed out by some researchers leads people to borrow too much; to the extent that over indebtedness can lead to suicides in extreme cases. The recent controversy in Andhra Pradesh shows that impact of micro finance needs to be more rigorously documented in order to convince policy makers and regulator that the movement should be supported.
- There are also problems for the MFIs in the form of regulatory and supervisory apathy leading to the financial exclusion of large segments of the poor people. The regulatory impediments hamper the effective use of innovative breakthroughs in delivering services to the actual clientele.
- So far the issue of higher interest charged by MFIs as compared to that by formal banking institutions continues to be vexatious discouraging the poor borrowers of micro-credit.
- The successful micro finance model of a particular context is blindly replicated in another context which is likely to be different one. For example, the just replica of "The Gramin Bank Model" developed in a small country like Bangladesh may not be successful in large country like India which is different in different contents".

Conclusion and Suggestions

With around 25 per cent of the total population in India below the poverty line and 75 per cent just above it, problem of financial exclusion is grave in India. Financial Exclusion is deep rooted in India's far-flung villages as well as the ubiquitously. A number of strategies have been designed and successfully implemented for enhancing the degree of financial inclusion in India, for instance, the SHG-Bank linkage model and association of banks with micro finance institutions. The Raghuram Rajan Committee has advocated the creation and promotion of small finance banks and strong linkage between large banks and small local entities to facilitate the retailing of large banks' financial products to small clients to create an inclusive banking structure.

Micro finance remains a powerful tool for development. It may not be panacea, but it has brought a sea change in the lives of many. Only spreading the outreach of micro finance will bring down the cost of capital and the operating costs and strengthen the bonding between micro finance and the Formal Financial System. Micro finance has been emerged as one of the need-based policies and programmes to cater to the neglected groups of society such as women, poor and deprived section of rural areas. Its concept is based on the empowerment of the poor and alleviation of poverty. It has been established as one of the best-known programmes among the administrators, NGOs and bankers. It has become now a useful additional strategy in poverty alleviation in the State and local circumstances. Several studies made by national international experts on micro finance have found the SHG profitable, viable and as a successful tool of social empowerment and no bank has reported any NPA under the SHG-Bank linkage.

In North Eastern States, this scheme has got slow momentum due to many reasons, e.g., lack of awareness due to illiteracy, lack of good NGOs, lack of motivation for formation of NGOs, lack of proper training to banks, NGOs and government officials, lack of cooperation between bank and Block officials, lack of sound credit structure of banks and lack of follow-up programmes which must be sort out very soon with the help of different agencies of SHGs and government machinery. Government can play a vital role in encouraging SHGs particularly SHG of women. So, the overall progress of micro finance is at a snail pace due to various constraints discussed above comparing to other parts of the country. At the same time, the SHG movement in North East India has started late comparing to other parts of the country. Very few social entrepreneurs are coming forward to take micro finance as an alternative. So, all-out effort should be made to promote the social entrepreneur to take initiative to make success the venture. Another reason is the high operating costs and low margins due to prevailing law and order situation in the region which has hampered investment in the micro finance sector. Government should take initiative to bring back the law and order situation into normalcy for overall growth of the economy. Thus, the vast segments of population particularly poor segments of society are out of the formal financial system and at the same time regional imbalances in the financial inclusion process is quite visible and there is a need for the micro finance movement to the broad based in North East India to make the financial inclusion more meaningful and inclusive.

REFERENCES

ADB (Asian Development Bank), (2000a), *Finance for the Poor: Micro Finance Development Strategy*, Manila

Gupta, Manoj Shankar, (2005), Poverty Eradication Through Micro Finance/SHG, in Singh, Ravishankar Kumar (ed), *Poverty and Sustainable Development: Third World Perspective*, Vol. II, Abhijit Publication, Delhi.

Kanwar, Gautam *et al.*, (2008), Microfinance in the Indian Scenario: A Study on the Existing Models, *The Indian Journal of Commerce*, The Indian Commerce Association, New Delhi, Vol. 61, No. 2, April-June 2008, pp. 19-40.

Khanka, S.S., (2010), Microfinance in India: From Evolution to Revolution, in Ahmed, J.U. (ed.), *Micro Finance in India: Issues and Challenges*, DVS Publishers, Guwahati, Assam, pp. 1-14.

Kilby, Patrick, (2002), *Micro Finance and Poverty Alleviation: The Dangers of a Development 'snake oil'*, National Centre for Development Studies, Australian National University, February.

Nayak, Sudarshan, (2006), *Empowerment of Poor through SHG and Micro Finance*, Cooperative Perspective, Vol. 41, April-March.

Neog, Bhupal, (2010), Exploring Micro Finance Models for Inclusive Growth in the North Eastern Region of India, in Ahmed, J.U. (ed.), *Micro Finance in India: Issues and Challenges*, DVS Publishers, Guwahati, Assam, pp. 169-178.

Pati, Ambika Prasad, (2006), Micro Financing and Empowerment of Poor in Meghalaya: The need for learning from the Experience, in Gautam, H.C. *et al.* (Ed.). *Rural Transformation in North-East India*, Department of Commerce and Department of Economics, Guwahati University, Guwahati, Assam, pp. 319-33.

Reserve Bank of India (2008), *Annual Report 2007-08*, Mumbai.

Website visited:

http://www.oecd.org/dataoecd/16/55/40339652.pdf accessed on 8/5/11

http://www.inafindia.in/Brochure—accessed on 10/8/11

http://www.nabard.org accessed on 25/5/09

http://www.microfinancegateway.org accessed on 28/5/09

http://www.planningcomission.nic.in/reports/genrep/rep_ppp.pdf accessed on 28/5/2009

http://www.skoch.in/images/stories/banking_knowledge/Financia Inclusion-Approach.pdf accessed on 26/6/11

Singha, R.K.P.G., (2009), Micro Finance in India: A Critical Analysis of SHG-Bank Linkages, Paper presented at the National Seminar on Micro-Finance Revolution: Understanding Its Success and Sustainability, organized by the Department of Management, NEHU, Tura Campus, Tura, Meghalaya held on 19th to 20th June.

Speech of Ms Usha Thorat, Deputy Governor, RBI at the HMT – DFID *Financial Inclusion Conference 2007*, Whitehall Place, London, UK, June 19, 2007.

18

Status of Microfinance in Nagaland

GAUTAM PATIKAR

Introduction

Microfinance is indeed a very traditional and familiar form of business. It is in general a practice of providing the poor with credit; savings and insurance facilities to set up or to expand income generating activities relating to agriculture and its allied activities and non-farm structure and thereby is a poverty reducing mechanism. It has turned out to be useful development assistance product. It reached out to millions of poor people and emerged as a revolution. It is a viable alternative that reached wither to undetach for their social and economic empowerment through financial and social intermediation.

Microfinance programme for women are promoted not only as a strategy for poverty alleviation but for women empowerment as well. Microcredit, which includes micro savings, is gradually emerging in Nagaland as one of the most effective strategies to alleviate poverty. It helps to generate employment and sustain the income of the households by giving them opportunities to work.

Microfinance scheme is generally dominated by self help groups-bank linkage programme aimed at providing financial services to the undetached poor based on the philosophy of peer pressure and group securing as collateral substitute. The SHG programme has been successful not only in meeting peculiar needs of the rural poor, but also in strengthening collective self help capacities of the poor at the local level, leading to their empowerment.

Self Help Group movement in Nagaland is an effective method for credit dispensations and has been SHG model which is quite successful. Through this chapter, an attempt has been made to review the present status of microfinance in Nagaland by highlighting its practices and progress.

Microfinance Practices

Microfinance in Nagaland is of recent origin. Unlike other parts of the country and general practice followed worldwide, the Microfinance programme in Nagaland is unique. Though, the programme is under the Department of Rural Development yet the approach is two fold, viz., Microfinance through Self Help Groups (SHGs) and Microfinance through Village Development Board (VDB).

Realizing the growing importance of SHG bank linkage programme and as per the recommendations of the NABARD Working Group, the RBI decided to extend SHG-bank linkage programme beyond the pilot phase and advised the banks to make it a part of their mainstream banking function. As an effect, microfinance through SHGs has gradually emerged in Nagaland. The State Governments and NABARD are playing a more proactive role in this area by identifying various NGOs/MFIs, organizing training programme for capacity building, etc.

Nagaland has been the pioneer in the concept of Decentralized Planning through active participation of the village community. The Village Development Boards are empowered in the entire process of implementation of all its rural developmental activities including Microfinance. This innovative approach to involve the VDBs in the process of credit related Microfinancial Intermediaries Activity is now firmly rooted in Nagaland. Almost all the VDBs are now involved as Microfinancial Intermediaries. In order to promote microfinance activities in Nagaland, initially, 25 VDBs were selected as Financial Intermediaries as Pilot projects. A Corpus Fund of Rs. One lakh was created through the contribution of VDBs, State Government, Central Government and NABARD at the rate of 40 : 20 : 20 : 20 respectively. With the successful implementation of the Pilot Projects, the State Government has decided to cover all

VDBs under this umbrella phase-wise. Till 2007-08, total number of 611 VDBs has been covered. During the year 2008-09, it was decided to cover 485 VDBs with a sanction amount of Rs. 485 lakhs. While for the year 2009-10, Rs. 24 lakhs was proposed to cover the remaining 24 newly recognized villages.

Progress under SHG-Bank Linkage

Savings is the positive difference between the income and consumption expenditure. Micro finance through self-help group encourages the saving habit of the SHGs members. Generally, increase in saving leads to increase in investment which in turn increases income. In Nagaland, there are 6057 SHGs available till the end of 31st March, 2009.

It is observed from Table 18.1 that out of 6,057 SHGs, 4,744 SHGs were registered with public sector commercial banks, 308 SHGs were registered with Regional Rural Banks and 1,005 SHGs were registered with Central Cooperative Bank. The total number of SHGs members registered with the Public Sector Banks stood at 30,435. The total savings of the SHGs was 157.65 lakhs as on 31st March, 2009. Out of the total savings, Public Sector Banks accounts for the largest share of 111.22 lakhs representing 70.55 per cent. RRB accounts for 11.51 lakhs representing 7.3 per cent, while Central Cooperative Banks accounts for 34.92 lakhs representing 22.15 per cent. It is, therefore, concluded that Public Sector Banks with large network in the State is responsible for assuming great responsibility for the SHG growth in Nagaland.

Out of 4,744 SHGs registered with commercial banks, 1,708 SHGs totalling 17,846 members were under SGSY and other sponsored Schemes with estimate saving of Rs. 53.54 lakhs. Till the end of March 2009, there were 1,384 women SHGs totalling 17,245 members registered with Public Sector Commercial Banks having Rs. 48.06 lakhs saving. It is estimated that 29.17 per cent of the total SHGs registered with the Public Sector Commercial Bank are exclusively for women. This indicates that women are gradually becoming aware of the fact that formation of Self Help Group can change their plight.

Table 18.1 : Progress under Microfinance- Savings of SHGs with Banks in Nagaland as on 31st March, 2009

(Amount in lakhs)

Sl. No.	Name of the Bank	Total savings of SHGs with Banks			Out of Total-under SGSY & other sponsored schemes			Out of Total SHGs- Exclusive Women SHGs		
		No. of SHGs	No. of Members	Amount of Savings	No. of SHGs	No. of Members	Amount of Savings	No. of SHGs	No. of Members	Amount of Savings
A.	*Public Sector Commercial Banks*									
1.	Allahabad Bank	152	1500	3.57	63	627	2.42	21	217	0.57
2.	Bank of Baroda	70	700	47.17	45	450	23.14	31	310	21.15
3.	Central Bank of India	124	1264	13.32	89	902	12.46	84	854	12.27
4.	State Bank of India	4,273	25758	46.63	1,466	15,452	15.28	1,215	15,528	13.92
5.	UCO Bank	55	561	0.16	34	353	0.14	30	308	0.13
6.	Vijaya Bank	70	652	0.37	11	62	0.10	3	28	0.02
Sub total		4,744	30,435	111.22	1,708	17,846	53.54	1,384	17,245	48.06
B.	*Regional Rural Banks*									
1.	Nagaland Rural Bank	308	NA	11.51	0	0	0	NA	NA	NA
C.	*District Central Cooperative Bank*									
1.	State Cooperative Bank	1,005	-	34.92	0	0	0	NA	NA	NA

Source : Status of Micro Finance in India. NABARD, 2008-09.

Table 18.2 : Progress under Microfinance—Bank Loan disbursed to SHGs in Nagaland during 2008-09

(Amount in lakhs)

Sl. No.	Name of the Bank	Total Loans disbursed during the year		Out of Total – Under SGSY & Other Sponsored Schemes		Out of Total – Exclusive Women SHGs	
		No. of SHGs	Amount	No. of SHGs	Amount	No. of SHGs	Amount
A.	*Public Sector Commercial Banks*						
1.	Allahabad Bank	16	11.82	16	11.82	4	3.48
2.	Bank of Baroda	29	14.08	19	8.23	8	6.98
3.	Central Bank of India	12	18.00	12	18.00	12	18.00
4.	State Bank of India	315	238.46	149	73.72	216	165.25
5.	UCO Bank	20	9.61	16	8.92	14	7.29
6.	Vijaya Bank	4	1.42	0	0.00	0	0.00
	Sub Total	396	293.39	212	120.69	254	201.00
B.	*Regional Rural Bank*						
1.	Nagaland Rural Bank	0	0.00	0	0.00	0	0.00
C.	*Cooperative Banks*						
1.	State Cooperative Bank-	—	—	—	—	—	—

Source : Status of Micro Finance in India. NABARD, 2008-09.

It is evident from Table 18.2, that Public Sector Banks in Nagaland are the key institution in promoting microfinance in Nagaland. The six public sector banks involved in providing microfinance loans in the State are Allahabad Bank, Bank of Baroda, Central Bank of India, State Bank of India, UCO Bank and Vijaya Bank. Among these banks, State Bank of India alone disbursed a total amount of Rs. 238.46 lakhs loan to 315 SHGs during 2008-09 out of which Rs. 165.25 lakhs was exclusively for 216 women SHGs and Rs. 73.72 lakhs to 149 SHGs under SGSY and other sponsored scheme. Vijaya Bank with Rs. 1.42 lakhs loan disbursed to 4 SHGs has the lowest share in the microfinance loan in Nagaland. Central Bank of India has the second largest share in microfinance loan with Rs. 18.00 lakhs to 12 SHGs exclusively for women under SGSY scheme, followed by Bank of Baroda with Rs. 14.08 lakhs loan to 29 SHGs. Allahabad Bank disbursed Rs. 11.82 lakhs to 16 SHGs and UCO Bank provided Rs. 9.61 lakhs to 20 SHGs.

Table 18.3 : Progress under Microfinance—Loan Outstanding against SHGs in Nagaland as on 31st March 2009

(Amount in lakh)

Sl. No.	*Name of the Bank*	*Total Bank Loans Outstanding against SHGs as on 31st March, 2009*		*Out of Total— Under SGSY & Other Sponsored schemes*		*Out of Total— Exclusive Women SHGs*	
		No. of SHGs	*Amount*	*No. of SHGs*	*Amount*	*No. of SHGs*	*Amount*
A.	*Public Sector Commercial Banks*						
1.	Allahabad Bank	64	32.57	63	31.39	10	6.88
2.	Bank of Baroda	70	47.17	45	23.14	35	23.65
3.	Central Bank of India	23	29.00	22	24.00	21	25.00
4.	State Bank of India	1,927	682.12	774	380.72	1,186	461.30
5.	UCO Bank	50	23.95	30	13.68	26	10.94
6.	Vijaya Bank	10	1.99	0	0.00	0	0.00
Sub Total		2,144	816.80	934	472.93	1,278	527.77
B.	*Regional Rural Bank*						
1.	Nagaland Rural Bank	14	30.00	NA	NA	NA	NA
C.	*Cooperative Banks*						
1	State Cooperative Bank	189	70.07	—	—	—	—

Source : Status of Microfinance in India. NABARD, 2008-09.

It is observed from Table 18.3 that the amount of loan outstanding was highest at Rs 682.12 lakhs with State Bank of India till the end of March 2009, followed by State Cooperative Bank with Rs. 70.07 lakhs and Bank of Baroda with Rs. 47.17 lakhs. The lowest of loan outstanding recorded at Rs. 1.99 lakhs with Vijaya Bank.

Financing under Swarnajayanti Gram Swarozgar Yojana (SGSY)

Swarnajayanti Gram Swarozgar Yojana (SGSY) is a centrally sponsored scheme. This scheme has been in implementation in the State since 1991-92 on a 75 : 25 funding ratio between the Centre and the State which has now been revised to 90 : 10 with effect from 15th September, 2008. The objective is to bring every assisted poor family above the poverty line within three (3) years through micro-enterprises activities. 30 per cent of the total poor families are to be covered within a period of five years. SGSY lays stress in cluster approach and focus on group approach. Under the programme, Self-Help Groups consisting of 10-20 members is formed and given a maximum subsidy of Rs. 1.25 lakhs per SHG whereas an individual Swarozgaris (beneficiary) gets a maximum subsidy of Rs. 10,000. The balance investment cost of the key activities is provided as bank loan. Table 18.4 gives an account of the physical achievement under SGSY during the period from 2002-03 to 2008-09.

Table 18.4 : Consolidated Statement of Physical Achievement under SGSY (2002-03 to 2008-2009)

Year	*Total No. of SHGs assisted*	*No. of SHG members assisted*	*No. of SHG members trained*
2002-03	163	1700	2925
2003-04	250	3161	4370
2004-05	118	1260	2652
2005-06	344	3052	5222
2006-07	287	2922	4063
2007-08	436	4288	5810
2008-09	753	6299	6916

Source : DUDA, Government of Nagaland.

It is observed from Table 18.4 that the total number of SHGs assisted under SGSY increased from 163 in 2002-03 to 753 in 2008-09. The total numbers of SHG members assisted were 1,700 in 2002-03 of which 710 were women and 8 were disabled. Out of 6,299 SHG members assisted in 2008-09, 3,275 were women and 19 were disabled. The number of SHG members trained under SGSY in 2002-03 were 2,925 and 6,916 in 2008-09. The number of women and disabled members trained were 1,213 and 9 respectively in 2002-03 which increased to 3,640 and 34 respectively in 2008-09.

Financing through NGOs

The major constraint in Nagaland has been the lack of credit linkages. In this regard, initiatives have been taken by various developmental agencies of the State Government as well as the Non-Governmental Organizations (NGOs) in mobilizing the people particularly the women folk in the rural areas for formation of Self Help Groups and introducing micro-credit programme that have been initiated by various Government Departments and Social Welfare Departments are being carried out independently under various developmental schemes / projects without any effort being made for sustaining such programmes (post project phase) by linkage with bank finance. There are several well established NGOs in the State that have been actively involved in spreading the concept of SHGs among the rural poor and in mobilizing them into SHGs in their area of operation.

A number of Self Help Promoting Institutions (SHPI) project were sanctioned to NGO by NABARD till 2008-09 due to dearth of good and credible NGOs in the State. However, in 2009-10, they deputed 88 functionaries of NGOs, KVKs and Government Department to a training centre of Mahila Shakti Kendra at Balipara of Tezpur district in Assam. Subsequently 6 proposals to 6 NGOs were sanctioned with the commitment of Rs. 37.50 lakh for promotion of 750 SHGs in 6 districts, viz., Dimapur, Mokokchung, Mon, Peren, Phek and Tuensang. The details of grant assistance sanctioned to SHPIs during the year 2009-10 are given in Table 18.5.

Table 18.5 : Grant Assistance to SHPIs during 2009-10

Sl.No	Name of the agency	For promotion of SHGs (Nos.)	District	Grant assistance sanctioned
1.	Prodigals' Home, Dimapur	100	Dimapur	500,000
2.	Mulung Women and Child Welfare Society, Dimapur	100	Mokokchung	500,000
3.	Chakhesang Women Welfare Society, Phek	150	Phek	750,000
4.	Eleutheros Christian Society (ECS), Tuensang	150	Tuensang	750,000
5.	Rongmei Baptist Association (RBA), Jalukie	150	Peren	750,000
6.	ANMA Integrated Development Association, Dimapur	100	Mon	500,000
	Total	750		37,50,000

Source : State Focus Paper NABARD Nagaland 2010-2011.

As a promotional measure, NABARD provides Revolving Fund Assistance (RFA) on a selective basis to good working NGOs on lending to SHGs. RFA of Rs. 10 lakh was sanctioned to one NGO in the State during 2007-08 for on lending to SHG members. Total RFA sanctioned till 2009-10 stands at Rs. 14.00 lakh.

Training Programmes of NABARD

NABARD has been conducting a series of awareness programme/ training programme capacity building, workshops, etc., covering as many districts for SHG members/NGO workers, Government officials and other stakeholders. As on 31st March, 2009, NABARD has conducted 42 training programme (6 Programme on SHG Awareness and Account Keeping, 1 programme on microfinance exposure visit to Bangladesh and the rest 35 were REDP & SDI programmes for SHGs covering 1068 participants on weaving, tailoring, mushroom cultivation, piggery, rabbit farming, etc.).

Table 18.6 : NABARD Support for Training and Capacity Building under Microfinance Sector in Nagaland as on 31st March, 2009

Sl.No.	*Training and Capacity Building Programme*	*No. of Participants till 2008-09 (Cumulative) Nagaland*
1.	Bankers	111
2.	NGOs	138
3.	Government Officials	14
4.	SHGs leaders/members	2,204
5.	Training for elected members of PRIs	57

Source : Status of Microfinance in India. NABARD, 2008-09.

Table 18.6 gives an account of the effort put by NABARD for training and capacity building under microfinance programme in Nagaland till the end of March 2009. It is found that the participants included in the training and capacity building programme of NABARD under microfinance were Bankers (111), NGOs (138), and Government Officials (14), SHGs leaders/members (2,204) and elected members of PRIs (57).

Microfinancing Activities through VDBs

The Government of Nagaland has declared VDBs as financial intermediaries for microfinancing activities. Out of the State programme allocation of Rs. 2,723 crore, an amount of Rs. 5.40 crore has been earmarked for giving financial assistance to 540 VDBs at Rs. 1.00 lakh to each VDB during 2006-07. This is a follow-up to the pilot project being implemented by 25 VDBs in the State. The Government of Nagaland proposed that players involved in the scheme may be limited to the concerned bank providing revolving fund assistance and the VDBs through their contribution of Rs. 1.00 lakh. State Bank of India (SBI), has already financed 220 VDBs. Additional finance will depend on Government of Nagaland's (Rural Development Department) feedback. It is learnt from the Special Secretary (Finance), Government of Nagaland that the Government will apprise regarding the performance of VDBs to SBI in due course. (Karmakar and Banerjee).

Table: 18.7 : District/State Total Corpus Fund, 2006-2008

(Rs. in lakhs)

Sl. No.	Name of the District	Total selected VDB		Total VDB corpus fund contribution		Total State share corpus fund		Total Central share corpus fund		Total fund	
		2006-07	2007-08	2006-07	2007-08	2006-07	2007-08	2006-07	2007-08	2006-07	2007-08
1.	Kohima	14	34	5.60	13.60	14.00	34.00	14.00	34.00	33.60	81.60
2.	Mokochung	19	44	7.60	17.60	19.00	44.00	19.00	44.00	45.60	105.60
3.	Tuensang	29	12	11.60	4.80	29.00	12.00	29.00	12.00	69.60	28.80
4.	Mon	62	22	24.80	8.80	62.00	22.00	62.00	22.00	148.80	52.80
5.	Zunheboto	47	13	18.80	5.20	47.00	13.00	47.00	13.00	112.80	31.20
6.	Wokha	49	6	19.60	2.40	49.00	6.00	49.00	6.00	117.60	14.40
7.	Phek	10	—	4.00	—	10.00	—	10.00	—	24.00	—
8.	Dimapur	98	33	39.20	13.20	98.00	33.00	98.00	33.00	235.20	79.20
9.	Kiphire	42	16	16.80	6.4	42.00	16.00	42.00	16.00	100.80	38.40
10.	Longleng	12	—	4.80	—	12.00	—	12.00	—	28.80	—
11.	Peren	4	20	1.60	8.00	4.00	20.00	4.00	20.00	9.60	48.00
	Total	386	200	154.40	80.00	386.00	200.00	386.00	200.00	926.40	480.00

Source : Directorate of Rural Development. Government of Nagaland Kohima.

With the launching of the microfinance programme through the VDB in the State, the respective VDB in the recognized villages has opened Corpus Fund Account. Table: 18.7 gives an account of the Corpus Fund position in the State during 2006-07 and 2007-08.

It is observed that the total number of VDBs selected during 2006-07 were 386 and during 2007-08 were 200. The total VDB corpus fund was Rs. 154.40 lakhs during 2006-07 and Rs. 80 lakhs in 2007-08. The share of the State and the Centre was Rs. 200 lakhs each in 2007-08 as against Rs. 386 lakhs each in 2006-07. The highest numbers of 98 VDBs were selected in Dimapur during 2006-07 with a total corpus fund of Rs. 235.20 lakhs and 44 VDBs were selected in Mokochung during 2007-08 with a total corpus fund of Rs. 105.60 lakhs.

Implications

In Nagaland, 21 (twenty one) out of the 52 Blocks are unbanked covering 421 villages. This indicates that more than 50 per cent of the rural areas do not have adequate banking infrastructure. The latest innovative venture to include the excluded in the development process through financial inclusion has been a revolutionary step. The microfinance initiative in the State has been made to declare the VDBs as "Financial Intermediaries" or Non-Banking Financial Intermediaries to integrate the ever important credit mechanism in the rural areas for foster economic development. The ramification to this approach, if successful, would ensure that grass root level organizations of Nagaland would control the credit/loan mechanism. Thus, the base of the economic progress of rural India will be determined by the poorest of the poor.

Microfinance through SHGs has been recognized as a powerful instrument for poverty alleviation and rural development. Besides, the social role of SHGs is highly impressive, as has been indicated in the subsequent paragraphs.

There are apparent synergies between SHGs and local politics since through membership of SHGs, or SHG clusters and federations, village women can gain experience of relevant processes (regular meetings, taking decisions, allocating money). They also become more "visible" in the village, which is important for campaigning. Woman SHG members also ran for local political office, i.e., in the Village Development Board.

The population of Nagaland is basically tribal. The society here is split by tribalism that has traditionally discriminated one tribe from the other. The fact that the majority of SHGs are single tribe groups is based on the principle of "affinity groups" and neighbourhood proximity. It is observed that members living nearby are able to get together more easily and village neighbourhoods are usually tribe based. The government's benefits for STs and SGSY subsidies have been easier to channel to the target population, since all members of a groups belong to the same tribe category.

SHGs seem uniquely placed to support their members on issues of social justice affecting women. Nevertheless, it is not found that SHGs are dealing regularly with issues of social justice. Nor did many groups report such actions. However, it is observed that some groups whose members already enjoy some "socio-economic" status are able to assist their own members or extent support to other vulnerable women in the village, while more disadvantaged ST groups and poorest groups provided correspondingly fewer instances of such action.

Women in SHGs are working together to address issues that affect not only their own members, but others in the larger community. But very few SHGs have been involved in community actions. These community services included improving education, health care, veterinary care and village road. Some SHGs are found to contribute finance and labour for new infrastructure and trying to stop sale and consumption of alcohol.

Conclusion

Considering the plight of the State the adoption and implementation of Microfinance Programme is noteworthy. Despite of making some headway, microfinance in Nagaland is still in its nascent stage. Microfinance yet remains a powerful tool for development. It may not be a panacea, but it has brought a sea of change in the lives of many. By reaching the unreached poor in the rural areas microfinance innovations are yielding results and giving hope to the large number of poor through providing credit.

The emergence of Microfinance and Self Help Groups in the State is a revolution and if properly managed can bring about further positive change not only in the economy but also in the quality of life of the large (general) masses. But in order to make the approaches more useful means for poverty alleviation and sustainable rural development, there is a need for sincere intervention by the promotional agencies particularly the banks and Block authority in the areas of awareness building, skill development and training. Considering the number of clients, range of services and the increase in the involvement of both formal and informal sector institutions, there is tremendous scope for the sustaining of microfinance development in Nagaland.

REFERENCES

DUDA, Government of Nagaland, Kohima.

Microfinance, (2006-08), Directorate of Rural Development, Government of Nagaland, Kohima.

Status of Microfinance in India, (2008-09), NABARD.

State Focus Paper, (2010-11), NABARD, Nagaland.

Sundaram, Satya, (2007), "Microfinance in India", New Delhi: B.R. Publishing Corporation.

19

Microfinance : A Tool for Accelerating Financial Inclusion

A Case Study in Manipur

THIYAM SURJIT MEITEI

Introduction

In fact 71 per cent of India's population is rural of which 29 per cent is below the poverty line. According to a 2005 World Bank estimate, 41.6 per cent of the total Indian population falls below the international poverty line of US $ 1.25 per day. According to a new UN Millennium Development Goals Report, as many as 320 million people in India and China are expected to come out of extreme poverty in the next four years, while India's poverty rate is projected to drop to 22 per cent in 2015. The report also indicates that in Southern Asia, however, only India, where the poverty rate is projected to fall from 51 per cent in 1990 to about 22 per cent in 2015, is on track to cut poverty in half by the 2015 target date. For reducing the poverty particularly in the rural areas Government of India has taken many programmes such as Integrated Rural Development Programme (IRDP), Swarnajayanti Gram Swarojgar Yojana (SGSY), Mahatma Gandhi National Rural Employment Guarantee Scheme (MGNREGS), Indira Awaz Yojana, National Rural Health Mission and National Rural Livelihoods Mission (NRLM), etc. NRLM will help self-help groups (SHGs) and enhance their livelihood options by providing easy loans, capital grants and skill training. Though government has taken many programmes poverty will remain as it is if there is no saving habit to the beneficiary. In this regard financial inclusion has taken a great role and microfinance will help it.

Microfinance refers to a broad range of financial services, primarily credit, made available to people who do not have access to formal banking services. Normally, these services would be required in areas with small population and "ticket-size" entailed would also be relatively smaller (factors making banks' presence unviable). Therefore, Microfinance institutions (MFIs) facilitate the reach of financial services at a more "micro" level. Microfinance takes an integral role to develop economic condition of the rural poor. It also gives the financial services to those who cannot access formal financial services. The poor skilled people who have no collateral security can also access microfinance loan easily for running their small business. Now-a-days the commercial bank knows the importance of microfinance and they introduced the microfinance as a part of their activities. They form the SHGs with no-frills account and give the micro loan through their account. It gives a great impact to the financial inclusion.

The term financial inclusion is not new but it is very important in these days. It is the delivery of financial services at an affordable cost to the vast sections of the disadvantaged and low-income households. The financial inclusion is an important tool for poverty reduction in developing countries like India. Access to finance by the poor and vulnerable groups is necessary for reducing poverty and social cohesion. It is an integral part to promote the inclusive growth in our society.

Objectives

The main objective of this chapter is *to find out how microfinance helps to the financial inclusions* and some of the sub objectives are:

(*i*) To study the importance of financial inclusion to alleviate the rural poverty.

(*ii*) To determine the relationship between microfinance and financial inclusion.

Methodology

To attain the above objectives, data were collected from both primary as well as secondary sources. Primary data are collected through personal interview with bankers and secondary data are collected from publications, books, journals and website, etc. The collected data are tabulated and restructured for clear and precise presentation to get the required information. For clear and precise presentation some statistical tools like, correlation, chi-square and graph, etc., are used.

Data Analysis

To ascertain the above stated objectives, the present study is discussing the collected data in different headings they are given below:

Savings of SHGs with Banks: Table 19.1 shows the number of SHGs in India having the saving account in different banks. According to RBI guidelines the commercial banks offer the no-frill account to the poor and needy people. It can reach the banking service to the every sections of the society and it is one of the major tools for financial inclusion. It clearly shows the number of SHGs in three different years having the bank account. The number of SHGs is in increasing trend, i.e., 50,09,794; 61,21,147 and 69,53,250 as on 31st March, 2008, 2009 and 2010 respectively. It means that the members of these SHGs get the banking facilities and they have the habit of saving to their respective account.

As we know there are 10 to 20 members in a group so that more than 10 crore people who are SHGs members get the banking facilities in India as on 31st March, 2010 through microfinance. It means that the poor who cannot open the normal saving account in the bank have the saving account through SHGs and can get the banking facilities even though they are poor. And now they have the habit of saving and repayment of loan as well as at least they get the banking education. From Table 19.1 it is also clear that among the different banking agencies commercial banks have the large number of SHGs, i.e., more than 55 per cent of the total SHGs bank linked in India are covered and rest are distributed to Regional Rural Banks and Co-operative Banks.

Banking Profile of Manipur: Table 19.2 shows the number of bank branches in the different districts of the State. Manipur has the highest population per bank branch in India with 33,000 population per bank branch against the all India average of 15,000 as on 31st March, 2009. And from Table 19.2 it is cleared that among

Table 19.1 : Savings of SHGs with Banks—Agency-wise Position in India

(Rs in crore)

Agency	*As on 31-03-08*			*As on 31-03-09*			*As on 31-03-10*		
	*No. of SHGs**	*Amount*	*Per SHG saving*	*No. of SHGs**	*Amount*	*Per SHG saving*	*No. of SHGs**	*Amount*	*Per SHG saving*
Commercial Banks (Public & Private Sector)	2810750	2077.73	7392	3549509	2772.99	7812	4052915	3673.89	9065
Regional Rural Banks	1386838	1166.49	8411	1628588	1989.75	12218	1820870	1299.37	7136
Cooperative Banks	812206	541.17	6663	943050	782.88	8302	1079465	1225.44	11352
TOTAL	**5009794**	**3785.39**	**7556**	**6121147**	**5545.62**	**9060**	**6953250**	**6198.71**	**8915**

Source : NABARD's Status of Microfinance in India 2009-2010.

*including SGSY

the nine districts Ukhrul has the lowest number of bank branches. Even Ukhrul has 4 bank branches and the 2 branches, i.e., RRBs are not functioning. Imphal west has the highest in number of banks with 35; Imphal East, Thoubal and Bishnupur are followed to this. It means that maximum number of the bank branches in the State are in the valley districts and only around 19 per cent of bank branches are in the hill districts. Against the bank branches maximum numbers are in the district headquarters and again the number of bank branches are not distributed equally to the nine districts. Statistically it is also proved, that is, the calculated value of chi-square at *df*. 8 is 68.040 it is much higher than the table value at 5 per cent level of 15.5, it means that there is the significant difference in distribution of number of bank branches in the nine districts of the State.

Table 19.2 : Number of Bank Branches in Manipur as on 31st March, 2011

Sl. No.	*District*	*Commercial Banks*	*Regional Rural Banks*	*Dist. Co-op. Banks*	*Total*
1.	Bishnupur	3	3	3	9
2.	Chandel	4	1	0	5
3.	Churchandpur	3	1	1	5
4.	Imphal East	8	4	4	16
5.	Imphal West	23	5	7	35
6.	Senapati	7	4	1	12
7.	Tamenglong	1	3	1	5
8.	Thoubal	4	4	2	10
9.	Ukhrul	1	2	1	4
	Total	54	27	20	101
		$\chi^2 = 68.040$	*df* = 8		

Source : 26th State Level Bankers Committee (SLBC) agenda report, Manipur.

SHGs and no-frills account in Manipur: Table 19.3 shows the district-wise number of SHGs and no-frills account of Manipur as on 31st March, 2011. According to 26th State Level Bankers Committee Report there are 19,007 banks linked SHGs operating in the State as on 31st March, 2011.

Table 19.3 : District wise position of number of SHGs-Bank linkage and no-frills account opened in Manipur, as on 31st March, 2011

Sl. No.	*District*	*SHGs*		*No-frills a/c opened*	
		No. of SHGs	*Percentage*	*No. of a/c*	*Percentage*
1.	Bishnupur	2,090	11	1,510	2
2.	Chandel	748	4	2,556	3
3.	Churchandpur	1,383	7	17,442	23
4.	Imphal East	1,854	10	3,070	4
5.	Imphal West	4,157	22	41,425	56
6.	Senapati	3,244	17	3,355	5
7.	Tamenglong	559	3	625	1
8.	Thoubal	3,820	20	3,488	5
9.	Ukhrul	1,152	6	698	1
	Total	19,007	100	74,169	100

Correlation between number of SHGs and number of no-frills account = 0.529

Source : 26th SLBC Agenda Report, Manipur.

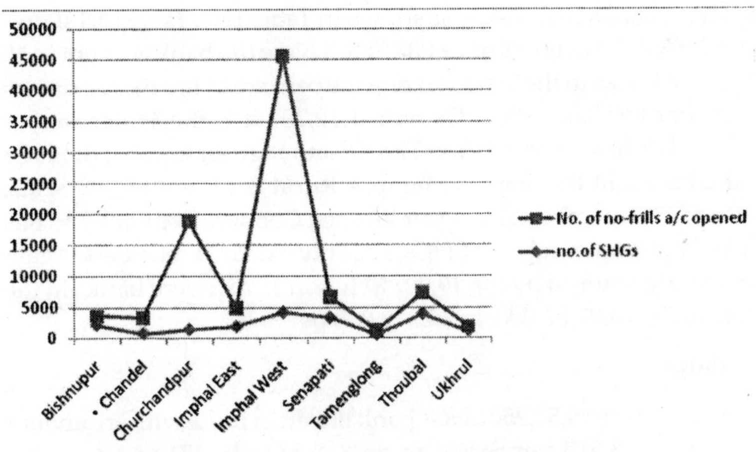

Figure 19.1 : Relationship between SHGs and no-frills account opened in Nine Districts of Manipur

From Figure 19.1 it is cleared that there is a closed relation between number of SHGs formed and number of no-frills account open in the different districts of the State.

Among the nine revenue districts of Manipur, Imphal West has the highest in number with 4,157 SHGs and Tamenglong has the lowest in number with 559 SHGs. In the same way Imphal West has the highest number in no-frills account with 41,425 and Tamenglong has the lowest in no-frills account with only 625. Again the calculated value of correlation between number of SHGs and no-frills account opened is 0.529; it is nearer to +1 so it is proved that the number of no-frills account opened and number of SHGs linked with bank are highly correlated. And it is also shown in the following Figure 19.1.

SHGs Bank Linkage in Manipur: All the SHGs formed are not linked with the bank in the State. There are different model of SHGs i.e., SHGs formed by Bank, SHGs formed by NGOs and SHGs formed by MFIs, etc. Those SHGs which are formed by the NGOs and MFIs are not all linked with bank, most of them are getting loan only from their respective NGOs or MFIs. According to SLBC report there are 19,007 SHGs as on 31st March, 2011 which have been linked with different banks in the State as shown in Table 19.4. Table 19.4 shows that 2, 88,752 members of 19,007 SHGs have the bank account in 15 different banks in the State. Among the banks, SBI has the maximum number of SHGs with 7,839 with 1,19,284 it is the 41 per cent of total SHGs linked with bank. The second highest number of SHGs linked bank in the State is Manipur Rural Bank with 5,293 SHGs with 85,237 members. Manipur Women Cooperative Bank Ltd has linked the least number of SHGs, i.e., only 5 with 74 members. Again the saving amount by the 19,007 SHGs in 15 different banks in the state is Rs. 18,92,82,000, i.e., Rs. 9,958 per SHG.

Findings

- There are 69,53,250 SHGs bank linked in India with an amount of Rs. 8,915 per SHGs as on 31st March, 2010 against this there are 19,007 SHGs bank linked in Manipur with an amount of Rs. 9,958 per SHG as on 31st March, 2011. It means after joining to microfinance they can save their money to the bank and improving their economic condition.

Table 19.4 : SHGs Bank Linkage in Manipur in different Banks as on 31st March, 2011

(Amount Rs. in lakh's)

Sl. No.	*Name of the Bank*	*Detail of SHGs saving with banks*		
		No. of SHGs	*No. of members*	*Saving Amount*
1.	Allahabad Bank	30	447	1.53
2.	Bank of Baroda	468	7,082	79.25
3.	Central Bank of India	234	3,890	6.87
4.	Indian Overseas Bank	9	144	0.09
5.	Punjab National Bank	87	1,293	21.10
6.	Punjab and Sind Bank	29	431	0.55
7.	State Bank of India	7,839	1,19,284	539.84
8.	United Bank of India	3,042	43,332	1,111.23
9.	UCO Bank	232	3,188	6.85
10.	Vijaya Bank	7	86	0.51
11.	Manipur Rural Bank	5,293	85,237	101.64
12.	Imphal Urban Co-operative Bank Ltd.	265	3,718	2.22
13.	Manipur State Cooperative Bank Ltd.	1,405	20,045	20.84
14.	Moirang Primary Co-operative Bank Ltd.	62	501	0.25
15.	Manipur Women Co-operative Bank Ltd.	5	74	0.05
	Total	19,007	2,88,752	1,892.82

Source : 26th State Level Bankers Committee Report, Manipur

- Imphal West has the highest number of bank branches with 35 out of total 101 as on 31st March, 2011. It is more than the total of four hill districts, i.e., 31 bank branches. Again population per bank branches in the State is much higher than the all India level. So there is the lack of bank branches in the State particularly in the hill districts.
- From this study it is found that there are 74,169 no-frills accounts and 19,007 SHGs bank linked in Manipur as on 31st March, 2011. By studying district-wise distribution they are

highly correlated, i.e., Imphal West has the highest number of SHGs as well as no-frill accounts in the same way Tamenglong has the lowest number of SHGs as well as no-frill account.

- In Manipur 15 different bank has linked with 19,007 SHGs as on 31st March, 2011. Against the 15 banks, SBI has the highest number of SHGs with 7,839 and Manipur Rural Bank and United Bank of India followed to SBI with 5,293 and 3,042 SHGs respectively.

Conclusions

From this study it is found that the number of bank branches in the State is least compared with its population (i.e., as on March 2009 population per bank branch is 33,000) and it is necessary to open more number of bank branches in the State so that to reach the banking facilities to the maximum population of the State. Again the number of SHGs bank linked and number of no-frill account open in different nine districts of the State are positively correlated it means if the number of SHGs is increased then the number of no-frill account open in nine different districts are also increased. In all over India there are around 6.9 million SHGs are linked with bank that is those members who are in this group have been getting banking services. Last but not the least it is also cleared that after joining to microfinance the members of the SHGs get the formal banking facilities in the simple and easy way. Therefore, it can be concluded that microfinance is the one of the best tool for accelerating the financial inclusion.

REFERENCES

January 2006, " *Reserve Bank of India Bulletin*", p. 73.

July-August 2011, *Economy at A Glance.*

Lead Bank Office State Bank of India Imphal, Manipur (2011), *26th State Level Bankers' Committee Meeting Manipur.*

NABARD (2010), *Status of Microfinance in India 2009-2010.*

NABARD (January 2008), *Report of The Committee on Financial Inclusion.*

NABARD, *Annual Report 2010-2011.*

SECTION - III

Financial Inclusion and Commercial Banks

20

Initiatives of Commercial Banks for Financial Inclusion : A Case of Selected Nationalised Banks in India

M. VASAN

Prologue

India occupies only 2.4 per cent of the world's land area but supports over 16 per cent of the world's population. About 70 per cent of the Indian population lives in villages. There are divergent demographic patterns, living standards, education levels and income levels as parameters of economic development. The rural India is yet to see the light of development and the results of planning process. The divide between the rich and poor is wide.

On one hand, due to liberalization, privatization and globalization of Indian economy there are drastically changing the banking field. While on the other hand, besides profit, social responsibility is also one of the prime agenda of commercial banks. The fact remains that the country cannot progress unless and until the basic infrastructure facilities reach to each and every citizen of the country. One of the important purposes of Indian planning is socialism and upliftment of poor. The downtrodden and poverty ridden mass has been excluded socially and financially even in independent India when planning and development process was basically meant for them. They should have been the beneficiaries of development.

The banking sector despite the fact that it has 67,000 branches does not lend to large sections of the Indian people. The average population per branch office is about 16,000. It is estimated that only 27 per cent of the cultivators have access to institutional credit.

About 22 per cent of cultivators get credit from money lenders and the remaining 51 per cent does not get any credit at all. Hence, financial inclusion drive is necessary which aims at reaching out to more people who deserve credit and who cannot access credit.

The "Financial Inclusion" is a must as it creates opening for other types of inçlusions. The development process starts with the reach of financial services. As per latest available report, the number of bank accounts per 100 populations is only 31. The number of accounts per 100 adult populations is only 59. As against such figures, the financial inclusion in developed countries like the U.K. is 90 per cent. There is, therefore, need for greater financial inclusion and to have bank accounts and infrastructure services. In case of financial exclusion is the unavailability of banking services to people living in poverty. It is believed to be one factor preventing poor people from existing poverty, by forcing them to manage their finances on a cash-only basis and restricting their access to·equitable sources of credit. The implications of financial exclusion which is captured in the following diagram:

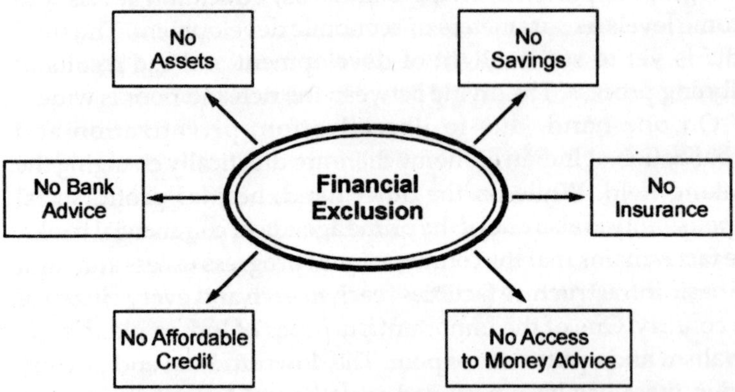

Fig. 20.1 : Implications of Financial Exclusion

The concept of financial inclusion in banking scenario is delivery of banking services at an affordable cost to vast sections of disadvantaged and low income groups. Banking services include credit, savings, insurance, payments and remittances which are essential and should be made available to the entire population without any discrimination. Financial inclusion is not only for social growth but a profitable proposition for banks.

There is a vast untapped market in India and the banks can reach out to cater to their financial needs. It is, therefore, imperative to roll out an action plan to cover the highly excluded areas/regions in a very definite, time bound manner. Hence, the overall strategy for financial inclusion, especially amongst the poor and disadvantaged segments of the population, should ideally comprise of:

- Ways and means to effect improvements within the existing formal credit delivery mechanism.
- Suggest measures for improving the credit absorption capacity especially amongst the marginal and sub-marginal farmers.
- Evolve new models for extending outreach.
- Leverage on technology solutions to facilitate large scale inclusion.

Scope of Financial Inclusion in Commercial Banks

In India, the focus of the financial inclusion at present is confined to ensuring a bare minimum access to a savings bank account without frills, to all. Internationally, the financial inclusion has been viewed in a much wider perspective. Having a current account/savings account on its own, is not regarded as an accurate indicator of financial inclusion. "Financial Inclusion" efforts should offer at a minimum, access to a range of financial services including savings, long and short term credit, insurance, pensions, mortgages, money transfers, etc., and all this at a reasonable cost.

Role of Commercial Banks and the Way Forward

The Family Resources Survey indicated that in 2002-03 there were 1.9 million households without a bank account of any kind, containing around 2.8 million adults. The Indian households can be broadly divided into two main groups, rural and urban. To have effective financial inclusion, the banks have to always keep in mind these target-groups and bring them to banking fold in such a way that it is a win- win situation for both. Commercial banks can step in to augment financial inclusion in two ways:

- providing banking and other related services; and
- providing non-banking services and support.

Banking and Other Related Services

To ensure banking services are attractive to those with low incomes, banking products must have features that meet the needs of this group of consumers. For this, the banks have to develop:

- Basic Banking Account.
- Low cost bill payment systems.
- Technology driven products.
- Biometric ATMs.
- Pre-paid Cards.
- Internet Kiosks.
- Deposit accounts, which offer an overdraft and an easy route to debt.
- Affordable insurance products.
- For individuals.
- For business enterprise.
- For Agro activities such as, weather/cattle/poultry.
- Retail Loans at all centres with simplified documentation and procedures through:
  - — Self Help Groups.
  - — Micro Finance Institutions.
  - — Loans to Small Medium Enterprise.
  - — Giving advisory services.

Once the banks have broadly decided on the range of products, they must customize it to suit the customer as per geographical area, method, and approach to be adopted.

Rural Areas

India has a rural population of about 780 million with limited or no access to financial services. The branch banking route apparently is not very practical due to the huge cost of opening the branches *vis-à-vis* volumes expected, high costs of operations, limited banking hours, illiteracy, non-availability of alternate channels in rural centres, etc. Further, financial inclusion through branch network may adversely affect customer service at branches due to increased traffic and larger number of people to be attended to within the limited hours of banking.

Therefore, the banks will have to provide technology driven products such as, ATMs, internet kiosks for successfully implementing financial inclusion. The involvement of Self Help Groups and Micro Finance Institutions is also must for development of effective financial inclusion models by commercial banks.

In the context of India becoming one of the largest microfinance markets in the world, especially in the area of women's savings and credit groups (SHGs) and the sustaining success of such institutions as demonstrated by the success of SEWA bank in Gujarat, low cost banking is not necessarily an unviable proposition. SBI alone, as on date, has credit linked over 850,000 Self Help Groups, lending approximately Rs. 4,000 crore to these groups. The NPA in this segment which is below 1 per cent is proof of the viability of such projects.

Urban Areas

Contrary to popular concepts of a predominantly rural India, an increasing percentage of Indian population lives in the urban areas. Over the last fifty years, while the country's population has grown by 2.5 times, in the urban areas it has grown by five times. High incidence marginal employment and urban poverty as reflected in 43rd of NSS revealed that 41.8 million urban people lived below the poverty line.

In spite of its prominent role in Indian economy, urban India faces serious problems due to population pressure. According to an estimate, nearly one-third of the urban India lives below poverty line. About 15 per cent of the urbanites do not have access to safe drinking water and about 50 per cent are not covered by sanitary facilities.

In this context, banks need to provide financial services which have to include savings, credit, insurance, leasing, money transfer, equity transaction, etc., to financial needs, life cycle, economic opportunities and emergency with the only qualification that (*i*) transaction value is small; and (*ii*) customers are poor. For this, banks can offer the same product range as in rural areas and can also provide smart cards such as pre paid cards or reloadable cards. These cards can be used by employers towards wage payment of contracted labour or other utility service providers.

Micro Enterprises

At the bottom of the SME pyramid, we have the micro enterprise segment. Financial inclusion of this segment has been the key concern of the Government and the regulators in most of the developing economies, including India.

In India, we have had several efforts to cover micro enterprises with bankable schemes. Some of them have been Government directed like, the efforts to grow Khadi and Village Industries, schemes like the IRDP, SEEUY, SUME, SEPUP. But the success story in this segment has been the voluntary development of the SHGs. The SHG movement has been gaining momentum in the country. In other developing economies like Bangladesh, Indonesia, Bolivia, etc. too, SHG movement has taken strong roots and has been a key to the financial inclusion of micro enterprises.

In India, the SHG funding or micro-finance, is directed towards the micro enterprise of the members of the group. It is the integrity of the members of the group that is essential for the commercial banks to support them. The funding to the SHGs in the form of micro-finance has to evolve into proper funding for the micro enterprises.

The process that can hasten this is the stabilization of the credit bureau(s), voluntary development of groups based upon socio-communal forces and support to the commercial banks from the regulators to have differential treatment for such banking coverage from the usual provisioning and regulatory norms. Success of financial inclusion depends upon the sustainability and not on subsidies and incentives.

Advisory Services

The banks have to take on the role of an advisor for poor and disadvantaged as the right advice at a difficult time can go a long way. This approach recognises the close two-way links between poverty and deprivation on the one hand and being unable to find and use appropriate financial products and services on the other.

The banks must advise on

- Reducing the vulnerability of low income families to financial exclusion and multiple debts in order to avoid them from becoming over-indebted and/or to lift them out of poverty.

- Improving access to high quality services for the most disadvantaged groups and individuals in rural communities.
- Managing problem debt and the other interlinked difficulties that people often face.
- Protection from loan sharks.
- Information about where to go to get expert help when people are in difficulty.
- Business related issues such as best insurance deals, availability of raw material, plant and machinery, agro inputs, helping in forming forward and backward linkages, providing information on various markets local as well as abroad and providing marketing inputs.

To provide above mentioned services, banks will have to restructure and look for IT enabled service providers such as, interactive internet Kiosks, help desk at strategic locations, wherever needed manned Kiosk, and telephone help lines/call centres.

Non Banking Activities

It is essential that an institution which uses resource of the society must contribute to society through its core business activities, its social investment and philanthropy programmes, and its engagement in public policy. The banks need to involve more actively in community service and voluntarily create funds to:

- Support social and philanthropic activities such as, education programmes for under-privileged, environmental projects related to, water harvesting, aforestation, pollution control, and sanitation.
- Support projects which may provide (*i*) sustained employment for vulnerable and disadvantaged groups; (*ii*) improving the confidence and skills of the most disadvantaged children and young people by conducting workshops or providing vocational training; (*iii*) health improvement programmes for people living in the most deprived communities; (*iv*) for upliftment of weaker sections of society; (*v*) creating jobs and enlightening women; and (*vi*) to remove superstition and ignorance.
- Support organisations which provide (*i*) for improving access to high quality services for the most disadvantaged groups

and individuals in rural communities by supporting small infrastructure projects and IT enabled services; (*ii*) support to particular client groups such as old, minority ethnic communities, lone parents, disabled people, careers, families with young children, people with mental health problems or learning disabilities; and (*iii*) services that may help solve problems of financial exclusion, such as, post offices, registered social landlords, housing, welfare rights and legal advice services, homelessness units and hostels, family learning projects, enterprise networks and local economic development companies, development trusts, GPs, community health services, hospitals, health voluntary organizations.

Business Model

The banking needs of these financially excluded people are mostly of limited transactions with low value in nature. Running a full-fledged rural outfit is not a viable proposition considering the involvement of huge operational cost. Business Correspondents (BCs) model is ideally the alternate viable business model in order to have a greater coverage of these people in rural and other areas. Under the set-up, the bank is permitted by RBI to outsource selected banking services through Business Correspondents (BCs) and their authorized agents. The customers shall have the freedom to use branch banking facilities even though the business correspondents are available in their locality or they were initially sponsored by the business correspondents.

Requirements for the Business Model

- A proven and tested software solution;
- Hardware and other equipments compatible to software application;
- Financially sound, established, experienced and reputed business correspondents with adequate expertise and manpower;
- Uninterrupted tele-connectivity;
- Features of the IT Solution;
- Low operational cost;
- Scalable;

- User friendly;
- Secured;
- Inter-operable;
- Compliant to legal system;
- Standardized;
- Viable and Profitable;
- Sustainable

Commercial Banks' Initiatives for Financial Inclusion

In India, the commercial banks are playing predominant role in financial inclusion. Some of the leading nationalized commercial banks' initiatives are presented hereunder:

SBI's Initiatives for Financial Inclusion

The objective of State Bank of India (SBI) in the present day context is to ensure financial inclusion of the whole population irrespective of areas and sectors. The 'inclusion' phenomenon cannot be confined to few pockets of area and people. The important question is increasing outreach and deepening penetration. There are two ways of doing it: (*i*) through the brick and mortar rural branches, (*ii*) outsourcing all the functions to a business correspondent in a particular area, viz., a state or with the help of business facilitators at a local level. Large scale rolls out and rapid scaling up again is not possible without suitable technology intervention which is easy to use, robust, and dependable and, at the same time, cost efficient.

SBI's answer to financial inclusion is the "SBI Tiny project", which can in simple terms be defined as a "Bank in a Box". The entire set-up consists of a cell phone which serves as POS machine, a finger print reader and a tiny printer, all of which can be packed into a 10 inch by 10 inch box. All these work on rechargeable batteries. SBI Tiny accounts (no frills accounts) are opened on the smart cards. The smart card is akin to an e-purse and stores information about the customer, the account number, finger prints as well as the balance in the account. The smart card can handle up to 16 accounts including loan accounts. This card is highly secured as it works on the bio-metric validation of the customer. The card works on the Radio Frequency Identification (RFID) technology.

SBI is today using this technology in our smart cards which work in conjunction with a mobile or a hand held connectivity device which works on Near Field Communication Technology (NFC). Transactions are possible both in on line and off line mode. It also permits the real time updation of balances in the card. By issuing a smart card to the rural customer, the cost of the transaction is reduced because we are dispensing with paper based transactions and shifting the actual operation of transacting on the account away from the branch to Customer Service Point / Provider (CSP) at the outlet in the location of the rural customer.

SBI is running pilots at several places like Aizawl (Mizoram), Medak and Warangal (Andhra Pradesh), Pithoragarh (Uttarakhand) and West Garo Hills (Megalaya). Andhra Pradesh has been identified by our bank for carrying out disbursements under National Rural Employment Guarantee Programme (NREGP) and other rural development schemes through SBI Tiny Card accounts in Warangal and Medak districts. The scheme is also being extended to areas like Chamoli and Pauri in Uttrakhand and Titabar in North East.

Bank of Baroda's Initiatives for Financial Inclusion

Bank of Baroda has adopted the "whole village approach" as part of its mandate for enabling for financial inclusion by extending banking services to the country's rural population. This though is not a new initiative for the Bank, since the passion for agriculture and rural development is ingrained in the Bank's philosophy since its inception in 1908. To give rural India access to finance and to enable economic independence, BoB has introduced a slew of services that extend credit facilities to small and marginal farmers, agricultural labourers and cottage industry entrepreneurs. Villages in Dungarpur district of Rajasthan were among the first 500 villages to benefit from the Bank's financial inclusion and total integrated village development programme.

In the past too, the Bank has taken a number of initiatives such as opening of specialised outlets of Gram Vikas Kendras (GVKs) and Multi Service Agencies (MSAs). The Baroda Swarojgar Vikas Sansthan (BSVS) was another initiative for capacity building and provided appropriate training for skill upgradation to unemployed youth and women for employment.

The Baroda Kisan Credit Card (BKCC) is yet another facility offered by the Bank to empower the farmer. The credit card designed exclusively for the benefit of the farmers aims to provide them the opportunity to manage and utilize their funds in the manner they deem fit. The Kisan Credit Card provides adequate and timely support to farmers for their production needs, which include among others, purchase of quality inputs, investment requirements like purchase of agriculture implements / tractor, etc., farming expenses towards farm maintenance, unforeseen family expenses and maintenance of non-farm activities.

As part of the Bank's commitment to Corporate Social Responsibility in its centenary year, i.e., 2007-08, BoB launched the Baroda Grameen Paramarsh Kendra (BGPK)—a centre for knowledge sharing, problem solving and credit counseling for the rural communities. The BGPK is an effort to narrow the "knowledge gap" in financial literacy, better farming practices and technology adoption. It offers rural communities a diversity of opportunities including market-linked prices, value addition services offered by various institutions, women empowerment and employment opportunities for rural youth.

The BGPK centre helps in spreading financial awareness among rural masses through village level meetings and helps them to choose suitable banking products. As part of information sharing and problem solving process, it holds interface sessions with the specialists from institutions like agriculture universities, Kisan Vikas Kendras and NGOs working in the rural development sector. The centre also provides extension services to the farmers by encouraging their participation in Grameen *melas*, and organising television and radio talks. Each of the BGVK centre also maintains a small library containing books, journals and audio-visual aids. Information on the prices of agriculture commodities in various *mandis* across the country is also provided, enabling the farmers to sell their products at the best prices. The farmers are also provided credit counselling on repayment pattern and rescheduling of loans and fresh credit during situations of rural distress.

Another important initiative is the Baroda Kisan Group Loan—a joint liability scheme—for purchase of heavy agricultural machinery like tractors, power-tillers, etc. either by farmers having larger holdings with irrigation facilities or group of farmers with irrigation facilities. The Bank also provides credit for purchase of second hand tractors to farmers interested in dry-land farming or having a small land holding. Production credit is also provided for raising various crops from the point of preparatory tillage till harvesting, for landowners or permanent tenants or lease holders or sharecroppers. It encourages the development of irrigation facilities; this covers sinking of wells/bore wells, lifting of water by installation of pump sets, transporting of water through field channels, water saving systems like drip irrigation/sprinkler irrigation, etc., for farmers. It also extends working capital to dealers/ distributors/traders of agricultural inputs like seeds, fertilizers, livestock inputs like cattle feed, medicine, etc., and supply of agriculture machinery/ irrigation systems.

Employment is provided to the unemployed technical personnel through the Agro Service Centre. The Bank also facilitates the setting up of agri-clinics and agribusiness centres by agriculture graduates. To address the needs of rural infrastructure the Bank provides credit for the construction of farm building/structures like cattle sheds, thrashing yards, fencing, etc., to the individual farmer or firms engaged in agricultural activity and are of long term nature. Credit is also provided for construction/expansion/modernization/ renovation of rural godowns and cold storages.

Other services provided by the Bank include, development of horticulture including production, processing and marketing of various fruit, vegetables, plantations and flowers, from the nursery to the point of market, by individual farmers, firms, organisations like co-operative societies. A number of allied activities, like dairy, poultry, fisheries, sericulture, mushrooms and apiculture are also encouraged by the Bank. To ensure financial inclusion for the Scheduled Castes and Scheduled Tribes who have been provided/ allotted land by the State government, the Bank finances their purchase of farm implements, irrigation systems and bullocks, etc.

The Bank has also allied itself with NGOs to encourage the formation of credit linked SHGs in the villages. Under the Dungarpur Project, the Bank works through the People's Education and Development Organisation (PEDO), a NGO working in rural development.

This initiative of the Bank has already brought about a change in the lives of people. Bank of Baroda has also announced plans of adopting more villages across the country. It plans to disburse credit worth Rs 1 billion, over the next three years in these villages. Of these, "Baroda Centenary Villages", as they will be called, 25 will be in Gujarat. The bank will also spend Rs 5 million to 7.5 million on these 25 villages for their social development. This will be done in consultation with the Panchayats and other voluntary bodies.

Canara Bank's Initiatives for Financial Inclusion

Over 48 Canara Gramin Vikas Vahinis fan out to villages across the country every day under the Canara Bank's financial inclusion initiative. After undergoing intensive training, the staff of rural and semi-urban branches use these vehicles to meet with villagers at their doorstep, explain the various extension products and services and then bring them into the banking fold. Accounts are opened instantly and loans sanctioned on the spot.

Canara Bank has adopted technology and co-developed bio-metric voice enabled Smart Cards along with the technology provider. The bank has also engaged the services of business correspondents who are able to reach out to the villages with hand held devices. In fact, the smart card has brought banking to the doorsteps of the villagers.

Financial inclusion is an important corporate goal of Canara Bank. Mobile voice-based ATMs, seven of which now operate nationwide, are part of the drive. The mobile ATM consists of a bus which has a voice-enabled, biometric money vending machine. The ATM accepts only the customer's fingerprint as password and also guides the customer to withdraw money through recorded voice instructions in the local language. These features make this ATM especially useful to cater to an illiterate clientele.

The bank is also assisting village artisans like blacksmiths, carpenters, leather workers, people engaged in servicing of agricultural implements and household equipments. In addition, the bank also has 36 training centres of which 14 impart training in special skills so as provide rural youth with opportunities for self-employment. The Bank also provides loans for setting up of such businesses.

It has also helped set up several women self-help groups (SHGs) and is providing training and other supports to empower the women and improve livelihood opportunities. Taking products to the market has always been a challenge for rural artisans. Recognising this, Canara Bank has provided a vehicle to the SHG with bar code facility so that they can take their products to areas of demand for sale. The vehicle doubles up as sales counter facilitating easy movement between points of sale.

It is not surprising then that Canara Bank is also extremely proactive on the CSR front as well. It has provided financial support for the construction of schools in over 100 villages at an average of Rs 1 lakh per school. It has also adopted 23 villages across the country where it has sought to upgrade infrastructure by providing roads, health care facilities, etc.

Corporation Bank's Initiatives for Financial Inclusion

Establishing banks at every village is not possible—it demands immense funds and huge workforce. The answer Corporation Bank has found is to go in for "branchless banking". It has used this model successfully in Chittoor district of Andhra Pradesh to bring more villages under financial inclusion in un-banked areas. The key to making this a success is linking banking with livelihood. According to the bank, financial inclusion is of no use if it fails to provide livelihood to the poor. With the help of technology, the poor need to be brought into the mainstream of growth.

In a joint project with National Dairy Development Board (NDDB), it has launched Milk Mitra cards in Chittoor district. Under this, women milk producers are given loans to enter dairy farming, the milk is supplied to NDDB and all payments are made directly to the bank account of each woman. These accounts can be accessed at the village level itself through the business correspondent, also a member of the local community.

It is a classic case of business at the bottom of the pyramid—and where commercial and social responsibilities can converge. This is clear if one looks at the successful implementation of the Milk Mitra card. The milk card scheme has also been replicated with the help of Smart Card for other produce also, like vegetables and flowers.

In fact, in Chittoor district, the Corporation Bank has added yet another dimension to this model, keeping in view the *mantra* of linking banking with livelihoods. It has been seen over time that branchless banking and better livelihood opportunities have inculcated the habit of saving in the villages. It is a clearly a win-win situation for both the bank and the people !

Such schemes have yet another positive spin-off. The section of the rural population that has benefited the most from these schemes is the women. They have grabbed the opportunity not only add to their family's finances but also have invested in their self esteem. The money they earn goes directly to their account and they can thus use it judiciously. The challenge for the bank was to take the more sophisticated technology to unsophisticated areas, as most of the rural areas are short of power and telephone connectivity. Added to this, the rural populace is not familiar with complicated machine operations.

Under the branchless banking model, basic banking services are provided without having to open an expensive branch. Each identified person is given a Smart Card which is akin to e-Purse. One of the villagers is appointed as "business correspondent" and he or she is given the branchless banking kit and cash to dispense basic banking services to the villagers. The kit is a handheld device with multiple connectivity options. The operations are carried out through radio frequency identification cards provided to business correspondents and the villagers. So, the model not only provides banking services to the villagers, it also opens an employment opportunity.

This model has yet another benefit. With the smart card, one can deposit or withdraw (money) at their own convenience. Additionally, there is no requirement to fill any forms or vouchers, which is quite useful for the illiterate segment that the scheme is seeking to target. The services are made available close to their homes, obviating the need to spend time and money on transport to reach the branch. The roll out and maintenance costs of this model are only a fraction of running a conventional branch.

This system is now proving to be a role model. Indian Institute of Management, Ahmedabad has evinced keen interest in the "Branchless Banking" model evolved by the Bank, which takes technology to the remotest villages of the country for providing banking facility. On its part, the Corporation Bank plans to extend this model to all villages in the country.

Punjab National Bank's Initiatives for Financial Inclusion

Tineri village is situated about 65 km from Patna under Masaurhi Block of Patna district, came into the limelight after Punjab National Bank (PNB) decided to make it the centre of attraction as part of its drive to foster greater financial inclusion in the country. Here, PNB decided to set up its branchless banking facility to serve the poor who had no idea about the diversified banking services.

The Tineri project was part of the 27 pilot projects (20 in rural areas and 7 in urban areas) launched by PNB across 13 States in the Indo-Gangetic Belt. The objective was to cover the Indo-Gangetic plain, where the bank has more inherent strength, not only in terms of outreach but also infrastructure availability.

Importantly, a key partner in the Tineri project was the local Panchayati Raj institution, which PNB felt was an essential to ensure the project's success. Panchayats have been key enablers, according to PNB, in motivating people to open accounts, the verification of which was undertaken by PNB. This was especially important when it came to motivating people to move away from traditional, but high-cost, lending sources like the money lender. PNB saw itself here as a catalytic agent, with an essential element here being peoples' participation.

The Tineri initiative was not only as part of PNB's social responsibility, but was also seen as a "holistic approach" towards providing basic banking facilities to the poorest of the poor in all corners of the country. The bank sees financial inclusion as a distinct opportunity and business proposition for future growth.

In Tineri and its surrounding there are 12 villages today, financial inclusion as per PNB's; directive is complete, with all residents having opened bank accounts, with an overdraft facility. This has effectively ensured that local people do not go to the moneylender to raise funds and suffer exorbitant interest rates in the process.

Though this was a pilot project to access the acceptability of basic banking services to the remote villagers, most of whom are illiterate and have little or no idea about the value for money, PNB sees in it a new window of opportunity. Under the project, each family in Tineri and its surrounding villages is provided with a biometric card, a thermal filter and a Near Field Communication (NFC) mobile handset at a total cost of only Rs. 110. In return, each customer is allowed to open a savings bank account even with zero balance. Also, all transactions are made with the biometric card and the NFC. The technology employed here is a mobile-base technology, an instrument that enables the bank to open the account and do the transaction as well.

Importantly, all SHGs of Tineri are being imparted training for knowledge building and entrepreneurship programme under various sectors through RUDSETI Patna. The same is also being extended to Nadaul and Punpun Panchayats. The bank's pilot projects show that two things have been done in Bihar. First, linking the people with the bank through the financial inclusion programme. Second, a tie-up which enables funding all the e-Seva Kendras through village level entrepreneurs. Such village level entrepreneurs will soon become individual business correspondents (BC) after due Reserve Bank of India verification. This will enable PNB cover 8,000 villages more.

To make PNB a household name in Bihar, the Bank has also established an e-Kiosk in each Panchayat with the collaboration of SREI Infrastructure Finance Ltd. The first such project was launched in Panapur village. Besides providing other services as per the requirement of the Panchayat, the Kiosk operator or Village Level Entrepreneur is seen working as a business facilitator for the bank for providing all types of banking services to the villagers. The success in Tineri has emboldened PNB to go ahead with its plans to bring about financial inclusion in Buxar, Rohtas, Gaya and Bhojpur districts of Bihar.

Challenges Ahead

Financial inclusion in a large scale is possible only if the banks join hands with like minded partners in their initiative. While business correspondent model introduced by RBI enables such partnerships to evolve, the major concerns would be as under:

- As there is no proven/tested model, the initial take off may be slow till sufficient experience is gathered.

- It is essential that the programme is viable for all the partners. However, payment of fee/commission, etc., to the business correspondent, has no precedence and will evolve over time.
- Risk management, operations, registration, credit, etc., are a major issue.
- Cash management by the business correspondents is also an issue which can affect the reputation of the bank.
- But these are not insurmountable. With experience and over a period of time, these can be sorted out and standards lay down.

Epilogue

Financial inclusion is not a one time effort; it is an ongoing process. It is a huge project which requires concerted and team efforts from all the stakeholders such as the Government, financial institutions, the regulators, the private sector and the community at large. From the sporadic attempts of today dispersed across the nation, it should gather momentum and grow in geometric proportions and develop into a focused and effective movement. If this is to be achieved, it requires the passionate involvement, dedication and commitment of all stakeholders. It requires a major mindset change in the minds of every individual involved—banker, bureaucrat, regulator *et al.*, and, therefore, creating awareness at all levels. At the same time, the role of technology in the whole scenario cannot be undermined either. It has to be admitted that today, more than even before, technology plays a vital role in bringing about integration in society of all social and economic classes. Accessibility, affordability, appropriateness and benefits determine how deep financial inclusion penetrates the social fabric of the village. Financial inclusion can empower even the poorest person and bring about a dramatic change in his fate.

REFERENCES

Alliance for Financial Inclusion, Workshop Report on Promoting Financial Inclusion through Innovative Policies, May 2009.

Financial Inclusion, The Indian Experience, speech by Smt. Usha Thorat, Deputy Governor RBI on June 19, 2007.

Honohan, Patrick, Measuring Microfinance Access: Building on Existing Cross-Country Data, Policy Research Working Paper No. 3606, Washington, The World Bank, 2005.

King, Robert G. and Ross Levine, "Finance and Growth: Schumpeter Might Be Right", *The Quarterly Journal of Economics*, Vol. 108 (3), pp. 717-737, 1993.

Kumar, Anjali; Thorsten Beck; Cristine Campos; and Soumya Chattopadhyay, "Assessing Financial Access in Brazil," Working Paper No. 50, Washington, The World Bank, 2005.

Rakesh Mohan, Reserve Bank of India—*Economic Growth, Financial Deepening and Financial Inclusion*, Nov. 2006.

Rangarajan C, *Report of the Committee on Financial Inclusion*, Jan. 2008.

Scottish Executive, Financial Inclusion Action Plan, 2005.

Shyamala Gopinath, *Reserve Bank of India—Inclusive Growth: Role of Financial Education*, Nov 2006.

The Hindu, Business column, December 24, 2010.

World Bank, *Banking the Poor: Measuring Banking Access in 54 Economies*, Washington, 2008.

www.inclusion.in

www.indiatoday.intoday.in/site/Story

www.planetd.org

21

Role of RRBs in Financial Inclusion in Tribal Areas : A Case Study of Langpi Dehangi Rural Bank in Assam Hills

RATAN BORMAN AND AYEKPAM IBEMCHA CHANU

PART - I

Introduction

The Regional Rural Banks (RRBs) have been in existence for more than three and half decades in the Indian financial system. The birth of Regional Rural Banks (RRBs) may be considered as an important phase in the history of modern Indian commercial banking because unlike the objectives of other normal commercial banks, the main objective of Regional Rural Banks is improving the efficacy of rural credit mechanism in India. The RRB Act 1976 clearly mentions that the RRBs are established with a view to developing the rural economy by providing, for the purpose of development of agriculture, trade, commerce, industry and other productive activities in the rural areas; credit and other facilities particularly to small and marginal farmers, agricultural labourers, artisans and small entrepreneurs and for matters connected therewith and incidental thereto. Hence, the geneses of the RRBs can be traced to the need for a stronger institutional arrangement for providing rural credit in order to boost the rural economy of India.

The Regional Rural Banks were established under the provision of an ordinance promulgated on 26 September, 1975 and RRB Act 1976, sharing ownership at the ratio of 50 : 15 : 35 by the Central government, the concerned State government and the sponsored bank. RRBs started functioning (some researchers refer it as reformed process) on 2nd October, 1975 with the formation of Prathama Gramin Bank; later, five other RRBs were established in the year itself. From a modest beginning of 6 (six) RRBs with 17 branches covering 12 districts in 1975, the numbers have grown into 196 with 14,446 branches working in 525 districts across the country in March 2006. However, as per the recommendation of the Vyas Committee (2004), the Government of India initiated the process of structural consolidation of RRBs by amalgamating RRBs which are sponsored by the same bank within a State. Under the process of amalgamation, 145 RRBs have been amalgamated to form 45 new RRBs. As a result, the number of RRBs has reduced from 196 to 133 in April 2007. In Assam, the Assam Gramin Vikas Bank came into the scene on 16th January, 2006 as a product of the amalgamation of four regional banks of Assam, viz., Pragjyotish Gaonlia Bank, Lakhimi Gaonlia Bank, Cachar Gramin Bank and Subansiri Bank. It has emerged the largest RRB in India covering highest number of districts in India. However, the Langpi Dehangi Rural Bank has remained the only regional rural bank that operates in the hill districts of Assam.

RRBs and Financial Inclusion

It is widely accepted in the policy circle that even during the post merger/amalgamation period also, the RRBs represented a powerful instrument for financial inclusion. Their, outreach *vis- à- vis* other schedule commercial banks particularly in remote regions and across population groups of the country is so impressive and it can be easily observed from the various reports published by the Reserve Bank of India. For example, today, RRBs has a large branch network in the rural areas forming around 43 per cent of the total rural branches of commercial banks. In case of deposit account in rural areas, RRBs has a significant share of 31 per cent of all deposit accounts of schedule commercial banks. The performance in the India's North Eastern region is also quite satisfactory. Since, RRBs has local ethos and regional based, it may become an important instrument for financial inclusion particularly in North East India. However, serious studies are to be conducted to know their real contribution in financial inclusion. This chapter is an attempt towards it. Here, the case of Langpi Dehangi Rural Bank is taken into consideration in order to know its contribution in financial inclusion in the two hill districts of Assam. This chapter is divided into different parts: the first part deals with an outline of the paper that includes introduction, RRBs and financial inclusion, objectives and research methodology; the next part is about the financial inclusion and some other consequences of financial exclusion. It is followed by a note on Karbi Anglong and LDRB; the next part shows about the findings of the study and ended with concluding remarks.

Objectives

Though, the banking industry has shown tremendous growth in volume and complexity during the last few decades, there are concerns that banks have not been able to include vast segment of the population, especially the underprivileged sections of the society, into the fold of basic banking services. Distribution of Commercial Bank Branches—Region/State/Union Territory (BSR, RBI, 2010)) shows that, there are certain under-banked States including Assam, where the average population per branch office continues to be quite high. In India, there is a scope for lending Rs 45,000 crores to approximately 400 million people in nearly six million villages and semi-urban areas where only 5 per cent have been served so far by the organized financial sector, with total disbursements of about Rs. 3,900 crore. (Agrawal, 2008) Hence, it is assumed that there is a wide variation with regard to degree of reach of financial services to the population. This precisely explains the reason for undertaking the present study.

The broad objectives, which the study seeks to achieve, are as follows:

- To examine the performance of Langpi Dehangi Rural Bank (LDRB) in delivering financial services in Assam Hills with reference to financial inclusion.
- To assess the challenges faced by Langpi Dehangi Rural Bank (LDRB) in rendering financial services in Assam Hills with reference to financial inclusion.
- To suggest measures for improvement in financial service delivery with reference to financial inclusion

Research Methodology

Area of Study: For the purpose of the study, Langpi Dehangi Rural Bank, the lone rural bank operating in Assam Hills has been selected. As the bank is spread over throughout the Assam Hills and capable of reaching vast segments of populace, the bank is taken for the study.

Data Collection: The study is mainly focus on secondary data, however primary data are also taken into consideration. Relevant data has been taken from various financial institutions including the Reserve Bank of India, Indian Institute of Banking and Finance, Langpi Dehangi Rural Bank, Lead Bank Reports of Assam Hills and NABARD. Survey of various reports submitted to the Government, literatures on financial inclusion are also conducted for the purpose of the study. To elicit further relevant information, interaction with bank officials, NGOs and beneficiaries have also been made.

Study Period : 2006-2010.

PART - II

Financial Inclusion

Financial inclusion has now become the buzzword in academic research, public policy meeting and seminars. Financial inclusion refers to a process that ensures the ease of access, availability and usage of the formal financial system for all members of an economy. It is the *delivery of banking services at an affordable cost to the vast sections of underprivileged and low income groups* (V. Leeladhar, 2005). In other words, it is the provision of affordable financial services, viz., access to payments and remittance facilities, savings, loans and insurance services by the formal financial system for the excluded section. Rangarajan Committee on Financial Inclusion (2008) defines it as *"the process of ensuring access to financial services and timely and adequate credit where needed by vulnerable groups such as weaker sections and low income groups at an affordable cost"*. Here, the term financial services include the entire gamut—savings, loans, insurance, credit, payments, etc. It facilitates efficient allocation of productive resources, helps in reducing the growth of informal sources of credit (such as money lenders) which are often found to be exploitative, bringing the savings of the poor into the formal financial intermediation system. However, at present, financial inclusion is mainly confined to ensuring a bare minimum access to a savings bank account without frills, to all.

Some Consequences of Financial Exclusion

Consequences of financial exclusion will vary depending on the nature and extent of services denied. Financial exclusion complicates day-to-day cash flow management—being financially excluded the low-income households as well as the micro and small enterprises deal entirely in cash and are susceptible to irregular cash flows. In case of low-income households, the absence of access to bank accounts and other saving opportunities will lead to lack of savings; low investments; lack of financial planning and security for old age; difficulties in gaining access to credit or getting credit from informal sources at exorbitant rates; increased unemployment due to lack of self –employment opportunities; higher incidence of crime, etc. The small business may suffer due to loss of access to middle class and higher-income consumers, higher cash handling costs, delays in remittances of money, lots of reliance on private money lenders for small credits. It may thus be advocated that financial exclusion not only widens the *Rich-Poor divide*, it also lead to *Social Exclusion*. Hence, inclusive financial system is required because it enhances efficiency and welfare by providing avenues for secure and safe saving practices and by facilitating a whole range of efficient financial services

PART - III

A Note on Assam Hills and Langpi Dehangi Rural Bank

Karbi Anglong and Dima Hasao Districts are two autonomous hill districts of Assam, falling under Schedule VI of the Indian Constitution and situated in the middle part of Assam. According to 2001 Census, total population of the districts was 10,01,390 persons and density of population was 78 persons per square km. Scheduled Tribe constitute the major segment of the total population in the hill districts representing 55.7 per cent of the total population of the district, sharing 13.7 per cent of the State of Assam. Agriculture and allied activities plays a crucial role in economic pursuit of the people of the hill districts. These two districts are known as "Assam Hills" (Goswami, 1988) and identified as "Special Region District" under category "An" Industrially Backward District by the Central Government (Cherunilam, 1982).

The Assam Hills has a banking network of 67 branches of which 64 branches are of scheduled banks including 43 branches of Regional Rural Banks, i.e., Langpi Dehangi Rural Bank (LDRB) and 3 branches of Assam State Co-operative Bank Ltd. Of these, 16 bank offices are located in the Dima Hasao district. The Lead bank of the district is State Bank of India and it formulates the Annual Credit Plan for the scheduled banks operating in the district. However, the LDRB has a dominant character having offices in many parts of hill districts and catering the need of banking services of the hills population.

LDRB, sponsored by State Bank of India was established on 27th January, 1982 under section 3(!) of Regional Rural Bank Act, 1976. The head office of the bank is located at Diphu of Karbi Anglong district. The bank's area of operation comprises of two hill districts of Karbi Anglong and Dima Hasao in the State of Assam. The bank has a total network of 43 branches and 1 satellite office, out of which 34 branches are operating in Karbi Anglong district and 9 branches and one satellite offices in Dima Hasao district. Out of 43 branches, 6 branches are situated in semi-urban centres and the remaining 37 branches and the satellite office are situated in rural areas.

PART - IV

Findings

(a) Analysis to know the Overall Performance Specially Branch Expansion of LDRB in Assam Hills

No further expansion of LDRB has been taken place in the Hills districts during the past ten years. After the amalgamation of all the

Table 21.1 : Progress of LDR Bank

(Rs. in lakhs)

Indicators	*March 2006*	*March 2007*	*March 2008*	*March 2009*	*March 2010*
No. of Districts covered	2	2	2	2	2
No. of Branches	43	43	43	42	42
(*a*) Rural	34	34	34	33	33
(*b*) Semi-Urban	9	9	9	9	9
Deposit	9891.23	12852.28	13314.21	16254.42	22903.88
Growth %	6.10	29.93	3.59	22.00	40.91
Gross Loan (O/s)	5954.15	7409.53	9195.13	11137.07	13422.04
Growth %	30.50	24.44	24.10	21.00	21.00
Loans to ST/SC	2615.34	6522.09	8243.65	8191.80	10396.64
% of Loan	43.92	88.02	89.65	73.55	77.46
Loan Issued (during the year)	3223.60	3513.01	4419.09	5412.35	5969.45
Growth %	28.45	8.98	25.79	22.48	10.29
Population per office (in 000)	25.58	25.97	26.37	27.90	28.50
Per Capita Deposits (Rs.)	899	1151	1174	1412	1912
Per Capita Credit (Rs.)	541	663	811	968	1120
CD Ratio %	60.2	57.7	69	68.5	58.6

Note : Number of Branches has reduced due to amalgamation.

regional rural banks of Assam, except LDRB under one umbrella as Assam Gramin Vikas Bank in 2004, many new changes have been taken place in the functioning of rural banks. However, no significant change can be seen in case of LDRB. In 2001, there were 43 numbers of branches of LDRB, comprising 37 branches in rural areas and 6 branches in semi-urban areas; it remains the same in 2010 covering 28.50 thousand populations per branch office against all India average of 14.50 thousand as on March 2010. Rather one rural branch has been closed down in 2008 claiming as the socio-political disturbances in the hills. This presents an unhealthy scenario in providing banking services in Assam Hills, as majority of population group lives in rural areas, in spite of being a rural push policy approach (Appendix Table 21.1), though, there are offices of 24 branches of Scheduled Commercial Banks in the districts; majority of offices (more than 50 per cent) are located in semi-urban areas (Table 21.2) catering the need of mostly salaried and business class populace.

Table 21.2 : Population Group and Bank Group-wise Offices of Scheduled Commercial Banks, March 2010

Population Group	*State Bank & Its Associates*	*Nationalised Banks*	*RRB Banks*	*Private Banks*	*Co-op Banks*
A. *Karbi Anglong District*					
Rural	5	3	29	—	—
Semi-Urban	5	3	4	—	2
B. *Dima Hasao District*					
Rural	1	2	7	—	—
Semi-Urban	2	1	2	—	1
TOTAL	13	9	42	—	3

Source : Compiled from Lead Bank Offices of Districts, 2010

(b) Analysis to assess the Degree of Reach of Financial Services to the Population

Here, the quantum of deposit accounts (current and savings) with ratio to the population is taken into consideration. In this context, the Population Census 2001 is taken into account and projected population of Assam Hills; (Table 21.3) clearly shows the ratio of

Table 21.3 : Financial Inclusion Coverage of Banking Services of L.D.R. Bank

Population Group	*Total*		*Rural*		*Urban*	
	2005	*2010*	*2005*	*2010*	*2005*	*2010*
A. *Population per Office*						
Karbi Anglong District	25889	29774	25820	27444	26407	46671
Dima Hasao District	22617	23965	25589	24957	12214	20490

(contd...)

Table 21.3 (contd...)

Assam Hills	25204	28529	25776	26627	21676	39941
B. *Deposits: Number of Savings Accounts per 100 persons*						
Karbi Anglong District	8.08	16.97	6.56	16.28	19.25	19.91
Dima Hasao District	8.48	11.80	5.67	9.79	29.12	20.37
Assam Hills	8.16	16.04	6.39	15.30	21.10	18.99
C. *Credit: Number of Credit Accounts per 100 persons*						
Karbi Anglong District	1.47	2.13	1.11	2.05	4.08	2.44
Dima Hasao District	0.90	0.86	0.54	0.63	3.53	1.83
Assam Hills	1.35	1.90	1.00	1.82	3.97	2.22

Sources : Compiled from Annual Reports of LDR Bank and Statistical Hand Books of Assam

deposit accounts to the total population was only 16.04 per cent as on March 31, 2010, as against all India average of 59 per cent. It is also observed that the ratio of Credit accounts has increased to 1.90 only in 2010 from 1.35 in 2006 which is 9.80 at all India level. In terms of number of accounts, there is a high growth of deposit accounts (120 per cent) between the periods 2006 to 2010; this may be due to mass scale opening of No-frill accounts, which numbers at 83,729 as on 31st March, 2010. There is also a growth of 31.80 per cent only during the corresponding period in case of credit accounts Table 21.4. Compared to the all India level, the coverage of financial

Table 21.4 : Population Group-wise Distribution of Deposit and Credit Accounts of L.D.R. Banks

Population Group	*No. of Offices*	*March 2006*	*March 2007*	*March 2008*	*March 2009*	*March 2010*
Deposit Accounts:						
Karbi Anglong District:						
Rural	30	50016	57674	61749	95700	129595
Semi-Urban	4	19563	15006	20138	31259	37165
Dima Hasao District:						

(contd...)

Table 21.4 (contd...)

Rural	7	10968	11748	11444	13612	17096
Semi-Urban	2	6743	5684	7937	6652	8346
Total	43 ^	87290	90112	101268	147223	192202
Credit Accounts:						
Karbi Anglong District:						
Rural	30	10107	13099	12899	14073	16316
Semi-Urban	4	4429	3168	4504	4372	4562
Dima Hasao District:						
Rural	7	1058	1537	1237	1355	1099
Semi Urban	2	891	859	799	773	750
Total	43*	16485	18663	19438	20573	22727

Note : * Number of branches reduced to 42 in 2009.
Source : Compiled from Annual Reports of LDR Banks.

services is also quite low. Though the RBI promoted no-frills savings bank account, having potentials to revolutionize rural agricultural economy, as well as usher in the banking habit amongst a large number of the less privileged population; the product was lost among a myriad of financial offerings and most banks have shown little verve and vitality in marketing it. Hence, the banking service continues to remain an elitist to lower middle-class pursuit. It is also observed that per capita deposit (Rs. 1,912) and credit (Rs. 1,120) is very low compared to all India average, deposit (Rs. 33,471) and credit (Rs. 24,230). This depicts a low level of performance and a scope for improvement.

(c) Analysis to know the Target Group of Customers for Services

It can be easily found from Table 21.5 which shows the Population Group-wise Distribution of Deposits and Credits of the Bank that during the period March 2006 to March 2010, there is an increasing trend on percentage share of deposits in rural and semi-urban areas. In contrast, share of credit is lower than that of deposits. It also seems that the credits are mostly offered to salaried income groups in order to ensure safety of loans and this clearly brings out bank's aspiration to earn good margins by investing funds into high potential areas, instead of strictly abiding by the RBI norm of priority sector lending to under-developed and undeveloped areas.

This reiterates the need of a holistic approach for financial inclusion.

The Distribution of Commercial Bank Branches in Assam Hills–Bank Group and Population Group-wise (Table 21.2) clearly shows

Table 21.5 : Population Group-wise Distribution of Deposits and Credit of L.D.R. Banks

(Amount in Rs. Lakh)

Population Group	*No. of Offices*	*March 2006*	*March 2007*	*March 2008*	*March 2009*	*March 2010*
Deposit Accounts:						
Rural	37	5152.28	6894.08	7082.19	9864.68	12831.07
%		52.09 %	53.64%	53.19%	60.69%	56.02%
Semi Urban	6	4738.95	5958.82	6232.02	6389.74	10072.81
		47.91%	46.36%	46.81%	39.31%	43.98%
Total	43^	9891.23	12852.28	13314.21	16254.42	22903.88
		100%	100%	100%	100%	100%
Credits:						
Rural	37	3407.97	4302.99	5526.93	6833.91	8581.17
		57.24%	58.07%	60.10%	61.36%	63.93%
Semi-Urban	6	2546.18	3106.54	3668.20	4303.16	4840.87
		42.76%	41.93%	39.90%	38.64%	36.07%
Total	43*	5954.15	7409.53	9195.13	11137.07	13422.04
		100%	100%	100%	100%	100%

Note : Figures in per cent indicate share of total.

* No. of branches reduced to 42 in 2009.

the dispersion of branches among rural, semi-urban by the various bank groups. It is evident from the table that LDR Bank which is the lone Regional Rural Bank operating in Hills District of Assam has 86.05 per cent branches in rural areas followed by State Bank group sharing with 46 per cent and other nationalized banks with a share of 56 per cent. This reiterates the need to sensitize the SBI groups as lead bank and nationalized banks to open more branches in rural areas looking at size of populace and to have a more participation from the rural areas.

From the analysis, it is easily found that though there is a strong initiative from the Government of India and the Reserve Bank of India for financial inclusion and financial reach to vast section of the especially weaker section of the society, the performance of the bank is not appeared to be satisfactory.

Some Challenges

The bank has shown growth in volume and complexity during the period, there are concerns that bank has not been able to include vast segment of the population, especially the underprivileged sections of the society, into the fold of basic banking services. There are many factors which have been acting as hindrance to reach financial services to vast sections. Some of the factors which could find out after conducting the survey of literature and interaction with the officials of Banks, NGOs and SHGs as barriers to access financial services coming from both demand side and supply side may be highlighted as follows.

From the demand side, the big challenges are the poverty, lack of awareness about financial services and products, financial illiteracy and social exclusion. Access to formal financial services also requires documents of proof regarding a persons' identity, income, etc. The poor people do not have these documents and thus are excluded from these services. Moreover, they may subscribe to the services initially but may not use them as actively as others because of high distance between the bank and residence, poor infrastructure, etc. which acts as non-price barrier. The unfriendly attitude of the banks to the customers also plays an important role in undermining the demand for financial services. On top of that, unreasonable and non-transparent fees, combined with burdensome terms and conditions attached to the financial products, also dampens the demand.

From the supply side, the main barrier is the transaction costs that the bankers perceive. Because of current low volumes, banks find that extending financial services is not cost effective and poor people don't utilize the financial services as they find financial services are costly and thus are unaffordable. Hence, even if financial services are available, the high costs deter the poor from accessing them. Furthermore, lack of communication, lack of infrastructure, language barriers and low literacy levels all raise the cost of providing services and prevent bankers from taking initiative from the supply side.

The Requirements

Deepening the financial system and widening its reach is crucial for both accelerating growth and equitable distribution, given the present state of development. After analyzing performances and challenges of LDR Bank, it appears that financial inclusion will not happen on its own and hence, effort should be made to combat various problems of the present Indian society like illiteracy, poverty, ignorance, cultural and psychological hurdles and simultaneously it is required to design innovative, lucrative and low cost banking products and services to lure public and to join the mainstream. Mass banking with no-frills accounts may become a win-win situation for both banks and clienteles. Dr. Vijay Kelkar, Chairman, Finance Commission in N.P. Sen Memorial Lecture at Hyderabad (dated 13/1/2008) said financial inclusion is a quasi public good. Hence, the Government, as facilitator, has to do a lot in this regard. The following measures may be considered for improvement in financial service delivery with reference to financial inclusion:

Giving Awareness and Financial Literacy: Efforts should be made for intensive awareness through education and promotion drive to create an in-depth impact on the masses. Government should promote introduction of basic banking – relevance, services, merits as a topic in secondary and higher secondary classes in all education institutions. Banks should design and organize aggressive education-cum-promotion campaigns in unbanked areas to enhance financial literacy and awareness, as well as to remove the doubts and apprehensions that the masses have towards the banking sector. Banks should involve the knowledgeable and well-informed local inhabitants in such activities. This will help the banks to consolidate and ensure, prompt and extensive response from populace and will drive them to open savings and current accounts. This will mark the beginning of basic banking in true sense.

Re-engineering Business Process: It has already proved at the international level that delivering banking facility to unbanked population that is the poor and weaker section of the society is not only bankable but also banking with them can be profitable. The bankers need to appreciate this realization and respond to the challenge of reaching out to this untapped potential. This would require banks to leverage the potential of technology, re-engineer their business processes and sensitization of their manpower toward this opportunity. It is also necessary that besides offering the conventional products and services they should set up teams who can understand the needs and requirements of the common man and design innovative products and services having greater suitability and desirability. Bank may also open small extension counters. This should simultaneously be supplemented by mobile banks. Wherever it is not economical to set up a branch, *credit camps* or *loan exhibitions* must be organized on weekly basis, to disburse small loans on easy terms. Greater use of technology should be made by the banks to improve their reach, speed of processing, as well as to reduce the operating cost.

Incorporation of other Constituents into formal Banking: The formal lines like no-frills accounts have appeared irrelevant as an instrument today due to absence of transactional value. Many transactions, particularly small borrowers, particularly of backward communities are still involved outside the formal banking system. Therefore, any policy for financial inclusion must be accompanied by a drive to bring other constituents like rural employers, merchants which facilitate payments, into the formal exchange mechanisms of the organized economy.

Collaboration with Other Segments and Introduction of ATMs in Rural Areas: As mentioned above, till today, no ATM facility is provided by the LDRB in the hill districts of Assam. There is an urgent need for collaboration with other segments of the society like co-operative societies; post offices, etc., to render financial services to the people living in remote locality as well as to extend the scope of financial inclusion with minimal intermediation cost. In this context, tying up with micro finance institutions especially SHGs may be a sustainable option. Since large sections of low income groups' transactions are related to deposits and withdrawals, ATMs with operating instructions and commands in vernacular language would greatly facilitate financial inclusions of rural populace as well as containing transaction costs.

Use of Defaults: This mechanism has been used to increase savings in many organizations (Agrawal). A similar mechanism could be deployed to increase usage of bank accounts. It is suggested that instead of giving cash transfers to the public, government should instead credit the bank accounts of the poor electronically. This will make people use their bank accounts. It has already been noted that some State Governments have started routing social security and National Rural Employment Guarantee Scheme through the smart cards. The smart cards are then linked to the bank accounts.

Simplify Procedures: It has been also seen in experiments that poor and weaker sections of the society generally avoids banks because of complicated forms, procedures, etc. Simpler structures will lead to higher footfalls to the banks. RBI along with banks should toil hard to reduce the amount of paper work in relation to the opening of an account as well as in getting small credits. Banks should make sure that local people are positioned in the front offices, so that the general public does not have to endure with language problem and does not have to suffer perceived/actual racial discrimination.

Addressing Social Issues: Promoting financial inclusion should be seen as an important part of wider towards social inclusion where vast sections of the society are engaged in unorganized activity. At the same time, market forces tend to focus more on profitable customers, while undermining those with lower perceived returns. This makes it even more important for policymakers in emerging markets. The initiatives of developing economies like Bangladesh, South Africa, and Bolivia, etc., that have been successful in financial inclusion should be studied to address social issues.

Broader Approach: Till today, the focus of policies has been so far on two areas—to open more bank accounts and providing more credit. But, this is a too narrow view. The poor people also need to invest their savings into financial products that get them higher returns than returns on savings account and fixed deposits. They also need other financial facilities like insurance, pension plans, etc., to manage risks and old-age. Rangarajan report has also mentioned the importance of looking at financial inclusion in a holistic manner and has mentioned the need to look into insurance and remittance needs of the poor. Meanwhile, few efforts have been made in the financial sector to provide financial products to the poor. UTI Mutual Fund tied up with SEWA to provide pension plans to the latter members. However, to make a holistic financial inclusion, removal of demand constraints (financial literacy, etc.) is very important.

Conclusion

The Financial Inclusion Task Force in UK has identified *three priority* areas for the purpose of financial inclusion, viz., *access to banking, access to affordable credit* and *access to free face-to-face money advice.* In the Indian context, Financial Inclusion becomes a serious issue because of its vast diversity and culture. There are problems to extending financial inclusion, but that can be overcome. To overcome the problem, there is a need for a holistic approach on the part of the banks in creating awareness about financial products and its benefits to the people. The banks would have to evolve specific strategies to expand the outreach of their services in order to promote financial inclusion. Banks need to redesign their business strategies to incorporate specific plans to promote financial inclusion of low income group treating it both a business opportunity as well as a corporate social responsibility. It may appear in the first instance that taking banking to the sections constituting "the bottom of the pyramid", may not be profitable but it should always be remembered that even the relatively low margins on high volumes can be a very profitable proposition. Financial inclusion can emerge as commercial profitable business. Financial inclusion is a win-win opportunity for the poor, for the banks and for the nation (Subbarao, 2009). In such a situation, the Regional Rural banks can play a significant role. The case study of LDRB easily shows about its performance and wide prospect of financial inclusion in the future. It is also fact that most of the financially excluded groups are from the rural areas. As RRBs are mainly concentrated in the rural areas of the country, a special focus may be given to RRBs with regard to financial inclusion. In the conclusion, it is also suggested that the government should take strong initiative for financial inclusion by formulating pro-poor people policy and programmes.

NOTES

The Government of India, Ministry of Finance issued nine notification on September 12, 2005 on amalgamation of 28 RRBs into nine new RRBs sponsored by nine banks in six States. These amalgamations have become effective from September 12, 2005.

The Reserve Bank of (RBI) and Government of India (GoI) has initiated several measures to achieve greater financial inclusion. Alternate financial institutions such as micro-finance institutions and Self-Help Groups have also been promoted in order to reach financial services to the excluded group. Some of these measures include:

- *No Frills Accounts:* In November 2005, RBI asked banks to offer a basic banking "no-frills" account with low or zero minimum balances and minimum charges to expand the outreach of such accounts to the low income groups. L.D.R. Bank has opened 83,279 numbers. No-frill accounts till 31st March, 2010.
- *Easier Credit Facility:* Banks were asked to introduce a General Purpose Credit Card (GCC) facility up to Rs. 25,000. The total number of GCCs issued by L.D.R. Bank as on end of March 2010 is 2,486.
- *Simpler KYC Norms:* In order to ensure that people belonging to the low income groups, both in urban and rural areas, do not encounter difficulties in opening bank accounts, the "Know Your Customer" (KYC) procedure for opening accounts was simplified for those accounts with balances not exceeding Rs 50,000 and credits thereto not exceeding Rs. 100,000 in a year.
- *Use of Information Technology:* Banks have been urged to scale up IT initiatives for financial inclusion speedily while ensuring that solutions are highly secure, amenable to audit, and follow widely accepted open standards to ensure eventual inter-operability among the different systems.
- *Electronic Benefit Transfer (EBT) through Banks:* To encourage banks to adopt Information and Communication Technology (ICT) solutions for enhancing their outreach, the RBI formulated a scheme to quicken the pace of adoption of the smart card-based Electronic Benefit Transfer (EBT) mechanism by banks with provision to reimburse the banks a part of the cost of opening accounts with bio-metric access/smart cards for payment of social security benefits, National Rural Employment Guarantee Act (NREGA) payments and payments under other Government benefit programmes which routed to persons belonging to below poverty line (BPL) families.
- *Business Correspondent (BC) Model:* In 2006, RBI permitted banks to use the services of non-governmental organizations, micro-finance

institutions, retired bank employees, ex-servicemen, retired government employees, Section 25 companies, and other civil society organizations as Business Correspondents in providing financial and banking services. In addition, RBI has also permitted banks to appoint the following as BCs (*i*) Individual *kirana*/medical or fair price shop owners; (*ii*) individual Public Call Office (PCO) operators; (*iii*) Agents of Small Savings Schemes of Government of India/Insurance Companies; (*iv*) Individuals who own Petrol Pumps; (*v*) Retired teachers; and (*vi*) Authorised functionaries of well run Self-Help Groups (SHGs) linked to banks. Till 31st March, 2010 L.D.R. Bank 118 numbers has been engaged as BF and 2,506 SHGs are promoted and linked to bank's credit.

- *Bank Branch and ATM Expansion Liberalized:* The RBI has totally freed the location of ATMs from prior authorization and permitted domestic scheduled commercial banks (other than Regional Rural Banks) to open branches in Tier 3 to Tier 6 centres (with population up to 49,999 as per Census 2001) without having the need to take permission from RBI in each case.
- *Expansion of Banks in the North East:* To improve banking penetration in the North East, the Reserve Bank asked the State Governments and banks to identify centres where there is a need for setting up either full fledged branches or those offering forex facilities, handling government business or for meeting currency requirements.
- *Financial Literacy and Credit Counseling:* RBI has advised the convener-bank of each State Level Bankers' Committee (SLBC) to set up a financial literacy-cum-counselling centre in any one district on a pilot basis, and based on that experience, to extend the facility to other districts in due course. So far, 154 credit counselling centres have been set up in various States of the country. These centres are expected to provide free financial education to people in rural and urban areas on the various financial products and services, while maintaining an arm's-length relationship with the parent bank.

REFERENCES

Agrawal, Amol (2008), "The need for Financial Inclusion with an Indian Perspective" *Economic Research*, IDBI Gilts Limited (A wholly owned subsidiary of IDBI Ltd.) Mumbai, March 3, 2008.

Bhandari, Amit K. (2009), "Access to Banking Services and Poverty Reduction: A State-wise Assessment in India", IZA Discussion Paper No. 4132.

Bose, Sukanya (2005), Regional Rural Banks: The Past and Present Debate http//wwwmacroscan.com

Chakra arty, K.C. (2009), "Pushing Financial Inclusion – Issues, Challenges and Way Forward" A presentation at 20th SKOCH Summit 2009, Mumbai on July 17, 2009.

Kelkar, Dr. Vijay, Chairman, Finance Commission in NP Sen Memorial Lecture at Hyderabad (dated 13/1/08).

Connolly, C., and K. Hajaj, (2001), *Financial Services and Social Exclusion*, Financial Services Consumer.

Developing Countries, paper presented at the conference, Access to Finance: Building Inclusive Financial Systems, World Bank, Washington, D.C.

Economic Growth, Financial Deepening and Financial Inclusion by Dr. Rakesh Mohan Annual Bankers' Financial inclusion an abiding virtue, *The Hindu*, Monday, Jan. 16, 2006

Kempson, E. (2006), Policy Level Response to Financial Exclusion in Developed Economies: Lessons for.

Leeladhar, V. (2005), "Taking Banking Services to the Common Man – Financial Inclusion", Commemorative Lecture by Deputy Governor, Reserve Bank of India at the Fedbank Hormis Memorial Foundation at Ernakulam on December 2, 2005

Malhotra Rakesh (2002), Performance of India's Regional Rural Banks: Effect of the Umblical Cord http://wwwalternate-finance.org.uk

Mohan, Rakesh (2006), "Economic Growth, Financial Deepening and Financial Inclusion" Address at the Annual Bankers' Conference 2006, at Hyderabad on Nov. 3, 2006.

Mohan, Rakesh (2006), "Agricultural Credit in India- Status, Issues and Future Agenda", *Economic and Political Weekly*, Vol. XLI, No. 11, March 18-24.

Policy Center, University of New South Wales.

Ramkumar, V. (2008) ,"Financial Inclusion: The Way Forward", CAB Calling, Vol. 32, No. 4, October-December.

Rangarajan, C. (2007), "Financial Inclusion: Some Key Issues", Lecture delivered at Mangalore University, Mangalore, August 10, 2007.

Report on Trends and Progress of Banking in India, RBI (various issues) www.rbi.org.in

Subbarao, Duvvuri (2009), "Financial Inclusion: Challenges and Opportunities", Speech at the Bankers' Club in Kolkata on December 9, 2009.

Thorat, Smt. Usha (2007), "Financial Inclusion—The Indian Experience", Speech at the HMT-DFID Financial Inclusion Conference, 2007, Whitehall Place, London, UK on June 19, 2007.

http://www.agvbank.co.in

www.finmin.nic.in

www.rbi.org

Banking Service and Financial Inclusion in Mizoram : With Special Reference to NABARD Activity

CHANAMBAM NALINI DEVI

Introduction

In India out of 100 persons, only 31 persons hold account in a bank. While in the North Eastern Region it is just 19 persons out of 100 that hold a bank account[1]. This finding is based on the assumption that one person has only one account, theoretically speaking while this assumption may not be correct as many persons could have more than one bank account. We find that on an all India basis 59 per cent of adult population in the country has bank accounts in other words, 41 per cent of the population is unbanked. In rural areas the coverage is 39 per cent against 60 per cent in the urban area. The unbanked population is higher in the North-Eastern region and the Eastern Region[2]. Generally in North Eastern region credit deposit ratio (CDR) is low as compared to the other parts of India. In case of Tripura, the CD ratio is 33 per cent against the national average of 73 per cent as on 31st March, 2011[3]. When compared to Tripura, Mizoram is a little bit higher that is 46.34 per cent.

1. Leeladhor, 2005
2. Thorat, 2007b
3. D. Subbarao

The figure reveals that there is lack of outreach of banking services to the population, at this junction financial inclusion services are doing well in bringing excluded population to the main stream of formal banking system. In India, most of the people are living in rural areas. Out of 203 million households in the country, 147 million are in rural areas and out of it 89 million are farmer households. 51.4 per cent of farm households have no access to formal or informal sources of credit while 73 per cent have no access to formal sources of credit[4].

The banking industry's penetration to unbanked areas is still found sluggish. The role of the Indian banker is challenging. At one end of his spectrum lies the demand to achieve financial inclusion as nearly 50 per cent of the population is yet to be covered under the formal system of banking and at the other end lay the task to fulfil the needs of the existing customer[5]. Financial inclusion is one of the important means for solving the disparity of rural and urban area and it is important for small enterprise mainly run by the weaker section of the society. The financial services include the grants, savings, loans, insurance, credit, payment, etc. The financial system has to provide its function of transferring resources from surplus to deficit, and its aim is to help them come out of poverty, however, it has been found that financial services are used only by a section of the population.

Technology and financial inclusion are the popular coinage in banking parleys in the country. Even if technological upgradation in the country is tardy financial inclusion is a major agenda for Reserve Bank of India (RBI) without financial inclusion banks cannot reach the unbanked. It is a major step towards increasing savings and achieving balanced growth[6]. Out of 6.9 billion people on the planet, just 30 per cent (2.1 billion) have bank accounts while 75 per cent (5.2 billion) people have mobile phones. In India, only 200 million people have access to bank account while 811 million have a mobile phone. For a population of 1.2 billion people, this

4. Ibid. 2.
5. K.C. Chakraborty, CII Conference.
6. Report of sixth Banking Tech Summit of Confidereration of Indian Industry, July 2011.

translates into 68 per cent having a mobile phone and only 17 per cent having a bank account. The numbers speak for themselves; when it comes to reaching the "un-banked" and extending financial inclusion for the large population mobile phone is the key[7]. As we look into the initiative the country is having with technological progress mobile banking has the potential to emerge as a game changer in terms of castes, convenience, and speed of reach.

The Financial Inclusion Fund (FIF) and Financial Inclusion Technology Fund (FITF) have been set up at National Bank for Agriculture and Rural Development (NABARD) for taking up various promotional and development activities and for supporting technological solution, respectively to give a momentum to the financial inclusion. These funds have a corpus of Rs. 500 crore each, with contributions from Government of India, RBI and NABARD Project involving grant of Rs. 40.95 lakh under Financial Inclusion Technology Fund (FITF) and it was sanctioned to Mizoram Rural Bank (MRB) for opening 40,000 accounts in districts (Aizawl to Kolasib) and of which, an amount of Rs. 20.47 lakh has been released. NABARD would also be supporting "core banking solution" project of Mizoram Rural Bank. For better performance of financial inclusion we need better performance of banking sector. The main focused of this chapter were, to study the number of banks operated in Mizoram (district-wise), to study the CD ratio, to study the number of no-frills accounts open under different banks, to study the financial inclusion performance, and to study the role of NABARD in financial inclusion.

Banking Services in Mizoram

Banking has always served as one of the most important instruments of economic development. In Mizoram, public sector banks have widen the horizon of banking activities especially, during the past two decades in tune with the socio-economic needs of the State, up to 31st March, 2007, there were altogether 96 number of bank branches in Mizoram. Out of this 26 were State Bank of India and 54 Regional Rural Banks, 2 are the other scheduled commercial

---

7. WimRaymackers.

banks, 11 are State Co-operative Banks. By February 2008, there are 107 branches of financial institutions in the State consisting of 36 commercial banks, 60 branches of Mizoram Rural Bank (MRB) and 11 branches of Mizoram State Co-operative Apex Bank and the branch of commercial banks and MRB in the State, account for 89 per cent of the total branch in the State. The co-operative credit structure in the State is 2-tier in nature. In addition to the banks, development financial institutions like NABARD, SIDBI and NEDFI also have their presence in the State. Out of 107 branches, 72 are in rural areas whereas the rest 35 are in urban/semi urban areas.

As on 31st March, 2011, the total number of Bank Branches in the State is 116. This is shown in the Table 22.1.

Table 22.1 : Bank Branches as on 31st March, 2011

Sl. No	*Banks*	*Rural*	*Semi-Urban*	*Urban*	*Total*
1.	SBI	19	7	0	26
2.	UCO	0	1	0	1
3.	Vijaya	0	2	0	2
4.	UBI	0	1	0	1
5.	Syndicate	0	2	0	2
6.	CBI	0	1	0	1
7.	BOB	0	1	0	1
8.	PNB	0	1	0	1
9.	IDBI	0	1	0	1
10.	Axis	0	1	0	1
11.	ICICI	0	1	0	1
12.	HDFC	3	1	0	4
	ACB-Total	22	20	0	42
13.	MRB	52	10	0	`62
14.	MCAB	7	5	0	12
Grand Total		81	35	0	116

Source : State Level Banker's Committee Report 28th June, 2011.

Table 22.2 : District-wise distribution of Bank Branches in Mizoram

Sl. No.	District	As on 31st March, 2011				Com Banks	RRBs	District Co-op.	Total	Total Population District-wise
		Rural	Semi-urban	Urban	Total					
1.	Aizawl	15	35	0	50	23	22	5	50	3,25676
2.	Kolasib	9	0	0	9	2	6	1	9	65,960
3.	Mamit	10	0	0	10	3	6	1	10	62,785
4.	Serchhip	11	0	0	11	3	7	1	11	53,861
5.	Lunglei	12	0	0	12	4	8	1	13	1,37,223
6.	Lawngtlai	6	0	0	6	2	3	1	6	73,620
7.	Saiha	4	0	0	4	2	2	1	5	61,056
8.	Champhai	11	0	0	11	3	8	1	12	108,392
	Total	78	35	0	113	42	62	12	116	8,88,573

Source : State Level Banker's Committee Report, 28th June, 2011, Mizoram.

The branch expansion programme of RBI was on in full swing. It aims to bring all villages with a population of 2,000 or more under banking coverage either by setting up branches or by appointing individual correspondents with specific responsibilities, for covering villages where there are logistic problems[8]. Lawngtali district is one of the least develop district in Mizoram and the total population of this area is 73,620. Under this district only six banks are operating, two commercial banks and three regional rural banks and one district co-operative bank. Again in Saiha district there are only five banks operating, two commercial banks, another two regional rural banks and one district co-operative bank and their total population is 61,056. In Mizoram, total number of villages are 817, i.e., eight (8) districts three (3) autonomous district council, twenty-three (23) sub-division, and twenty-six (26) Rural Development Block (2001 Census Report). However, the total number of bank branches is only 116. According to provisional Census report (2011) of the State, the total population is around 10,91,014 but up to June 2011, the total number of bank branches is only 116, as compared to other parts of India. (Table 22.2)

8. D. Subbarao (RBI, Governor).

Table 22.3 : Bank Deposits/Advances and Credit Deposit Ratio

Bank	*31st March, 2005*		*31st March, 2006*		*31st March, 2007*		*31st March, 2008*	
	Deposit	*Advance*	*Deposit*	*Advance*	*Deposit*	*Advance*	*Deposit*	*Advance*
SBI	476.14	240.98	581.26	323.13	722.87	448.73	1493.00	791.60
UCO	21.94	2.74	30.03	4.41	30.67	7.84	37.33	15.89
Vijaya	133.49	49.84	177.55	58.12	182.20	57.79	193.08	48.62
IDBI	—	—	—	—	11.35	0.00	0.00	0.00
UBI	—	—	—	—	3.90	2.05	97.03	10.37
Axis	—	—	—	—	18.59	3.62	63.38	9.13
Syndicate	—	—	—	—	—	—	4.39	1.88
CBI	—	—	—	—	—	—	15.34	5.63
BOB	—	—	—	—	—	—	43.11	1.40
PNB	—	—	—	—	—	—	12.21	12.33
ICICI	—	—	—	—	—	—	6.63	1.43
HDFC	—	—	—	—	—	—	50.36	6.19
MRB	147.10	80.21	166.02	108.54	198.85	128.33	655.75	293.89
MCAB	130.73	86.48	159.18	95.93	176.69	111.88	316.78	186.34
Gr. Total	909.40	460.25	1114.04	590.13	1345.12	760.24	2988.39	1384.70
CD Ratio	50.61	—	52.97	—	56.52	—	46.34	—

Source : *Ibid.*, Table 22.1 (data for 2008, 2009, and 2010 are not available).

Deposit and Credits

The Credit Deposit (CD) ratio generally gives an idea about the extent to which deposit resources have been locally deployed to propel the economy. Though, in itself, it has its own limitations, nevertheless it gives a clue regarding the credit absorption capacity of the local economy provided other things remain favourable.

Generally in North Eastern Region, CD ratio is low as compared to other parts of India. In case of Tripura, the CD ratio is only 33 per cent against the national average of 73.6 per cent. In Mizoram CD ratio is 46.34 per cent. Bank-wise deposits/Advances and credit deposit ratio is shown in Table 22.3. It shows that, CD ratio in the State is decreasing; CD ratio is 50.61, 52.97, and 56.52 in 2005, 2006 and 2007 respectively but in 2011 ratio is only 46.34 it shows that the financial inclusion programme is not sufficient in the State it needed to be strengthened.

Table 22.4 which shows number of no-frills accounts opened under different banks shows that the number of persons is minimum as compared to the State population and the number of SHG linked account is also minimum that is 2,854 only. We need to improve on this sector as well. In Mizoram, the role of NABARD is promising, this bank implemented many schemes under the Central government and they have been collaborating with State government in implementing some schemes for overall development in the State and also process for the implementation of financial inclusion plans in all the districts with particular reference to Lawngtlai district, which is the financially least included district in the State. Besides this, they have been planning increase agricultural credit, production credit and investment credit in coordination with banks, NGOs and government. Not only this they also have been trying to strengthen micro-finance by increasing linking of SHGs and JLGs, up scaling of Farmers' Club and implementation of rural infrastructure development projects in a planned manner.

Financial Inclusion in Mizoram

The term financial inclusion is perceived in different ways under different contexts. First, it is a view that only access to credit is treated as financial inclusion, whereas, the other view includes all the services extended by the financial institutions. Apart from that,

Table 22.4 Number of no-frills account opened under different banks

Banks	No. of No-frills account opened			No. of SHQ linked			No. of Banking Correspondents			Total deposit at the bank branch (As in lacs)		
	Last quarter	ADD	Q.END	Last quarter	ADD	Q.END	Last quarter	ADD	Q.END	Last quarter	ADD	Q.END
SBI	4684	658	5342	196	–25	171	2	0	2	49478	99822	149300
UCO	253	4	257	13	0	13	0	0	0	3327	406	3733
Vijaya	0	0	0	0	0	0	0	0	0	16938	2970	19308
UBI	324	29	353	25	0	25	0	0	0	8923	780	9703
Syndicate	340	3	343	0	0	0	0	0	0	453	–14	439
CBI	548	2	550	35	0	35	0	0	0	2072	–538	1534
BOB	340	17	357	27	0	27	0	0	0	1621	2690	4311
PNB	2546	954	3500	11	1	12	0	0	0	876	345	1221
IDBI	12	0	12	0	0	0	0	0	0	0	0	0
Axis	119	0	119	0	0	0	0	0	0	6251	87	6338
ICICI	117	–2	115	0	0	0	0	0	0	539	124	663
HDFC	6	3	9	0	0	0	0	0	0	4963	73	5036
	0	0	0	0	0	0	0	0	0	0	0	0
MRB	65225	29239	94464	1958	77	2035	0	0	0	55216	10359	65575
MCAB	6302	214	6516	527	9	536	0	0	0	29093	2585	31678
Total	80816	31121	111937	2792	62	2854	2	0	2	179750	119089	298839

Source : *Ibid.*, Table 22.1.

financial inclusion by banks and other institutions must target, apart from personal/private investment requirements of individuals and groups, the universal public investment requirements necessary for development of infrastructure, social sector services, public utilities and productive forces/capacity building efforts etc. On 29th December, 2003, former UN Secretary General Kofi Annan has stated that the stark reality is that most poor people in the world still lack access to sustainable financial services, whether it is savings, credit or insurance. The great challenge before us is to address the constraints that exclude people from full participation in the financial sector. Together, we can and must build inclusive financial sectors that help people improve their lives. The United Kingdom was one of the first countries to realize the importance of financial inclusion. The Reserve Bank of India has set up a commission (Khan Commission) in 2004 to look into financial inclusion and the recommendation of the commission was incorporated into the mid-term review of the policy (2005-2006). In the report RBI exhorted the banks with a view of achieving greater financial inclusion to make available a basic "no-frills" banking account.

In India financial inclusion first featured in 2005, when it was introduced, that, too, from a pilot project in UT of Pondicherry, by K.C. Chakraborty, the Chairman of Indian Bank. Mangalam Village became the first village in India where all households were provided banking facilities. In January 2006, the Reserve Bank permitted commercial banks to make use of the services of non-governmental organizations (NGOs/SHGs), micro-finance institutions and the other civil society organizations as intermediaries for providing financial and banking services. These intermediaries could be used as business facilitators (BF) or business correspondents (BC) by commercial banks. The RBI asked the commercial banks in different regions to start a 100 per cent financial inclusion campaign on a pilot basis. Mizoram State level banker's committee report dated 28th June, 2011, has reported that the bankers have decided to achieve 100 per cent financial inclusion in the Aizawl district as a pilot project, however so far the achievement made by the bankers have not been made public[9].

9. State Level Bankers Committee Report 28th June, 2011.

No Frills Accounts

In November 2005, RBI asked banks to offer no-frills savings account which enables excluded people to open a saving account. Normally, the savings account requires people to maintain a minimum balance and most banks now even offer various facilities with the same. No-frills account requires no (or negligible) balance and is without any other facilities leading to lower costs both for the bank and the individual. The number of no-frills account has increased mainly in public sector banks from about 0.4 million to 6 million between March 2006 and March 2007. The number of no-frills accounts in private sector banks also increased from 0.2 million to 1 million in the same period[10]. We should work towards bringing nearly 400 million citizens to the formal fold of the banking sector. It is not just about opening no-frills accounts. As of today, 75 million no-frills accounts have been opened but there are hardly any transactions in term. Banks need to work towards providing a full range of financial services and this would need a lowest, reliable, easy to use and secure technology backbone linking six lakhs villages in the next four-five years[11].

The brief account structure under the no-frills policy of RBI in the State under the different commercial and regional banks operated in the State is shown in Table 22.4, under this policy the total number of account opened under the no-frills account is 1,11,937 at the end of the March 2011, and number of self-help group linked accounts are 2,854 only. The maximum number of no-frill account holder is seen in Mizoram Rural Bank. The total number of account holder is 96,499 and in Mizoram Co-operative Apex Bank Ltd. The number of account holder is 7,052 with number of SHG linked account and this is the second highest account holding bank. However, in Vijay Bank there are no accounts opened under the no-frill account. SBI has 5,515 accounts which are opened with SHG linked and they are further link to other two banking correspondent.

SBI is the only bank which have banking correspondent. In case of HDFC they have only 9 SHG link account are opened. Under the no-frill account opened in PNB it is little better than the other

10. Anmol Agrawal, March 3, 2008.
11. K.C. Chakraborty, CII Conference July 2011.

remaining banks, i.e., 3,512 account. In case of CBI they have 585, BOB-384, UBI-378, Syndicate-343, UCO-270, Axis-119, ICICI-115, IDBI-12, etc. Table 22.5 shows current, saving and SHG deposits under different banks.

Table 22.5 shows that under these two banks IDBI and HDFC, there is no any type of deposits from the private as well as SHGs. The SHG Bank linkage programme can be regarded as the most potent initiatives since independence for delivering financial services to the poor in a sustainable manner. The programme has been growing rapidly and the number of SHGs financial dealing increased to 29.25 lakhs on 31st March, 2007. For the North Eastern region, there is need to evolve SHG models suited to the local context of such areas. SHGs have been credit-linked with banks, benefiting more than 400 lakh poor families. There is a need for further depending and up sealing of micro-finance interventions. In India out of the total SHGs, women groups are 86 per cent represent.

Table 22.5 shows the least number of SHG opened and operated in the State. For example, Vijaya Bank, Syndicate, IDBI, Axis, ICICI, HDFC. At the end of 31st March, 2011 the total number of 2,854 SHGs which have opened their accounts under different banks and their total amount of deposited money is 891.89 lakhs and the advances given to them by these different banks are 3402.16 lakhs.

Under the PNB, 12 SHGs have opened their account and their deposited amount is 1.70 lakhs but they are not giving any credit advances to them. And in the case of Canara Bank of India, 35 numbers of SHGs have opened their accounts and their deposited amount is 2.15 lakhs but their credit advances is also very minimum only 0.42 lakhs. Under the UBI, 25 member of SHGs are opened their account and their deposited amount is 0.78 lakhs but their advances to them is little higher than the above two banks, i.e., 8.78 lakhs. Under the UCO bank only 13 number if SHGs have opened their account and their deposited amount is also very minimum only 0.03 lakhs, however, this bank give advance to them at the tune of 8.72 lakhs. In the case of SBI, 171 SHGs are opened their accounts and their deposited money is 20.95 lakhs and their outstanding in this sector is 511.60 lakhs. Mizoram Rural Bank taking a very good role in the banking services in the State. Under

Table 22.5 : Current, saving and SHG Deposits under Different Banks

Banks	Current Deposits Quarter end		Saving Deposits Quarter end		SHG Deposits (Rs. in Lacs)			
	(i) No	(ii) Amount	(i) No	(ii) Amount	No. of SHGs Q.END	No. of SHGs Members Q.END	Amount Q.END	Total SHG Advance (outstanding) Q.END
SBI	1172	46566.88	101246	61935.24	171	2511	20.95	511.60
UCO	143	214.19	3348	1117.48	13	104	0.03	8.72
Vijaya	425	1833.00	11335	6064.00	0	0	0.00	00.00
UBI	123	327.00	2427	4729.00	25	238	0.78	8.78
Syndicate	35	56.18	1352	273.76	0	0	0.00	0.00
CBI	127	166.64	1304	565.37	35	350	2.15	0.42
BOB	25	2.15	191	38.57	27	270	0.41	1.61
PNB	96	438.05	4253	312.48	12	170	1.70	0.00
IDBI	0	0.00	0.00	0.00	0.00	0.00	0.00	0.00
Axis	425	1755.00	5059	4259.00	0.00	0.00	0.00	0.00
ICICI	48	330.17	1829	375.88	0.00	0.00	0.00	0.00
HDFC	0	0.00	0.00	0.00	0.00	0.00	0.00	0.00
MRB	1553	3154.82	239018	37083.40	2035	27572	844.42	2844.76
MCAB	7303	1577.46	62251	18820.29	536	7246	21.45	26.27
Total	11476	56421.54	433613	135574.47	2854	38461	891.89	3402.16

Source : *Ibid.*, Table No. 1.

this bank, maximum number of SHGs has opened their accounts this stood at 2035 and their deposited amount is 844.42 lakhs and their credit advances to them are 2844.76 lakhs. Mizoram Co-operative Apex Bank is also taking a good role. A total number of 536 SHGs have opened their accounts and their deposited amount is 21.45 lakhs and their credit advance to them is 26.27 lakhs.

Role of NABARD in Mizoram

National Bank for agriculture and rural development (NABARD) was established by an Act of the Parliament on July 12, 1982. NABARD was set up by Government of India as development bank with a mandate for providing and regulating credit and other facilities for the promotion and development of agriculture, small scale industries, cottage and village industries, handicrafts and other rural crafts and other allied economic activities in rural areas with a view to promoting integrated rural development and securing prosperity of rural areas. During the just concluded financial year (2010-11) National Bank of Agriculture and Rural Development (NABARD) achieved all time high performance in Mizoram State[12]. Some of the achievement of NABARD is given below:

Refinance for Investment Credit: NABARD provides medium term and long term refinance to Commercial Banks, Regional Rural Banks and Co-operative Banks for various investment purposes like minor irrigation, horticulture, land development, animal husbandry, forestry and wasteland development and also to non-farm sector including rural housing, agro-processing, etc. Refinance amounting to Rs. 23.05 crore was disbursed during the current year against the achievement of Rs. 10.60 crore during the last year as per details given below.

Central Government Sponsored Schemes: NABARD has been facilitating implementation of various centrally sponsored credit linked schemes with particular reference to animal husbandry schemes. As envisaged under these schemes, NABARD is the convener of the State Level Sanctioning and Monitoring Committee (SLSMC) for guiding their implementation. The Subsidy under these schemes is also administered by NABARD.

12. Dr. P.M. Ghole.

Sl. No	Agency	2009-2010	2011-2012
1.	CBs	44.35	222.64
2.	MRB	0.0	620.20
3.	MCAB	1016.31	1461.79
	Total	1060.66	2304.63

Source : NABARD Annual Report 2010-11.

Venture Capital Fund for Dairy and Poultry Projects: Besides this, interest free loan of Rs. 18.11 lakh was also disbursed to SBI in respect of 107 borrowers and under Dairy Entrepreneurship Development Scheme, capital subsidy of Rs. 1.00 lakh was disbursed in respect of 1 borrower.

Sl. No	Agency	As on 31-3-2010		As on 31-3-2011	
		No. of Units	Interest free loan sanctioned	No. of Units	Interest free loan sanctioned
1.	SBI	289 (Dairy)	433.50	301 (Dairy)	451.50
2.	MCAB	18 (Dairy)			
		7 (Poultry)	48.50	20 (Dairy)	65.00
			—	8 (Poultry)	—
3.	MRD	3 (Dairy)		3 (Dairy)	9.50
		2 (Poultry)	9.50	2 (Poultry)	—
	Total	319	491.50	334	526.00

Source : NABARD Annual Report 2010-11.

Pig Development, Small Ruminants and Poultry Development: Following subsidy claims were sanctioned by SLSMC. The amount would be released on receipt of funds from GoI.

Sl. No	Agency	As on 31-3-2011	
		No. of Units	Interest free loan sanctioned
1	MCAB	1 (Piggery)	0.25
2	MRB	292 (Piggery)	50.56
	Total	293	50.81

Source : Annual Report 2010-11.

Refinance for Production Credit: For the first time in many years, Mizoram Rural Bank was sanctioned a credit limit of Rs. 80 lakhs to support its loans granted for seasonal agriculture operations (Crop Loans) and the amount has been fully disbursed.

Promotional Programmes under Rural Non-Farm Sector: NABARD provides grant support to NGOs for promotion of rural non-farm sector. The main activities support is skill development/ upgradation, technology upgradation, construction of Rural Haat, cluster development etc. The details are given below:

Sl. No	*Programme*	*2009-2010*		*2010-2011*		
		No. of Prog	*Amount*	*No. of Prog*	*Partic-ipants*	*Amount Disbursed*
1.	Skill upgradation programme	22	10.7	21	540	9.38
2.	Support for marketing	0	0.0	1	20	0.47
3.	Rural *Haat*	4	10.7	5	4000	14.92
4.	Cluster Development	1	2.71	1	Weavers 200	4.21
5.	Innovative project	0	0	1	2	3.78
6.	RSETI	0	0	1	7	3.73
7.	Rural Mart	0	0	1	SHG 1	0.33
	Total	26	24.11	31		37.15

Source : NABARD Annual Report 2010-11.

An innovative project for development of prototype of portable grass cutting-cum-drilling machine was sanctioned for the first time in the State. Again for the first time, one Rural Mart was sanctioned to Kalkidan SHG, Durtlang for marketing of products of SHGs and rural artisans.

1. ***Farmer's Clubs:*** Farmer's Club is an informal forum of progressive farmers coming together to organize technology transfer, credit and marketing for carrying out their activities. NABARD provides grant support for maintenance of such clubs and for taking up various promotional activities by the clubs. The clubs are formed by banks or NGOs including KVKs. So far, 103 farmers' clubs have been formed in the State, of which 21 FCs were formed during the current year.

2. ***Farmers Technology Transfer Fund (FTTF):*** With a view to create awareness about improved crop technology for major crops, animal husbandry schemes, farmer's clubs, SHGs, JLGs, financial literacy, etc. One project for installation Solar Drier, Solar Water Heating System and Solar Lighting System for processing of organic turmeric was also sanctioned to a co-operative society under FTTF.

3. ***NABARD Consultancy Organisation:*** New Land Use Project (NLUP) is a flagship programme of the government of Mizoram. Under NABCONs, one consultancy assignment regarding preparation of detailed project reports for 2 identified clusters in a comprehensive and integrated manner is expected to serve as a model for development of agriculture and rural areas of Mizoram State. Further, MPLADS study of Kolasib District was conducted by NABARD during the year. Seven District level awareness programmes on "Forward Market Trading" were also organized at different district headquarters during the year.

4. ***Financial Inclusion:*** Financial Inclusion is the process of ensuring access to the timely and adequate credit and financial services by vulnerable groups such as weaker sections and low income groups at affordable cost. Financial inclusion is a national agenda. Two dedicated funds, viz., financial inclusion fund and financial inclusion technology fund (FITF) has been set up at NABARD for taking up various promotional and developmental activities and for supporting technological solution, respectively to give a momentum to financial inclusion. These funds have corpus of Rs. 500 crore each, with contributions from Government of India, Reserve Bank of India and NABARD Project involving grant of Rs. 40.95 lakh under financial inclusion technology fund (FITF) was sanctioned to Mizoram Rural Bank (MRB) for opening 40,000 accounts in two districts (Aizawl and Kolasib) and of which, an amount of Rs. 20.47 lakh has been released. NABARD would also be supporting 1 crore Banking Solution Project of Mizoram Rural Bank.

5. ***Micro-Finance:*** SHG-Bank linkage is the largest micro-finance programme pioneered by NABARD. SHG Bank linkage has proved to be an effective strategy for reaching the unreached population of our country. Considering its advantages to both banks and borrowers, the participating banks have adopted this as their mainstream activity. NABARD, on its part has taken up various initiatives to promote SHG-Bank linked Progragmme, the details of which are as under:

Sl.No	Programme	No. of Programmes	No. of Participants	Amount
1.	Training on SHGs	12	190	2.62
2.	Micro-enterprise developmont programme	14	270	1.65
3.	Marketing intervention	4	(8 SHGs) 60	0.84
4.	JLG promotion	2	41	0.32
5.	SHG promoting institution	8	36 (SHGs)	1.92
	Total	40		7.35

Source : NABARD Annual Report 2010-11.

* Sponsored NGO/SHG stalls in Anthurium Festival at Reiek in Mamit District, Kohima (Nagaland) and Bhimthadi Jatra (Pune).
* Organised training-cum-exposure visits on micro-finance to Bidar (Karnataka) and Puri (Odisha) for Board of Directors of MCAB, bank officials, NGOs, KVK and progressive farmers.

During the year, NABARD promoted the concept of Joint Liability Groups (JLGs), which is a group of 4-10 persons with homogeneous background, coming together to avail loans from banks for undertaking a similar economic activity and the members of which are jointly liable for repayment of the loan at all members. The economic activities could be in farm or non-farm sector. In order to promote this concept, state level and district level workshops on JLGs were conducted by NABARD and pamphlets have been printed on JLGs for use by bankers and borrowers. One JLGPI Project was sanctioned to MCAB for promoting 120 JLGs. MCAB has made a beginning under JLGs in financing targeted group.

Conclusion

For development of any nation, the role of banking is very important, without the proper functioning in the banking sector there is difficult to setting development target. So, banking performance and developmental activities go hand in hand. Today, banks are already offering services over mobile to communities that have been historically unbanked. In rural areas, where accessibility is a problem, banks are using the micro-finance network and business correspondents and facilitators to bring more people under the ambit of banking services. Capitalizing on the huge untapped potential in smaller towns and cities and rendering financial services to this segment of people poses a big challenge, few banks have explored technology solutions to increase the scale of their micro-finance portfolios, with the use of smart cards and core banking solution. However, often a multitude of operational issues and quoted as reasons for lagging behind in financial inclusion targets. Till such time complete technology integration takes place on all fronts, there are bound to be areas where intermediate brick-and-mortar structures need to be in place. Even with Business Correspondents (BCs) issues arise regarding their supervision and customer grievance redressed. Certain accounting issues in this regard also needed to be addressed. All these operational issues and many more can be resolved if banks begin to look at financial inclusion as business opportunity rather than an obligation to fulfil their corporate social responsibility.

North Eastern Region is lacking behind in almost all the sectors like infrastructural facilities, industrial sector and service sector which include under this sector mainly hospital facilities and banking facilities. For all round development we need to develop proper facilities for banking service in different areas in this region. Recently, D. Subbarao has stressed that "Credit Flow" in North East is a major challenge and said, "the RBI would prioritise this as a major task to stimulate growth of industry, trade and commerce in the region". Low credit deposit ratio in the region is an area of concern. In case of Tripura, the CD ratio is 33 per cent against the national average of 73.6 per cent on 31st March. "Our target is to ensure that CD ratio in Tripura should rise to 40 per cent at the end of this current financial year", he said. In Mizoram CD ratio is 46.34 per cent. This is a little bit higher than Tripura but it is still low when compared to the national average. However, in other developed countries CD ratio is more than 90 per cent. At present in Mizoram, the number of bank branches operated in the State is only 116 and according to provisional Census report (2011) total population of the State is around 10,91,014. So, the banking figure is not sufficient and needed more and more number of bank branches for achieving the financial inclusion programme in the State.

REFERENCE

Financial Inclusion and Empowerment of Indian Rural Households, B.B. Barik.

Financial Inclusion and Micro-Finance in India: An Overview—Jayasheela, Dinesha P.T. and Basil Hans, available in http://ssrn.com/abstrct=1089680

Financial inclusion, UN available in, http://en.wikipedia.org/wiki/financial inclusion

Financial Inclusion—RBI initiatives—Dr. K.C. Chakraborty (National Seminar of Launching a National Initiative for financial inclusion, organized by DFS, GoI at New Delhi Sept. 2009.)

Financial Inclusion—The Indian Experience—Usha Thorat (RBI monthly bulletin, July 2007).

Major role of technology in financial inclusion, Oommen A. Ninan,*The Hindu*, July 11, 2011.

Mizoram Statistical Handbook 2011.

NABARD, Regional Office Report, Aizawl (2010-2011).

National Bank for Agriculture and Rural Development Committee to Rural Prosperity 2009.

Rangarajan Committee Report on Financial Inclusion in India, 2008.

RBI plans branches in all seven States—*Hindu* Special Correspondent, *The Hindu*, 20/5/11.

Reserve Bank of India, speeches published on financial inclusion and rerated topics in its following, monthly bulletin during 2006-2007.

State Level Banker Committee Report (June, 2011).

The need for financial inclusion with an Indian perspective- Economic Research (IDBI Gilts) Amol Agrawal-2008.

Use technology to achieve financial inclusion"—*Hindu* special correspondent, *The Hindu*, 26/6/11.

23

Regional Rural Bank and its Role in Financial Inclusion : A Case Study of Meghalaya

SHANKAR SARMA AND TH. CHAOBA SINGH

Introduction

The major segment of Indian population lives in the rural area and most of them are not availing benefits of financial institution, only 41 per cent of the adult population of the country has access to the benefits of financial institution (RBI GHY, 2008). In other words we can say that 59 per cent of the adult population is outside of the purview of the financial inclusion. Our nation has introduced several reforms to inculcate the formal financial habit of the excluded people. In the Eleventh Plan idea of financial inclusion has received a deep attention of financial regulators, government and the banking sector, like many other nations.

In India rural credit policy was framed in keeping two main objectives in mined: (*i*) To include a large number of population within the formal financial system; and (*ii*) By using credit instrument for poverty eradication. To achieve these goals, Government of India and RBI had introduced series of measures but failed to achieve the goals. A working group was constituted in the year 1975 by Government of India under the Chairmanship of M. Narasimham to explore the possibilities of an alternative rural credit agency. Following the recommendations of the above said Committee, the Reserve Bank of India (RBI) was set up first on 2nd October, 1975. As on 31st March 2010, there were 82 RRBs with a network of 15,475 branches spread over 619 districts in 26 States and 1 Union Territory.

Reserve Bank of India (RBI) vides its circular No. RBI/2005-06/288 on January 25, 2006 has enabled banks to use the services of Non Governmental Organization/Self-Help Groups (NGOs/SHGs), Micro Finance Institutions (MFIs) and other Civil Society Organizations (CSOs) as intermediaries in providing financial and banking services through the use of business facilitator and correspondent models. This has furthered the scope of extending banking facilities in untapped/ non banked area.

Financial inclusion is the delivery of financial services at an affordable cost to low income household. The term "financial inclusion" has gained importance since the early 2000s, and is a result of findings about financial inclusion and its direct correlation to poverty. Financial inclusion is now a common objective for many central banks among the developing nations. Financial Inclusion includes assessing of financial products and services like:

- Savings facility.
- Credit and debit cards access.
- Electronic fund transfer.
- All kinds of commercial loans.
- Overdraft facility.
- Cheque facility.
- Payment and remittance services .
- Low cost financial services .
- Insurance (Medical insurance).
- Financial advice.
- Pension for old age and investment schemes.
- Access to financial markets.
- Micro credit during emergency.
- Entrepreneurial credit.

Objectives and Methodology of the Study

The objective of the study is to analyze the performance of Meghalaya Rural Bank (MRB) in Financial Inclusion. For the purpose of analyzing the performance of MRB, both primary and secondary data have been collected from the annual report of the Banks and various journals, articles published by Government and non-Government agencies. The parameters used for measuring the performance of MRB in Financial inclusion are, volume of deposit, volume of loan and advances disbursed, Branch expansion of MRB and Number of accounts.

Meghalaya Rural Bank

Meghalaya Rural Bank was established on 29th December, 1981 under the provision of the RRB act 1976. The initial name of MRB was KA BANK Nong.Kyndong RI Khasi Jaintia. The operation of the banks was confined to Khasi and Jaintia hills only. On May 2007, the Bank was renamed as Meghalaya Rural Bank and the area of operation was also expanded to Garo Hills. At present the area of operation cover six districts of the States, namely, East Khasi Hill, West Khasi Hills, Jaintia Hills, RiBho, East Garo Hills District, West Garo Hills District. The MRB has been playing a significant role for the welfare of the people and for the economic development of the State. MRB was established to catch the credit needs of the various sections of the people of State especially for small and marginal farms, lenders, labours and rural artisans.

Analysis

Keeping parity with the objectives as stated above authors have made an attempt to analyze the performance of MRB in the financial inclusion. To get the candid idea about the branch expansion of MRB during the last decade the authors have constructed the following Table 23.1.

Table 23.1 : Branch Expansion (Coverage of MRB)

Year	Total no. of branch	Rural	Semi Urban	Urban	Metropolitan
2001-2002	51	42	7	2	NA
002-2003	51	42	7	2	NA
2003-2004	51	42	7	2	NA
004-2005	51	42	7	2	NA
2005-2006	51	42	7	2	NA
2006-2007	51	42	7	2	NA
2007-2008	52	42	8	2	NA
2008-2009	54	42	10	2	NA
2009-2010	55	42	10	3	NA

Source : Annual Report of Meghalaya Rural Bank—Various issues.

The aforesaid figures have also been presented through the following Figure 23.1.

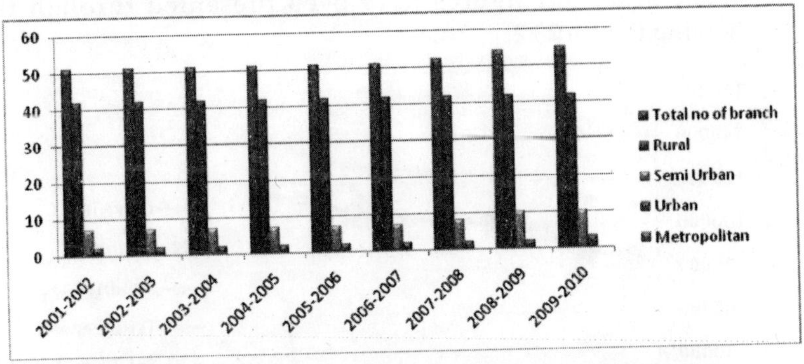

Figure 23.1 : Branch Expansion of Meghalaya Rural Bank

The branch expansion was stagnant for the first six years in the last decade and the expansion took place in the last 3 years of the study period. The branch expansion took place mostly in the semi-urban area and the number of branches increased by 3 branches. In the rural area the branch expansion was constant except in the year 2009-2010 where the number of branches increases by one branch only.

Having discussed about the branch expansion the authors now proposed to measure the performance of MRB by taking accounts of the customer as one of the parameters. To get lucid idea about the different types account maintained by the customer the author has constructed the following Table 23.2.

Table 23.2 : Number of Account Holder

Year	*Current A/C*	*Saving A/C*	*Sundries A/C*	*Term deposit*	*Special Term deposit*	*R. Deposit*	*Total*
2000-2001	1564	85359	5	6695	11252	2806	107681
2001-2002	1934	88345	7	6562	12438	2725	112011
2002-2003	2819	96928	4	8677	12371	2827	123626
2003-2004	2303	101270	5	5385	12156	3060	124179
2004-2005	2366	102843	8	5363	11330	2544	124454
2005-2006	2549	103680	12	6903	11444	2606	127194
2006-2007	3199	107387	10	4880	10191	2058	127725
2007-2008	3897	111956	10	6443	9709	1964	133979
2008-2009	4445	116315	204	7854	10363	2175	141355

Source : Annual Report of Meghalaya Rural Bank—Various issues.

The aforesaid figures have been presented through the following Figure 23.2:

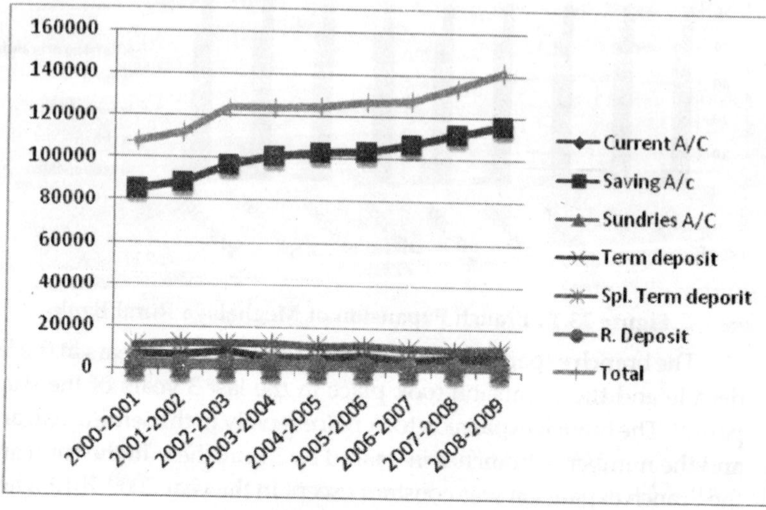

Figure 23.2 : Number of Account Holders

Total number of bank account was 1,12,011 in 2001-2002 which has increased to 1,41,355 in 2008-2009. Registering an increase by 1.26 times, the total number of account consist of current account, savings account, sundries account, term deposit account Special term account and recurring deposit account. The number of current account, savings account, sundries account, term deposit account Special term account and recurring deposit account. has increased by 2.30, 1.32, 29, .14, 1.20, 0.83, 0.80, 1.26 times respectively during the study period.

Table 23.3 : Deposit Accepted by MRB

(Rupees in thousand)

Year	*Current A/c*	*Saving A/c*	*Sundries A/c*	*Term deposit*	*Spl. Term deposit*	*Recurring deposit A/c*	*Total*
2000-2001	187642	480688	16	122870	423304	11773	1226293
2001-2002	147869	621465	7	145285	502400	15158	1432184
2002-2003	115709	714506	740	177619	527012	18373	1553959

(contd...)

Table 23.3 (contd...)

2003-2004	200773	756964	350	214165	565791	20084	1758127
2004-2005	303357	1000441	1074	255302	618337	20685	2199196
2005-2006	373706	1139503	336	214759	742559	23222	2505085
2006-2007	383981	1362052	779	296836	737388	20349	2801385
2007-2008	278311	1685299	1540	359967	814177	20555	3159848
2008-2009	380039	2185104	932	382486	1067692	23192	4039445

Source : Annual Report of Meghalaya Rural Bank—Various issues.

Having discussed about the number of accounts the authors now proposed to measure the performance of MRB by taking into account of the volume of deposit customer as one of the parameters. To get a vivid idea about the volume of deposit accepted by the bank, the author has constructed above Table 23.3

The aforesaid figures have been presented through the following Figure 23.3.

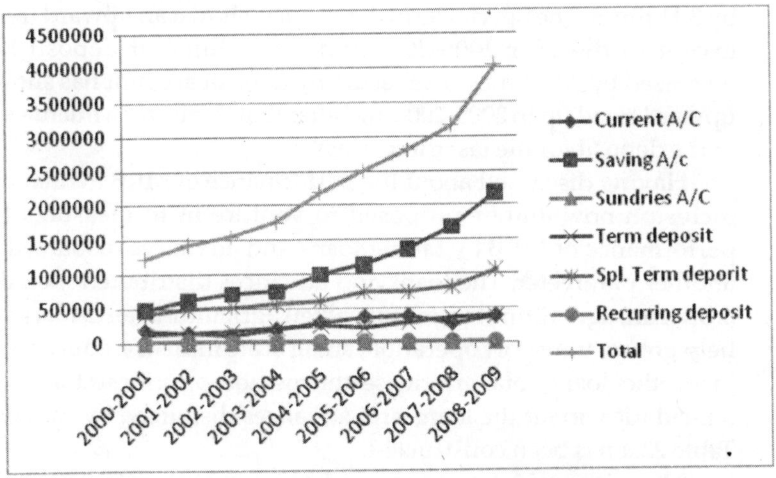

Figure 23.3 : Deposit accepted by MRB

From the analysis of Table 23.3, it is found that the total deposit accepted by the bank was Rs. 12,26,293 thousand in 2000-2001 which has increased to Rs 40,39,445 thousand in the year 2009-2010, thus registering an increase by 3.29 times since 2000-2001. The total deposit was gradually increasing and has shown an upward trend since 2000-2001. The total deposit consists of deposit in current account (A/c), savings A/c, Sundries A/c, Term deposit A/c, Special term deposit and recurring deposit.

The deposit in the current account was Rs. 1,87,642 thousand in 2000-2001 and increased to Rs. 3,80,039 thousand in 2009-2010 thus registering an increase by 2.03 times. The deposit in current account was not satisfactory in 2002-2003 and 2007-2008 as the volume of deposit decreased in both the years as compared to its previous years. The Savings Bank account has shown an upward trend and the deposit in the Savings Bank account was Rs. 4,80,688 thousand in 2000-2001 which has increased to Rs. 21,85,104 thousand registering an increase by 4.55 times.

Sundries deposit was Rs. 16 thousand in 2000-2001, which has increased to Rs. 932 thousand in 2009-2010 thus registering an increase by 58.25 times and growth rate of deposit has shown a wide fluctuation. The term deposit account has shown upward trend except in the year 2005-2006 and the deposit have increased by 3.11 times. The Special term deposit has shown an upward trend except in the year 2006-2007 and the volume of deposit has increased by 2.52 times. The recurring deposit account has shown upward trend up to 2005-2006 and after that there was a fluctuation in the deposit for the last three years.

Having discussed about the performance of MRB in financial inclusion now author proposed to venture in to measures the performance of MRB by taking loans and advances disbursed as another parameter. The loans and advances distributed includes crop loan, agricultural term loan, allied agricultural term loan, self help group, transport operation, small scale industry, educational loan, other loans, total priority sector and non-priority sector. To get a lucid idea about the loans and advances disbursed by the bank Table 23.4 has been constructed.

The aforesaid figures have been presented through the following Figure 23. 4.

The total loan and advances was Rs. 123,616 thousand in the year 2000-2001 which has to Rs. 6,93,140 thousand in the year 2008-2009, thus registering an increase by 5.61 times. The volume of loans and advances disbursed has shown an upward trend up to 2006-2007and in the year 2007-2008 the volume of loans and advances has reduced to Rs. 4, 68,180 thousand and after the volume

Table 23.4 : Loans and Advances

(Figures are in thousand)

Year	Crop. Loan	Ag. Term loan	Allied Ag. Term loan	SHG	Retail Trade/ Small business	Trans-port Opera-tors	SSI	Hous-ing	Educa-. tion Loan	Others	Total Priority Sector	Total Non Priority Sector	Total
2000-2001	11572	794	3391	627	15024	21699	13765	NA	NA	4578	71450	52166	123616
2001-2002	13133	798	2326	1047	18437	21823	15753	108	NA	5221	78646	73515	152161
2002-2003	16531	875	3582	2493	14499	23463	7336	8329	191	NA	77281	94367	171648
2003-2004	18023	603	3357	3762	22429	31560	10608	6770	191	228	97531	92580	190111
2004-2005	30744	3441	3624	3351	22169	34387	12587	5911	150	3687	120051	128543	248594
2005-2006	100642	38591	48577	8775	64850	64507	49762	42370	375	10854	429303	237397	666700
2006-2007	133772	38355	41310	35224	90689	52314	55484	86909	1862	8124	544043	281314	825357
2007-2008	85951	19425	4996	9149	46334	22264	33134	43250	1871	6879	273253	194927	468180
2008-2009	117005	20336	7556	9749	82727	44015	34303	37820	2194	7236	392945	330195	693140

Source : Annual Report of Meghalaya Rural Bank—Various issues.

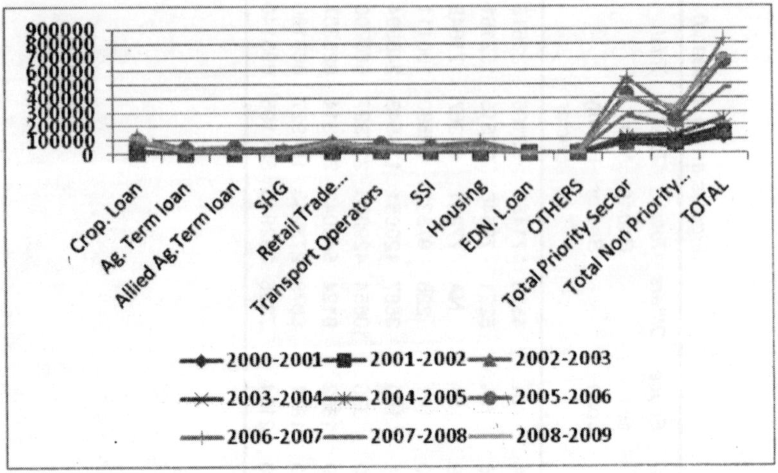

Figure 23.4 : Loans and Advances

loan and advances disbursed has shown an upward trend. Loans and advances disbursed include crops loan, Agriculture term loan, Allied agricultural term loan, self help groups, retail, trade/small business, Transport operations, small scale industries, housing, educational loans, other loans. Loans and advances to priority sector and non-priority sector. The priority sector consists of crop loan, Agriculture term loan, allied agricultural term loan, self-help group, retail trade/small business, small scale industries, Housing, Educational loan, other loan. The crop loan has increased by 10.11 times, Agriculture term loan by 25.61 times, allied agricultural term loan by 0.45 times, self-help group by 15.55 times, retail trade/ small business by 5.51 times, small scale industries by 2.49 times, Housing by 350.12 times, Educational loan by 11.49 times, other loan by 1.59 times, total priority sector by 5.50 times and non-priority sector by 6.33 times during the study period. Apart from the above mentioned loan, MRB has implemented various schemes to provide financial services to the rural people. These are Swarna Jayanti Gram Swarozgar Yojana, Kisan Credit Card, Gram Udyog Rojgar Yojana, Self Help Group/NGOs, public housing finance, national agricultural insurance scheme, deposit insurance and credit guarantee scheme.

It is evident from the above discussion that the role of MRB in financial inclusion is not satisfactory. The reason for poor performance may be attributed as follows:

- Being mostly agrarian economy, hardly has scheme which lend for agriculture.
- Illiteracy and the low income savings and lack of bank branches in the rural areas continue to be a road block to financial inclusion.
- Not economic viable because of low scale (population).
- Limited manpower.
- Lack of technology.
- Security problems to Business correspondent.
- Logistic problem.
- Cash (big) handling problem in rural areas.

Initiatives taken by MRB: There is sincere effort made by MRB to improve the financial services in the rural areas. Some of the measures are hereunder:

- Introduction of Mobile Van.
- Local NGOs for taking up business correspondent at village level.
- Organizing of financial literacy camp in village involving local administration. (*Dorbar shonang*).
- Appoint one person from local areas is compulsory to communicate.
- No frill account facility given in large number and giving credit linkage to Credit Card and Loan.
- Introduction of Non Public Banking Working Day (NPBWD) in rural area but not in semi urban and urban.
- MRB is trying to issue ATM card in near future.

Suggestions

On the basis of findings from the analysis following suggestions are made:

- The bankers should be customer friendly and should do the work efficiently.
- In the rural branches local language can be used for all sorts of transaction as most of the people are not much educated or literate.

- The bank can held some awareness programme to motivate the people to come under the purview of financial inclusion.
- The procedure for opening bank account and the procedure for granting loans and advances can be simplified.
- Proper security should be provided to the business correspondent.
- Latest technology like mobile banking can be introduced in the rural areas as people are living scatterly due to geographical condition.
- Special camp can be arranged to change the mind set of the rural people regarding the banking.

Conclusion

From the research enquiry it has been gathered that the volume of deposit, The volume of loans and advances disbursed, number of account opened has shown an upward trend and the growth rate of increases was marginal as compared to our neighbouring States. The branch expansion was almost stagnant except in the last two years. Therefore it is very much necessary to explore the ways and means to provide financial services to the rural and poor people as rural development has direct bearing in the overall economic development of the country.

REFERENCES

Annual Reports, *Meghalaya Rural Bank, 2000-2001 to 2008-2009*.

Agrawal Amol (2008), "The need for financial inclusion with an Indian Perspective", *Economic Research*, IDBI, Mumbai.

Choudheri, P.C. (2007), "Total financial inclusion Various Approaches" *Indian Journal of Agricultural Economics*.

Deshpande, Rani, (2006), "Safe and Accessible:, bringing poor savers into the formal financial system." *Focus Note 37*, Washington, D.C.

Gandhi, Riddima, (2010), *Calling on Mobile Banking, Financial Inclusion in Rural India* Center for Strategic and International Studies Washington, D.C.

K.C. Chakraborty, (2006), *Financial Inclusion Concept, Issues and Roadmap*, Institute for Development and Research in Banking Technology, Hyderabad.

K.C. Chakrabarty, (2010) *"Creating Competition the Only Solution for Financial Inclusion"*, *The Economic Times*, 5th July, 2010.

SECTION - IV
Financial Inclusion and ICT

24

Information Technology Application Models for Financial Inclusion

L.S. SHARMA

Introduction

Development theories has been concentrated on land, labour and capitals the factors of production. Most of the leading theories assume that the markets are perfect and there are no frictions present in the environment. But if these theories were correct then there was very little reason for financial markets to exist (Agarwal, 2008). The later studies showed that there were imperfections in these markets and financial institutions help to reduce these imperfections.

Finance has been recognized as the brain of the economic system and most of economies strive to make their financial system more efficient. It also helps to make the system to be always in the lookout for discrepancies which could freeze the entire economy and bring fallout. Earlier researchers were focused on the development of the economy through finance and now-a-days research is showing that financial inclusions are as important.

Rangarajan Committee defines financial inclusion as the process of ensuring access to financial services and timely and adequate credit where needed by vulnerable groups such as weaker sections and low income groups at affordable cost. The financial services include the entire gamut of savings, loans, insurance, credit, payments, etc. In order to understand the term "financial inclusion" one also needs to understand the term "financial exclusion". Financial exclusion means those sections of the population who do not avail the financial services provided by the institutions. The exclusion may be in terms of rural, poor regions and those living in harsh climatic conditions where it is difficult to provide these financial services. Rangarajan Committee includes financial exclusion to those sections of the population particularly those living on low incomes, which cannot access to mainstream financial products such as bank accounts, low cost credit, remittances and payment services, financial advisory services, insurance facilities, etc.

The financial system today in India encompasses a host of institutions including 75,170 branches of commercial, mainly public sector banks across the country; 15,612 branches of 82 Regional Rural Banks; 14,000 or so co-operative bank branches; 95,626 outlets of Primary Agricultural Credit Co-operative Societies, NBFC's mutual fund companies *et. al.*, yet the problem of exclusion from access to formal financial services are so acute that despite the penetrative outreach of the financial system 50 per cent of the country is still unbanked (Joshi, 2011). One of the primary reasons has been due to the high cost of the financial services. To open an account in Cameroon, the minimum deposit required is over 700 dollars, an amount higher than the average GDP of the that country while no minimum amount is required in South Africa. Annual fees charges exceed 25 per cent of the GDP per capita in Sierra Leone while no such fees are required in Philippines. In Bangladesh, Pakistan, and Philippines to get a small loan, the process takes about a month while it takes a day only in Denmark (World Bank Report, 2008).

About 40 per cent of India's population possesses bank account and just about 10 per cent of thc population are covered under life insurance. The proportion of the population who are covered under non-life insurance is very low to the extent of 0.6 per cent. Further, the data reveal that a large segment of India's population continues to remain deprived from the basic banking services. Moreover, just 10 per cent of people are having any kind of life insurance cover and the proportion of population having non-life insurance is as low as 0.6 per cent. Further, only 13 per cent of population possesses debit cards while people possessing credit cards comprise mere 2.0 per cent (Reddy, 2010). All these indicate towards the low level of financial inclusion in the country. There is still limited access of basic financial services such as savings, loan, remittance and insurance services by the huge population in the rural and unorganised sector is a concern. When access to basic and affordable financial services is provided, it not only expands opportunities for livelihood but also provides empowerment to the poor. The extent of financial exclusion is a major concern given the fact that around 81 per cent of Indian households save a portion of their income. In spite of many initiatives taken at various levels and inculcating strong saving habits of households, a large section of population across the country still remain excluded from any kind of financial services.

Another reason for the financial exclusion is the non-price barriers created for the customers. Opening an account requires documents relating to the identity of the person, residence proof, age proof, income statement, etc. The poor section of the population does not have evidences of such documents. In order to get a loan, margin money is required to be deposited as collateral which again is a barrier for the poor section. Distances between the banks and the customers, poor infrastructures are also some of the deterring factors. Financial services also use a different set of financial terminologies, various documents and terms and conditions are usually placed before its user. The poor sections of the population are not educated on these terminologies.

Moving towards universal financial inclusion is the national commitment and RBI's policy priority. Financial access is necessary as it enables access to financial savings, credit, remittance, insurance, pensions from formal financial institutions at cheaper cost. Taken together this enables movement from the margin to mainstream. It allows a paper trail of transactions effected through the banking system and thus curbs illegal transactions. The inhibitors to this process are the small character of loans. Low value, high volume nature of transactions in the penny economy makes administration of loans and recoveries costly. Once appropriate technological solutions are in place, then technology can be leveraged effectively to overcome the barriers of geography. RBI emphasizes a bank led model of financial inclusion relying on information technology solution.

Technological developments in the form of telecommunications and internet technology have helped to extend the banking services in the remote areas. Technology has enabled to reach out to the customers and instead of making customers approach towards banks, with the development of technology using hand held devices connection through GPRS /GSM /CDMA /landline networks. Technology will have to play a vital role if financial inclusion has to be successful.

Lack of adequate number of bank branches and service delivery models has been one of the hurdles in catering to the financial services of the underprivileged. A branch-based delivery mechanism is not feasible as it entails huge costs. Hence, there arises the need as well as demand for trying out with new types of technology based delivery mechanisms.

Inclusive growth can be achieved if all available resources, including technology and expertise are geared to include more people under financial inclusion. The need for enhancement of the financial inclusion in order to achieve inclusive growth and eradicate poverty has been widely accepted in India. With this regard, initiatives have been taken by the RBI and the government in past few years to enhance financial inclusion across the country. Although these initiatives have paid off to a certain extent in terms of increased network of bank branches in rural area and priority sector lending, a sizeable portion of population particularly rural and economically vulnerable groups, continue to remain excluded from the even basic banking services. Besides, lack of financial awareness and language barriers, various demand or supply specific factors act as key barriers to financial inclusion. Despite several initiatives taken up by government and RBI in past, we are far away from desired level of financial inclusion. Government and RBI are required to take some more concrete steps to realize full potential of financial inclusion. Technological innovation can play a major role in enabling a broader reach for various banking and financial services while also bringing about an improvement in the quality of the services and lowering transaction cost.

Literature Survey

The works of Nobel laureates Joseph Stieglitz and George Akerlof led the economists to think about the role of financial markets in the real economy on the basis of asymmetric information and principal-theory agents. Michael Jensen and William Meckling (1976) found that in the world of imperfect information and principal agent problems, the capital structure of the firm could be used as a tool by themselves to which the incentives of the managers with the shareholders interest can play an important role.

In the chapter entitled "Towards Building an Inclusive Financial Sector: Lessons from South Africa", Arora and Leach (2005) examines the South African case which substantiates the efforts taken by an economy characterised by significant social and economic divides to bring previously excluded population segments into the mainstream financial sector. The researcher has showed that the South African counterpart has chosen to follow market-led approach. The study indicates some differences in approaches followed by India and South Africa and suggested some useful lessons from the South African initiatives.

In the chapter entitled "Accelerating Financial Inclusion through Mobile Phone Technology: Opportunities, Challenges and Policy Options for India" Sumanjit (2011) mentions that technology is the key for financial inclusion because it can reduce cost significantly and reach the masses. The study deals with the use of mobile phone technology as the most suitable for banking the unbanked. The study also explores the opportunities and challenges of the adoption of mobile technology. The researcher also discusses the policy options for the equitable access to financial services for all.

Jalal-Karim and Hamdan (2010) in European, Mediterranean and Middle Eastern Conference on Information Systems discussed the impact of information technology on improving banking performance matrix by taking Jordanian banks as case study. The study measures the impact information technology on five parameters and found that there is an impact of information technology in the market value added, earnings per share, returns on assets and net profit margins.

Gandhi (2010) in the newsletter of Centre for Strategic and International Studies stated that the mobile phone revolution is sweeping across India and has the potential to dramatically transform the lives of the nation's rural poor but an estimated 8 million rural Indians who own mobile phones do not have access to banks. She opines that this gap could be bridged by using the mobile banking technologies. The study also analyses the role of regulators, financial institutions, technology and service providers for improving the access and deliverability of mobile banking services to India's rural poor.

Technological Application Model

India is one of the word's largest and fastest growing telecom market, with about 771.18 million at the end of January 2011, can also leverage the mobile technology to reach out to the large unbanked population in remote areas (Joshi, 2011). Moreover, providing branchless banking services through mobile phones will help banks to penetrate with less investment. However, user friendly applications which could be used in the most basic mobile phones instead of sophisticated applications on expensive phones would facilitate successful implementation. Today, WiMax technology is providing villages with wireless connectivity. Advent of 3G will further enhance the mobile broadband penetration among people residing in rural regions. Moreover, local language applications will increase the pace of financial inclusion. As the telecom market emerges, it will help in connecting to the central database and provide services to the consumers of the rural consumers.

The Rangarajan Committee having discussed extensively the issue of using technology as a driver is of the opinion that the requirement of rapid financial inclusion as a national goal can only be achieved by using appropriate IT. The creation of a national database, sectoral, geographic and demographic reports, and also a payment system among the card holders to benefit the under privileged unbanked population of the country is not possible without extensive use of IT. This alone can bring down the costs of the small ticket transactions and make nationwide financial inclusion a reality.

Rangarajan Committee has laid down the devices to be used in several forms such as Simputers (Simple Inexpensive Multi-lingual Computers)/personal digital assistants, programmed mobile phones, etc. These devices also uses bio-metric as for identification and authentication. Rural ATMs which have been introduced by banks and found to be very popular among rural masses as it is much easier to use and does remove some of the social-psychological barriers.

The committee also has recognised the fact that RBI has set up an advisory group for IT-enabled financial inclusion to facilitate development of IT solutions for delivery of banking services. The group has an advice for certain minimum parameters and standards that are essential for setting up robust interoperable systems on open platforms for financial inclusion. The technology suppliers and banks should evolve common minimum standards for ensuring inter-operability between their systems.

The Committee is of the view that nearly all models converge on certain essential components and has laid down the processes to be followed in the technology application. The essence of all these models consists of:

- the issue of a smart card to the rural consumer on which all his transactions are recorded;
- a hand-held terminal with the business correspondent (BC) at the village level; and
- a Central Processor Unit (CPU) linking the smart cards and BC terminals with the banks.

The committee also ensures to take precautions so that every transaction made is accompanied by a print-out being provided to the farmer. There are also other models where smart cards are dispensed with and mobile telephones, etc., are used.

The operating costs of these models are expected to be minimal and can be easily absorbed by banks to increase the volumes and will justify the absorption of incremental operating costs. Also, the costs of the models are substantially lowered if the infrastructure is shared. It is, therefore, Rangarajan Committee has recommended that a shared infrastructure of different banks enabling nationwide financial inclusion for the participant banks would confer large scale benefits and also enable effortless transfer of funds between the card holders of the various banks.

Essentially, the start up costs is the initial investment costs comprising cost of the smart card, terminals to the BC and the CPU. The Committee is of the view that the Financial Inclusion Technology Fund can provide the necessary support for defraying technology application and hardware costs of technology adoption. The cost of smart card is estimated to be around Rs. 100 and the terminal with BC will cost between Rs. 10,000 to Rs. 20,000 depending upon the features and accessories like printers. The cost of server with capability of serving various accounts would be around Rs. 35 lakhs in today's price. This cost in comparison to the cost of setting up a physical branch office will be much more economical and will help to overcome some of the barriers.

The Committee is of the opinion that the existing banking infrastructure and NGOs which have already developed extensive inroads into rural areas should be made optimal use of for enabling outreach of banking services. The BF/BC models backed by technology applications should encourage a role for the small players and integrate them into the national system. The Committee is of the opinion that State Governments should make payments to NREGP and Social Security Payments through such technology-based solutions like smart cards.

Rangarajan Committee laid its foundations for technological application model to provide financial services in rural areas through BC model using simple IT solutions. The system consists of two layers: a central infrastructure and a field based system to access the central database by field correspondents. The account holders use a Multi-application smart card for banking and non-banking transactions. For authentication, biometrics will be used primarily through hand-held devices carried by BC. Essentially various models will have the following components, viz., a smart card (contact or contact less), BC with a simputer/handheld device/ mobile phone with banking services, merchant establishments as point of service with a computer terminal, a computer system, the bank and a centralized card management system for all of the above.

(*a*) *Model using Smart Card (FINO):* FINO Ltd. uses the best standards comparable to EMV and CEPS standards. It also uses biometrics for authentication meaning using the fingerprint to identify and authenticate the user. The system also provides a PIN like number called the Unique Relationship Number (URN) which helps him to identify products and customers. The model also uses security standards using the 3-DES scheme that prevents unauthorized access to the card. The card will have the data of the customer like the demographic profile, health details, and net worth of the customer which will make it ready for transaction. The smart card should also enable multi application platform operations like banking, financial services, remittances, community welfare programmes like PDS, MNREGA, etc. The card may also have a PIN and it could be used to the available POS like ATM and other point of sales.

There has been several pilot projects carried using this model. The Krishna Bhima Samruddi Local Area Bank uses a model called Pigmy Collection Terminal. The model creates small terminals by using laptop computer. Its main activities are to collect instalments on the advances taken, making deposits for pigmy schemes as well as other deposits like fixed deposits, savings etc. Each of the Pigmy Collection Terminal can store up to 1,000 accounts and receipts are printed and given to the customer immediately after a transaction is made.

Krishna Bhima also uses another model which makes the use of simputers. This model is also known as simputer model. Simputer are simple computer or Simple Inexpensive Multi Lingual Computer. It is a kind of net book which is simple to use and because it does not require to be literate to operate the system. It uses touch, audio and visual to interact with the user. It also supports multiple language text and speech output which guides the user. The mode of operation is the customer goes to a simputer-ATM, the BC helps the customer to enter the data and carries out a transaction and immediately after the transaction a printout is taken as a receipt and given to the customer.

FINO Ltd. uses a hand-held device which is known as Hand-held device Model. The hand held device is a compact portable device with a 2 to 4 line display and a keypad of 16 keys, which has embedded thermal printer and the system has a battery life for 8 hours. This device is suitable for far off rural areas where electricity is not available and the infrastructures are not well developed. One advantage of this model is that it is a capable of operating in offline mode and update whenever connectivity is available. The model also uses biometrics for authentication and validation of the customer and access is restricted through this biometrics. It also supports to read the smart cards issued to the customers. The model also allows deposits, remittances, withdrawals, transfers, etc., for financial as well as non-financial transactions.

Another model for technology application is using the mobile phones and Little World Pvt. Ltd. uses this technology. The model consists of a central database of various accounts including no-frill zero-balance account holders at the central computer with the facility to connect to the bank's host computer. It is based on the new generation Near Field Communication (NFC) mobile phone technology; contact less radio frequency identification (RFID) enabled smart cards and the biometrics. These cards store the ID profile of the customer, allows multiple accounts, last known balance and the past few transactions. These are also RFID tag to identify the cardholder. The operator uses portable equipment for authentication along with biometrics. All the devices used are battery operated with battery life of 10 days without recharge. The transactions are conducted through online *via* GPRS or encrypted SMS to the bank's host. Offline transactions are carried out in batch processing which allows deposits and withdrawals. The transactions are immediately completed with the business correspondent (BC). The model also allows the audit trail to be taken for the transactions that had occurred.

(*b*) *IT-enabled Financial Inclusion Model (ALW):* The IT-enabled Financial Inclusion Model is basically revolved around the business correspondent (BC) and Business facilitator (BF). The model works in the following manner. A potential customer is met by the BF and passes information to the Business Correspondent. BC enrolls the customer into the customer account for the bank. The bank then carries out a know your customer (KYC) scrutiny check and arranges for a Zero Balance Savings bank account for the customer with the relevant information. The information includes the photograph of the customer, fingerprints and signature which is optional. The information collected is encrypted and embedded in a smart card.

As soon as the smart card is handed to the customer then the card is activated with the fingerprint identification. During the activation, the balance available in the bank is also recorded in the smart card. Then the smart card can be used for operation. The customer operates the smart card in the following manner. Whenever the customer wants to withdraw or deposit money to the bank using the smart card at the terminal of the business correspondent, he will undertake a biometric identification and then the transaction will be carried with the help of BC. Once the transaction is over a printout of the transaction will be made. These transactions are free from office hour time limit meaning anytime 24 × 7 transactions can be carried out. In case the BC does not have any balance to provide to the customer, he can issue a printout stating that no cash is available at the BC's end and the information will be passed to the bank and cash will be replenished. It also acts a cheque which allows the BC to operate even if balance is not available so that the services to customers are not denied. The terminals with the BC are operated with rechargeable battery and are not totally dependent on electricity as rural areas lack regular power supply. This model also allows making use of the smart card as a debit card in normal POS. The system works in integrated village level terminals, through POS with banks. Then it is integrated to the core banking system for various support services to the customers. Every BC can handle to the tune of 500 to 1,000 accounts and the cost of transactions is very low.

This model uses store and forward mechanism used for uploading field transactions originating on handhelds. It also generates agent/entity-wise detailed transaction reports for all the transactions. This model integrates with core banking system and other third party systems through customized interfaces. It also supports for pushing back end updates to smart card such as interest run, charges, blocking of cards, etc. It also allows remote parameter configuration such as maximum daily withdrawal amount, maximum cumulative account balance, etc. The system supports for settlement among multiple banks using the same infrastructure. This technology based on remote banking models can be used for outreach for the following purposes:

- Micro savings (no-frills pre-paid account),
- Disbursal of Government benefits,
- Microcredit (GCC),
- Farmers credit and benefits,
- Micro-insurance,
- Cash withdrawals,
- Wage disbursements for NREGA,
- Pensions,
- Cashless payments to merchants,
- SHG saving-cum-credit accounts,
- Passbook,
- Equated monthly instalments (EMI), and
- Utility payments.

Some Experimental Initiatives on financial Inclusions through use of Technology

There have been several initiatives taken by the commercial banks in India. Some of the well known pilot projects undertaken are:

State Bank of India Tiny Initiative: The State Bank of India experimented a project called SBI-Tiny in the States of Mizoram, Uttarakhand and Andhra Pradesh. A non government organization was appointed as the business correspondent (BC). The NGO started with coverage of 9 villages and registered 2,400 customers in the first phase. Each village was served by a SBI-Tiny customer service point (CSP). The CSP is the gateway for delivering banking services to the customers. The CSPs provide the application forms and the prospective customer come to the CSP and fills the forms. The CSP then collects the filled forms, enters the data in the computer and captures a photo of the customer as well as two fingerprints of each customer. Then the CSP sends the forms to the nearest SBI branch office for approval and enrolment cards are sent the card production centre to print the cards. The printed cards are then sent to the CSP and the CSP hands them over to the customer after verification of the fingerprint and photo. The cards are issued for a validity period of 10 years. The card contains data of biometric finger prints, last known balance and history of recent transactions.

The banking facility operates in the following manner. The business correspondent uses a portable equipment, viz., a mobile unit, a fingerprint unit and a transaction printer. All these equipments operate on a portable battery which has a stand-by time for 10 days. The authentication of the customers takes place by matching the photo and fingerprints. Once authenticated, the chip embedded in the card gets charged. Once the card is charged, it is brought near to the mobile device, and then message templates for deposit, withdrawal and balance enquiry are generated. The business correspondent then selects the relevant option and the transaction is carried out by authenticating with the server and sends a message to the mobile, which in turn writes to the card. When the card is brought near to the printer, a transaction report is printed in triplicate. The BC carries cash physically for making payments to the customer. The available services include savings product (SBI-Tiny no-frills pre-paid account), microcredit, micro-insurance, cash withdrawal and as well as used for routing Government payments.

Government of Andhra Pradesh (GoAP) Project on Social Security Payments through Smart Cards: In order to make payments directly to the widows, handicapped, old and eligible weavers, the government of Andhra Pradesh took up a project to ensure payments to the above beneficiaries. The payments were made through smart card and business correspondents. The pilot project involves six banks comprising of SBI, Union Bank of India, UTI Bank, State Bank of Hyderabad, Andhra Bank and Andhra Pradesh Grameen Vikas Bank. The project was launched in April 30, 2007 where social security payments were disbursed to 127 beneficiaries in 3 villages through intermediaries. Andhra Pradesh government covered more schemes including Andhra Pradesh Rural Employment Guarantee Scheme and expects to cover 5 million beneficiaries (Rangarajan Report, 2008). This is an initiative where the transfer of funds is directly reached to the ultimate beneficiaries. This is an initial step taken up to increase the financial inclusion and as well as to curb corruption. The technology used is similar to SBI-Tiny project except that the card stores six fingerprints. The transaction process is similar except that beneficiary lists are issued by the Andhra Pradesh government to the banks and the banks issue the smart cards. The government transfers the money to the bank for making payments to the beneficiaries. The customer service points (CSPs) are selected from the voluntary organisations. The Andhra Government has experimented by making payments through intermediaries and smart card technology.

Appraisal: Technology that delivers value and convenience to the users is readily accepted by consumers. It was seen that both pilot projects were successful in bringing bank to the doorstep of the consumers. The initial cost of the investment in the financial inclusion project is seen to be very high in view of their low returns; the cost of transaction is very low in comparison to traditional banking methods. The banks will require training of the beneficiaries, CSPs and BCs to the enrolment and transaction process.

Although the cost of acquiring accounts may be seen high in view of low returns but the cost of transaction is very low when compared to traditional banking methods; it is believed that this model will gain acceptance when more products of the banks are routed through them. Banks would need to deploy substantial resources for enrolment process and making of smart cards during the initial stage. BC capacity building is the biggest challenge in financial inclusion as the potential of technology in this area is already proven.

This model can engage the government machinery for routing payments so that a multi benefit can be derived from the exercise. The process will reduce the possibility of corruption in the transfer of money to the beneficiaries. The benefits that will derive from the routing of government payments through such model are that additional resources can be generated by banks to fund these exercises. It will further open up the market for micro-insurance which is still untapped. Banks also can transfer their several products to the form of smart cards for small loans, vehicle loans, artisan loans etc.

The Reserve Bank of India has constituted a group to look into the standards for data storage and transmission of biometric data as these will be the most important authentication data. There will be a requirement of the uniform standard for capturing, storage and transmission of biometric data. The RBI committee has given a recommendation suggesting to align the standards to the ISO-IEC (International Organisation for Standardization—International

Electro Technical Committee) international standards. This will help to ensure that biometric data can be used for other applications.

In order to ensure secrecy and non-repudiation, biometric cards are found to be appropriate for identification of individuals. But the major problems may occur as the card holders by virtue of their professions which may involve hard work with their hand so may not have clear finger prints. It may be, therefore, necessary to have a PIN associated with the card when biometric fails so that it can be used in infrastructures like ATMs and POS terminals.

Regarding the business correspondent's (BCs) activities, the accounting procedures to be followed and arrangements of cash needs to be planned out in advance. Supply of spares, consumables and maintenance services would have to be meticulously planned by technology providers, BCs and banks. Here again, with time and larger volumes of independent suppliers may come up. In cases where intermediaries are used, the banks and their unions may not like the arrangement and a dialogue may have to enter into with the bank unions.

Conclusion

The above study points to the importance of financial inclusion and highlights various technological experiments which have been adopted to reduce the gap of financial exclusion. It has been seen that an overwhelming majority of rural India do not avail the financial services from banks. Although most of them are aware of the benefits of the basic financial services, they are not able to reap the benefits as the transactions cost and necessary requirements for opening an account cannot be fulfilled easily. So the financial institutions have to be tailor made the services for the beneficiaries. Once the transactions cost is brought down to a minimum, the services can be provided by bringing down the price of the services. Opening an account requires documents relating to the identity of the person, income statement, age proof, residence proof, etc. The vulnerable section of the population does not possess and properly keep evidences of such documents. The Unique Identity Number (UIN) is expected to be a major breakthrough and it may be used as the documentation proof for access to financial services.

As per the IISS survey opines that if any payment mechanism's transaction volume increases the transaction costs becomes lower. This is called the network effect and such payment system increases its credibility. For such a system to work the regulatory system must guarantee authenticity, non-repudiation, security, confidentiality and stability.

In the coming years mobile phones are likely to be the primary mode of payment system. In order to work the payment system more functional, smart card, mobile phones and a computer would be used. The smart cards should be able to inter-operate with different systems of banks and issues relating to "switching and messaging" have to be carefully addressed. Issues relating to minimizing the risks involved in financial transactions have to be made. The business models should try to reduce the transaction cost so that the beneficiaries get the facility at affordable prices. The financial inclusion model should also try to give least strain to the technology. By adopting the ISO standards the problem of interoperability can be curbed. One of the problems of using biometrics is that the fingerprints may not function as the beneficiaries are vulnerable people who work by hand as their fingerprints may not be recognized due to hard labour, therefore, another additional form of recognition may be used such as PIN. Overall the system should be amenable to audit as a responsibility of the banks. Apart from initiatives such as smart cards for opening bank accounts with biometric identification, disbursement of social security payments under the National Rural Employment Guarantee Scheme, through such smart cards, mobile ATMs, coverage of post offices under electronic payments systems in remote areas increase the financial inclusion. So the challenge now lies in taking greater advantage of new technologies and effective implementation of the model to expand the coverage of the banking and financial system. Thus, the overall success of the financial inclusion will depend on the right choice of technology and model to be used.

REFERENCES

Agarwal, A., (2008), *The Need for Financial Inclusion with an Indian Perspective*, Economic Research, accessed on http://www.oecd.org/dataoecd/16/55/40339652.pdf

Akula, V., (2009), The Time for Mobile Banking for Financial Inclusion is Now, *Hindustan Times*, August 07.

Arora, S.S.; Leach J., (2005), Towards Building an Inclusive Financial Sector: Lessons from South Africa, *Economic and Political Weekly*, Vol. 40, No. 17 (Apr. 23-29), pp. 1726-1730

Beck, T.; Demirgue-Kant, A.; Peria, M.S.M., (2006), *Banking Services for Everyone? Barriers to Bank Access and Use around the World*, World Bank Policy Research Working Paper 4079.

Chakrabarty, K.C., (2009), *Technology, Financial Inclusion and the Role of Urban Cooperative Banks*, Address by Dr, Deputy Governor of the Reserve Bank of India, at the Foundation Day and Inauguration of the "Core Banking Solution Project" of the A.P. Mahesh Co-op Urban Bank Ltd., Hyderabad, 9 August, 2009.

French, S.; Leyshon A., (2004), The New, New Financial System? Towards a Conceptualization of Financial Reintermediation, Review of International Political Economy, Vol. 11, No. 2 (May), pp. 263-288.

Gangopadhayay, S., (2009), "How Can Technology Facilitate Financial Inclusion in India? A Discussion Paper", *Review of Market Integration*, Vol. 1, No. 2, pp 223-256.

Gandhi, R., (2010), Calling on Mobile Banking: Financial Inclusion in Rural India, *South Asia Monitor*, 143, July 01, 2010.

IBA, (2007), Approach Paper on IT Enabled Financial Inclusion: How to Leverage Technology for Broad Basing Financial Inclusion Initiatives, IBS-Sub Committee on IT Enabled Financial Inclusion, Department of Social Banking.

Jalal-Karim, A.; Hamdan, A. M., (2010), *The Impact of Information Technology on Improving Banking Performance Matrix: Jordanian Banks as Case Study*, European, Mediterranean & Middle Eastern Conference on Information Systems, April 12-13, 2010, Abu Dhabi, UAE

Jensen, M.; Meckling, W. H., (1976), Theory of Firm: Managerial Behaviour, Agency Costs and Ownership Structure, *Journal of Financial Economics (JFE)*, Vol. 3, No. 4.

Joshi, D.P., (2011), "Financial Inclusion, Financial Deepening and Economic Growth", *Yojana*, August 2011.

Leasi, P., (2010), "Financial Inclusion and Mobile Banking in Samoa", *BIS Review*, September, 2010.

Mahadeva, G.I.M, (2008), Financial Growth in India: Whither Financial Inclusion? *Margin*—The Journal of Applied Economic Research, 2:2. pp. 177-197.

Misra, S.K.; Wickamasinghe, N., (2004), "Security of Mobile Transaction: A Trust Model", Electronic Commerce Research, Vol. 4, No. 4, pp. 359-372.

Neralla, D., (2010), Director, Atom Technologies, Mobile Technology Led Financial Inclusion Jenien-ICRIER Conference Review, Seminar dated Feb. 8, 2010.

Okunoye, A.; Bada A.O.; Frolick M., (2007), *IT Innovations and E-Service Delivery: An Exploratory Study*, Proceedings of Ninth International Conference on Social Implications of Computers in Developing Countries, Sao Paolo, Brazil, May 2007.

Prakash, N., (2009), *Financial Inclusion with Mobile Banking*, Computer Express, April 10.

Rangarajan, C., (2008), Report of the Committee of Financial inclusion, NABARD, Mumbai, accessed on http://www.nabard.org/pdf/report_**financial**/Full%20Report.pdf

Reddy, N. S. N. *Financial Inclusion—Role of Information Technology*, accessed on http://www.allbankingsolutions.com/Articles-NSNR-Financial-Inclusion-Role-of-IT.htm

Reserve Bank of India (2008), *Mobile Payments in India: Operative Guidelines for Banks*, accessed on http://www.rbidocs.rbi.org.in/rdocs/Content/PDFs/84978.pdf

Richard, N.; J.S. Arora; Sumanjeet, (2009), "The Evolution of e-Banking: A Study of Indian and Kenyan Technology Awareness", *International Journal of Electronic Finance*, Vol. 3, No. 2, pp. 149-165.

Singh, S., (2009), *Mobile Remittances: Design for Financial Inclusion*, Lecture Notes in Computer Science, Springer: Berlin.

Sumanjeet, (2011), Accelerating Financial Inclusion through Mobile Phone Technology: Opportunities, Challenges and Policy Options for India, *Man and Development*, 33:2, June 2011.

25

Microfinance and ICT Infrastructure in Rural India : Accelerating Financial Inclusion through Innovative Technologies and Alternative Channels

H. RAMANANDA SINGH AND N. DHANESHWAR SINGH

Introduction to Microfinance in India

The majority of poor people in rural areas around the world lack access to financial services. Indian accounts for an estimated 40 per cent of poor of the world. India continues to have highest concentration of poverty with more than 285 million people—about 26 per cent of the population living below the official poverty line. About 70 per cent of Indian villages lack access to appropriate, affordable and safe financial products and services.

Microfinance has been recognized as the most viable, efficient and result-oriented mode of financially empowering the poor. Microfinance is basically refers to a broad range of financial services such as deposits, loans, money transfers and insurance to the poor, low income households and micro-enterprises. In the recent past, financial inclusion through microfinance has become global movement for providing access to financial services at affordable cost to the rural and the poor.

The microfinance sector in India has made tremendous progress in terms of size and magnitude, outreach and dimensions of socio-economic impact in the recent years. From mere 500 SHG under pilot phase by NABARD in 1992, SHG-Bank Linkage programmes of NABARD has now achieved the spectacular growth in as much as 6.1 million SHGs with outstanding saving of Rs. 54,556.2 million and loan outstanding of Rs. 2,26,798.5 million as on 31 March, 2009. Moreover, many MFIs of different legal forms have also contributed for exponential growth of this sector through innovative technology driven financial products and services.

One of the key challenges in extending access to financial services in under-served rural markets has been the high "cost to serve". This includes the costs associated with origination; supervision and continuous monitoring that are incurred in these markets. Increasingly, technology is being viewed as key to a low-cost banking strategy for the rural market.

If the current structure of the bank branches were to be used to cater to the need and requirement of the rural population, it would mean setting up a bank branch in virtually every village. The cost of such a large network would not justify the revenues generated from it, given the nature of transactions. Thus, the challenge for banks/ MFIs is to innovate a low-cost network/delivery channel with a high outreach and flexibility with respect to the timing of its operation. Thus, the two key challenges that must be overcome to extend banking to the rural and poor population are:

- Elimination/reduction of cash handling; and
- Low cost delivery channels

Information and Communication Technology (ICT) can address both of the above challenges. MFIs are now using new information and communication technologies (ICTs) to improve their operations in three main areas: Expanding their customer base and extending their reach into underserved areas, establishing secure identities for customers and lowering transaction costs. With new software's specially designed to cater to the needs of the MFIs, mobile phones, efficient Management Information Systems, among others, technology can and will in the near future bring about a paradigm shift in the domain of microfinance.

Objective

The objectives of this chapter are given below:

- To explore the extent to which ICT infrastructure can contribute to the development of microfinance sector.
- To determine innovative delivery channels for reaching the rural poor.

- To discuss the issues and challenges of adopting new technologies and alternative delivery channels.

Research Methodology

The research methodology adopted for achieving the above stated objectives is exploratory in nature. The development of conceptual framework of this chapter is entirely based on secondary data available up to March 2010.

ICT Infrastructure in Rural India

India now has a population of over 1 billion of which its rural population is approximately 70 per cent. Much of the rural population does not have access to common infrastructure like connectivity, electricity, health and drinking water. Complex characteristics of rural India include inaccessible terrain and geographically dispersed hamlets / villages.

ICT is one of most important infrastructure for connecting people and places beyond the geographical boundaries. There have been debates on role of Information and Communication Technology (ICT) in developing a connectivity backbone in rural India to address urban-rural divide. ICT has been recognized as an infrastructure in developed countries and its use has shown the path of rapid socio-economic development. However, in developing countries, especially in India, ICT interventions are still on concept stage. Many pilot projects are experimented in isolation and scaling up strategy is yet to be formulated.

Despite many initiatives taken up, India stands as per the report, 37th among 82 nations with network readiness index (NRI) as 3.89 (7 Point Scale), 70th for ICT infrastructure. This indicates that a lot of improvement is needed in the national scenario.

In order to improve ICT infrastructure in rural areas, various policies and reforms such as "National Telecommunication Policy", "Indian IT Policy", "Indian Infrastructure Policy" and "Policy on Convergence" have been formulated by the Government of India in the recent past. National Telecom Policy (NTP99) was framed in 1999 with an objective to increase tele-density of 7 per 100 by 2007 and 15 by 2010. A very important decision came up in this policy was Universal Service Obligation (USO). Under this policy it is aimed at ensuring universal access to every citizen at affordable prices. Information, Communication and Entertainment Bill (ICE) was also another milestone in the history of Indian telecommunication having special focus on private service providers in the areas of ISP, Paging, VSAT and public mobile trunk operators.

Telecom growth in India has been fuelled by wireless growth. The wireless subscriber base has grown from 1.6 million in 1999 to 90.14 million in March 2006 and is nearly double the subscriber base of 50.18 million of fixed service users. The mobile sector grew at 72.6 per cent in comparison to 8.6 per cent growth in the fixed sector over the year between March 2005-06.

Another initiative of Government of India to improve ICT infrastructure in rural India and last mile connectivity is State-wide Area Network (SWAN) projects under e-governance which are being implemented in various States. Under this scheme, optical fibre line will be provided up to Block level and last mile connectivity through radio link. This will enable provide connectivity backbone for e-governance at all the levels.

Mere provision of hardware and software components will not help the rural population draw benefits, but a systematic and convergent approach of policy makers, business drivers would be necessary for its use. Innovations are necessary for adoption of this technology since it can be viewed as a tool to improve the efficiency and effectiveness of the process that exists for the development of rural population and economy. Such processes could be providing basic information to the public for good governance, creating an atmosphere of transparency in pricing, marketing products, providing education and addressing disaster mitigation issues, etc. Reaching the rural population where the other infrastructure relating to connectivity like rail, road is limited can be made possible through ICT infrastructure.

Leveraging ICT: Breakthrough for Rural Outreach

Some of innovative business model for rural outreach by leveraging the existing rural ICT infrastructure in India are given as under:

- ***E-Choupal:*** e-choupal is information Kiosk totally owned and set up by ITC basically designed to support ITC's agricultural products supply chain. e-choupals are set up with solar power backup and VSAT connectivity. They also provide access to local market (*mandi*) prices and global market price information on various agricultural products to allow farmers to compare prices. In fact, farmers view ITC as treating with greater respect and dignity than is the case in traditional *mandi* interactions.

- ***n-Logue:*** It is promoted by TeNeT Group, IIT Chennai research group headed by Professor Ashok Jhunjhunwala. The core innovation at the heart of n-Logue's operations is a WLL technology, Cordect, which provides joint wireless Internet and voice connectivity. n-Logue is the second largest organization in this field, supporting over 500 rural IT-Kiosk. The focus of the company is to drive Internet and Telecom services in small towns and rural areas of India, thereby realizing its vision of "significantly enhancing the quality of life of every rural Indian by driving the digital revolution profitably".
- ***e-Grama:*** NABARD has part funded establishment of 13 Village Information Centres (e-Grama centres) through an NGO in Davanagare district of Karnataka to help SHGs/villages to have access to Information Communication Technology. These e-Grama centres make available information on areas like weather conditions, crop inputs, product prices, land records, etc. Besides this, add-on services like book-keeping of SHGs, DTP, scanning, etc., are also being provided.
- ***Computer Munshi:*** Proper book-keeping of SHGs is one of the gray areas owing to the illiteracy among the group members. NABARD sanctioned financial assistance of Rs. 0.61 million to PRADAN—an NGO to develop system and local resources to address the issue. It involves training skilled local youth in computer operations and specially designed software to maintain SHG accounts. The project is being implemented in 4 districts (9 units) in Jharkhand and 1 district (1 unit) in Orissa.

The pioneering breakthroughs in adopting ICT solutions have been made by MFIs which have attained financial and institutional stability and sustainability enabling them to have well defined MIS systems and a clear vision of what IT can do for their organizations. These organizations have been able to either raise funds from donors or fund them from their own funds, e.g., SEWA

(Self Employed Women's Association) Bank, or else take assignment to develop IT software like BASIX (Bharatiya Samruddhi Financial Services) has done with International Finance Corporation (IFC). Some of MFIs who have successfully integrated ICT and MIS into the design and planning of the MFI and its operations are BASIX and Swayam Krishi Sangham (SKS). The Activists for Social Alternatives (ASA), Development for Humane Action (DHAN) Foundation, etc.

Though ICT is mainly adopted by the New and Large MFIs, yet there is a small but increasing trend of small MFIs adopting ICT primarily with support from partner agencies (such as CARE's CASHE programme) and or from SIDBI.

Innovative Delivery Channels for Financial Inclusion and Reaching the Rural Poor

Financial Inclusion refers to providing access to financial services at affordable cost to the rural and the poor. Being remoteness, wider geographical areas, difficult terrains, sparsely populated and poor physical infrastructure in the rural areas, the biggest challenges for Financial Inclusion (FI) today is outreach to poor with cost effective. ICT has been recognized as one of the most cost effective tools for the financial inclusion.

Many of the thousands of microfinance institutions (MFIs) worldwide recognize that technology is essential, not only to reach new people, but also to make the business of microfinance more cost-effective and sustainable. Mobile phones, ATM machines, and a host of new innovations promise to help MFIs more efficiently provide services to people typically considered "unbankable".

With wireless communications networks growing and technology costs falling, electronic payments (e-payments), rather than cash or cheque-based payments, have emerged as a powerful tool with which financial institutions can build national scale and manage small lending risks. Banks and MFIs can use the hardware and communication networks that process e-payments transactions, such as (ATMs, POS, mobile phones and internet–base banking) and point-of sale (POS) terminals, to serve people who cannot access, or who choose not to use, bank branches.

Branchless Banking : Emerging Business Model

One of the key challenges for MFIs is providing financial services to clients in remote areas including rural areas where the population density is low, the market is smaller and providing service entails high costs. Branchless Banking through Business Correspondent (BC)/Business Facilitator (BF) model—whereby a bank links itself with third party merchants located in remote areas—has emerged as a solution for this problem of outreach. Correspondents manage transactions on behalf of the partner institution and are remunerated on a fee-for-service basis. Bank Correspondents are expected to be having long-term businesses, and should be respected and trusted in their communities. The Bank Correspondents should also be "ICT-enabled"; generally equipped with equipments such as an Electronic Funds Transfer at Point of Sale (EFTPoS) device, barcode readers and/or keypads, a personal computer, etc. They are linked to the partner institution's servers using a telephone line, cable or satellite link. Post offices, supermarkets, general stores, grocery stores, tele centres, etc., are good examples of Banking Correspondents.

In India, commercial banking entities like State Bank of India, HDFC, have tied up with the respective Service Centre Agencies (SCAs) in the States under the framework of National e- Governance Plan (NeGP) to provide Banking Correspondent status to the Common Service Centres (CSCs) equipped with ICT infrastructure and provide microfinance services through them. Detailed guidelines and circulars on BC and BF model were also issued to all the commercial banks by RBI to mitigate various possible financial and operational risks.

Branchless banking followed by a number of nationalized banks like SBI, UBI, Indian Bank, PNB who have collaborated with technology based companies providing solutions not only to enhance outreach but also to give microfinance services through different technology options. These agencies include Financial Information Network & Operation Ltd, (FINO), Zero Mass Foundation and Atom Technologies.

Many of MFIs operating in India have already tie-up with nationalized banks to act as BC in favour of parent bank. This model is purely based on sound business model which has been widely implemented in many parts of the country through active participation of banks, MFIs, technology provider, etc. It is the clear example of collaborative and convergent of many stakeholders in a single platform to reach the rural mass with the help of existing ICT infrastructure.

A unique ID (identification) for each citizen would also help accelerate this model for easy identification of clients remotely as required by Know Your Customer (KYC) norms of RBI. Setting up a Unique Identification Authority of India for maintaining UID for every citizen by 2012 is a positive step for providing better services to poor. In the recent Union Budget 2010, Government of India has already made budgetary allocation of Rs. 1, 900 crores for UIAI.

M-Banking : Future of Microfinance

Cellular phones, especially with GSM backbone, due to its accessibility and affordability are becoming an indispensable communication tool for the poor in the developing countries. As per the World GSM Association report, during the year 2003-2006, more than 800 million mobile phones were sold in developing countries. Mobile phones in today's scenario have become the only option for communication from being one of the options because of the ubiquity of its use and popularity even among the poorer section of the society.

Mobile phones have become mobile wallets by facilitating electronic payments in exchange for goods and services. Mobile Phone Banking (m-Banking) has assumed tremendous significance under the circumstances and this development in m-Banking has positively affected the microfinance industry also with usages like facilitating savings deposits, loan repayments and other funds transfers.

Indeed, one of the most used devices by both microfinance providers and their clients is the mobile phone. With the number of African and Asian users increasing by tens of millions each year, many organizations are looking for ways to best utilize mobile phones as a tool for microfinance.

m-Banking has the potential to be transformational because:

- It uses existing mobile communications infrastructure which already reaches unbanked people.

- It reduces the cost and risk inherent in dealing with cash.
- It may be driven by new players, such as telcos, with different target market from traditional banks.
- It may harness the power of new distribution network for cash transactions, such as airtime merchants, beyond the conventional merchant POS or ATM network of banks.
- It may be cheaper than conventional banking, if the offering is competitive.

The extent to which will mobile banking will in fact be transformational in a country will depend in large measure on whether the environment is enabling.

M-Banking is the hottest area of development in the banking sector and is expected to replace the credit/debit card system in future. In past two years, m-Banking user has increased three times if we compare the use of either debit card or credit card. Moreover 85-90 per cent mobile users do not own credit cards.There is at least 36 per cent of population that are literate having mobile phones and have no access to credit. This is the potential market that would appreciate mobile banking solutions.

"m-Money" is money that can be accessed and used *via* mobile phone. Today, mobile subscribers in markets such as South Africa, in Kenya *(P-Pesa)*, Philippines *(G-Cash)*, Japan, and elsewhere are beginning to use mobile money for transactions and services including domestic and international remittances, bill payment, payroll deposit, loan receipt and repayment, and purchases of goods and services ranging from prepaid airtime to groceries to bus tickets to micro insurance. Some examples of m-Money are:

m-Pesa, in Kenya: When Vodafone and Safaricom launched their m-payment service m-Pesa in Kenya in March 2007, they gained 2.37 million subscribers in little over one year. According to Dr. Nick Hughes, Head of International Mobile Payment Solutions for Vodafone Group, this is "an uptake which has surprised us but shows the need in the marketplace for very simple, secure and low-cost services".

g-Cash in Philippine: In the Philippines, the Central Bank collaborated closely with Globe and SMART, the country's two mobile operators, to develop a framework for mobile banking that incorporated consumer protection into mobile-operator business model. The Central Bank issued guidelines in 2005, shortly after the launch of Globe's g-Cash product, and it continues to engage with a variety of stakeholders today, including most recently the equity stake that Globe took in one of the country's saving banks.

m-Chek, India: is one of pilot project for m-Banking in India taken up by mChek India Payment Systems Pvt. Ltd and Grameen Koota-Micro Finance Institution to implement mobile payments in the micro credit sector. To take this beyond the pilot phase, mChek needs to tie up with a bank. Under Reserve Bank of India (RBI) norms, mobile payments have to be routed only through bank or credit card accounts.

There is lot of potential for harnessing benefits of m-banking technology for inclusive growth as mobile penetration in rural India has witnessed a rapid growth in the past. m-Banking is at a very initial stage of pilot testing by most of MFIs. However, some progress has been made in the recent past through collaborative efforts of banks, telecos and MFIs. In the absence of any common regulatory framework or guidelines, m-Banking in India will take some more time to pick up at national level as one of effective tools for financial inclusion. The Reserve Bank of Pakistan has taken a proactive approach and established transparent and detailed guidelines for banking agents and mobile banking well-ahead of any large-scale implementation. It recently joined forces with the country's telecommunication authority and set up a joint regulatory committee to propose medication to the mobile banking regulatory framework. The bank also created a cross-industry, multi-sector "Stakeholders Group" to address product, operational and technical issues for mobile banking. If RBI can follow a similar collaborative, proactive and risk-based approach to craft supportive guidelines, it would remove one the major obstacles for MFIs to develop transformational delivery channels in India.

Considering large number of mobile phone subscribers in rural India, m-banking will be the *future of microfinance* in India for accelerating financial inclusion provided there is collaborative and convergent efforts of all the stakeholders such as policy makers, regulators, banks, telecos, MFIs, etc. supported by enabling environment backed up by adequate ICT infrastructure in rural India.

Issues and Challenges of Adopting New Technologies and Alternative Delivery Channels

The promise of technology to enable breakthrough in the way microfinance is delivered around the world is quite encouraging, but there is still some important obstacles to be overcome in the near future. Some of issues and challenges for adopting new technology and alternative delivery channels are discussed below:

High Capital Cost: Generally the greatest barrier to information technology is the cost. Most of the MFIs in India are lacking capital except a few big MFIs. High initial capital investment required for any technology solution has been one of big challenges for many MFIs in India. SIDBI and NABARD financial support to MFIs for new technology adoption is appreciable. Open software solution of MIFOS, Grameen Foundation which are made available to small MFIs at free of course is also one solution to this challenge. Share of resources, through common ICT infrastructure under consortium of MFIs can also drive down the cost of the solution, making it affordable to deliver financial products and services to those living in rural areas. One of such example is FINO software solutions which can provide core banking solution for all the MFIs under one platform and IT infrastructure.

Technology Integration and Risk: Indirect channels such as ATM, agents, smart card, POS, mobile-banking, etc., require integration and data synchronization between third-party platforms and those of the MFI. For example, an MFI's banking application must "talk" to the partner's IT system using the same communication protocol. For mobile banking, an MFI needs to connect to a mobile operator's platform either directly or, more likely, through the black box of a mobile-technology vendor that provides application development and switching capability. Experience has shown that, though manageable, this is one of the biggest hurdles to overcome. The security in relaying a customer's personal and financial data to the MFI is another concern, and, depending on the risk threshold set by the RBI and the MFI's own risk unit. MFIs must ensure that an adequate level of encryption and safe storage employed so that data cannot be intercepted or otherwise compromised.

Manpower Problems: Many MFIs have ambitions to explore different innovations but fall short on actual execution. Small or start-up MFIs in particular is often understaffed for all the initiatives being pursued, and managers lack the bandwidth necessary to manage the milestones, budget and scope. To obtain channels expertise in the short-term, MFIs can hire external consultants. Channel consultants should ideally have a broad understanding of multiple delivery channels and their implementation so that they can recommend appropriate channel solutions for the institution and support the MFI to bring them to fruition.

In the long-run, training and capacity building for MFI staff will be necessary for multi-channel strategies to become the norm for MFIs. Some conference, such as the Mobile Money Transfer series organised by Clarion Events, now include comprehensive workshops on everything from customer adoption to technology-vendor selection for mobile banking. Other centres that already offer training such as Micro Save, Sa-Dhan, etc., could expand their offering or provide separate training on channel development and implementation.

Regulatory Constraints: Though a number of leading or large MFIs have become NBFC under RBI regulation, majority of MFIs are still unregulated thereby limiting launching of alternative channels. For example, NGOs cannot legally offer savings accounts; they cannot offer useful services, such as account-to-account transfers, utility payments, or cash-in or cash-out transactions through retail-agent channels. Thus being NGO (and sometimes being a finance company) limits the types of financial services the institution can offer and thus curtails its ability to launch transactional payment channels.

In India, for example, the regulators permit only full-fledged commercial banks to offer mobile banking services and develop banking-agent programmes; even regulated non-bank finance companies are not allowed to develop these channels. One of the reasons for mobile operators to partner with banks is "regular cover", but non-bank MFIs cannot provide this. Moreover, NGOs cannot be a member of the major payment networks, such as Visa and Master Card, and can only access these networks through partnerships with member banks.

Infrastructure Bottleneck: Finally, the infrastructure in the country or region that is needed to support certain alternative channels is not always reliable. This includes sporadic power supply, a weak wireless telecom infrastructure and the limited availability of a national switch to process electronic transactions across multiple payment platforms. Almost all well-developed ATM networks, for example, rely on these three characteristics to allow customers real-time access to their funds in nearby locations.

Improving the country's energy and communications infrastructure is imperative for certain remote channels to flourish, though naturally financial inclusion is but one of the many infrastructure-dependent activities which government decision-makers must consider, and infrastructure typically takes years to improve to a satisfactory level. In the mean time, MFIs may have to consider alternatives—such as back-up power generators, fixed-line communications, and multiple interfaces with bank (in lieu of a broad switch)—that allow them to offer a robust and reliable banking channel to their customers.

Conclusions

ICTs will continue to impact microfinance operations worldwide. As prices of relevant technology like ATMs, biometrics, voice recognition, smart-cards, and PDAs continue to fall, more MFIs will be able to take advantage of the benefits they offer. New technologies and applications are constantly being developed aimed at increasing the reach and efficiency of microfinance organizations. Improvement will make operations more secure, increase transparency (and thus scalability), reduce repetitive tasks, and provide data mining capabilities that will allow MFIs to compete effectively and better manage their operations.

While mobile money is now in its emerging stages, it is rapidly moving toward consolidation and growth. Industry leaders are clear that what is needed now is sustained action: experimentation and innovation by firms with mobile money business models and by government in the regulatory framework to make them possible. It is important to sustain and even diversify the opportunities for mobile network operators, banks, technology providers and other interested firms to share experience and learn about business and technology innovations in the mobile money space. At the same time, it is important to establish and support similar forums for regulators to exchange policy innovations across countries.

Many of the more promising alternative channels will require building relationships, agreements, and alliances—sometimes with parties unfamiliar to MFIs—and thus multi-sector dialogue and collaboration will be a key skill that all stakeholders will need to enhance. Ultimately, MFIs and other stakeholders need to develop mutually beneficial channel solutions that both create business value for the institution and enhance the availability, accessibility and affordability of financial services to poor.

A stable and conducive policy environment is necessary for other initiatives such as single credit bureau, biometric IDs or smart cards and weather stations. The sector at this stage needs a *laissez faire* environment; policy makers should be on continuous vigil and deliver concurrent improvement in policy and regulation. All organizations engaged in microfinance should be brought together under a single legal status and regulatory authority.

Providing connectivity to rural India provides the much-needed access to information and power. Active participations and collaborative efforts of various agencies like banks, MFIs, corporate houses, telecoms, Government, regulators, etc., are needed for systematic integrations and harmonic synchronization between microfinance and ICT infrastructure for accelerating financial inclusion in the coming years. It will create the necessary atmosphere to create wealth and enable rural India. We now need to build on this and work towards empowering India.

REFERENCES

Beth Kenkins, *Developing Mobile Money Ecosystems*, Washington, DC: IFC and the Harvard Kennedy School.

Bhatnagar, Subhash and Robert Schware, (2000), *Information and Communication Technology in Development: Cases from India*, New Delhi, Sage Publications.

CGAP, *Using Electronic Payments to Build Inclusive Financial Systems*, (draft), CGAP, USA 2005 (E)

CGAP, *Focus Notes*, "Banking through Network of Agents".

Cheryl Frankiewicz, AfriCap, *Information Technology as a strategic tool for Microfinance in Africa—A seminar Report*, Calmeadow.

David Cracknell, (2004), "*Electronic Banking For the Poor: Panacea, Potential and Pitfalls*, Micro saves.

Department for International Development (DFID), "*The enabling environment for mobile banking in Africa*".

Insight –ACCION –"*Accelerating Financial Inclusion through Innovative Channels*".

Insight, ACCION Prta Credit: "*Increasing MFI Efficiency with Technology*".

Laura I. Fredrick (2005)," *Information Technology Innovations for Scaling Rural Microfinance Outreach*", exchange

Nirvikar Singh, "*Information Technology and Rural Development in India*", University of California, Santa Cruz, USA.

Payal Malik, (2006), "*An Analysis of the Reform of India's Telecommunications Industry: Policy, Regulation and Indicators.*"

www.accion.org.

www.trai.gov.in

www.infodev.org

www.cgap.org.

www.microsave.org

www.nabard.org

SECTION - V
Financial Inclusion and Micro Insurance

26

Micro Insurance-tailor-made for the Poor

SREEMOYEE GUHA ROY

Introduction

Micro insurance, the subject matter of this chapter, is the most recent in the wave of micro movements that have been sweeping international development thinking and practice in recent years. Founded on the basic principles of the micro credit revolution, micro insurance extends social security mechanisms and insurance products to groups that are in dire needs but have been historically bypassed by these services. Recognizing the poor as willing and capable agents in their own socio-economic change, micro insurance seeks to incorporate marginalized and low income groups in the mainstream capitalist economy by providing them with insurance products that address their security needs and purchasing capacities.

Micro-insurance is a key element in the financial services package for people at the bottom of the pyramid. The poor face more risks than the well-off, but more importantly they are more vulnerable to the same risk. Usually, the poor face two types of risks – idiosyncratic (specific to the household) and covariate (common, e.g., drought, epidemic, etc.). To combat these risks, the poor do proactive risk management—grain storage, savings, asset accumulation (especially bullocks), loans from friends and relatives, etc. However, the prevalent forms of risk management (in kind savings, self-insurance, mutual insurance) which were appropriate earlier are no longer adequate. Poverty is not just a state of deprivation but has latent vulnerability. Micro insurance should, therefore, provide greater economic and psychological security to the poor as it reduces exposure to multiple risks and cushions the impact of a disaster. There is an overwhelming demand for social protection among the poor. Micro insurance in conjunction with micro savings and micro credit could, therefore, go a long way in keeping this segment away from the poverty trap and would truly be an integral component of financial inclusion.

In recent times the case for micro insurance is strong as it tries to create a partnership between the development and corporate sector for the purposes of development and poverty alleviation. This is particularly pertinent for countries like India, which have denationalized banking and insurance sector.

This chapter provides an overview of the micro insurance market in India, covering the service providers in the market, the distribution models employed, the products offered and their uptake among the low-income population. The market in India is overwhelmingly formal as informal insurance systems are relatively unknown in the country. While traditional systems of insurance do not exceed beyond the small degree of guaranteed return, other NGO-managed community based insurance systems provide more significant benefit to those covered. While there are few around the State, their focus is almost entirely on health risk and the overall numbers of those insured by such systems are still miniscule relative to the large proportions of the population that do not have any form of insurance cover.

Salient Features of Micro Insurance Market in India

Product Characteristics—Micro insurance products in the market have short policy contract terms and are generally underwritten on group basis.

Health Prominence—Health insurance is prominent in community-based systems because health risk is generally seen as potentially the most devastating type of systematic risk likely to upset the lives and economic livelihoods of the low-income population.

Low Outreach of Community-based Insurance—Community-based health insurance systems managed by NGOs are available but, except in couple of cases, has miniscule outreach.

Dominance of Loan Linked Product—This is the largest product in the market driven by the compulsion of borrowers to purchase insurance schemes mainly to protective cover to MFIs.

Micro Insurance Category—The advent of separate micro insurance guidelines provided by the insurance regulator has seen the launch of new micro insurance products in the formal market.

New Distribution Models—Rural and social sector obligations imposed on formal insurers by the market regulator have compelled insurance companies to experiment with new distribution models through NGOs, MFIs and the rural banking network.

Adviceless Selling—Micro insurance is sold overwhelmingly without advice while the higher end of the insurance market is served by brokers providing advice. Micro insurance agents are specifically restricted to working with a single life and single non-life insurer.

Insurance Providers

Formal insurance service providers that are the insurance companies legally registered with the government and supervised by the industry regulator. The Insurance Regulatory and Development Authority, dominate the insurance market in India. Micro insurance is in its infancy in the country but growing fast through the activities of the formal insurance companies under the impetus provided by the rural social sector obligations imposed by the IRDA. A considerable effort is now being made by these companies to design innovative products but even more so to experiment with the distribution channels. In addition with the increasing economic growth in India the government has become concerned about the exclusion of the low-income population from the growth process. It is within this framework that the government is increasingly turning its attention to insurance as a form of social protection. This has led to the launch of a number of country-wide pilots for health and/or life insurance for the poor and even some experiments with State-wide schemes.

Formal Sector Insurance

Despite the recent advent of the government into insurance as a social security mechanism for low income families, the formal insurance companies are still the dominant providers of insurance services in India. In March 2006, there were 15 companies registered with IRDA for providing life insurance and 12 general insurance companies along with two specialist public sector insurers, the Export Credit Guarantee Corporation and Agricultural Insurance Company. This industry structure has emerged out of a public sector insurance monopoly, the Life Insurance Corporation of India and four general subsidiaries of General Insurance Corporation. The insurance monopoly was ended in 2000 when the IRDA relaxed the barriers to entry specifically for the purpose of attracting private and foreign companies in the insurance sector. However, during 2006-07, the micro insurance business of these companies represented less than 1 per cent of their total turnover. The IRDAs micro insurance guidelines were, of course released only in November 2005. However, in September 2007, there were only 12 micro insurance products registered with the IRDA by 6 companies. Currently there are not much formal insurance companies focusing exclusively, or even extensively, on the micro insurance market but the rural and social sector obligations have compelled them to take a close look on the micro insurance market and there is an increasing degree of experimentation with it.

Community Insurance Schemes

There are a variety of community and cooperative insurance schemes available in the country. A survey undertaken by the International Labour Organization (ILO) in India identified about 50 such schemes. But mostly are all health insurance schemes with a few having add-on under-writing of life, housing and/or productive assets. The schemes vary in size from the 1.5 million beneficiaries of Karnataka's Yeshasvini Trust to relatively small schemes with just a few hundreds covered. The insurance is offered either directly by NGOs or cooperatives or in partnership with insurance companies. In a number of cases the aggregator provides insurance to its members directly and the risk not necessarily passed on to an insurance company. These are often referred to as in-house insurance providers. Thus then aggregator becomes underwriter in this model.

Social Security

Social Security insurance is available in the market, mainly for the middle and upper income segments. These products are mostly linked to mutual funds and are known as Unit Linked Insurance Products with life cover. Efforts to provide social security to low-income households or unorganized sector are at a nascent stage. There have been government initiatives both at State and national levels for below poverty line households but these have had limited success, so far, due to the lack of client education and information as well as inappropriate product design. The Government of India has also launched its social security initiative—Aam Admi Bima Yojana, for poor families that do not own agricultural land.

Distribution

The limiting features of micro insurance products is low premiums, on the one hand and high transaction costs (for insurers) on the other, which makes it necessary for these products to be offered through special vehicles that have been variously described as "nodal agencies" or "aggregators". These are agencies that already have access to and commercial and financial relationships with large groups of low-income families in a certain geographical area. These agencies form an essential part of the delivery mechanism for micro insurance in India. These are:

- Microfinance Institutions;
- Non-Governmental Organization;
- Self-Help Groups;
- Co-operative societies; and
- Other community benefits institutions.

In addition to the above agencies, other organizations or persons who have regular interactions with low-income families, such as Panchayati Raj Institutions have also been targeted to deliver micro insurance products. IRDA, realizing the importance of these delivery agencies has referred them as "micro insurance agents" in the Micro Insurance Regulations, 2005.

The restriction to only one company of each type is based on the assumption that the complexity of insurance products is high and that "too much information" would be a burden for the MI agent and the client. This restriction makes it impossible to combine the best products from different companies into a bouquet that will suit the needs of particular types of clients.

There are four main models for delivering the micro insurance services to the target segment which are given below:

Partner Agent Model: Here insurers utilize Microfinance Institutions delivery mechanism to provide sales and basic services to clients. This involves no risk and limited administrative burden for Microfinance Institutions. This is most commonly used model but as seen in many cases it involves some delays in claim settlement.

Full Service Model: Here the provider is responsible for all aspects of product design, sales, servicing, and claim assessment. Besides, the insurer is responsible for all insurance related costs and losses but, retain all profits.

Community-Based Model: Here the policy holders own and manages the insurance programme, and negotiates with external healthcare providers.

Provider Model: In this model the service providers and insurers are the same that is hospitals and doctors offers policies to individuals and groups.

Micro Insurance Products

Micro insurance may be offered for a wide variety of risks. These include both health risks and property risks.

Life Insurance—It provides coverage against death (accidental and natural). Beneficiaries receive compensation upon the death of the policy holder, who is typically the primary bread winner.

Health Insurance—It provides reimbursement towards following hospitalization expense for illness/diseases sustained by the insured person.

Crop Insurance—It covers the loss of crops due to natural disaster, fire, and lightning; strike etc. The cover of crops insurance is restricted to the cost of production up to the point when production is lost.

Livestock/Cattle Insurance—Under the livestock policy, cover is provided for the sum insured or the market value of the animal at the time of death whichever is less.

Asset Insurance—It provides cover against loss of assets or stock of rural entrepreneurs due to fire, flood, riots, strike, etc.

Customer Expectation

Despite the involvement of NGOs, the customers still have bad claim experience. In some schemes the attrition rates are high, but concealed by new client acquisition. The caps on claim payment and the floor premium levels are not acceptable to the customers. The scenario relating to risk coverage for rural communities looks promising in terms of the interest shown by several organisations both in the financial sector and in the service sector. However, there are some fundamental issues that need to be addressed in more concrete terms. The insurance cover available in most cases is compulsory, having been sold by the MFI or NGO acting as the distributor. The customer rarely has made any informed choice of a particular policy or even a type of risk. The insurance is mostly to cover the credit risk of the lending organisation than to mitigate any identified risk of the customer. In a few cases the commission income to the distributor has been a major consideration; not whether the policy is best suited product for the customer. While there are few products custom designed for specific needs after considerable study, many products sold in the micro insurance market suffer from deficiencies. The staffs of MFIs / NGOs do not have full knowledge of the product as also the claim processes. The delay in settlement of claims or refusal thereof alienates the customer. Client dropouts increase costs to the company as well as to the customer.

Centre for Microfinance (CMF) has carried out a study of barriers to household risk management. Low participation is typical in Indian market with 5 to 10 per cent households buying insurance. But the study found that it would increase to 20 to 30 per cent especially through visits by insurance marketers. Additional information creates a need in households to obtain risk cover. Lack of funds is the reason given by 64 per cent of those without insurance. The study concludes that insurance is price sensitive and liquidity sensitive. Building trust and confidence increases demand for insurance. Higher levels of literacy influence demand for insurance significantly.

Recommendations of the Study

There is a need to conduct the insurance awareness campaign and the members who benefited out of insurance can better explain the schemes.

- Micro insurance products must have the features of simplicity, availability, affordability, accessibility and flexibility.
- Training should be given to all the micro insurance intermediaries regarding the product features, enrolling formalities, premium collection and claim processing.
- There is a need for establishing credibility of private player.
- Mass media like television, radio and newspapers have to be used effectively to create awareness about the micro insurance product among rural areas.

Conclusion

Micro insurance is the key component of poverty alleviation. But, the penetration of insurance products among the poor is very low. This is mainly because of lack of awareness about the benefits of insurance and reluctance of insurers to sell insurance to the poor due to high delivery costs. Keeping this in view, insurance companies should go beyond devising new products to improving their processes for building awareness, marketing enrolment, premium collection, claim settlement and renewal among the hitherto unreached. Micro insurance will also require a regulatory framework that is flexible enough to allow Insurers, NGOs, and Self Help Groups to innovate in product design and delivery models to make insurance affordable to the poor and still be economically viable. In the golden words of C.K. Prahlad, "Improving the lives of the billions of people at the bottom of the pyramid is a noble endeavour. It can also be lucrative".

REFERENCES

Bhat Ramesh and Jain Nishant (July 2006), "Factor Affecting the Demand for Health Insurance in a Micro Insurance Scheme", IIM Ahmedabad, W.P. No. 2006-07-02.

Ganesan Dr. S. and Jayaprakash Dr. S. (July 2007), "Micro Bank Assurance Models for India" Eleventh Annual APRIA Conference at National Chengchi University, Taipei, Taiwan

Ito Seiro and Kono Hisaki (2007), "Why the take-up of microinsurance is so low? Evidence from a health insurance scheme in India" *JEL Classification*: F35, O19.

MacCord Michael J. (March 2008), "Vision of the Future of Microinsurance and Thoughts on getting there" *Microinsurance Note#9*.

Malika Mark and Kuriakose Anet T. (2008), "Social Fund Innovation Notes" *World Bank 2008*, Volume 5, number 2.

Pierro Rachele (2008), "Micro Insurance & drr: Challenges and Opportunities in the context of Climate Change".

Rajivan Anuradha (April 2007), "Engaging the Private Sector to Insure the Poor", UN Business Focal Point.

Rao Koli N. (2008), "Risk Management as a Pillar in Agriculture and Food Security in India", Food and Agriculture Organization for the United Nations.

Roth Jim, MacCord Michael J. and Liber Dominic (2007), "The Landscape of Microinsurance in 100 Poorest Countries", the Microinsurance Center, LLC.

Wiedmaier Martina-Pfister (August 2004), "Regulation and supervision of Micro Insurance", Division 41 Financial System Development.

27

Micro Insurance for Micro Entrepreneurs of Manipur: The Way Forward

A. RAJMANI SINGHA

Introduction

Over the last few decades despite of sustained efforts, Government of India has failed to make any significant improvement in its poverty figures, with over 400 million — more than the total in the poorest African nations — still struck in poverty. India's rank in UNDPs Human Development Index has moved to 119 in 2010 against 127 in 2005. Though India has jumped few positions during the last five years, it continues to have high absolute poverty of people living below USD 1.25 per day along with high incidence of multidimensional poverty which is characterized by lack of access to health, education and living standards.

Of late, the micro credit-microfinance-microenterprise movement has been making a silent revolution in the upliftment of rural India through the emergence of vibrant Self Help Groups (SHGs) and it has become an effective tool to address the problem of poverty and empowerment. These provisions have enabled the poor households to increase their income and build their own assets, employment and empowerment. But, still they are vulnerable to withstand unexpected events and remain exposed to multiple risks, which take away the gains made due to their association with the SHGs. Besides, the poor living in risk prone area (floods and drought), are not willing to invest further for their enterprise development fearing that their business assets are exposed to risks. To overcome such unexpected risks micro insurance (MI) will be the best option to ensure them a social and economic security. MI is the provision of insurance cover to the low income households.

Micro Insurance in India

In 2006, the then President of India, Dr. A.P.J. Abdul Kalam had launched a special scheme for covering the risks of the rural poor through micro insurance by the Life Insurance Corporation of India. The CNRI (confederation of NGOs) was vested with the responsibility of collecting the insurance premium. The Scheme introduced was named *"Jeevan Madhur."* It has been implemented in various States like Tamil Nadu, Kerala, Maharashtra, A.P., Gujarat and U.P. Initially, the main focus of micro insurance has been on life, in-patient health care and property. SEWA (Small Enterprise Women's Association) (life, in-patient health care and property), LIC, India (Life) representing from the public sector undertaking and Birla, Tata AIG, micro insurance from private insurance agencies in the country ranging different insurance products to meet the demand of the clients.

India is having a huge potential and prospects for micro insurance and this sector is considered a good profitable niche. The country alone, the untapped market is estimated to range between $1.4 billion and $1.9 billion, covering life and non-life services. This is possible to achieve the expected growth only when insurance is better understood among potential clients and a wider range of risks are recognized as insurable by them. Insurance currently covers only 2 per cent of the poor in India. More than 90 per cent of the population of the country, or 950 million people, are excluded from this service—a huge missing market.

Earlier, in India, the Micro insurance initiative was on a bank-driven basis. The assets (mainly dairy animals, sheep and goat) created under the poverty alleviation programmes by the banks were insured and the lives of the beneficiaries were covered by Government of India under a group insurance policy. As most of the non life insurance companies had master policy with the banks at the apex level, the claim servicing was not given attention in the field, which resulted inordinate delay in settlement of claims and a negative image was created about the insurance companies among the poor.

Micro-Insurance Models

A key concern in the pricing of an insurance product is the element of cost of acquisition and its delivery. Obviously, the delivery costs have to be contained to keep the cost of insurance sufficiently low to attract the poor and to incentivize the insurer to venture into this segment viewing it as a genuine market opportunity.

The Committee studied four different models for delivering micro-insurance services to the targeted clientele:

Partner—Agent Model

- Insurers utilize MFIs' delivery mechanism to provide sales and basic services to clients.
- There is no risk and limited administrative burden for MFIs.

Full Service Model

- The provider is responsible for all aspects of product design, sales, servicing, and claims assessment.
- The insurers are responsible for all insurance-related costs and losses and they retain all profits.

Community-Based Model

- The policy holders own and manage the insurance programme, and negotiate with external health care providers.

Provider Model

- The service provider and the insurer are the same, i.e., hospitals or doctors offer policies to individuals or groups.

Micro insurance sector is very infant stage in Manipur. Private micro insurance such as Birla and Tata Aig play the significant role in the field of micro insurance in Manipur during 2007-08. However, in hilly districts of Senapati and Chandel, Life Insurance company play the important role in providing services of micro insurance in the areas of health and crop insurance.

Imphal west district is capital district of Manipur. Among the nine revenue districts, Imphal west is the most developed district in Manipur. As on 31st March, 2010, there are 17,908 Self Help Groups directly performing microfinance activities in nine districts. Among the nine revenue districts, Imphal west district covered the maximum number of SHGs in the State with 3,821 numbers. The present study is also confined to this district.

Objective of the Study

Following are the objectives of the study:

- To find out the awareness level of micro insurance among the SHGs formed in the State in general and more particularly the Imphal west district.
- To identify the impact of micro insurance on their financial lives especially to those who are deals with micro enterprises.
- To examine the reason behind the less popularity of micro insurance in Manipur.
- To evaluate the contribution of micro insurance among the first generation micro entrepreneurs.

Methodology

The Sample size of the study is comprised of 198 micro entrepreneur respondents working under different SHGs in Imphal west district of Manipur. Out of the total 3,821 SHGs, 50 SHGs have been selected on the basis of cluster random method for the present study and further 4 SHG members deals with economic oriented activities *vis-à-vis* micro entrepreneurs are selected on the recommendation of the respective SHGs office bearers. Primary data were collected through a pre tested questionnaire under direct interview method. The study was conducted in the month of September and October 2010. The collected data are classified, tabulated and interpreted into the present form. Further, secondary data were collected from the books, journal, annual report and website.

Data Analysis

On the basis of collected primary and secondary data, the researcher has classified and presented in the following manner:

District-wise Position of Self Help Groups in Manipur: Table 27.1 shows the district-wise position of Self Help Groups formed in Manipur. As per State Level Bankers Committee Report there are 17,908 SHGs working in nine different districts of the

State. Out of these total, 15,730 SHGs are operated by women folk in the State. Hence, the participation of women in SHG formation *vis-à-vis* micro finance activities in the State is very high. It is also found that almost all the SHGs formed in the State are engaged on economic-oriented activities. Imphal west district accounts the highest number of SHGs formed in the State and Tamenglong district falls the lowest formation of SHGs deals in microfinance activities in the State. It has directly related with the most developed district and the most backward district in the State. Besides different NGOs deals with the rural development activities in the State also forming a large number of SHGs which are not included in the present number of SHGs formation in the State.

Table 27.1 : District-wise Position of Self Help Groups in Manipur as on 31st March, 2010

District	*No of SHGs formed*	*No. of women SHGs*	*No of SHGs taken up economic activities*
Imphal west	3,821	3,216	3,821
Imphal east	1,670	1,331	1,670
Thoubal	3,734	3.494	3,734
Bishenpur	1,787	1,564	1,787
Chandel	686	599	686
Ukhrul	1,127	999	1,127
Churachandpur	1,336	1,031	1,336
Senapati	3,193	3,005	3,193
Tamenglong	554	491	554
Total	17,908	15,730	17,908

Source : 22nd State Level Banker's Committee Meeting, Manipur, p. 10.

Classification of Micro Entrepreneur's Age-wise: Below given Table 27.2 is compiled from the primary data collected through the distributed questionnaire. Among the classified age group, age between 41-50 accounts the highest number involved in SHG formation *vis-à-vis* involved in economic-oriented activities to maintain their families. The aged group above 60 years is representing only 4 respondents against the highest of 86 out of 198 respondents. It is also found that the age group between 21-30 accounts only 7.07 per cent of the total respondents joined in the process of formation of SHGs due to their family problems and other reasons.

Table 27.2 : Age-wise Classification of Micro Entrepreneurs

Age (Yrs)	*Frequency*	*Percentage*
21-30	14	7.07
31-40	58	29.30
41-50	96	48.48
51-60	26	13.13
Above 60	4	2.02
Total	198	100.00

Source : Primary Data.

- 48.48% of the respondents are in the age group of 41-50.
- 2.02% are in the age group of above 60.

Gender-wise Classification of Micro Entrepreneurs: Table 27.3 highlights the gender-wise classification of micro entrepreneurs selected for the study. Women play the important role in socio-economic development of Manipur. Out of the total respondents 91.92 per cent are women micro entrepreneurs and only 8.08 per cent are male micro entrepreneurs.

Table 27.3 : Gender-wise Classification of Micro Entrepreneurs

Gender	*Frequency*	*Percentage*
Male	16	8.08
Female	182	91.92
Total	198	100.00

Source : Primary Data.

- 91.92% of females have responded to the questionnaire.
- 8.08% of males responded to the questionnaire.

Micro Insurance Schemes Implemented in the District: Few common micro insurance schemes are implemented in the district like other parts of the State and the country. Among the various schemes of micro insurances implemented in the district, it is found out that health insurance accounts the highest number of respondents. It implies that large number of respondents are more concerned on their health besides their day-to-day earnings. Further it is also found out that the crop insurance scheme is adopted as another important scheme in the district and considered as second highest micro insurance scheme in the district. Most of the respondents are agricultural farmers and they prefer to insure their micro insurance to protect from failure of crop due to too much rain or too little rain in a season. More than 60 per cent of the respondents are under these two schemes.

Table 27.4 : Micro Insurance Scheme Covered

Schemes	*No. of respondents*	*Percentage*
Life Insurance	24	12.12
Health Insurance	76	38.39
Livestock insurance	17	8.58
Crop insurance	43	21.72
Asset Insurance	16	8.08
No insurance	22	11.11
Total	198	100.00

Source : Primary data.

- 38.39 % are contribution from health insurance.
- 08.08% are contributed from assets insurance.

Awareness of Micro Insurance: Table 27.5 is developed on the basis of a question asked to the respondents like: have you ever heard or avail the services of micro insurance or not? On the basis of it, it is found that 61.11 per cent or 121 out of 198 total respondents replied that they were aware of the term micro insurance and remaining 38.89 per cent says no. The above statistics is what they have responded to the questionnaire, but more important is how depth they were aware on the different issues of micro insurance which has helped directly in the process of eradication of poverty.

Table 27.5 : Percentage of Respondents Aware of Micro Insurance

Sl. No	*Awareness*	*Frequency*	*Percentage*
1.	Yes	121	61.11
2.	No	77	38.89
	Total	198	100.00

Source : Primary Data

- 61.11% of respondents are aware of micro insurance.
- Only 38.89% are unaware of micro insurance.

Reasons Behind the Less Popularity of Micro Insurance in Manipur: Table 27.6 is drawn from the multiple answer responded by 198 respondents for the present study collected from Imphal west district of Manipur. More specifically, "the products are not matching our needs" accounts the highest in rank followed by 49 respondents with "do not know the agent which sells the product". Most of the respondents gave their opinion in two or more reasons behind the less popularity of micro insurance in Manipur, as a result the total number of respondents rose to 341. The results of the Table 27.6 is more significant from the micro insurer point of view. On the basis of it various strategies can be developed by the implementing agencies.

Table 27.6 : Popularity of Micro Insurance in Manipur

Sl. No.	*What target poor told*	*Respondents*
1.	Not aware of the micro insurance product	16
2.	Cannot afford to pay the premium	23
3.	Our income flow is highly uncertain	34
4.	Do not know the agent which sells the product	49
5.	The products are not matching our needs	76
6.	Have to pay the premium every year If nothing happens, it is a loss	34
7.	Do not trust the insurance company as they have rejected a genuine claim earlier in our neighbourhood	26
8.	We have not initiated any micro enterprise of our own and hence we do not have any business assets of insurable nature	38

(contd...)

Table 27.6 (contd...)

9.	Documents needed for making a claim are difficult and it involves expenses and more time.	45
	Total	341

Source : Primary data

- 76 respondents gave their opinion as the products are not matching their needs.
- 16 respondents gave their opinion as they are not aware of the micro insurance

Willingness to Pay Premiums towards Micro Insurance: Six different closed ended premiums rate had been asked to the respondents to know their willingness to pay premiums against the insured micro insurance scheme. Very interestingly, it is found that Rs. 85 per annum premium accounts the highest number of respondents preferred followed by Rs. 90 per annum and least one is Rs. 100 with 10 respondents out of 198 respondents.

Table 27.7 : Percentage of Respondents willing to pay Premiums towards Micro Insurance

Premium per annum (Rs. per head)	*No. of Respondents*	*Percentage*
75	27	13.64
80	39	19.70
85	67	33.84
90	43	21.72
95	12	6.06
100	10	5.05
Total	198	100.00

Source : Primary Data

- 33.84% of respondents are willing to pay Rs. 85 per annum towards Micro insurance.
- 5.05% of respondents are willing to pay Rs. 100 per annum.

Table 27.8 : Economic Activities engaged by the Micro Entrepreneurs

Activities	*No. of respondents*	*Percentage*
Food processing units	37	18.69
Handloom weaving	81	40.91
Handicrafts	15	7.57
Animal rearing activities	11	5.56
Agricultural aclivilies	23	11.62
Small shop vendors	18	9.09
Others	13	6.56
Total	198	100.00

Source : Primary data

- 40.91% of respondents are engaged with handloom weaving activities.
- 6.56% of respondents are engaged in other activities (excluding above 6 activities).

Finding of the Study

Following are the main findings of the study:

- Of the available listed insurance products, all are covering only a single risk; there is lack of double or multiple risk micro insurance in the district as well as in the State.
- Private insurance such as Birla and Tata Aig, have more products as well as more area coverage than public sector insurance companies.
- Among the different micro insurance products, health and crop insurance are two most popular risks for which insurance is demanded. Other products such as life, livestock, business assets and accident risks are not actively marketed by those companies nor demanded by the clients in the district.
- The study reveals that majority (48.48%) of respondents are in the age group 41-50 years. This implies that people become conscious of micro insurance more particularly on health insurance during this age group and start realizing the importance of an insurance cover.
- The study also shows that majority (91.92%) of respondents are females. This shows that females take the significant role in the socio-economic development of their respective families.

- Out of the total respondents selected for the present study 40.91 per cent of the respondents were engaged with handloom weaving activities.

Suggestions for Further Improvement

The following suggestions will be of much help to the NGO/ insurers, who will be taking up the micro insurance in Imphal West district of Manipur in particular and State in general. However, the NGOs/insurers can adopt these practices to suit to their context.

Enrolment: Before launching a scheme of micro insurance for its members, NGO/MFI/SHPI shall take up a small survey of its SHG member's deals with micro enterprise activities to know what type of risk to be covered on a priority and level of willingness to pay. This will be a big input, while negotiating with the insurers for a customized product package.

Awareness: While enrolling for micro insurance, each micro entrepreneurs should be given a brief/pamphlet (in local language), mentioning all the important policy terms. Members should be explained about the exclusion clause (e.g., what are all the diseases not covered and so on in case of health insurance).

Premium Collection: Micro entrepreneurs' clients find it easy to pay premium in small amount in different instalments. But, for the service providers, it adds to its transaction cost. Hence, the SHG can pay the premium from its funds/or it can lend it to its members and the member entrepreneurs will pay to the group in easy instalments with or without interest as per the group's choice. Different method for payment of premium can be adopted which should be client friendly not insurer friendly.

Product Features: The present product features on micro insurance in Manipur is limited to certain areas. For example of health insurance, expenses are limited to the hospital expenses only without covering the other expenses like transport, room rent and so on.

Processes: Proposal forms and claim forms should be made available in local language. It will help in faster processing and timely submission by the clients. Further, as far as possible the process should be in simple and easy way so that each and every client must easily understand without depending on other agents. A continued dialogue with the insurers and SHG members is highly needed which will help in bringing out improvements in product features/processes based on the feedback from the clients.

Claim Administration: Claim processing by a specified person at the NGO level and at the insurance office level, both of them has undergone training/exposure visit respectively. So, both of them understands each other's constraints better and acts accordingly. Timely and actual insured amount payment will set up a confidence among the clients and between clients and insurers.

Capacity Building: Peer education–SHG members who benefited out of insurance schemes go and explain the schemes, which results in better acceptance of the insurance concept by the community. Awareness campaign is not a one shot exercise. It should be followed up by the NGO, after the initial briefing by the insurance company. Training for NGO staff, federation and SHG leaders on product features, enrolling formalities, premium collection and claims processing. Exposure visits for front line staff of insurance companies, who deal with the micro insurance to bring out a change in their mindset.

The Way Forward

As the Micro insurance sector in Manipur is in its infancy stage, all the stakeholders, viz., government agencies, regulator, insurers, banks, MFIs, SHPIs, and NGOs & SHGs have to put in their concerted efforts in building the sector into a new height. The significant and important of this sector and linkage with other sectors such as micro lending, micro credit, and micro finance and micro enterprise should be made aware to all the stakeholders. Here, government both central and State shall launch a Micro Insurance pilot project in a few selected subdivision or district level to demonstrate to the mainstream insurers that micro insurance can be profitably delivered to the poor in a sustainable manner provided needed flexibilities are in-built in the products and processes customized for the target market. Government shall dedicate a Special Fund for innovations which will assist the pioneering stakeholders, to experiment with the innovative products, flexible processes.

Even though the recent IRDA guidelines on micro insurance have recognized the SHGs working for at least 3 years, as micro insurance agents, it has not recognized the SHGs as an eligible entity to take the insurance cover in its name. IRDA has to recognize all SHGs/CBOs as an informal entity and allow the insurers to transact business with the SHGs/CBOs as done by the RBI in case of SHG Bank linkage programme. IRDA shall revise its guidelines and bring the Community managed insurance programmes, under regulation, as they are real innovators. IRDA shall prescribe a lower capital requirement as in Uganda and Sri Lanka, so that the international micro insurers will be attracted into India and they will bring their expertise to take the sector forward. IRDA shall designate selected institutions as Resource Institutions on MI and they may be given the responsibility of nurturing the small NGOs and help them in putting the systems and procedures in place for effective management of the MI programme.

The insurers should customize the products to different market segments according to their felt needs. Insurance companies should organize exclusive capacity building programmes to their management and field staff. Such training programmes should also include exposure visits to the successful micro insurance programme. Rationalizing the procedures and simplifying the operational processes will lead to cost efficiencies. Routine works can be outsourced from the NGOs/MFIs, retaining the core underwriting work alone to the insurance companies. MI is now only NGO/MFI driven. The alternate channels like bank branches of commercial banks, RRBs, co-operatives, in the rural areas, Post Offices, Agro input dealer networks, SHG marketers shall be developed to increase the outreach. For the poor to make it affordable, the premium should be as low as possible.

Conclusion

From the above analysis and results derived, it is concluded that micro insurance is in infancy stage in Manipur and it is not so widely aware by the SHG members and micro entrepreneurs. There is a huge untapped market for micro insurance in Manipur, more particularly the Imphal west district. Micro insurance should be linkage with micro credit, micro finance and micro enterprise in a compulsory way for making a lesser degree of risk on financial investment in any field. With appropriate delivery channels, types of coverage, product simplicity and easy premium collection methods and concerted efforts of all the stakeholders, this huge unreached market can be reached by insurers. Thus, if judiciously used, micro insurance will go a long way in eradicating poverty. If the various micro insurance models with client friendly schemes are implemented effectively by insurers, MFIs, NGOs, SHPIs, SHGs, health institutions, donors and co-operatives, the BPL population will lead a peaceful and secured life.

REFERENCES

Allianz AG, GTZ and UNDP Public Private Partnership (August 2006), Micro Insurance Demand and Market Prospects India

Devadasan, N., (2005), "Micro Health Insurance in India—Lessons learnt and the way forward"— Presentation at the Round Table Conference on Micro Insurance Regulations, held at Hyderabad and organized by FICCI & IRDA in Feb. 2005.

Garand, Denis, (2005), CGAP Working Group on Micro Insurance — Good and Bad Practices Case Study No. 16 "VIMO SEWA, INDIA", Oct. 2005.

Gunita Arun Chandhok, (2009) Insurance—A Tool to Eradicate and a Vehicle to Economic Development, *International Research Journal of Finance and Economics*, Issue 24.

Hennie Bester *et al.*, (2010), Micro Insurance in Brazil Towards A Strategy for Market Development.

IRDA, (2004), *Annual Report 2003-04 Insurance Regulatory Development Authority*, Hyderabad, 2004.

IRDA, (2004), Concept Paper on Need for Developing Micro Insurance in India.

Mallikarjun & Krishnamurthi, *Micro Insurance in India—The Life-saving Boy for the Small Man*, Icfai University Press, December 2007, p. 22s.

Michael J. McCord and *et al.*, (2001), *Micro Insurance: A Case Study of an Example of the Full Service Model of Micro Insurance Provision*, Self-Employed Women's Association (SEWA).

Micro Insurance Update Newsletter (2005), Oct. 2005, Issue: 2, "Strengthening the Micro Health Insurance Units for the Poor in India", Project.

Rao, G.V., (2005), "Investment Portfolio: Life", *IRDA Journal*, Nov. 2005, Vol. III, No. 12, pp. 8, IRDA, Hyderabad.

Roth, J. and G. Ramm, (2005), "Micro Insurance—Demand and Market Prospects—India", Micro Insurance Centre, Apr. 2005.

UNDP, (2007), *Micro Insurance Can Build Security for the Poor in India*.

SECTION - VI

Financial Inclusion and Rural Development

28

Financial Inclusion : Its Need in Rural Development of Manipur

O. DEEPAK KUMAR SINGH

Introduction

Manipur is one of the seven sisters of the North East India; it has a total area of 22,327 sq. km forming 0.7 per cent of the total of Union of India. The State has 352 km long international border with Myanmar on the east and 502 km long border with adjacent States of Nagaland, Assam and Mizoram. As per 2001 Census, total population of the State was 23,88,634, out of which urban population was 5,70,410 and the rural population was 18,18,224. The urbanization process is found to be very slow, the urban population has increased from 5.06 lakhs in 1991 to 5.70 lakhs in 2001. Thus, most of the population resides at the rural areas and rural development cannot be taken lightly in any strategy. In the light of rural development, the need for a well developed banking system and provision for financial inclusion cannot be underestimated.

Meaning of Financial Inclusions

Rangarajan's Committee on financial inclusion defines it as the process of ensuring access to financial services and timely and adequate credit where needed by vulnerable groups such as weaker sections and low income groups at an affordable cost (Rangarajan, 2008).

It includes savings, banking services, loans, insurance, financial counselling and credit at an affordable cost to the vast sections of disadvantaged and low income groups. The financial system has to provide its function of transferring resources from surplus to deficit units but both deficit and surplus units are those with low incomes, poor background, etc. These services were provided to help the poverty. So far, the focus has only been on delivering credit and has been very successful. An efficient society is also characterized by the availability of banking services to the entire population without any discrimination.

Finance has been a factor for growth and development, since time immemorial, even though it was not well recognized. It can be refer to as life blood to an economic system and most economies strive to make their financial systems more efficient. In the research conducted by Patrick Honohan (of Trinity College, Dublin), developed/advance economy reflects higher financial indices. Financial inclusion cannot be regarded as sole ingredient, but it is an important factor for rural development.

The Reserve Bank of India's conception of financial inclusion appear to have even more restriction, "the midterm review of October 2005 had urged all banks to make basic banking facilities accessible to vast sections of population with a view to achieving greater financial inclusion (Reddy Y.V., 2000).

Financial Inclusion in Indian Context

In November 2005, RBI asked banks to offer no-frills savings account which enables excluded people to open a savings account. Normally, the savings account requires people to maintain a minimum balance and most banks now even offer various facilities with the same. No-frills account requires no (or negligible) balance and is without any other facilities leading to lower costs both for the bank and the individual. The number of no-frills account has increased mainly in public sector banks from about 0.4 million to 6 million between March 2006 and March 2007. The number of No-frill accounts in private sector banks also increased from 0.2 million to 1 million in the same period. No significant increases were there in foreign banks. This is understandably so as majority of rural and sub-urban bank offices are in public sector banks.

Banks have been asked to consider introducing General Purpose Credit Card (GCC) facility up to Rs. 25,000 at their rural and semi urban branches. The Interest rate on the facility is completely deregulated. A simplified mechanism for one-time settlement of overdue loans up to Rs. 25,000 has been suggested for adoption. Banks have been specifically advised that borrowers with loans settled under the one time settlement scheme will be eligible to reaccess the formal financial system for fresh credit.

In January 2006, banks were permitted to use other rural organizations like Non-governmental Organizations, self-help groups, micro-finance institutions, etc., for furthering the cause of financial inclusion. Information technology can also be used to increase financial inclusion in India by introducing following facilities.

- Using of smart cards for opening bank accounts with biometric identification.
- Mobile banking services to ensure that the transactions are recorded in the bank's books on real time basis.
- The use of IT also enables banks to handle the enormous increase in the volume of transactions for millions of households for processing, credit scoring, credit record and follow-up.

RBI has been taking an important role to increase financial literacy in the country. It has set up a multilingual website in 13 languages explaining about banking, money, etc. It has started putting up comic strips to explain various difficult subjects like importance of saving, RBI's functions, etc. These comics explain myriad and complex concepts in an entertaining manner.

The Reserve Bank of India has undertaken a project titled "Project Financial Literacy". The objective of the project is to disseminate information regarding the central bank and general banking concepts to various target groups, including, school and college going children, women, rural and urban poor, defence personnel and senior citizens.

RBI will implement policies to encourage banks which provide extensive services while demotivating those which are not responsive to the banking needs of the community, including the underprivileged.

The nature, scope and cost of services will be monitored to assess whether there is any denial, implicit or explicit, of basic banking services to the common person. "The concept of financial inclusion extends far beyond the question of newly bringing all cultivators including the small and the marginal into the fold of institutional credit as the current officials discourses on the subject seem to suggest. The points are that financial inclusion needs to be contextualized" (N.A. Majumdar, 2007).

Objectives of the Study

- To stress the need for financial inclusion in Manipur.
- To find the reasons for being financially excluded.
- To trace the consequence for being financially excluded.

Methodology of the Study

The study was based on the data collected through a survey of 120 rural people, scattered around the districts of Thoubal, Bishnupur, Jiribam Sub-Division of Imphal East District and Machi Block of Chandel District, whose occupation were related to either agriculture and its allied activities or Khadi and Village Industries. Secondary data comprised of various publication and reports of the State and Central Government, Census 2001, *Economic Survey 2007*, etc. The main occupation of the State has been still dominated by agriculture and its allied activities.

Limitation of the Study

The information collected from 120 number of rural people cannot represent the entire State but correspondingly the data represent the profile of the rural people whose occupation are related either with agriculture and its allied activities or village industries or micro enterprises or handloom and handicraft. Most of the respondents have less educational qualification, other Backward Class, Scheduled Tribes and Women. Therefore, there will be reciprocal relation to the collected data with the whole State.

Table 28.1 : Profile of the Respondents

Occupation	*Women*	*Men*	*OBC*	*ST*	*SC*	*General*
Agriculture and its Allied	12	24	15	9	7	5
Village Industries	8	19	13	7	3	4
Entrepreneur	5	3	4	1	0	3
Micro enterprises	10	15	12	8	0	5
Handloom and Handicraft	16	8	10	8	2	4

Sources : Field survey

Financial Service in Manipur

The total number of scheduled commercial banking offices in Manipur was 81 as on 31st March, 2011 of which commercial banks accounts for 54 offices and Manipur rural banks had the highest number of offices in the State with a total of 27 offices, followed by SBI and UBI with 18 and 15 respectively in the State. Imphal west accounts the highest number of commercial banks with 23 and 5 RRBs followed by Imphal East with 8 commercial banks and 4 RRBs. Among the hills district Senapati district represent the highest number of commercial banks with 7 and 4 RRBs.

There are four other general reasons namely bad recovery climate, weak collateral security, Law and Order and low banking habit. The whole atmosphere has three other implications as well:

- Low profitability;
- Low eligibility; and
- Low ground level actual credit (leakages).

The recovery-performance speaks of the efficiency and maturity of the financial sector. Because delay is costlier and interests amount over time. The recovery is fairly low in Manipur. This speaks of the lack of "pre-investment appraisal" of the proposed unit of investment.

Table 28.2 : Highlights of Banking Scenario in Manipur (2006-07)

Number of Bank Branches	77
Population Per Bank	38127
Credit Deposit Ratio (%)	53.40
Per Capita Credit	Rs. 2556
Per Capita Deposit	Rs. 4781

Source : Statistical Abstract Manipur 2007.

Table 28.2 presents the banking scenario in Manipur and one can see the emphasis on having banks in the rural sector. RBI has made efforts to make commercial banks open branches in rural areas. Priority sector lending was instituted to provide loans to small and medium enterprises and agricultural sector. Further special banks were set up for rural areas like Rural Cooperative Banks, Regional Rural Banks.

Financial Exclusion

The demand for financial services cannot be available in all the sections of population in the State. Financial services are excluded mainly to poor and rural regions. Due to lack of transport and communication facility many rural areas in the State are excluded from financial services. In most of the developing countries, financial services such as saving account, credit from formal financial institution is restricted to a large part of the population (Manoranjan Sharma, 2008).

The excluded population then has to rely on informal sector (moneylenders, etc) for availing finance that is usually at exorbitant rates. These lead to a vicious cycle. First, high cost of finance implies that first poor person has to earn much more than someone who has access to lower cost of finance. Second, the major portion of the earnings is paid to the moneylender and the person can never come out of the poverty. "The absence of adequate infrastructure hampered the people, particularly in the rural areas, from benefiting fully from the development efforts initiated since the initiation of economic planning in the country" (Kulwant Rai Gupta).

There is always a colliding situation between poverty and permanent financial exclusion. Both poverty and financial exclusion result in a reduction of choices which affects social interaction and leads to reduced participation in society. There are certain phenomena indirectly related to financial exclusion, namely financial discrimination, financial illiteracy, financial exploitation etc.

1. Poor people do not utilize the financial services as they find financial services very costly and thus are unaffordable to them. Hence, even if financial services are available, the high costs deter the poor from accessing them.

2. Access to formal financial services also requires documents of proof regarding a person's identity, income, etc. The poor people do not have these documents and thus are excluded from these services. They may also subscribe to the services initially but may not use them as actively as others because of high distance between the bank and residence.
3. The reasons are sometimes people may find difficulty in understanding language, various documents, requirements and conditions that come with financial services. It also depends on the level of literacy of the people.

The above reasons show that, it is not enough to assume that financial inclusion will happen on its own.

Table 28.3 : Showing Trends of Financial Exclusion in Manipur

Reasons of Financial Exclusion	*No. of Response*	*Percentage of Response*	*Remarks*
Financial Illiteracy	23	19.17	Need for Awareness
Complex Formality	31	25.83	Need of Documents/Guarantor
Inability to Give Security Deposit	42	35.00	Due to Poverty
Non Existence of Financial Institution	8	6.67	Less coverage at remote areas
Corruption	12	10.00	Dishonest Officer
Any Other	4	3.33	Ignorance/time saving
Total	120	100.00	

Source : Field Survey.

Agriculture has been a dominating occupation in the State, the respondent have access to financial sources through either bank or local financial institution or some informal sources, i.e., relatives or moneylenders but, majority of the farmers / Agriculturist have no other means of sources or they use their own source. The new strategy for agricultural growth and diversification of agriculture from traditional crop cultivation to horticulture, etc.; would require more investment in cold storage, rural road, communication, marketing network and facilities, warehouse, etc. Simultaneously, efforts should be made to revitalize agriculture through introduction of biotechnology and other innovations. This would require substantial increase in investment in research and development for agriculture (GoI 2003).

Table 28.4 : Showing Sources of Finance to Various Groups

Occupation	*Bank/ Financial Institution*	*Local Financial Institution*	*Informal Sources/ Money lender*	*Own Sources/ No other Sources*	*Total*	*Remarks*
Agriculture/Farmer	7	4	11	14	36	
Village Industries	14	0	3	10	27	
Entrepreneurs	5	2	0	1	8	
Micro Enterprises	2	8	7	8	25	
Handloom and Handicraft	9	2	2	11	24	
Total	37	16	23	44	120	

Sources: Field Survey.

Village industries includes shoe making, bee rearing, carpentry who are either assisted by KVIC or some other sources. Most of the identified village industries got assistance from KVIC, but only a few rely on either local sources or own sources.

Out of 8 entrepreneurs identified, 5 have opened bank account and rely on it. They have better knowledge of financing business. 2 of the respondents prefer local financial institutions which have become more common in the State in the form of micro credit institution, private bank or financial institution.

Many of the micro enterprises established in the rural areas of the State in the form of groceries, garments house, restaurants and food corner do not access to bank financing as it proves to be time consuming as compared to the extent of benefit derived from it.

The occupation of handloom and handicraft were mainly done by womenfolk in the State. Women have been taking an important role in the society by adopting handloom and handicraft as their profession. Most of them rely through own sources or self finance while many of the weaver were also involved in the SHGs.

Another way to analyze the financial inclusion is to see the region-wise distribution of the bank offices, credit and deposit ratios. Lower financial deepening in rural areas. In urban areas the population per bank office has declined in all the regions except Western region.

Table 28.5 : District-wise Banking Performance in Manipur as on 31-3-2004

Particular	*Sena-pati*	*Tmng-long*	*Ccpur*	*Cha-ndel*	*Ukh-rul*	*Imphal East*	*Imphal West*	*Bishn upur*	*Thou bal*
No. of Bank Branch	12	4	5	5	4	11	32	8	10
Agri & Allied Activities									
No. of A/c	1219	57	305	605	70	1335	3745	1124	1516
Amount of Advance (Rs. In lakhs)	413	4	97	106	86	259	1549	450	419
Small Scale Industries									
No. of A/c	104	47	127	137	64	890	2333	1226	518
Amount of Advance (Rs. In lakhs)	40	12	83	87	9	586	1648	441	91
Services and Others									
No. of A/c	1766	516	1167	939	206	3219	13582	3335	3203
Amount of Advance (Rs. In lakhs)	806	194	789	248	106	1459	11822	1210	1001
Total No. of A/c	3089	620	1599	1681	340	5444	19660	5685	5237
Total Advance (Rs. In lakhs)	1259	210	969	441	201	2304	15019	2101	1511

Statistical Abstract 2007 (Manipur)

In all India statistics, despite of the rural policy-push, majority of the population continues to be financially excluded. The efforts were further intensified by RBI and its Annual Policy (2005-06) mentioned:

Access to insurance by different sections of rural people also comprised to financial inclusion, but still many people were excluded from finance. Many of the villagers have found to be less aware about the knowledge of general insurance which is shown in Table 28.6. 40 respondents out of 120 populations are covered to life insurance. 70 of them have neither General Insurance nor to Life Insurance.

Table 28.6 : Showing Access of Insurance to Various Levels

Occupation	*Life Insurance*	*General Insurance*	*No. Insurance*
Agriculture/Farmer	11	4	29
Village Industries	8	0	23
Entrepreneurs	7	0	1
Micro Enterprises	14	0	23
Total	40	4	76

Sources : Field Survey.

Prospects of Financial Inclusion

Demand constraints imply that people do not come forward because of number of factors. One of the causes as well as consequences of poverty and backwardness is inadequate access to different sources of credit. In the 2008-09 budget statement, the Finance Minister proposed two more measures: one to add at least 250 rural household accounts every year at each of their rural and semi-urban branches of commercial banks (including regional rural banks) and two, to allow individuals such as retired bank officers, ex-servicemen, etc., to be appointed as business facilitator or business correspondent or credit counsellor.

People seldom know what lies in their best interests and often end up making non-optimal decisions. The various experiments used to understand this behaviour point that people do not select the best choice given the options. Hence, it is better to include a default amidst various options, with default being the choice that leads to a better choice. The default means if the consumer is unable to choose, the default option will be applicable.

This mechanism has been used to increase savings in many organizations. Earlier, employees had to opt in for the pension plan and most preferred not to opt for the pension plan. The choice was rephrased with help from Behavioural research. Unlike previously, employees had to select whether they wanted to opt for the pension plan, this time the employees were enrolled automatically in pension plans. So, if they did not want to take the plan, they had to opt out of the plan. The default option had changed and the onus was now on the employee to opt out of the saving plans and most knowing the benefits, preferred to stay with the scheme. This led to increase in the pension savings in many organizations. A similar mechanism could be deployed to increase usage of bank accounts in India. It is suggested that instead of giving cash transfers to the public, government should instead credit the bank accounts of the poor electronically.

This will make people use their bank accounts. Now, this may work in developed economies but is going to be difficult to implement in developing economies like India. Nevertheless, it could be pilot-tested in a few urban regions.

It has seen that people are reluctant to go to banks as they are not clear of the directions, processes, etc. Business Economics experts suggest that measures like giving people a map showing the direction of the bank, asking for a time for appointment with the banker, etc., would lead more people to come to the bank. Another important finding is that poor people avoid banks because of complicated forms, procedures, etc.

Instead of opening a saving account separate account could be opened called education account, vehicle account, etc., to enable a person to know the purpose of the saving. Due to compulsorily transfer of salary to the employee of government department many of the people have more access to financial institution. In certain flagship programme of the Central Government of India like National Rural Health Mission (NRHM) and NREGA, the trends of financial inclusion has tended to increase as according to guidelines.

These suggestions have come from research in developed economies. The emerging markets need to set up their own behavioural economies research centres. These centres will need to conduct surveys, conduct experiments, etc., to understand the behavioural nuances keeping people away from subscribing to various financial services.

Women are better savers than men and financial inclusion is more likely to succeed when they are given more aware. Manipur has a diverse demographic profile which needs to be made a part of the financial inclusion policies. This makes it even more important for policy-makers to have their own behavioural research centres in emerging markets. The situation is very different from that in developed economies (where financial exclusion is a minority) and may require some adjustments to make the solution more workable. The Financial Inclusion report also shows how a few developing economies like Bangladesh, South Africa, and Bolivia, etc., have achieved financial inclusion. The policymakers in these economies would have also faced similar kinds of problems. The research literature covers the various initiatives that have been successful in these regions. The research should also document how the social issues (if any) were addressed in these economies.

The focuses of policies have been so far on two things—one, to help people open more bank accounts and two, providing credit. The first makes people belong to the formal financial system and also gives them an identity. The second helps them get some financial capital and enables them to carry on some business activities to manage their livelihoods. However, this is too narrow a view. The poor people also need to invest their savings into financial products that get them higher returns than returns on savings account and fixed deposits. They also need other financial facilities like insurance, pension plans, etc., to manage risks and old-age.

One of the criticisms against the microcredit movement has been the focus on credit. Most MFIs do not offer savings services beyond the compulsory savings linked to credit. However, the fact that the poor are capable of weekly repayments shows that the poor are capable of savings, even if it is only in small amounts. One of the reasons why the poor might not save in financial form might be the lack of appropriate products.

It is also important to look into insurance and remittance needs of the poor. The Mutual Funds have also been offering schemes that allow people to invest with just Rs 50. The schemes are called micro-SIP (Systematic Investment Plan) where a person would be required to invest regularly and minimum withdrawals are allowed. This will lead people to save regularly and withdraw judiciously.

Though this point has been noted above, it needs separate mention. Financial inclusion alone will not be enough. The reforms in financial sector have taken centre stage in Indian polity with substantial media coverage to the same. It is true that access to finance is important but so is the access to real assets. The efforts have to be made to enable people to create real assets (plant, machinery, etc.) with the access to various financial services.

It is widely felt Indian economy has changed but policies pertaining to financial sector are still very restrictive (some even term it as draconian). However, it is just one side of the argument. The reforms in financial sector have been much more progressive than the reforms in real sector.

This implies it is much easier to get credit in India than other business processes like starting a business, licenses, etc. In fact, latest report indicates that one area where India has been a major reformer is "Getting credit". Therefore, it is not fair to assume India will grow on the basis of reforms in the financial sector alone. The reforms in the real and financial sector need to go hand in hand.

Conclusion

The above research points to the importance of financial inclusion in the State. There is another very important point to the entire exercise—the spirit of financial inclusion. A few commentators have also pointed to the similarity between sub-prime crisis and financial inclusion. The sub-prime market was originated to provide finance to people with weak credit histories (financial inclusion).

The population is largely financially excluded and it needs to be more careful. Therefore, it is necessary to cover all the villages by Bank after making an accurate household survey. The need of the time is to properly assess the products of various financial inclusions. Never yet experience facility of the financial products in the State includes No Frill Saving Bank Account, Small over Draft Facility for General Consumption, General Credit Card for Income based activity, micro insurance life and disability cover health insurance cover, mutual fund, etc. But these financial products available in the rural people of the State are limited only to the private sector and cannot be easily afforded by rural poor.

Financial Inclusion has far reaching consequences, which can help many people come out of adverse poverty conditions. The financial markets must act responsibly and ensure that the spirit of financial inclusion is not breached in the future.

announcements (Manishankar Aiyer and Jay Ram Ramesh) on the proposed South Asian Union and the trade corridor *via* North East.

- Manage the HR
- Recruit
- Retrain
- Retain (get the stone age mentality out).

Few lessons from -Toffler, Drucker (management leaders) Phelps (Nobel Laureate of 2006) and Stiglitz (Nobel Laureate of 2001).

Therefore the question here arises is that with creating more wages and entrepreneurship, it generate more employment (Phelps, 2006). We need to take lessons from the above stalwarts in recruiting, retraining and retaining the workforce to compete globally. Since an ever migrating workforce (like a herd or a hunter/gatherer) will only stagnate the knowledge bank rather than bringing increments. Unlike a farmer who cultivates and nurtures the seed to the fruit as observed by evolutionary biologist. The fascinating inter-disciplinary world of business and biology !

Conclusion

More Financial literacy outreach to be conducted by financial institutions both public as well as private. And more banking correspondents to be deployed in rural areas. To develop awareness in schemes of government, subsidies and loans, microcredit and finance. One of the authors has been involved with the rural planning and credit department of Reserve Bank of India (RBI-NE) in these exercises. RBI opening 6 new sub-offices in the 6 States of North East India, except Assam which has its regional office in Guwahati since 1949. Agartala in Tripura has inaugurated its office on 18th May, 2011.This is to encourage the other public and private banks to be operational so as to include the 70 per cent population who are financially excluded in North East India.

REFERENCES

Das, G., (2002), *India Unbound*. New Delhi. Random House Publication.

Drucker, P.F. (2001), *The Essential Drucker*. Great Britain. Butterworth-Heinemann Publications.

Edmund S. Phelps, *Modern Macroeconomics* (November 2001) by Philippe Aghion, Roman Freedman, Joseph Stieglitz, and Michael Woodford–web article.

Friedman, T., (2000), *The Lexus and the Olive Free*. New York. Anchor Books—Random House.

Sachs, J., (2005), *The End of Poverty*. England. Penguin Publications.

Stiglitz, J., (2004), *The Roaring Nineties*. London. Penguin Publications.

Toffler, A., and Toffler, H., (2006), *Revolutionary Wealth*. New York, Random House Inc.

Wikepedia., (2007), searchcio.techtarget.com/sDefinition/0,,sid19_gci826478,00.html - 55k.

Younkins, E., (2007)., http://www.wju.edu/academics/bus/iscm/Younkins.asp

Minister, Department of MSME, Textiles and Tourism, Government of West Bengal felt that agility and dynamism should be infused to ensure steady growth of the sector. Moreover, he also suggested that there should be a perfect balance between the *Traditional Sector* and the *Sunrise Sector*.[2]

The study of Lyngdoh and Pati (2010) revealed that *there is a significant relationship between financial inclusion through Micro Financing and economic transformation, social outcomes, political participation and decision making*.[3]

Sikkim is the highest, steepest, remotest and wettest State in the country with formidable mountain specific constraints of remoteness, fragility and marginality being acutely visible. Tough terrain, heavy monsoon and frequent landslides make any development work during the five monsoon months a daunting task.

For the proud indigenous people of this State, unskilled labour work would not appear very attractive and for some would have demeaning connotations as well. To make the scheme popular and mass-based, the Chief Minister – Shri Pawan Chamling—gave the maxim "***Afno gaon, Afai banaun***" (let us build our village ourselves). This State Policy of positioning SRDA as a nation building activity resulted in a dignity of labour and ensured large scale participation of the rural folks.

Sikkim Rural Development Agency (S.R.D.A.) is an organization registered under the Registration of Societies Act vide Registration No. 16, Memo No. 12(4) 1975-76/3108 dated 12/11/1975. The main objective of establishment of this organization is to involve the rural poor (BPL) in the developmental process, which is based on the philosophy that all the people should equally share the benefit of development. This organization is making all out effort to identify the local needs and resources. The Head Office of SRDA is located at Gangtok. This organisation implements a number of poverty alleviation schemes under ***Swarnajayanti Gram Swarojgar Yojana*** (SGSY)

The SGSY is a holistic programme covering all aspects of self employment such as organization of the poor into self–help groups, training, credit, technology, infrastructure, marketing, etc. The SGSY gives emphasis on group financing for poverty alleviation by organizing the rural poor living under BPL category into self help groups (SHGs). Accordingly the bulk of assistance under SGSY is expected to be provided to SHGs for supporting the group level micro enterprises and individual enterprises established by their members. The SGSY seeks to promote self employment opportunities to rural people through promotion of micro enterprises in clusters which would facilitate proper implementation and monitoring of the activities effectively. The objective of SGSY is to bring the ***swarozgaris*** above the poverty line by providing them with income generating assets through mix of Bank credit and Government subsidy by ensuring appreciable sustained level of income over a period of time.

The families Below the Poverty Line (BPL) in rural areas constitute the target group of the SGSY. Out of the total *swarozgaris* assisted 50 per cent should be SCs/STs, 40 per cent women and 3 per cent disabled persons, and minorities 15 per cent of the total target. The rural poor are encouraged to be organize into self help groups. Each group consists of 5-20 members. Only one member from a family is eligible for membership of a group.

Subsidy is only an enabling element of the SGSY scheme. Subsidy is backing ended, i.e., to be kept by Bank in Subsidy Reserve Fund Account. The quantum of subsidy for individuals is 30 per cent of project cost or Rs 7,500 whichever is less. The subsidy for SCs/STs and disabled persons is 50 per cent of project cost or Rs. 10,000 whichever is less.

Skill Development Trainings undertaken by SRDA, Sikkim: The SRDA Sikkim provides training in the following traditional and non-traditional trades to prospective youth of the State since its establishment. Many educated youths of the State have started their own enterprises after getting skill development training organized by Sikkim Rural Development Agency.

- Thanka Making
- Thunga Making Training
- Candel Making Training
- Cane and Bamboo works
- Motor Driving Training
- Carpet Weaving Training
- Pickle Making Training

Younkins wrote how society tends to have negative attitudes towards entrepreneurs, and this is reflected in cinema, art, and scholarly works. This view goes a long way since Plato, down to Kant, and till today. But this is not the reality, let me share with you that not all entrepreneurs are exploiters. Dr. Edward Younkins wrote:

> "Business in a free society rewards businessmen who are honest, trustworthy, understanding, self-reliant, rational and hard working. While practices such as lying, deception, fraud, and theft might lead to short-term gains, such practices would certainly lead to ruin in the long run. A businessman only... benefits by offering goods and services that others are willing to buy. If he does not cater to the desires of others, he will not prosper. He enables others to attain what they want and to pursue their visions of happiness. The businessman is an appropriate symbol of a free society. Capitalism inspires business behaviour that is prudent, diligent, prescient, innovative, imaginative, and virtuous. The successful businessman must be a risk-taking man of ideas and moral action".

- Private public partnership.
- Government as a regulator.
- Interdependent economy.
- Foreign Direct Investment.
- Venture capital.
- Intellectual Property Right (Patent).
- Infrastructure.

We like the word moral action here. It gives an idea that an entrepreneur that wishes to be successful in the long term must be ethical. But to avoid another Enron, World Com or Tyco kind of a scandal (corporate scams) we need to keep the above key points in practice.

Globalization is a term that was invented in order to emphasize that the globalization of a product is more likely to succeed when the product or service is adapted specifically to each locality or culture it is marketed in. The term combines the word globalization with localization. (An earlier term for globalization in terms of product preparedness for international marketing is internationalization.)

The term first appeared in the late 1980s in articles by Japanese economists in the Harvard Business Review. According to the sociologist Roland Robertson, who is credited with popularizing the term, globalization describes the tempering effects of local conditions on global pressures. At a 1997 conference on "Globalization and Indigenous Culture," Robertson said that globalization "means the simultaneity—the co-presence—of both universalizing and particularizing tendencies."

The increasing presence of McDonald's restaurants worldwide is an example of globalization, while the restaurant chain's menu changes in an attempt to appeal to local palates are an example of globalization. Perhaps even more illustrative of globalization: For promotions in France, the restaurant chain recently chose to replace its familiar Ronald McDonald mascot with Asteroid the Gaul, a popular French cartoon character. (Wikepedia, 2007). Friedman (2000) in his book the *Lexus and the Olive Tree* mentions that it is very important for us to maintain a balance between the cultural practices and the new age globalization.

- Change attitude.
- Mind set.
- Work Culture.
- Financial literacy.

"Stop doing favours like the white masters did" no one is the white man's burden—as Rudyard Kipling quoted a hundred odd years ago.

We remember Gurcharan Das in his book "*India Unbound*" said that India's future does not depend on politicians who only preach reforms on their lips, but rather, depends on the millions of ordinary Indians who dare to take up the entrepreneurship challenge creating wealth not only for themselves, but also for their country, and in turn creating jobs; more efficiently than any government employment guarantee schemes could provide or promise.

Gurcharan Das now heads a venture capitalist fund that becomes angel investor to various start ups. He said interestingly, venture capitalist initiatives can become a better form of philanthrophy than any other charitable initiatives. If one opens a welfare centre, one can only say in Confucius words "give a man a

To conclude, the Sikkim Rural Development Agency (SRDA) plays a crucial role in achieving the dream of inclusive growth in Sikkim. It has been felt that SRDA has a considerable positive impact on the socio-economic conditions of the rural poor. Virtually, it has increased the self-confidence and is obsessive with narcissism of development of the lower strata of the population of Sikkim.

NOTES

Lyngdoh, B.F, and Pati, A.P., (2010), Financial Inclusion, Women and Inclusive Growth, *the Indian Journal of Commerce*, Vol. 63, No. 2, April-June 2010.

Silponnati for Micro and Small Scale Enterprises, April 2010, Vol. 33 Issue 04, Federation of Associations of Cottage & Small Industries (FACSI) Kolkata, page 19.

The Sikkim Budget 2009-10.

SECTION - VII

Financial Inclusion and Entrepreneurship Development

issues, he agreed with him that intellectual contemplation was man's highest activity.

Much later, the eighteenth century German philosopher, Immanuel Kant, taught that if a person acts in order to gain benefits, the act has no moral value. It follows that since the goal of business is to make profits, then business cannot be said to have moral worth. In essence, Kant removed prudence from the province of morality, thus debarring business from any chance for respect.

The avowal of self-interest renders the businessman and the business system suspects. Once business has been deprived of its moral standing, it was not long before people began questioning and renouncing as evil its inherent profit motive and means of seeking wealth through capitalizing on people's earthly desires. It is impossible to separate business from its goals.

Universal Bias

The views of the above philosophers were only the beginning. There has been an almost universal bias against business and the businessmen on the part of intellectuals, historians, writers of fiction and non-fiction, film-makers, socialists, the popular culture, the Church, cartoonists, etc. To this day television, radio, newspapers, magazines, books, and plays tend to portray the businessmen as evil, greedy, crooked, and immoral. Even business ethics texts usually say that self-interested behaviour leads to immoral actions and caution businessmen to restrain their self-interested behaviour. It is no wonder that business activities are regarded with cynicism by the public at large when what they are exposed to are largely unfavourable, untrue, and incomplete images of business. The public image of business includes many villains but only a handful of heroes.

In truth, businessmen are as good or as bad as the average man. Businessmen do not always behave morally. Some lie, cheat, and act irresponsibly or with impunity, but in the long run such behaviour is certainly unwise. Capitalism rewards business behaviour that is honest, civil, fair, compassionate, diligent, prudent and heroic. In a free society, people in business are neither better nor worse than those in other professions. There are good and bad in all walks of life and certainly no justification to believe that all business people are evil. Moral principles which are valid for all people are equally valid for those in business.

Hostile public opinion may result from the absence of adequate and true information and the presence of misinformation regarding business. Most businessmen earn their rewards by personal ability and free trade in a free market. Business is essentially decent, but corruptible. Business provides earthly well-being. Business supplies a rational and humane system of rewards in exchange for individuals' productive efforts. Wealth is the result of a creative process. The purpose of business is not to help mankind by producing and selling goods and services. Businesses do benefit others but this is only a secondary consequence of their actions. Although businesses thrive from satisfying customers, their primary purpose is to generate profits for their owners who want to be happy and live well. In a free economy, people can advance their own lives by pleasing customers who through their voluntary actions determine the distribution of rewards.

The Right to Private Property

The moral justification for business profits is the right to private property. Men must be permitted to act to ensure their own survival and pursue their own flourishing. Living well involves all that makes us human. To survive and thrive on earth requires a concern for one's material well-being. Material prosperity enables a man to cultivate his mind and spirit, to seek wisdom, and to develop his character. Business is a natural moral consequence of this concern and an essential activity of what is required to live a full life. When people are criticized for acting selfishly, they are oftentimes being derided for exercising their right to pursue their own happiness.

So-called intellectuals, those who deal with ideas expressed in words, disproportionately oppose capitalism and business. These social critics report, interpret, analyze, and comment on public affairs. They include scholars, professors, journalists, literary critics, novelists, playwrights, film-makers, television newsmen, political staffers and speechwriters, and others who see part of their function as observing, finding faults, and proposing societal changes. Unlike the man in the street that tends to be ambivalent toward business, most intellectuals take great joy in maligning business and

The goal of many business critics appears to bring down the more able to the level of the less able and to make the producers feel unearned guilt for their accomplishments. This envy can be viewed as an egalitarian outcry against the reality of individual differences in abilities, attainments, and rewards. These critics appear to be opposed to the departure of business and the free market from their unattainable ideals of egalitarianism and collectivism. They also do not like the fact that capitalism permits moral pluralism. Many social critics would prefer a universal ethical code imposed by fiat or at least by consensus.

Most professionals are mainly viewed in terms of services provided and only secondarily in terms of their profits. Businessmen, on the other hand, are primarily perceived in terms of its profits. Many people do not seem to understand that to be a businessman is to serve others. Businesses must satisfy their customers if they are to survive. Service is a prerequisite of profit. Businessmen create goods and services for themselves and others. Every product and service that sustains and improves human lives is made possible by the world's creators. Businessmen should take pride in their achievements and their virtues of rational thought and productive work that make them possible. Business is a noble calling. There is no justified reason for an honest businessman to be ashamed of his profession or to feel guilty about his earnings.

Too many misconceptions and misstatements have been disseminated about business. Business has rarely been treated fairly or accurately. We need to proclaim the truth about business. Many Americans and Canadians are uninformed about the workings of business, the free market system, and the nature of government powers. They have not been taught the concepts underpinning free enterprise. Many do not realize that our economy has moved away from capitalism and, thus, they frequently blame capitalism and businessmen for faults of the mixed economy. Each of us needs to do our part in words and deeds to improve the image of business and the businessman. Our goal should be to match the image of free enterprise with its reality.

If India wishes to be Competitive, it needs to produce more and more Entrepreneurs.

But what are the necessary attitudes in society to produce entrepreneurs? We believe it all lies in the attitudes towards finances. India is land of paradox when it comes to money; we remember reading Nehru's speech condemning the culture of commerce and money. We also recall in the caste system, the commercial traders are not held in high esteem. But at the same time India has a goddess for wealth, *Laxmi* isn't it? It seems when it comes to money, there is a hate-love relationship in the Indian psyche as a collective nation.

We wonder how the Chinese (our prospering neighbours view money?) does we don't know for sure, but we think their civilization has a long history and developed competency in managing finances and perhaps positive attitudes towards money due to that. We recall it is their civilization that came out with "paper money".

A tentative problem statement, we wish to propose is as follows. Is there a "robust entrepreneurship spirit" in a particular society *versus* their money attitudes?

- Our advantages in a disturbed Zone (North East India).
- Women (participation and dialogues) power.
- Cultural practices.
- Art and music.

We think cultivating an entrepreneurship spirit is a very important in a country. It is a mean to empower the poor societies. Entrepreneurs are the main agents to create a robust economic activity between nations, societies. When nations, societies, individuals actively trade with each other, there will be less thought of "pointing a gun" towards each other. We realize we are interdependent. War is pointless. If I kill you, I in turn kill my own self. You and I are one. We need each other like the activities in NE India.

But it is true that the only reason we have not become Afghanistan, Somalia, Bosnia-Serbia is because of our egalitarian attitude towards women, the nourishment of art and culture and the festivities of the various ethnic groups of NE India.

Recently we came across the works of Andrew Bernstein, Dr. Edward Younkins and Michael Novak that documents how entrepreneurship brings peace, create wealth and help in the moral development of the ethical entrepreneur.

- Wood Carving Training
- Beautician Training
- Doll/Toy Making Training
- Computer and Tailoring
- Mushroom Training
- Embroidery Making
- Milk Product Item
- Blanket Weaving
- Handloom Weaving
- Soap Making
- Sanitary Fitting
- Khada Making
- Mobile Repairing
- Sinki, Gundruk, Kinema
- Jute Product Training
- Broom making
- Medicinal Herbal
- Bakery
- Vegetable Plantation
- Traditional Hanky and Mat Making
- Bag, File Board and Cover Training
- Ginger Candy
- Bee Keeping
- Knitting
- Carpentry Training
- Bamboo Basket Making
- Fruit Juice
- Banner Making
- Decorative Dry Flowers
- Donut and Nimki Making
- Phenyl Making
- Dhup Making
- Papad Making
- Dry Meat Making
- Block and Screen Making
- Security Service Training
- Cushion Cover
- Peloong Making

- Daka, Topi, Choli Making
- Gugdri, Pira Making
- Beodhan (carpet) Making
- Sanitary Napkins

Besides providing the above list of activities, SRDA have undertaken 24 different areas of activities under SGSY as on 31st March, 2010. The amount of unit cost sanctioned under SGSY is given below:

Table 29.1 : Activities Taken Up under SGSY (2010)

Sl.No.	*Activity*	*Unit Cost in Rs.*
1.	Large Cardamom	25,805
2.	Cardamom (rain fed)	20,080
3.	Gladiolus	27,100
4.	Amliso Plantation	20,700
5.	Ginger	22,000
6.	Dairy	30,000
7.	Piggery	37,200
8.	Goatery	14,500
9.	Pony	18,000
10.	Bullock	19,000
11.	Yak	14,800
12.	Poultry	76,500
13.	Mixed Vegetables	15,400
14.	Fisheries	25,000
15.	Carpet Weaving	18,500
16.	Handloom Weaving	13,750
17.	Cutting and Tailoring	14,700
18.	Knitting	17,200
19.	Carpentry	13,000
20.	Wood Carving	13,000
21.	Blacksmith	11,400
22.	Bamboo Works	11,400
23.	Broom Making	11,500
24.	Toy Making	12,500

Source : Sikkim Rural Development Agency, Government of Sikkim, Tashling Secretariat, Gangtok.

fish." Thus the recipient of charity keeps on becoming dependent.

But if one becomes a venture capitalist, he invests his money to fund start ups by budding entrepreneurs who have what it takes to succeed except money. The money invested in such start ups is used to till the start up could stand on its own to feet. Then the VC sells his stake and profits and use the money to fund another start up. This is a better model because it creates businesses, nurtures the entrepreneurs in a society and in turn creates jobs.

Spectra mind is one of the start ups funded by Chrysalis, the venture capitalist fund headed by Gurcharan Das. Today Spectra mind creates jobs and wealth for Pune, regardless of how we think about BPO jobs; at least it is better than seeing our young people unemployed.

Chrysalis has sold their stake on Spectra mind, and now has started to fund another business idea by other budding entrepreneurs. This is what Gurcharan Das calls a higher form of Philanthrophy. It is the true way *"to teach a man to catch fish, so that he can eat forever, without depending on others."* If this is not empowerment then what is?

Gurcharan Das said that the scarcest resource in a country are not gold or minerals, but entrepreneurs. We think to measure the true wealth of a nation, one need to count how many entrepreneurs it has. The study above could be our contribution to crack the codes of what makes an entrepreneur successful. We think one of them is the attitudes towards money.

We think in many ways, negative money attitudes of certain communities in India, has resulted in the scarcity of entrepreneurs coming out from that society. This is true for my tribe (Jesson's tribe) in Sabah, Malaysia. I see (Jesson) the same thing among the North Easterners. Is this the reason for our poor economic development?

Surprisingly, the words a Marwari, Gujarati, and other business communities are often using as a "swear word" and have a stigma attached to negative emotions. But these are people who are on the front lines of Indian Business. We think it is due to the money attitudes that their community has passed down to them that made them excellent entrepreneurs.

Other aspect to money attitudes is a recent study by Brendan Burchell of Cambridge University, trying to explain the behaviour of financial aversion. He thinks that it has three possible explanations. The first explanation could be in the realm of neuroscience. Where financial aversion or a strong avoidance towards financial management is due to a phenomenon called Dyscalculia. This is a condition similar to Dyslexia, but more in the context of dealing with numbers. It is an inability to deal with numerical and mathematical concepts.

The second explanation is derived from economic psychology. These areas are emerging fields ripe for research inquiry; and thirdly, innovate and manage knowledge.

A poster boy for ethical entrepreneurship in India is Narayana Murthy and Azim Premji. Imagine, if 100 Narayana Murthys and Azim Premji's created in India. How much change could that bring to a billion Indians?

But the future came too fast for us to handle this transition landing us in a future shock (Alvin Toffler, Future Shock,1969) and there onto the new age "Revolutionary wealth" (Toffler and Toffler, 2006). We became a consumer society or rather a prosumer society (one who produces as well consumes) and amputee few of our cultural contexts in the race. Therefore, we need to relearn, redesign the curriculum and sensitize the Indian knowledgeable workers to these change agents and encourage horizontal growth of skills. As knowledge is non rival, intangible, non-linear, relational, mates with other knowledge, portable, can be compressed into symbols, smaller and smaller, explicit and implicit and hard to bottle, e.g.,Yahoo (David Filo/Jerry Young) and Federal express (Fred Smith), e.g., of social enterprises, free play, Rugmark and Rubicon.

Strength in North East India

- Biodiversity.
- Service industry.
- Tourism.
- Craft.
- Trade route.

For example, South Asian union, Trans-Asian Railway from Burma to Bulgaria–28 nations 80,900 km (NE-315 missing link).

Entrepreneurs and leaders in NE must take advantage of the recent proposal by the Central Government (Union Minister's recent

REFERENCES

Basic Statistics of North Eastern Region, (2006), Evaluation and Monitoring Sector North Eastern Council, Secretariat, Government of India, Nongrim Hill.

Datta Ray, Gurudas Das, (2004.), *Dimensions of Rural Development in North-East India*, Akansha Publishing House, New Delhi.

Government of India, (2008), *Report of the Committee on Capital Formation in Agriculture*, New Delhi, March, p. 21.

Kulwant Rai Gupta, (2005), *Rural Development in India*, Atlantic Publishers and Distributors, New Delhi, p. 14.

Manoranjan Sharma, (2008), *Dynamics of Indian Banking: Views and Vistas*, Atlantic Publishers and Distributors, New Delhi, p. 389.

N.A. Majumdar, (2007), *Inclusive Growth "Development Perspective in Indian Economy"*, Academy Foundation, New Delhi.

Rangarajan, (2008), *Report on the Committee on Financial Inclusion*, January 2008.

Reddy Y.V., (2006), *Annual Policy Statement for the Year 2006-07*, Reserve Bank of India, April 18, p. 56.

Statistical Abstract of Manipur, (2007), Government of Manipur.

29

SRDA and Inclusive Growth in Sikkim

S.S. MAHAPATRA

Introduction

India is a country of rural base economy. More than 70 per cent of the total populations are living in rural area. Rural development is must for overall development of the country. Speaking on the auspicious Republic Day function at Gangtok, the Governor of Sikkim underscored the imperative need of *inclusive growth* for ushering in all-round development of the State in particular and country in general. He elaborated the vision of the Government and various measures contemplated by it in the Eleventh Plan for inclusive growth of the State.

Further, presenting the State Budget for 2009-10 in Sikkim Legislative Assembly, Dr. Pawan Chamling, who is also Minister-in-Charge, Finance, Revenue & Expenditure, said in his budget speech: "The State Government will endeavour to achieve all the socio-economic targets through inclusive development. Services of all sectors within and outside the government shall be roped in for comprehensive development of the State.[1] the Budget 2009-10 aimed at inclusive growth driven by rural renaissance.

Speaking in a Seminar on Inclusive Growth Role of MSMEs in Indian Economy organized on 24th March, 2010 in Kolkata which was organized by Federation of Associations of Cottage & Small Industries (FACSI) in association with Ministry of MSME, Government of India, Mr. Manabendra Mukherjee, the then Hon'ble

Index

verbalizing anti-capitalist viewpoints. They look down on businessmen and wonder why they did not choose to use their talents to achieve social goals.

Many people do not seem to understand that to be a businessman is to serve others. Businesses must satisfy their customers if they are to survive. Service is a prerequisite of profit. Businessmen create goods and services for themselves and others.

Businessmen appear materialistic, unreflective, and mundane to the intellectual. Intellectuals are also apt to think of wealth as a finite quantity and to view it as stolen if made and as underserved if inherited. They also see business proficiency as in opposition to the moral tradition of duty which says that we must sacrifice selflessly and serve others. The doctrine of altruism says if a person possesses something needed by another, he must surrender it or be guilty of theft. Strong believers in Marx's labour theory of value, most intellectuals perceive the relationship between employer and employee as one of exploiter to victim. To the business moralist, success in the market looks like exploitation. The businessman is also frequently blamed for depressions and recessions. Intellectuals also like to promote the idea that political crusaders and humanitarians, rather than businessmen, are responsible for America's well-being.

Unfair System

Intellectuals have a hard time giving the market its due credit. After all, in their minds the market system does not appear to be fair to the intellectuals themselves. They were the most valued, rewarded, and successful in school where standards differ from those in the free market. Whereas schools reward intellectual achievements and verbal ability, the market rewards business skills and character traits such as honesty, friendliness, rationality, practicality, realism, creativity, self-reliance, hard work, etc. They, therefore, resent the capitalist system in which they are not held in as much esteem as when they were in school and are not rewarded financially as much as many businessmen. Intellectuals are predisposed to perceive the market as too disorderly and to prefer rewards to be centrally distributed like they were in their schooldays.

Many novels, films, plays, and television programmes are not representative of the real business world. These media have often been unflattering in their depiction of business and capitalism, have attacked business for destroying an old communal order based on equality, and have lamented the businessman's preoccupation with material success and the domination of large organizations in people's lives. The businessman has been depicted with hostility and derision and has been portrayed as materialistic, greedy, miserly, villainous, corrupt, unethical, hypocritical, insecure, insensitive, anti-cultural, exploitative, smaller-than-life, depersonalized mechanized, repressive of emotions, and subservient to the system.

A small percentage of our society's fictional works have characterized the businessmen in a more favourable light by emphasizing: the possibilities of life in a free society; the inherent ethical nature of capitalism and the good businessman; the strength, courage, integrity, and self-sufficiency of the hardworking businessman; and the entrepreneur as wealth creator and promoter of human progress. A few positive images do exist, but more are needed in order to illustrate the value of free enterprise, innovation, and personal initiative. People should be shown the positive and honourable qualities of business, businessmen, and careers in business.

A Noble Calling

Although businessmen represent one of the leadership groups in society, they tend to feel uneasy, self conscious, and even guilty about their positions. After all, Western culture has frequently derided and criticized the free enterprise system and generally holds business in low esteem. Although the benefits of business are welcomed, there has been a general prediction for people to begrudge productivity and those who cause it. As a result, many businessmen believe that if they are to earn respect, they must do so by doing more than performing well in business. Many attempt to prove their value by giving back to education, the arts, the community, etc. There is a tendency to defend their profession by pointing to socially responsible activities such as charity or to external consequences of their commercial activities such as jobs created or taxes paid to the government.

30

Entrepreneurship Development and Financial Inclusion in North East India : Past, Present and Future Challenges (Look East Policy)

KONWAR N. AND FELIX M. J.

Introduction

Dr. Edward Younkins says that throughout history, Western culture has been ambivalent and oftentimes has been disdainful regarding the moral merits of business. Of those engaged in various professions, businessmen have been the most denounced, vilified, and misunderstood. The hostility toward gains and contempt for commerce can be traced to cultural inheritances from the days of the Greek philosophers who emphasized the essentially vulgar characteristics of retail trade.

From Plato to Business

Plato consigned the trader to the lowest level in his ideal society. He ranked men from the bottom up beginning with workers, tradesmen, and artisans whose function was to provide life's necessities. Warriors were assigned a higher status and philosophers were at the top. Plato valued rational ability over courage and declared that the philosophers should rule. Contemplation constituted the worthy life. Plato's otherworldly dualism denigrates man's worldly nature and assigns the intellectual and spiritual dimensions of man to a higher level. The mind is thus held to be morally and ontologically superior to the body. Although Aristotle disagreed with Plato's otherworldliness and on many other philosophical